TOY CONFIDENTIAL

ALED LEWIS

HOW BOOKS

Cincinnati, Ohio
www.howdesign.com

Published by HOW Books, an imprint of F+W Media, Inc., 10151 Carver Road, Suite 200, Blue Ash, Ohio 45242. (800) 289-0963. First edition.

For more excellent books and resources for designers, visit www.howdesign.com.

16 15 14 13 12 5 4 3 2 1

ISBN-13: 978-1-4403-2043-9

Distributed in Canada by Fraser Direct
100 Armstrong Avenue
Georgetown, Ontario, Canada L7G 5S4
Tel: (905) 877-4411

Distributed in the U.K. and Europe by F&W Media International, LTD
Brunel House, Forde Close, Newton Abbot, TQ12 4PU, UK
Tel: (+44) 1626 323200, Fax: (+44) 1626 323319
Email: enquiries@fwmedia.com

Distributed in Australia by Capricorn Link
P.O. Box 704, Windsor, NSW 2756 Australia
Tel: (02) 4577-3555

fw media

Edited by Megan Patrick and Scott Francis
Art directed by Grace Ring and Ronson Slagle
Production coordinated by Greg Nock

THANKS

To family and friends for supplying encouragement, toys and suggestions. Thanks to Megan for taking this chance on me and thanks to anyone on the Internet who has liked, reposted, voted on, blogged about or featured my work. It's been invaluable in allowing my goofy ideas to be seen.

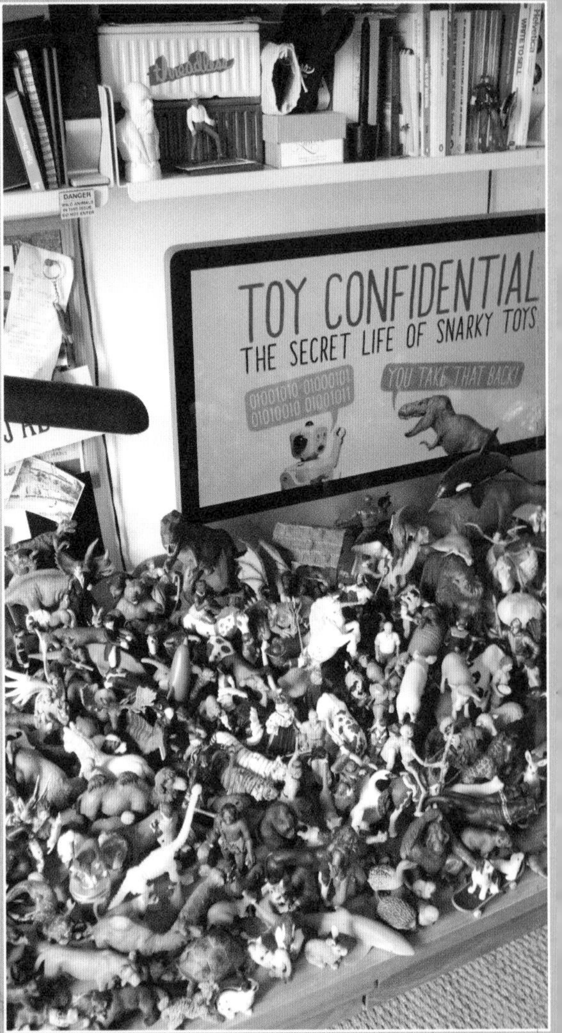
DANGER
TOY CONFIDENTIAL
THE SECRET LIFE OF SNARKY TOYS
01001010 01000101
01010010 01001011
YOU TAKE THAT BACK!

Dedicated to Abigail for her unwavering support in each of my questionable endeavors and for sharing our small London flat with thousands of toys without complaining once.

INTRODUCTION

It all started in a toy store when I saw a figure of a unicorn rearing up as though he was showing off his magnificent horn. I arranged some of the other horse figures around him looking suitably displeased at his show-off antics and it amused me enough to make it a project!

The process of making this book was pretty much a regression back to early childhood and that theater of the mind where the toys are the players and where a conversation between a doll and a dinosaur is perfectly normal. This is my first truly solo project and it's been a really fun way to express my sense of humor. Expect some observational comedy, the occasional wordplay, and an unabashed vein of popular culture running through the core.

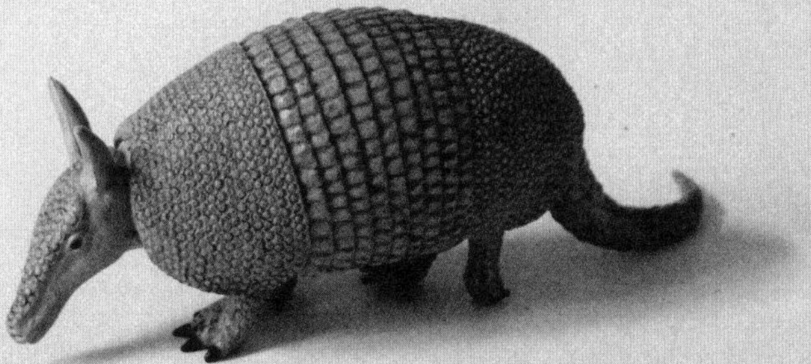

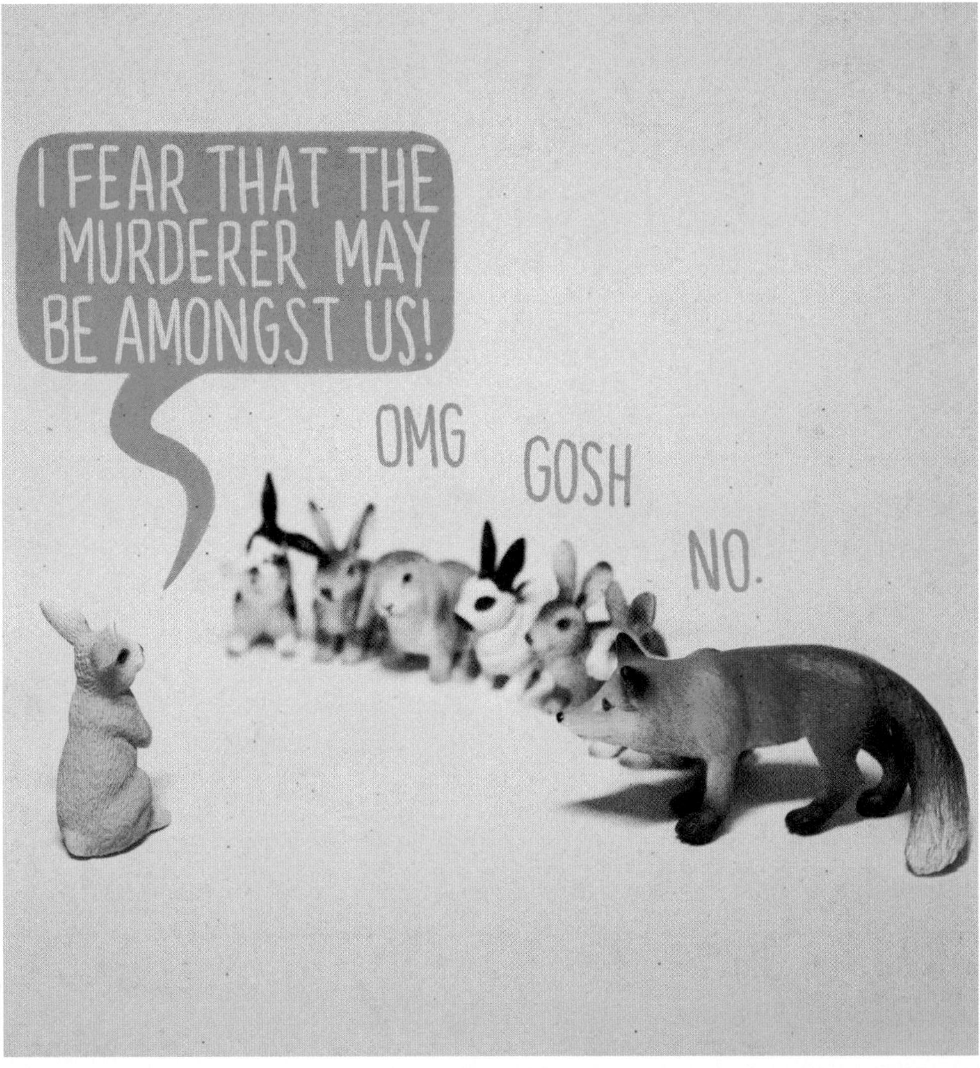
I FEAR THAT THE MURDERER MAY BE AMONGST US!
OMG
GOSH
NO.

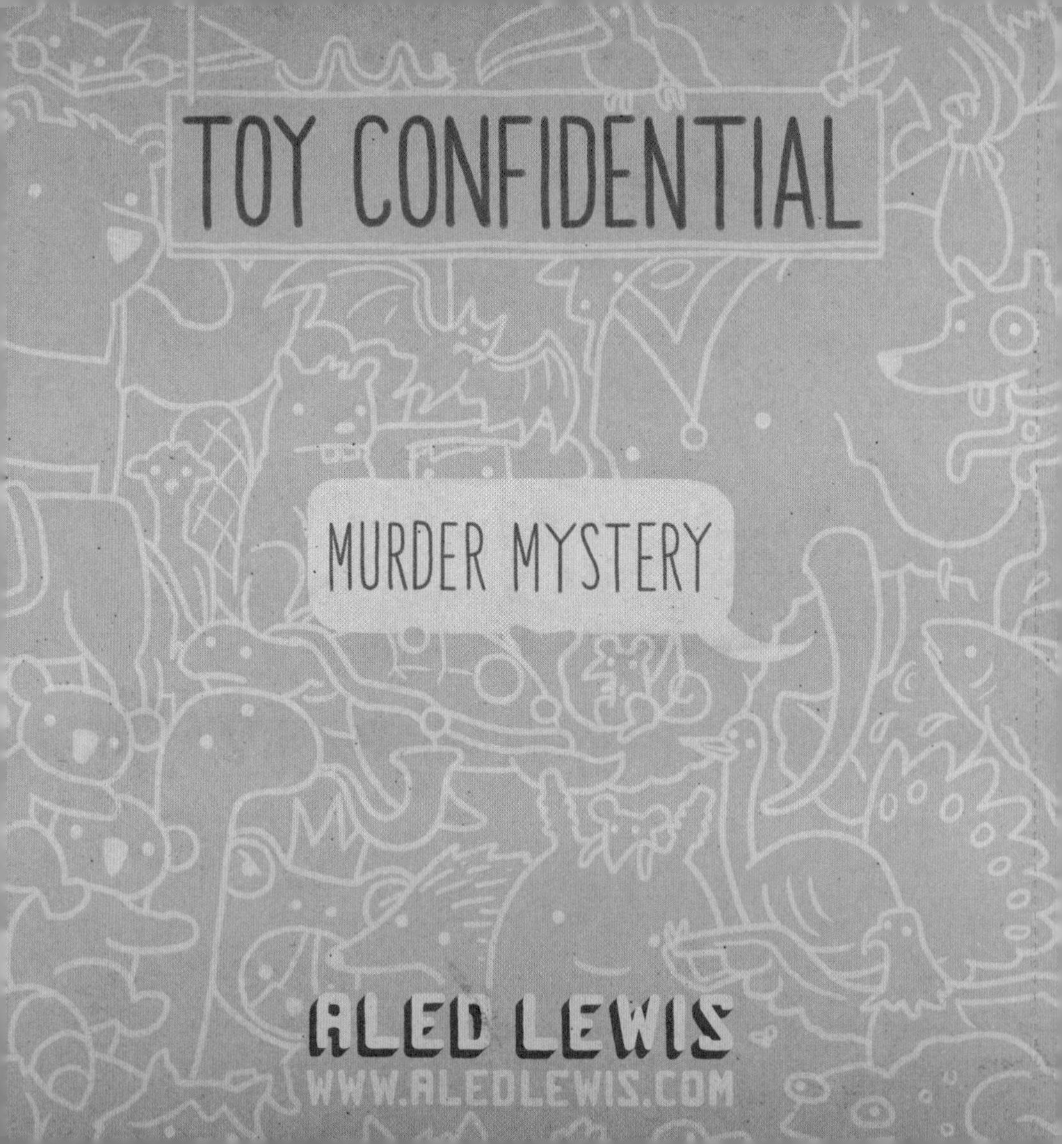
TOY CONFIDENTIAL
MURDER MYSTERY
ALED LEWIS
WWW.ALEDLEWIS.COM

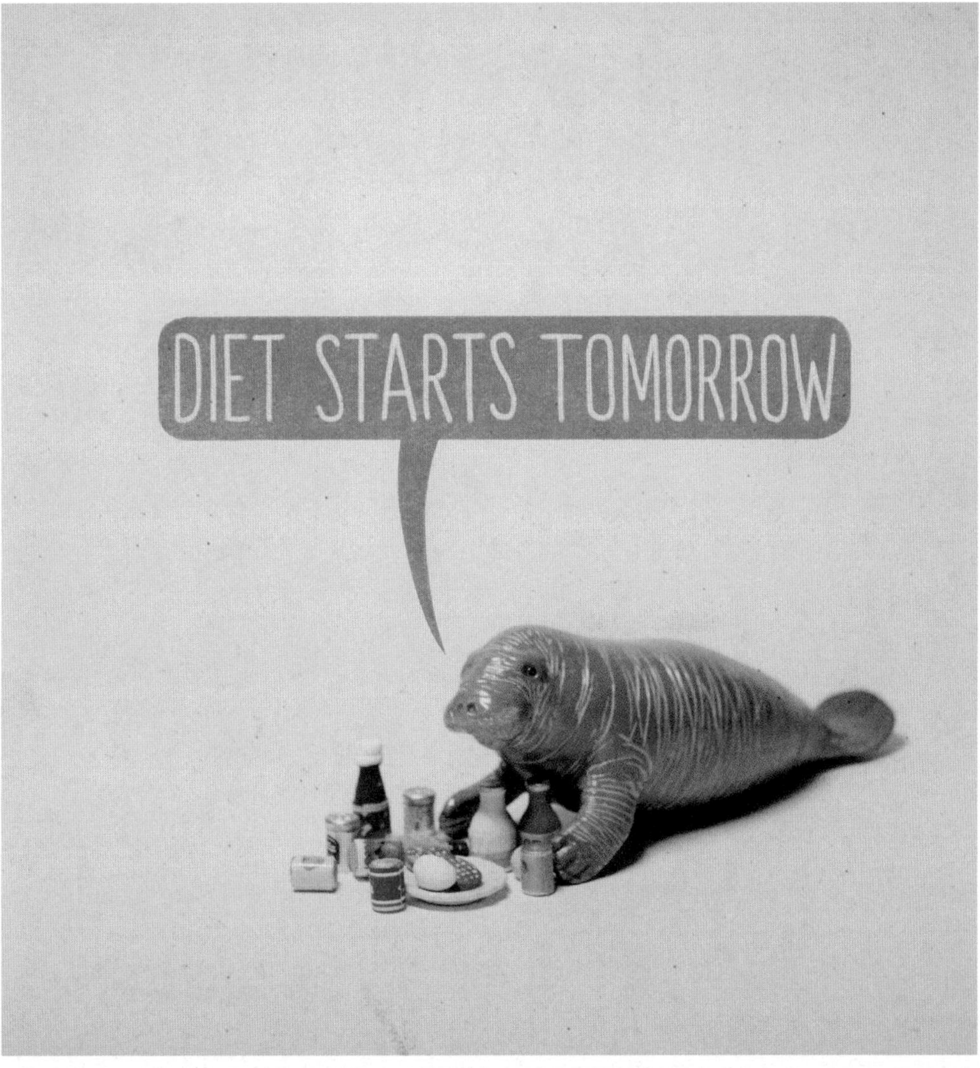
DIET STARTS TOMORROW

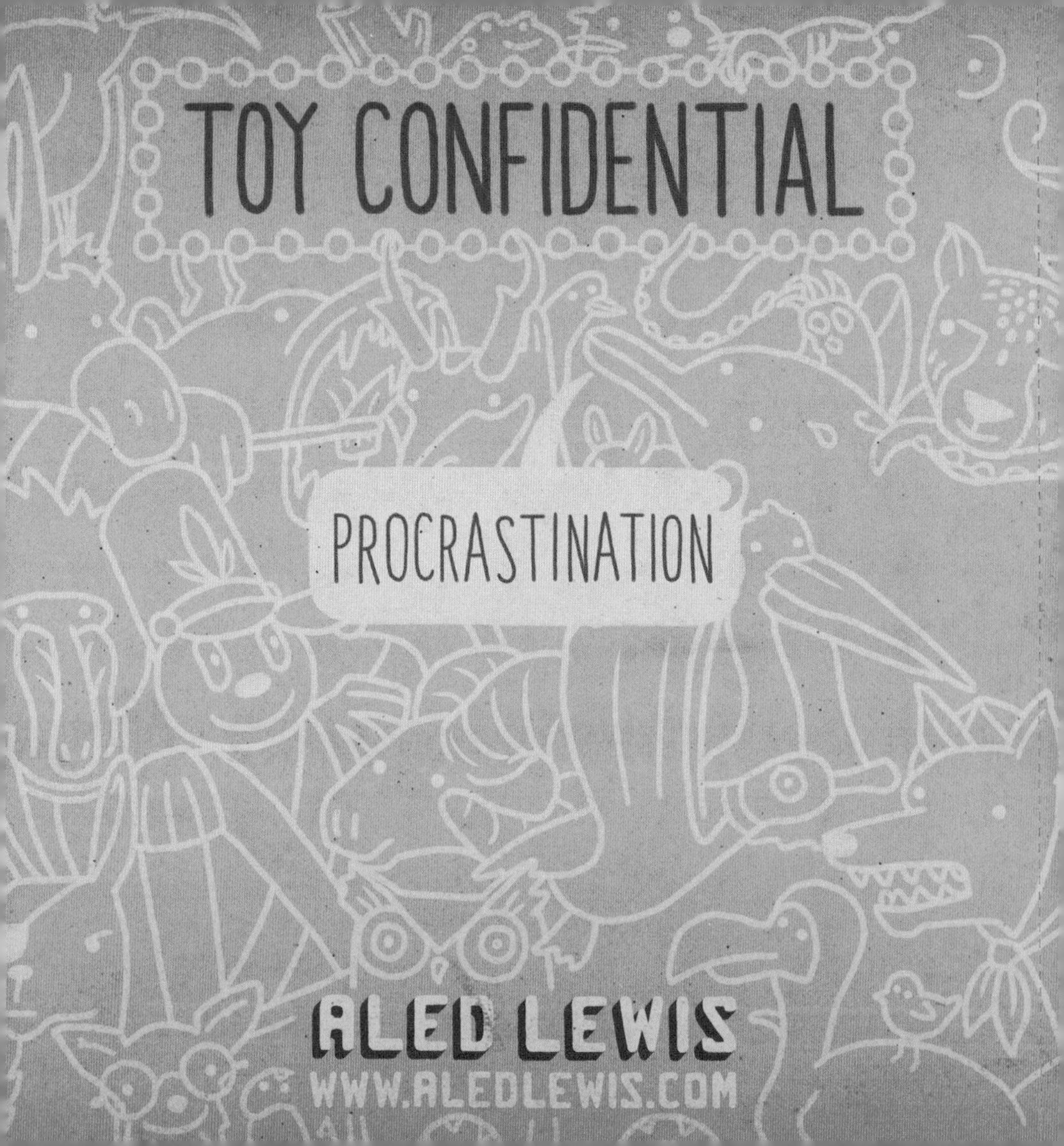
TOY CONFIDENTIAL
PROCRASTINATION
ALED LEWIS
WWW.ALEDLEWIS.COM

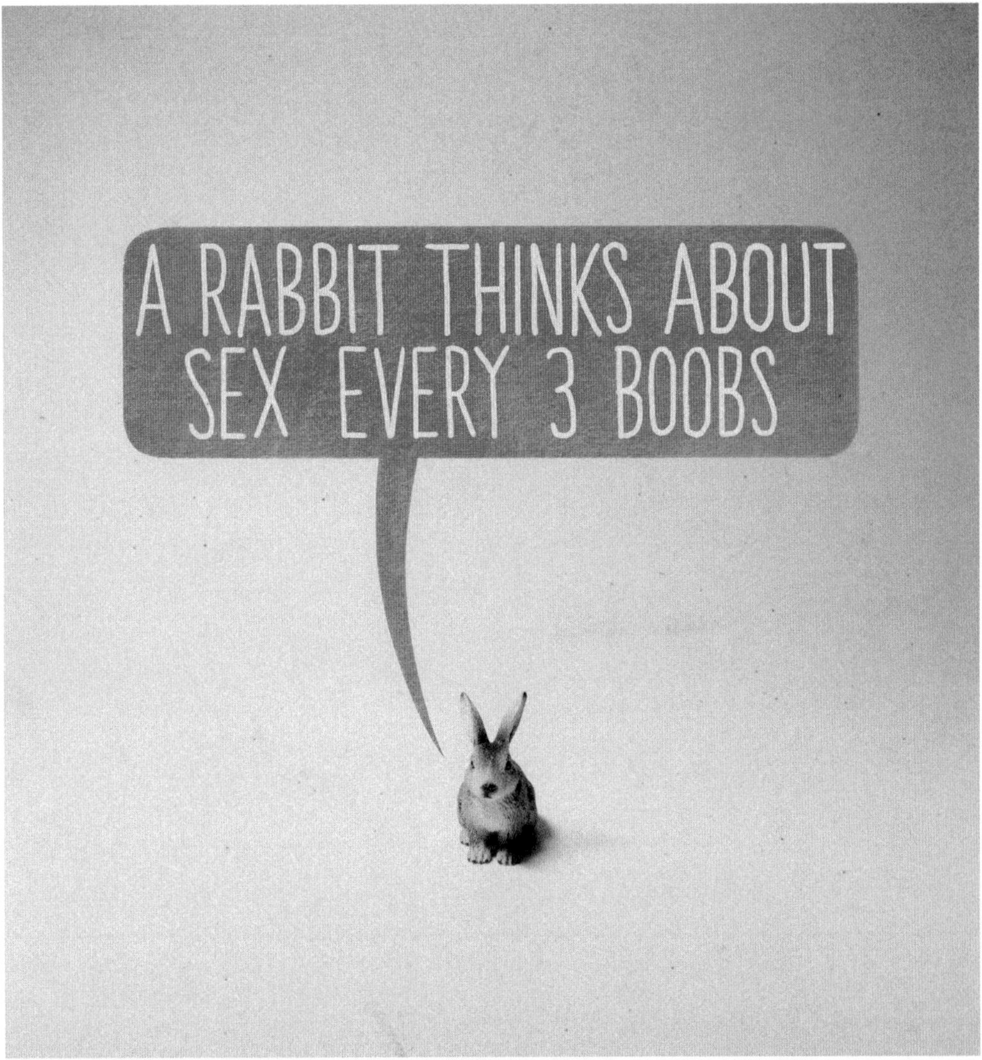
A RABBIT THINKS ABOUT SEX EVERY 3 BOOBS

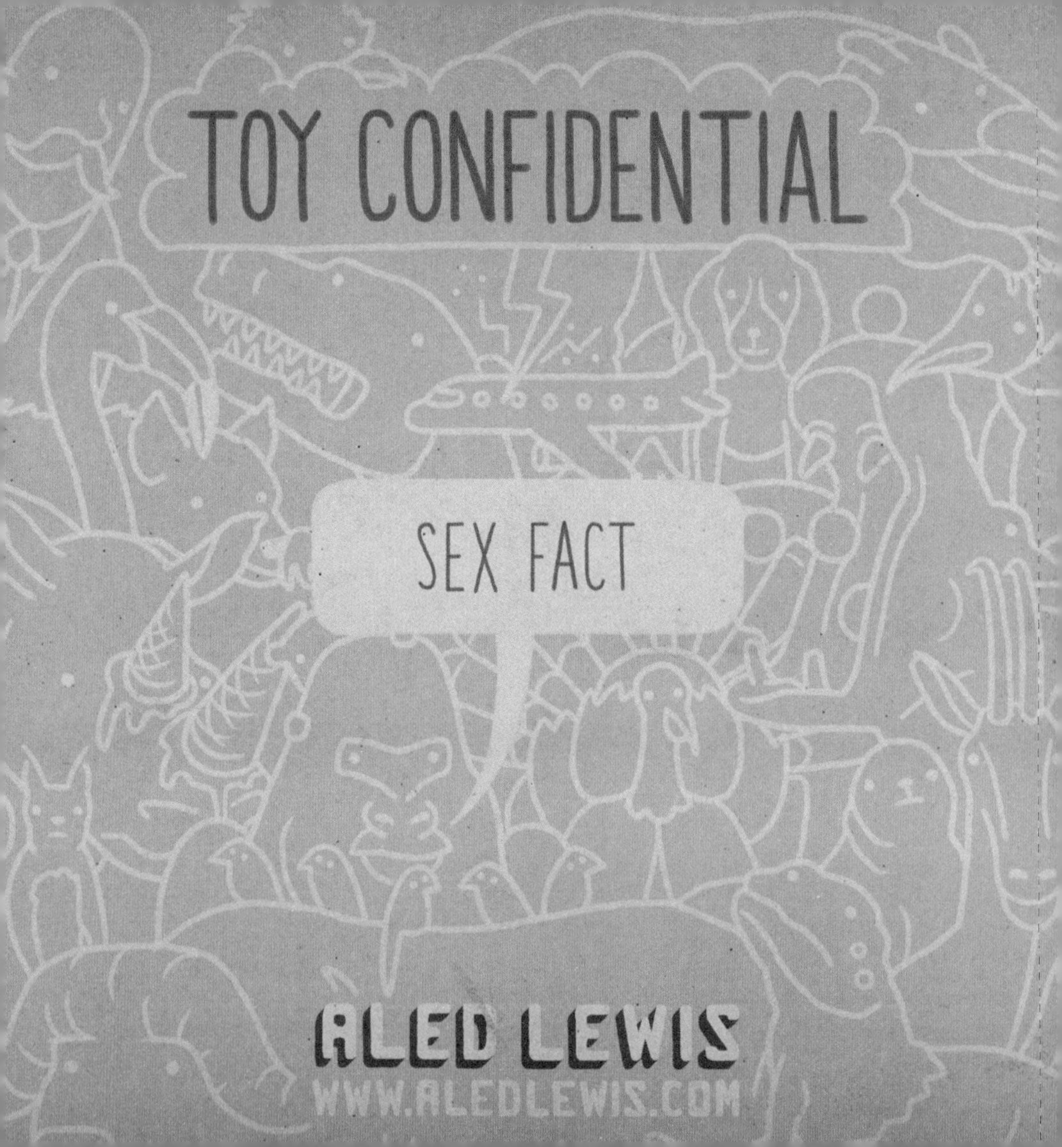
TOY CONFIDENTIAL
SEX FACT
ALED LEWIS
WWW.ALEDLEWIS.COM

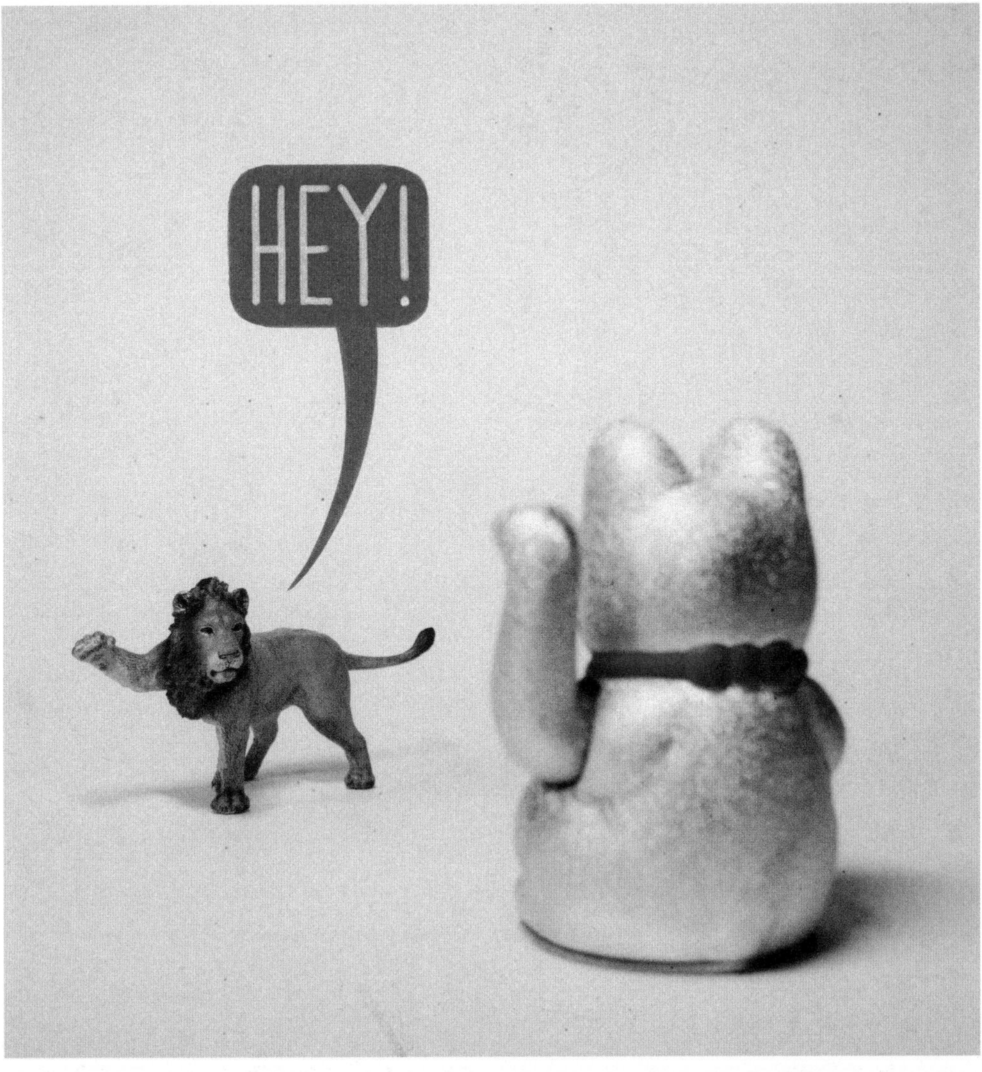
HEY!

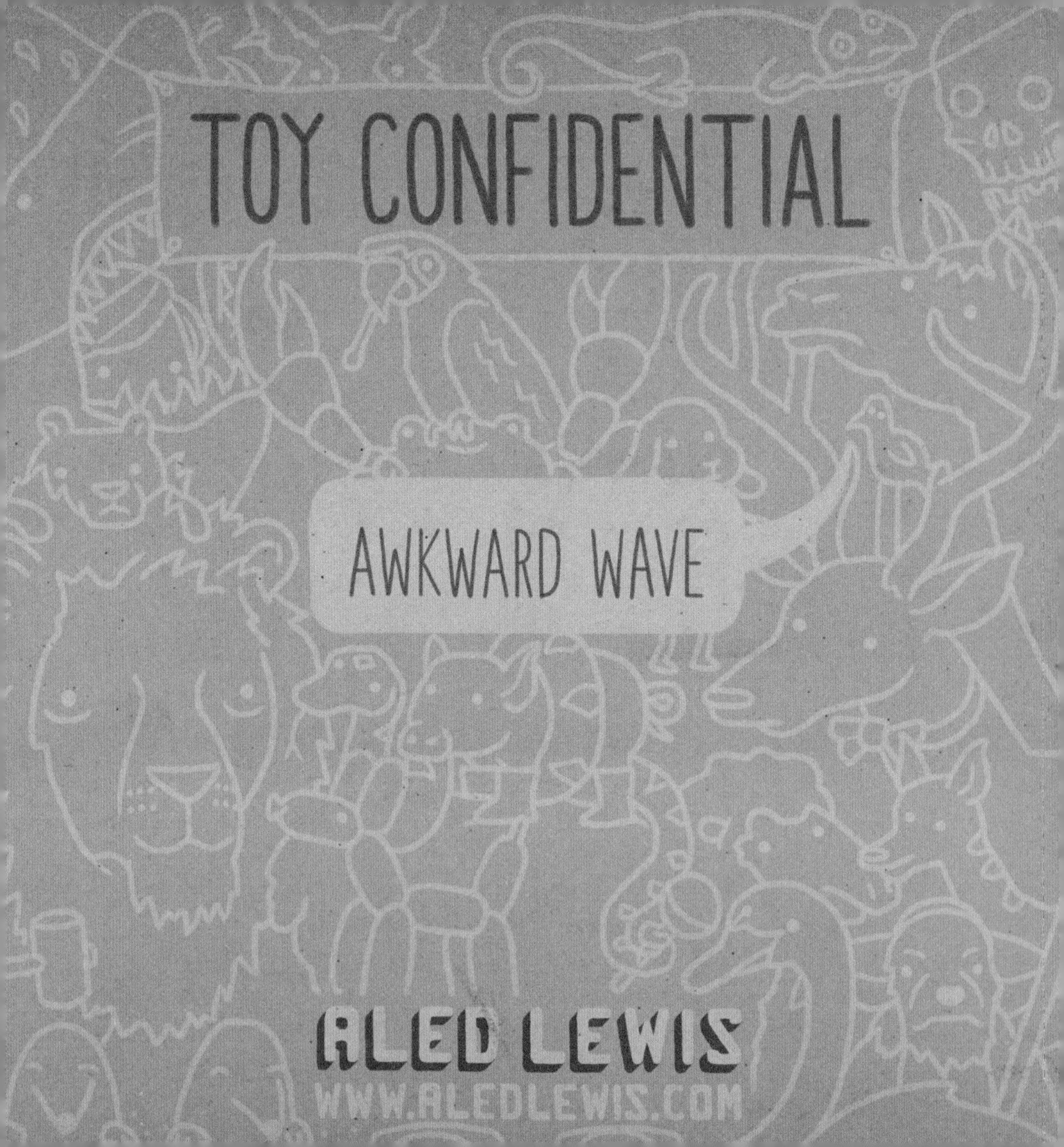
TOY CONFIDENTIAL
AWKWARD WAVE
ALED LEWIS
WWW.ALEDLEWIS.COM

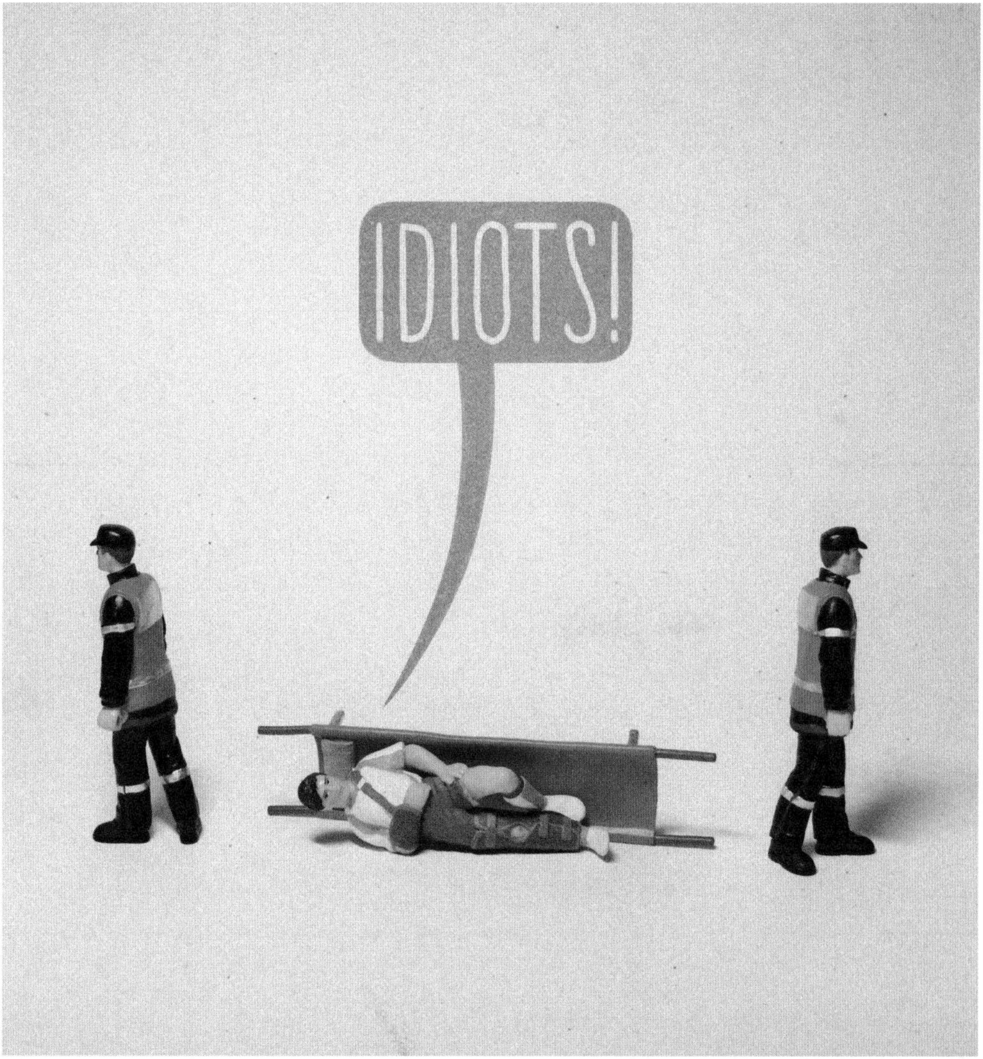
IDIOTS!

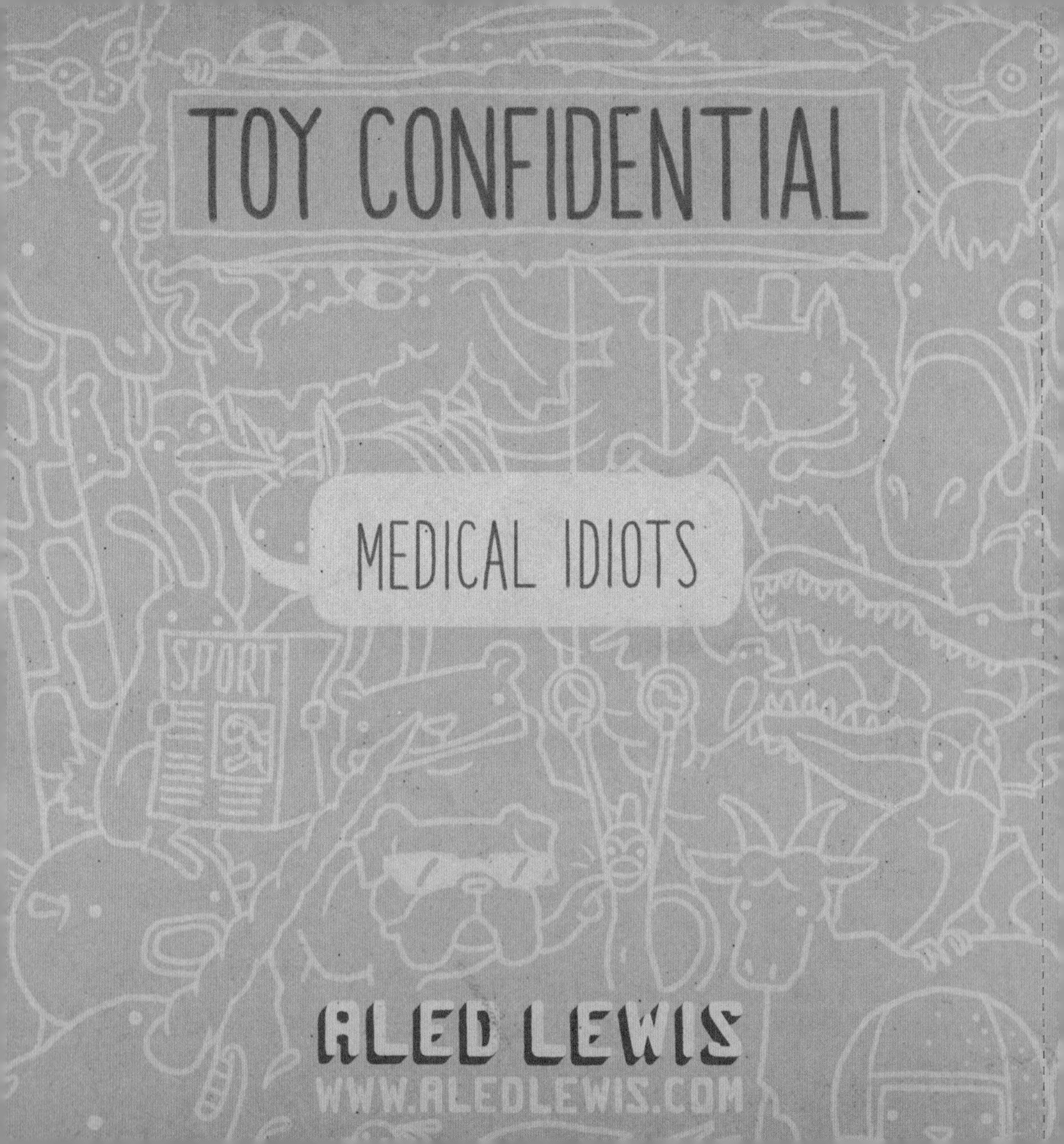
TOY CONFIDENTIAL
MEDICAL IDIOTS
SPORT
ALED LEWIS
WWW.ALEDLEWIS.COM

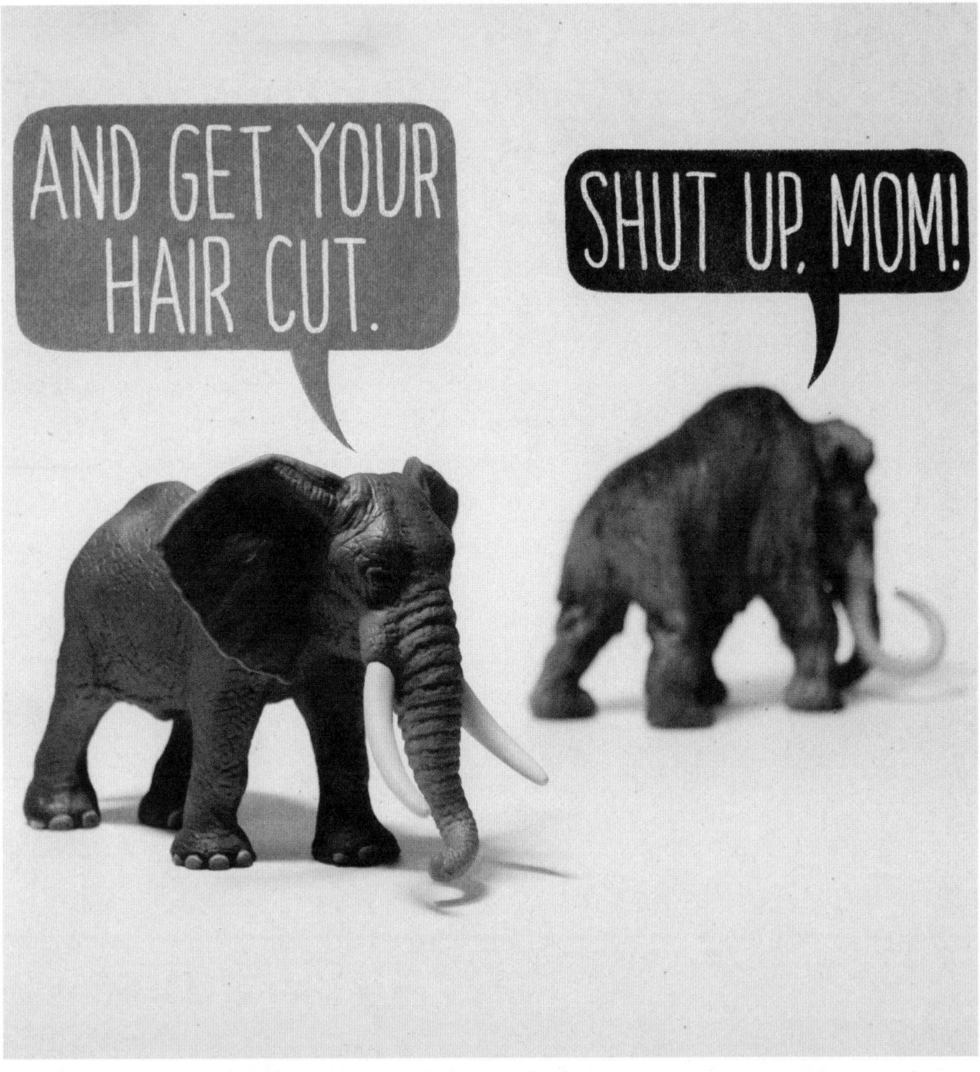
AND GET YOUR HAIR CUT.
SHUT UP, MOM!

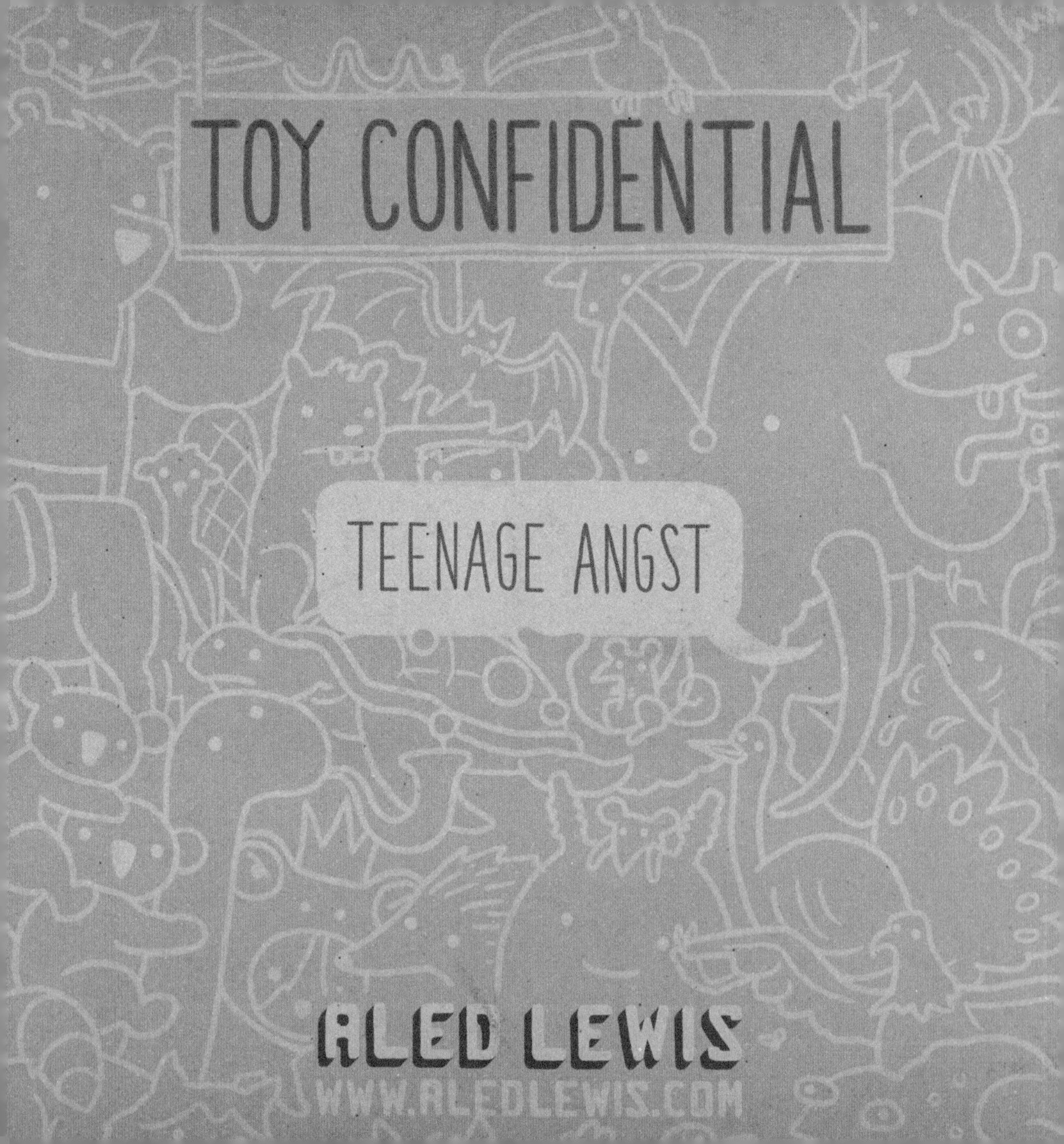
TOY CONFIDENTIAL
TEENAGE ANGST
ALED LEWIS
WWW.ALEDLEWIS.COM

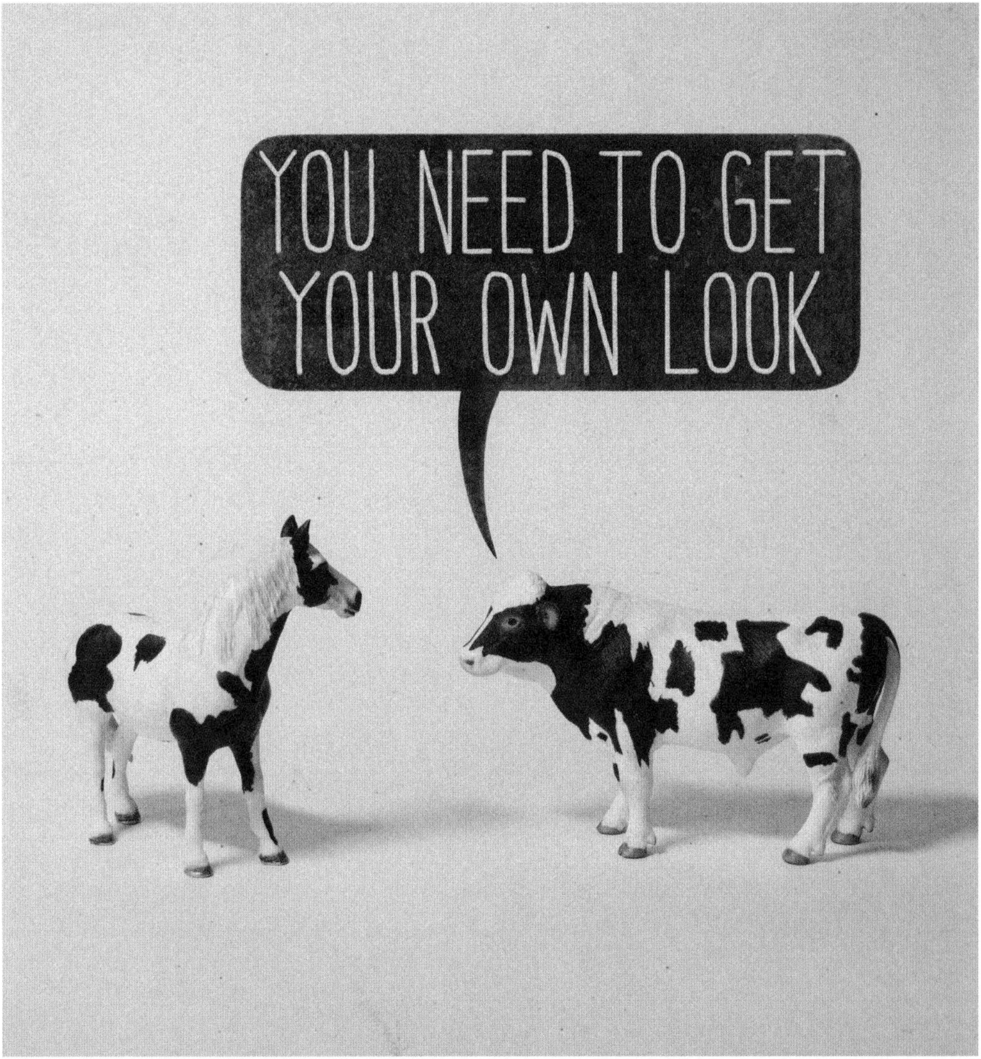
YOU NEED TO GET YOUR OWN LOOK

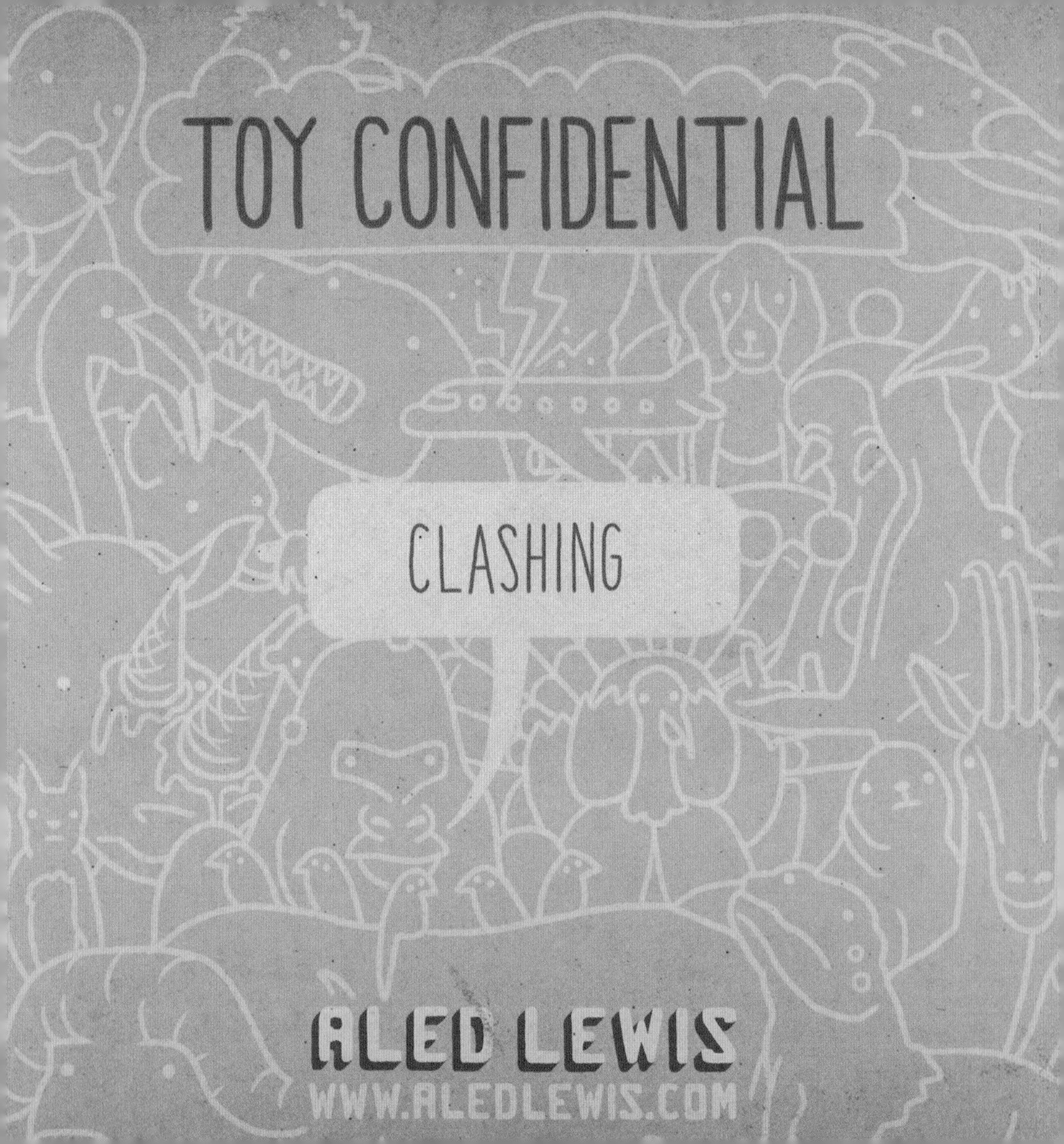
TOY CONFIDENTIAL
CLASHING
ALED LEWIS
WWW.ALEDLEWIS.COM

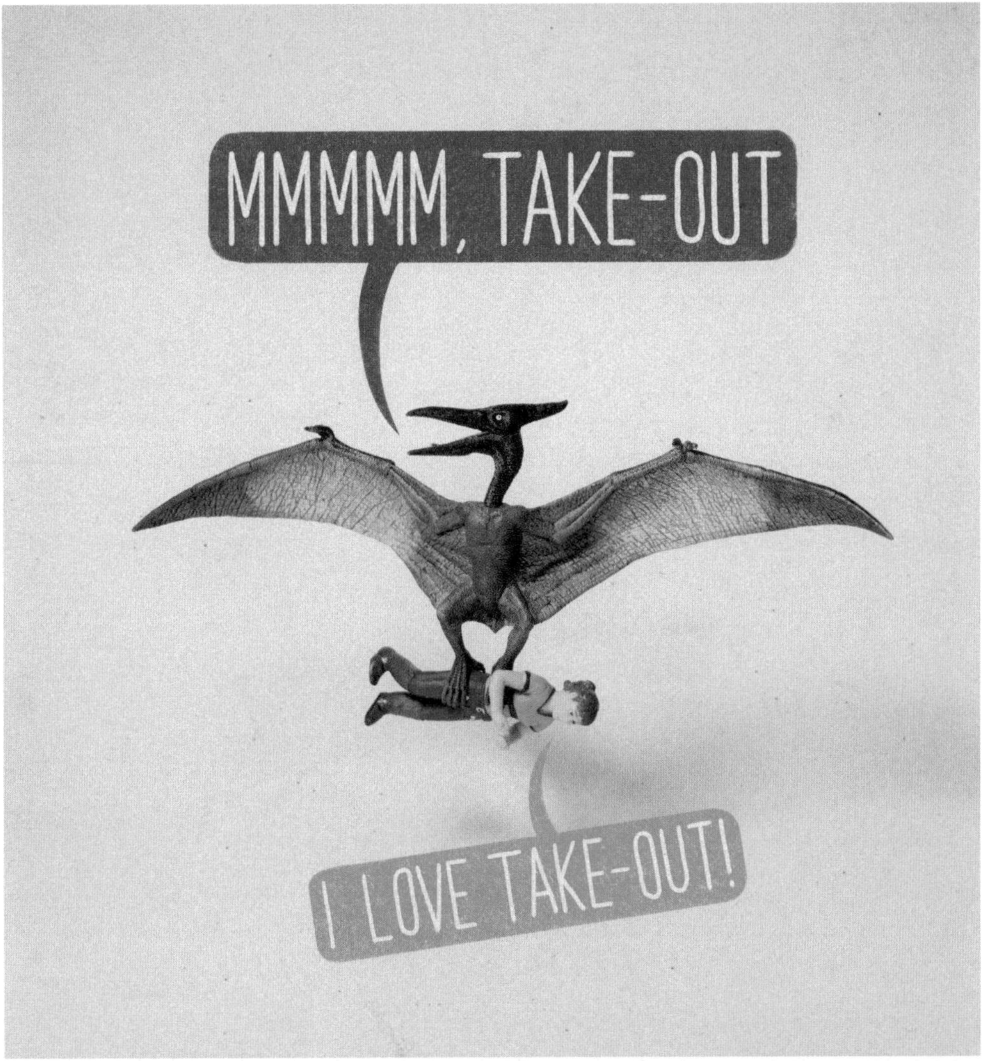
MMMMM, TAKE-OUT
I LOVE TAKE-OUT!

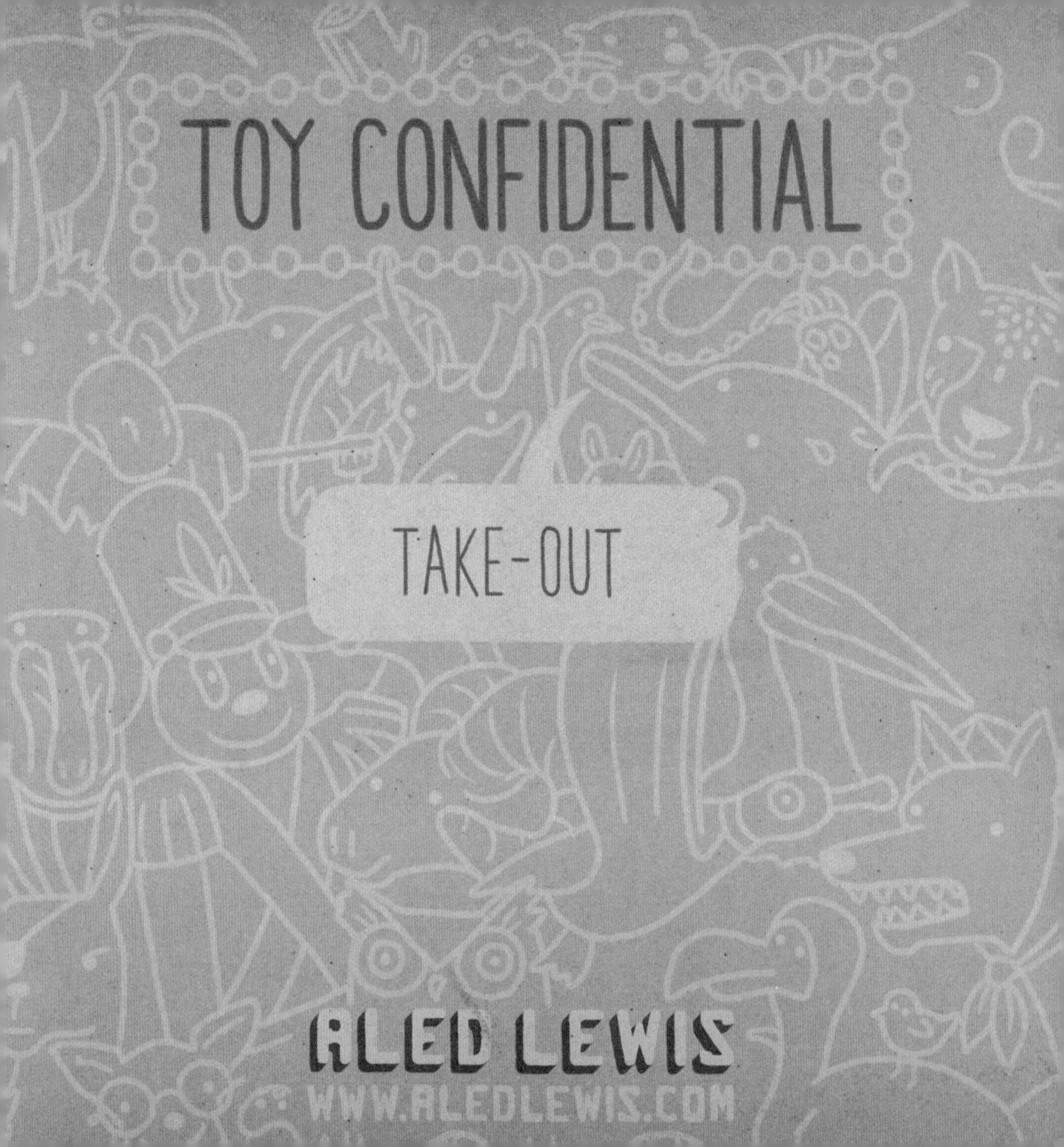
TOY CONFIDENTIAL
TAKE-OUT
ALED LEWIS
WWW.ALEDLEWIS.COM

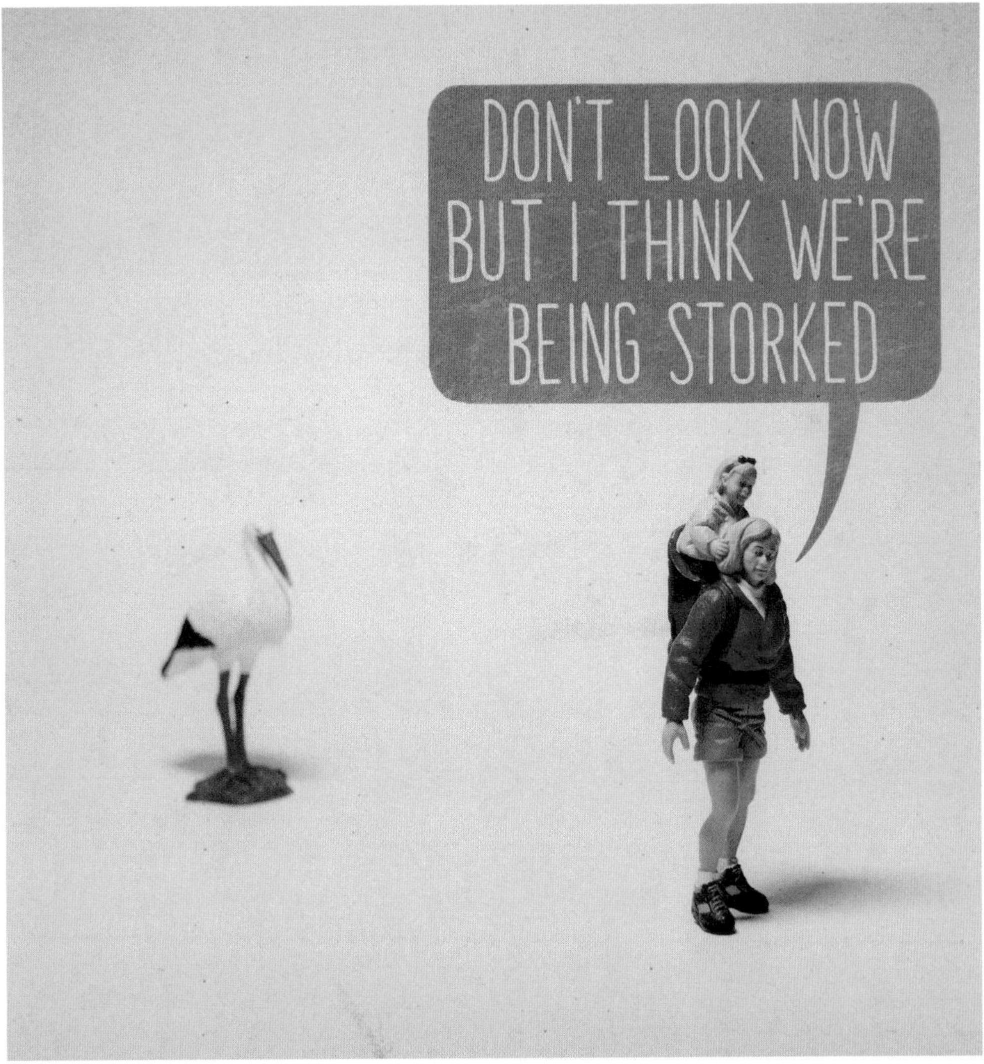
DON'T LOOK NOW BUT I THINK WE'RE BEING STORKED

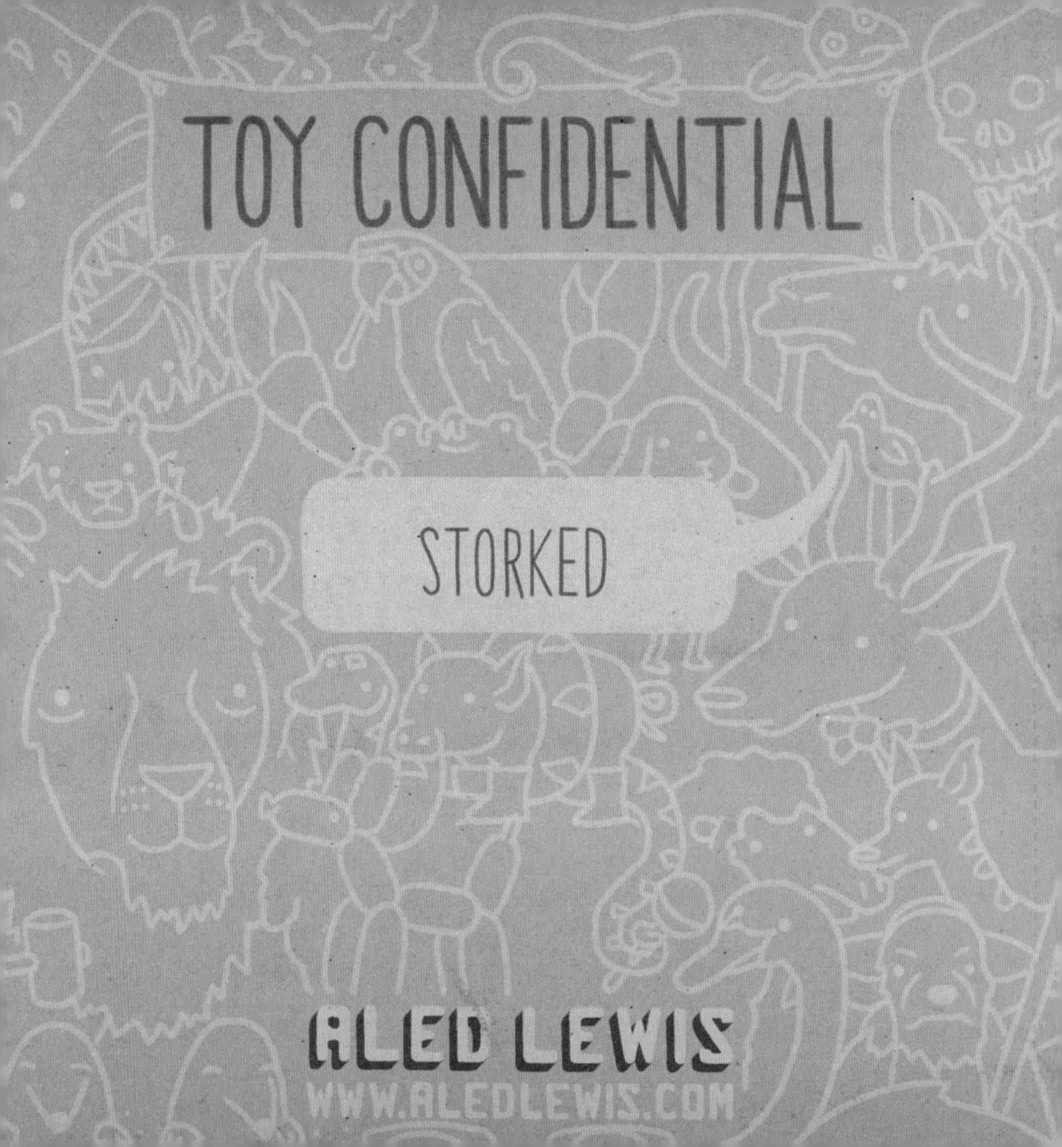
TOY CONFIDENTIAL
STORKED
ALED LEWIS
WWW.ALEDLEWIS.COM

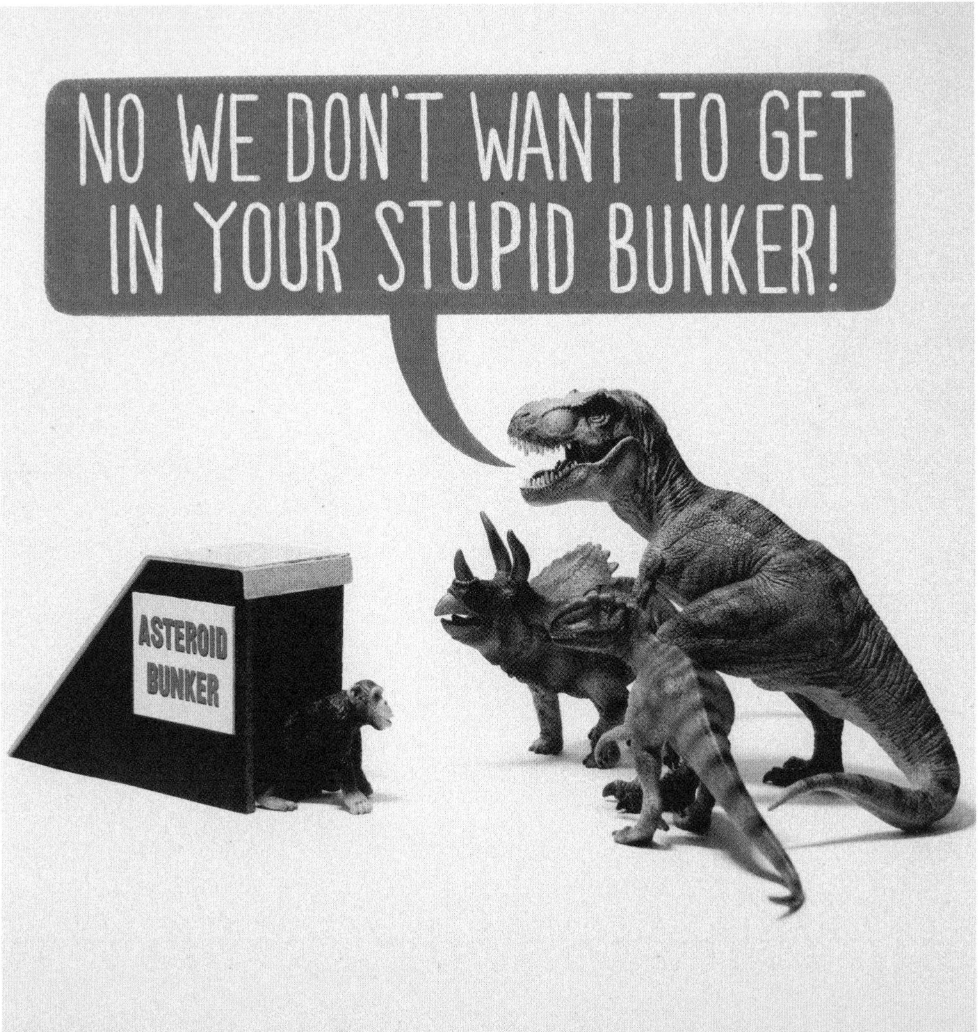
NO WE DON'T WANT TO GET IN YOUR STUPID BUNKER!
ASTEROID BUNKER

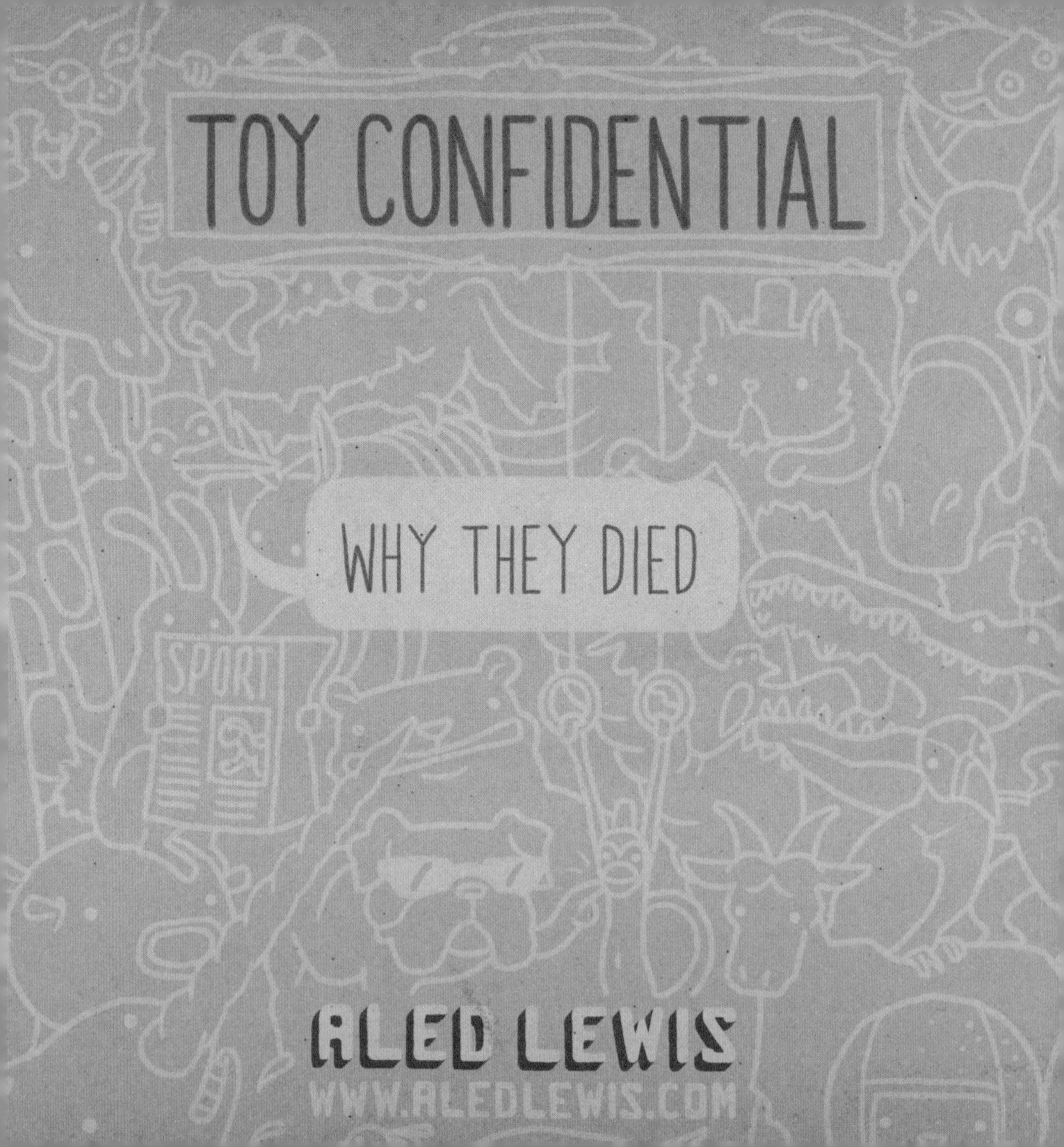
TOY CONFIDENTIAL
SPORT
WHY THEY DIED
ALED LEWIS
WWW.ALEDLEWIS.COM

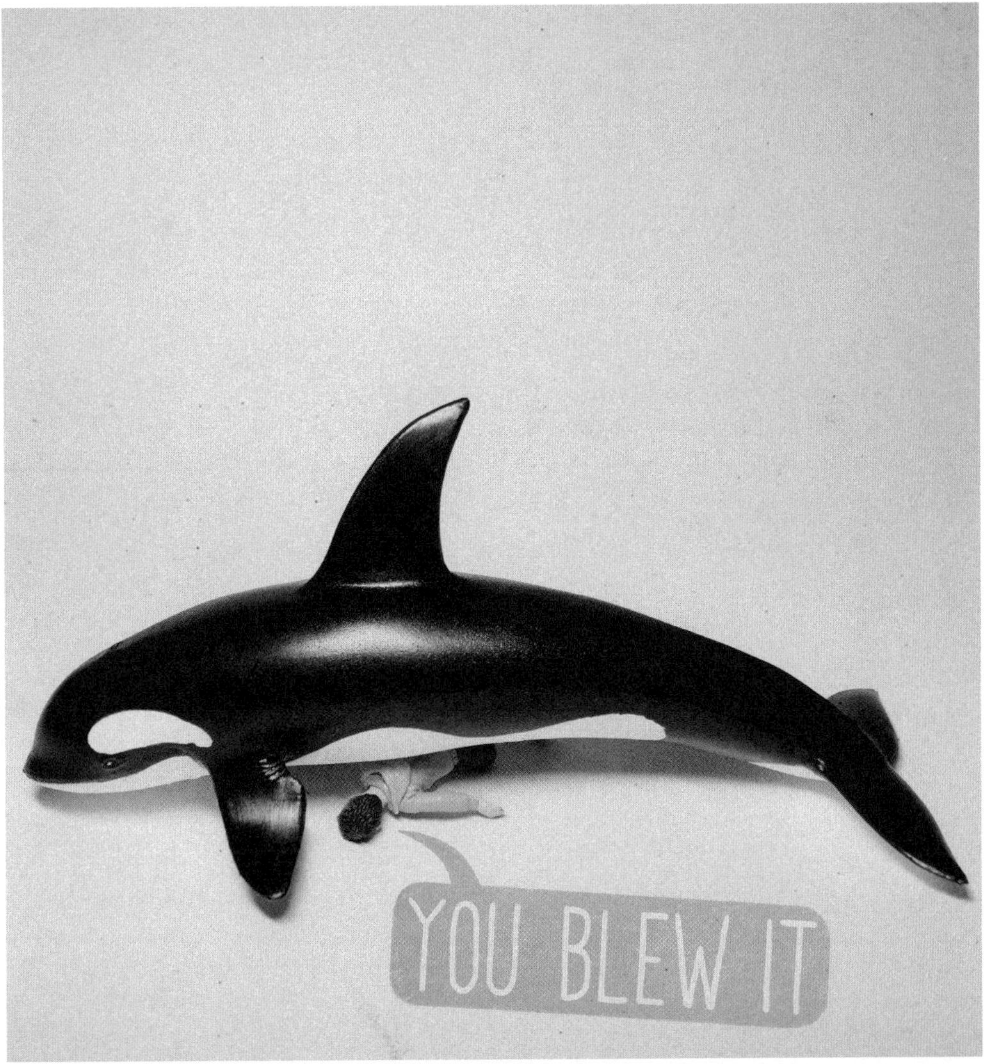
YOU BLEW IT

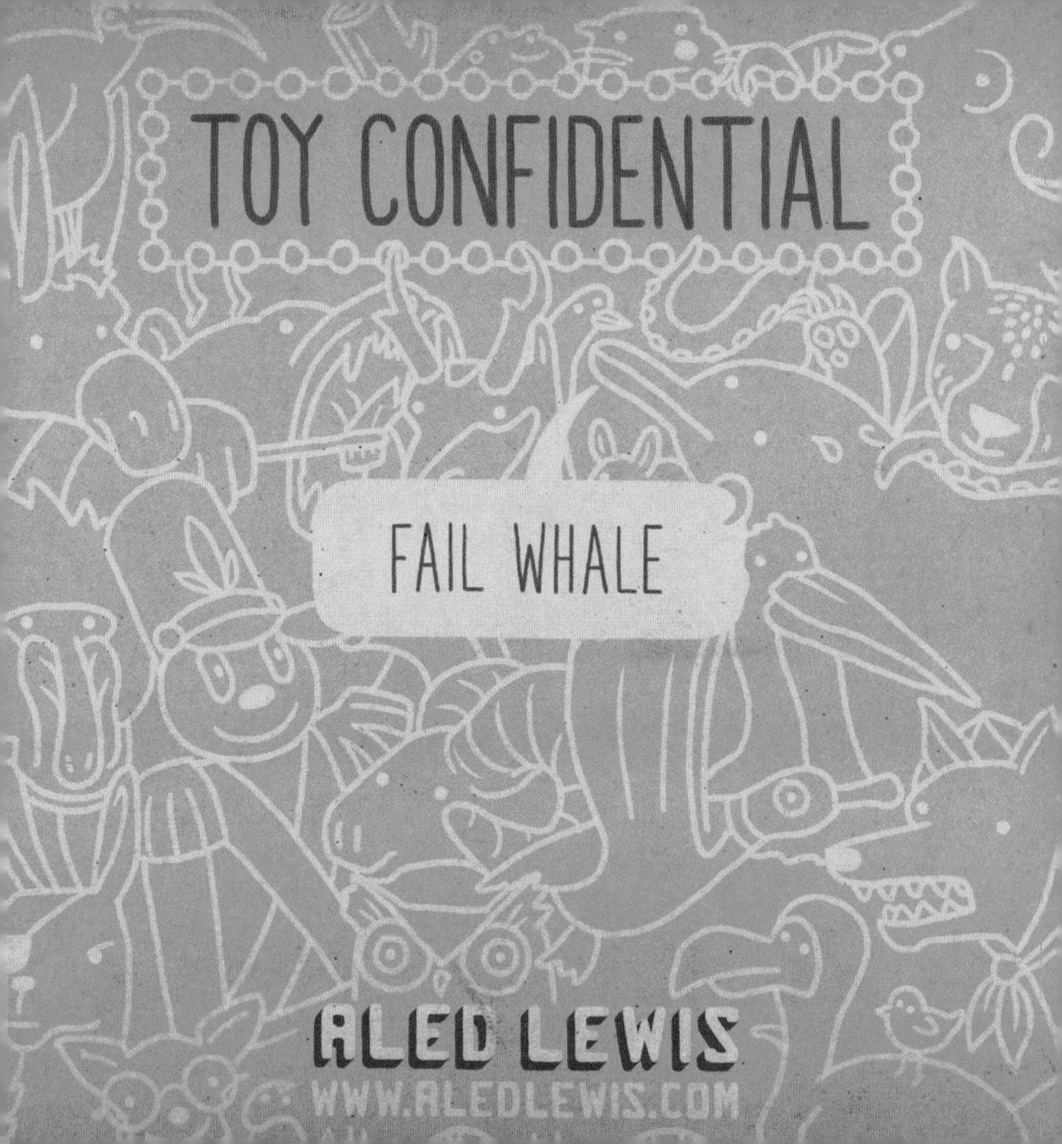
TOY CONFIDENTIAL
FAIL WHALE
ALED LEWIS
WWW.ALEDLEWIS.COM

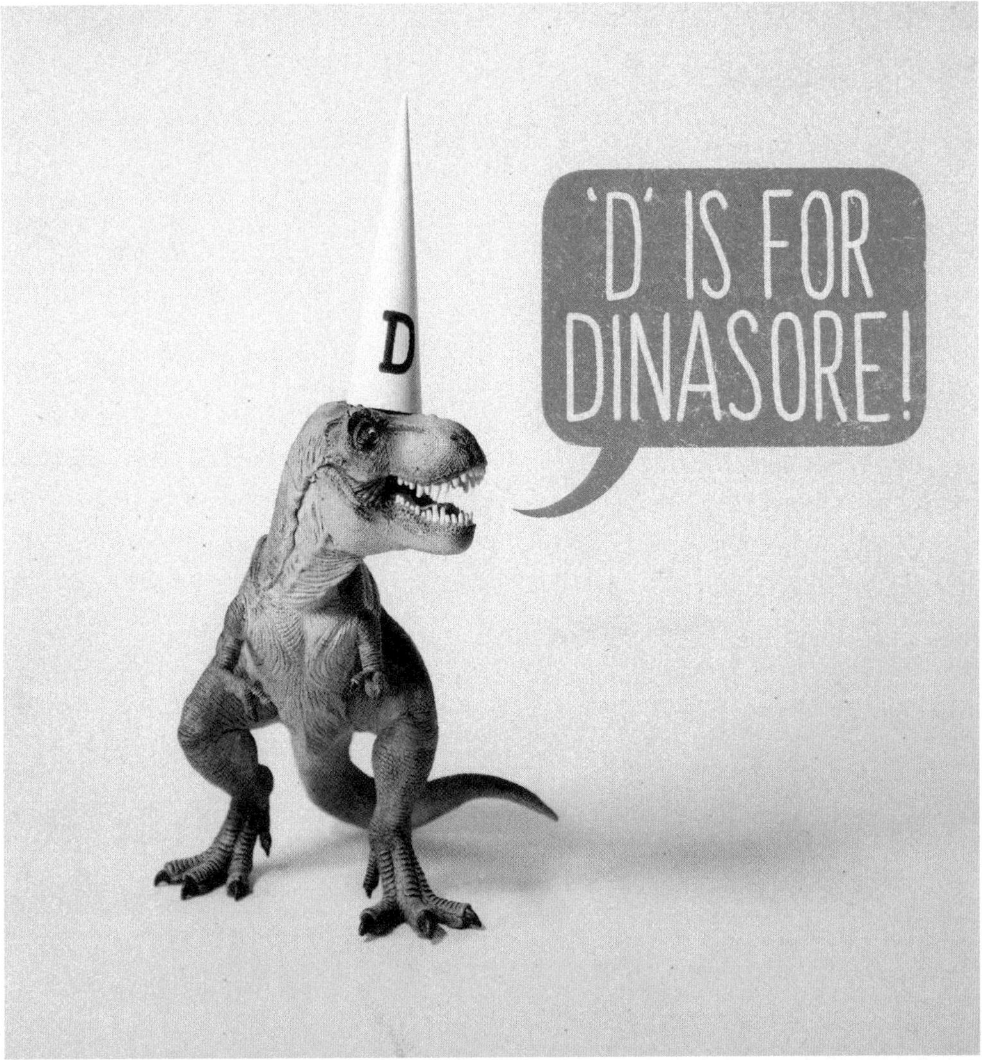
D
'D' IS FOR DINASORE!

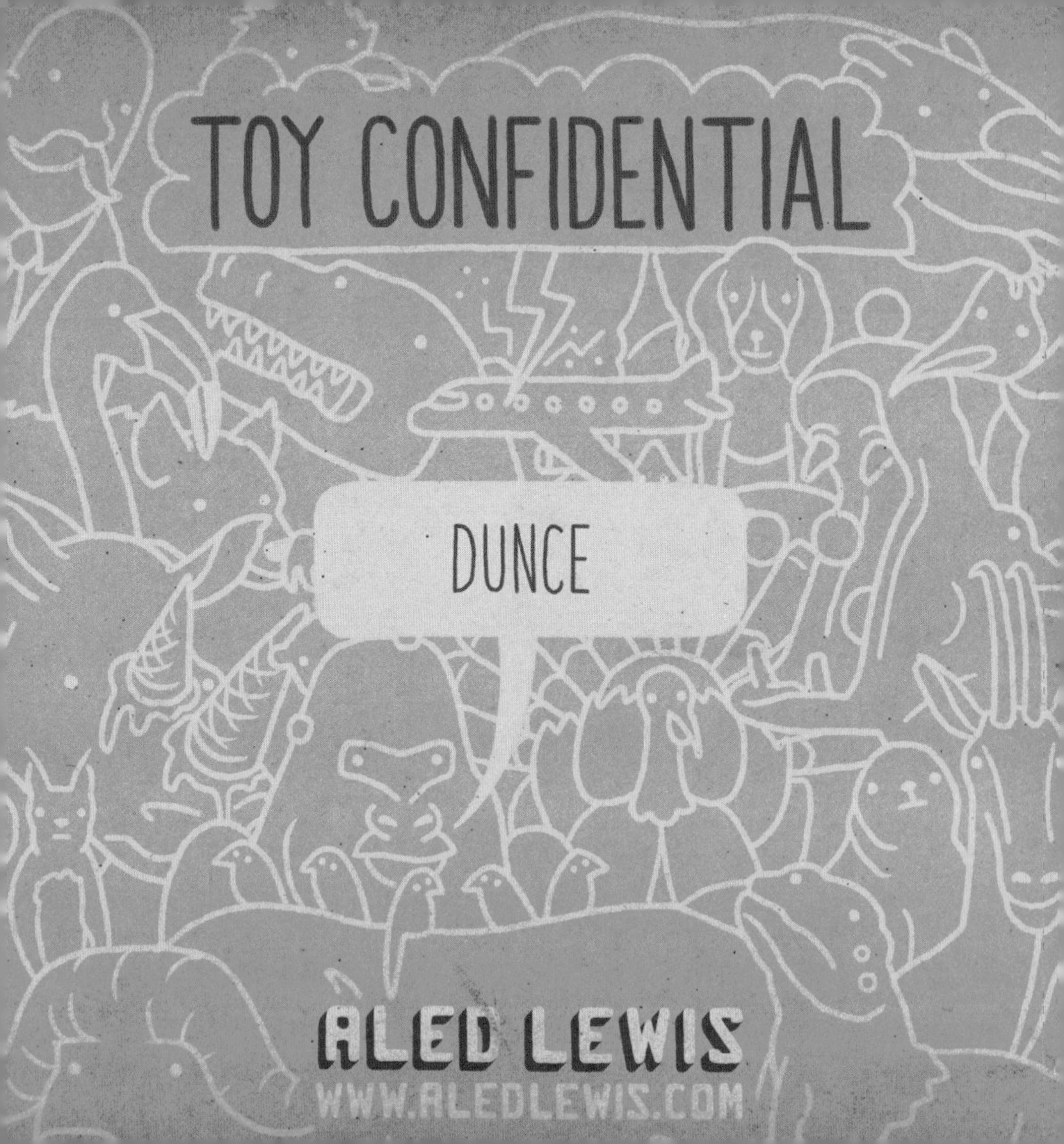
TOY CONFIDENTIAL
DUNCE
ALED LEWIS
WWW.ALEDLEWIS.COM

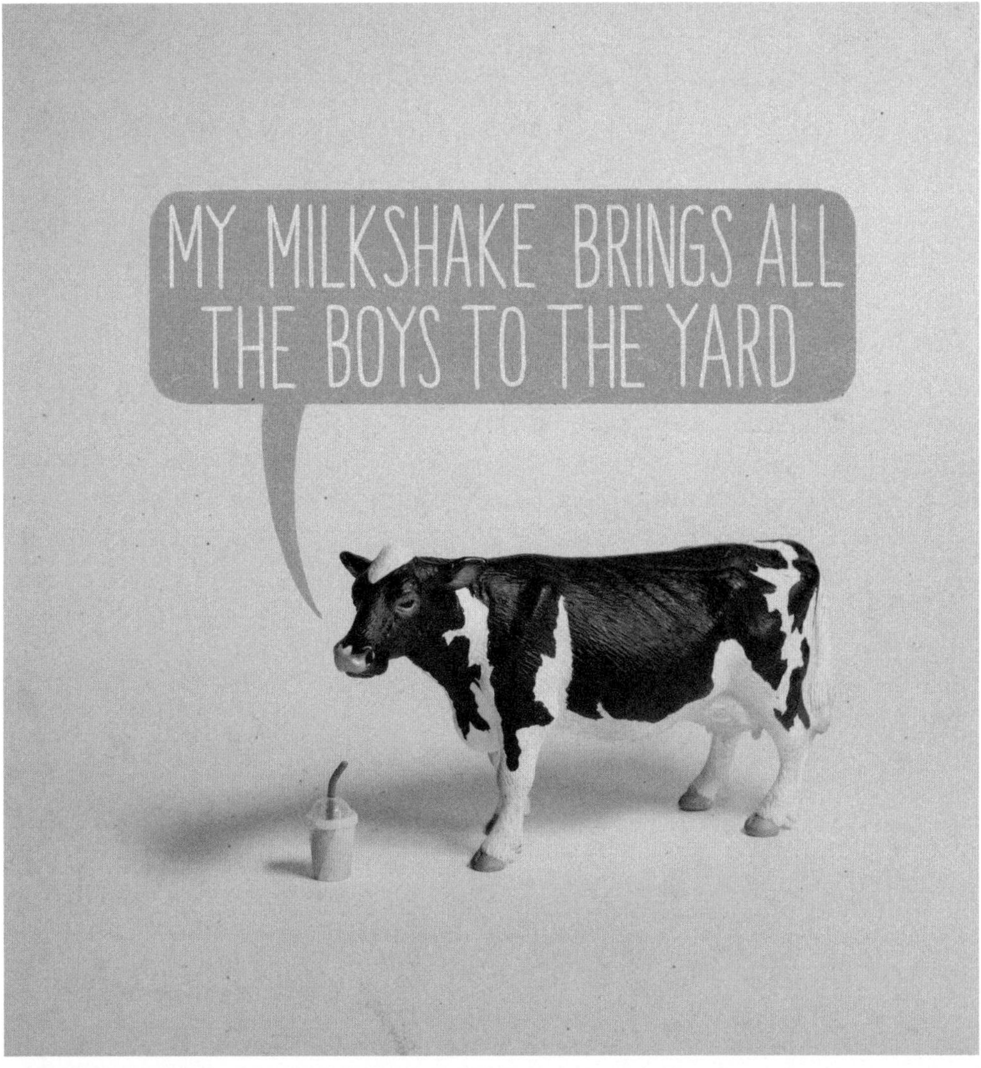
MY MILKSHAKE BRINGS ALL THE BOYS TO THE YARD

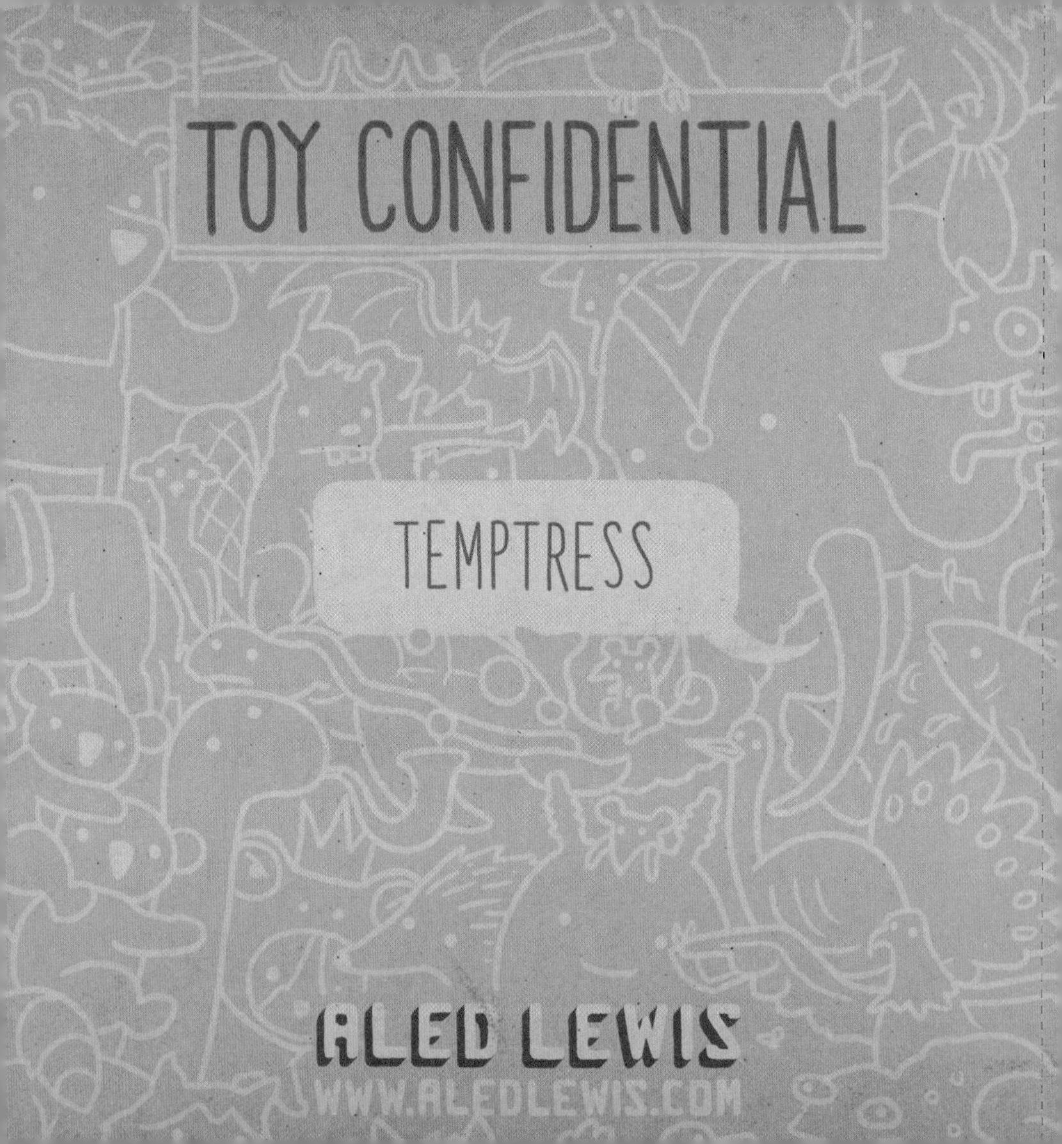
TOY CONFIDENTIAL
TEMPTRESS
ALED LEWIS
WWW.ALEDLEWIS.COM

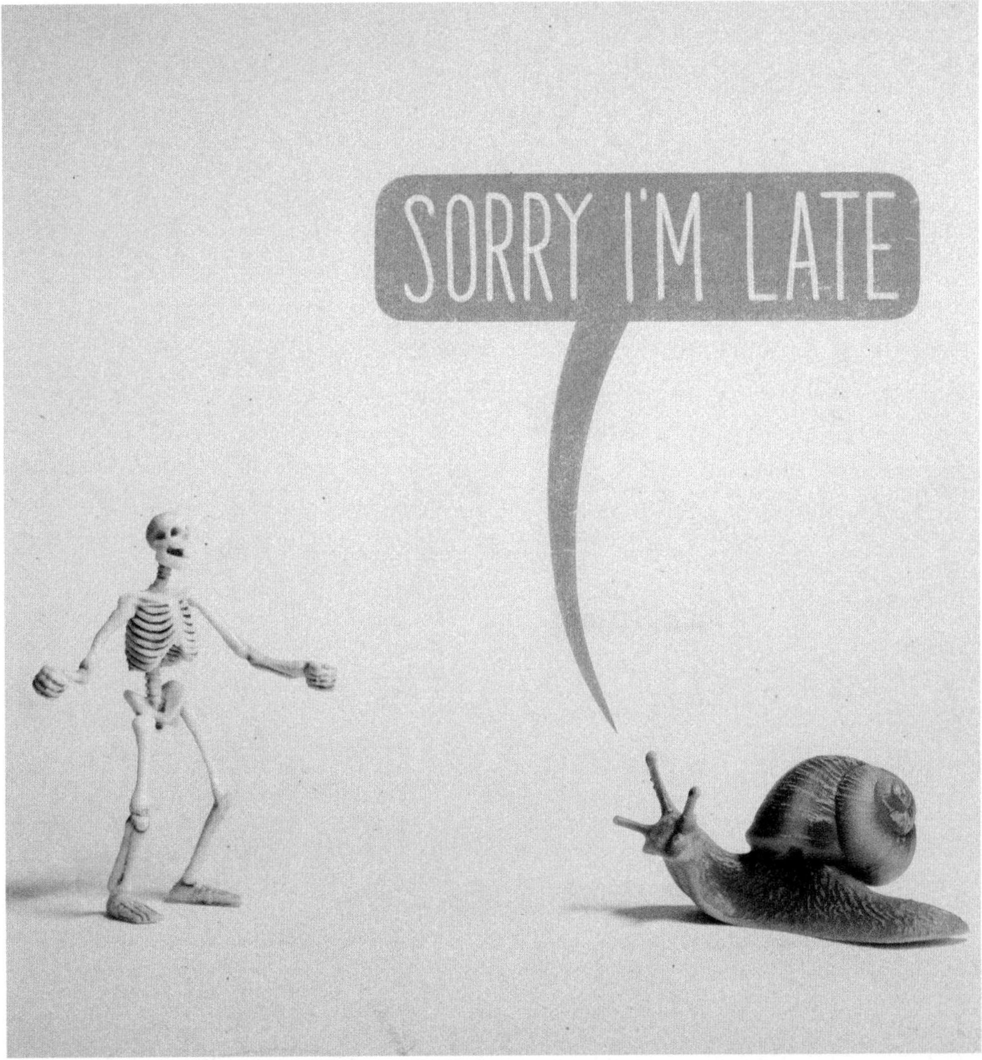
SORRY I'M LATE

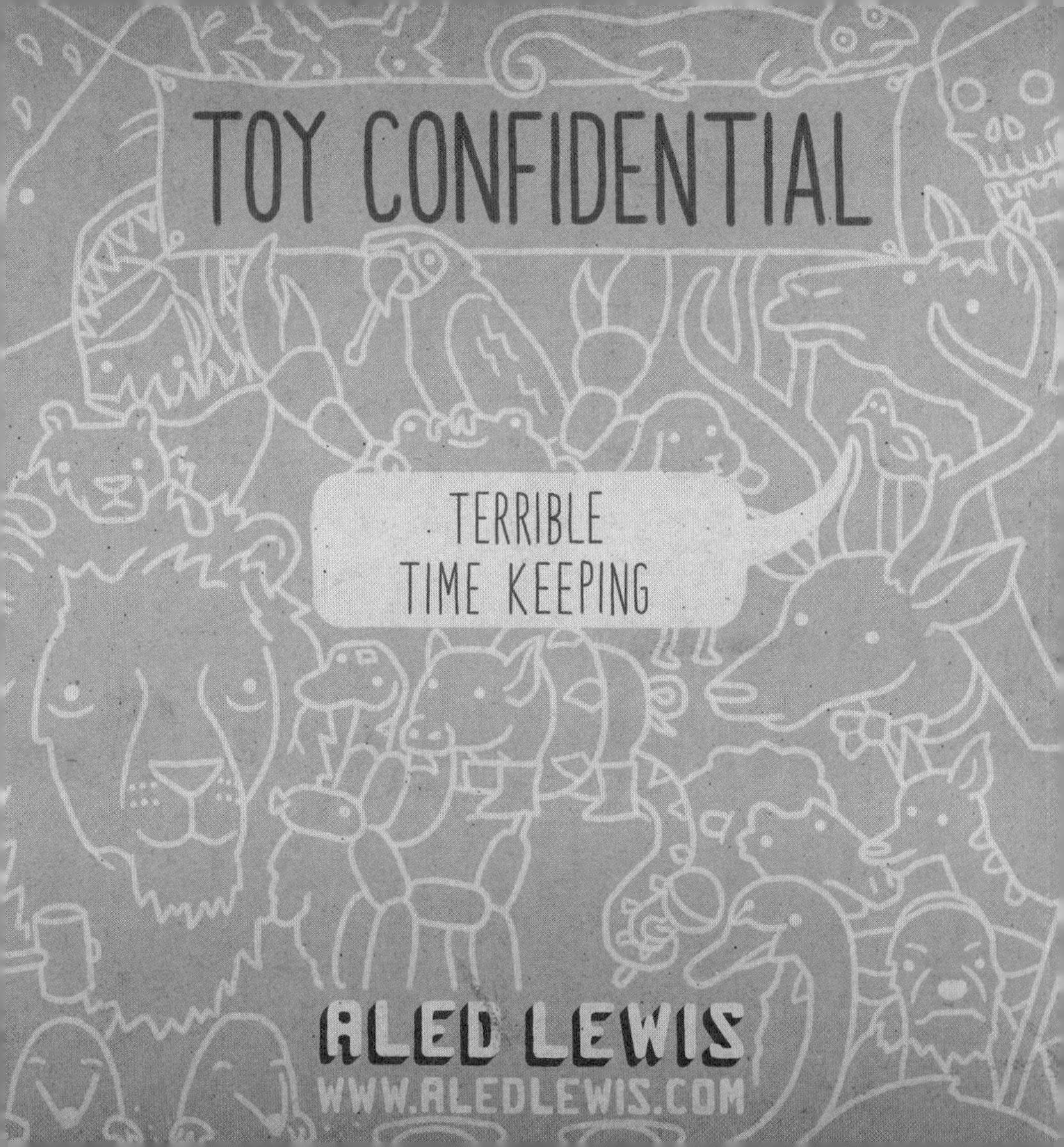
TOY CONFIDENTIAL
TERRIBLE
TIME KEEPING
ALED LEWIS
WWW.ALEDLEWIS.COM

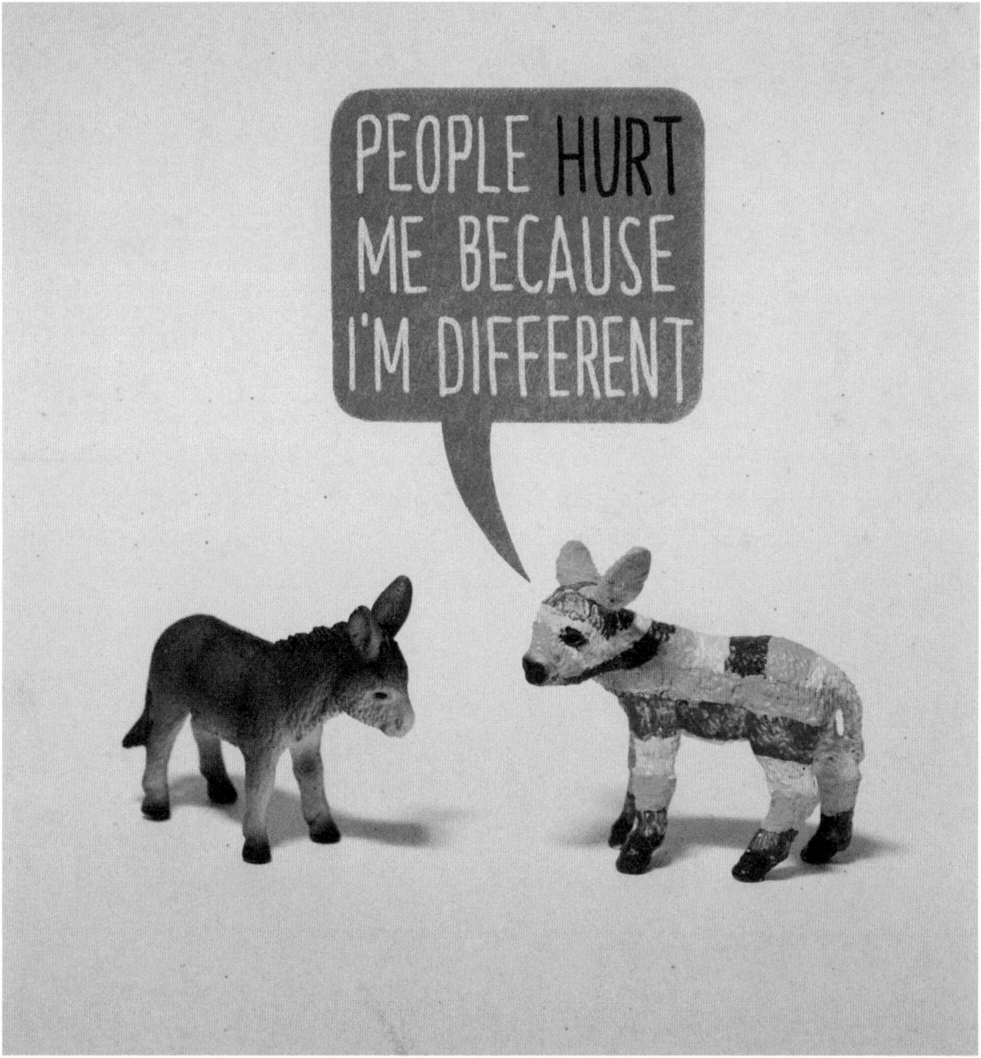
PEOPLE HURT ME BECAUSE I'M DIFFERENT

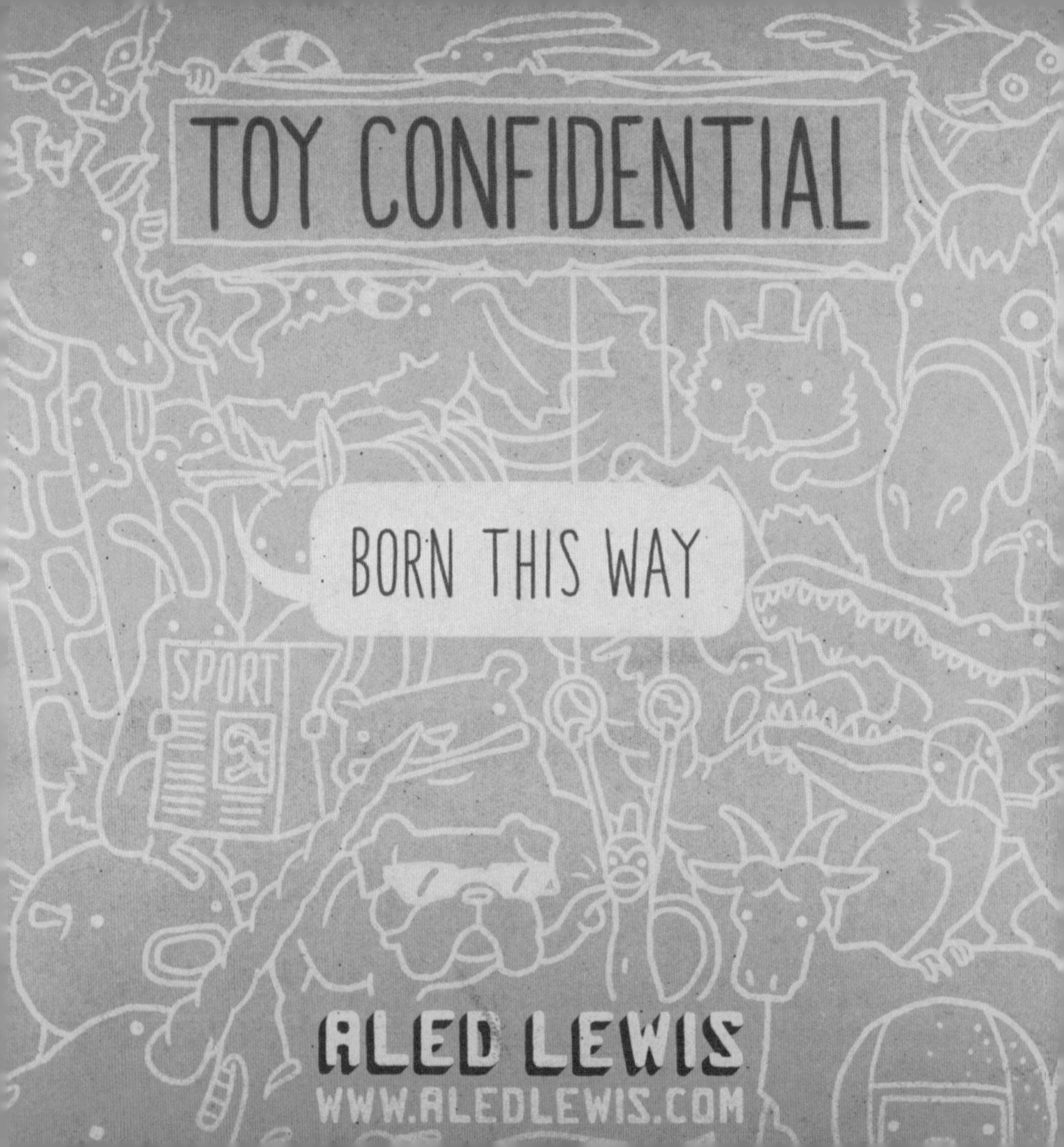
TOY CONFIDENTIAL
BORN THIS WAY
SPORT
ALED LEWIS
WWW.ALEDLEWIS.COM

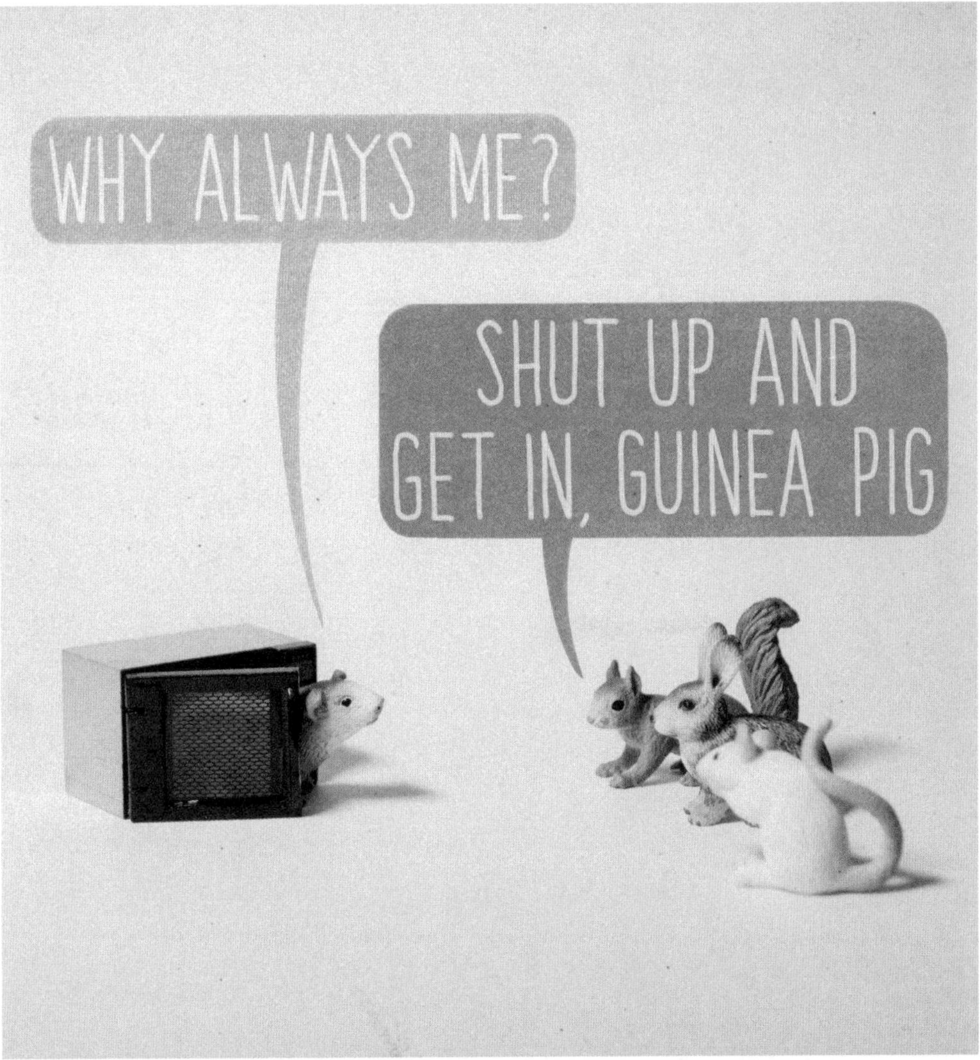
WHY ALWAYS ME?
SHUT UP AND GET IN, GUINEA PIG

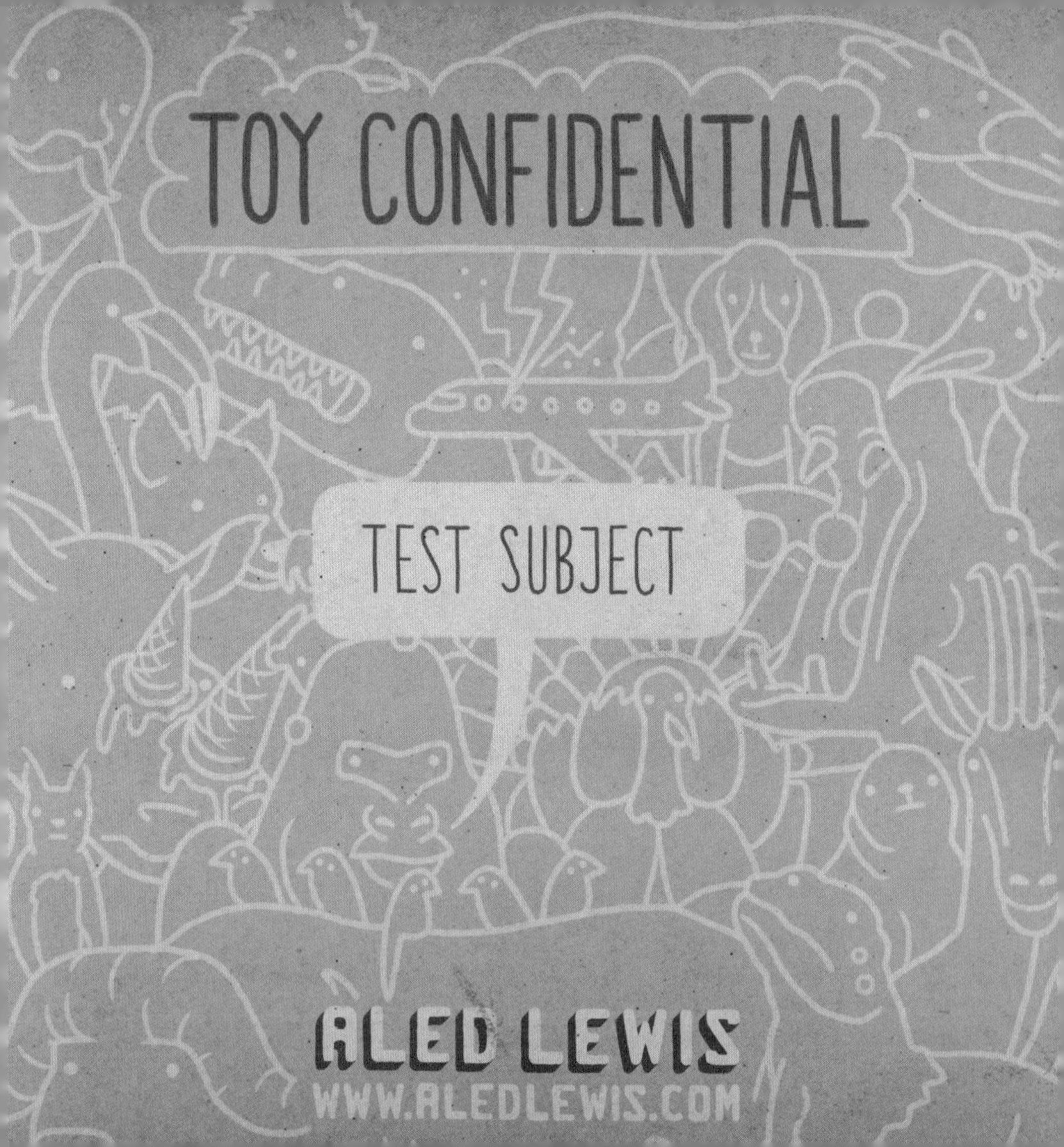
TOY CONFIDENTIAL
TEST SUBJECT
ALED LEWIS
WWW.ALEDLEWIS.COM

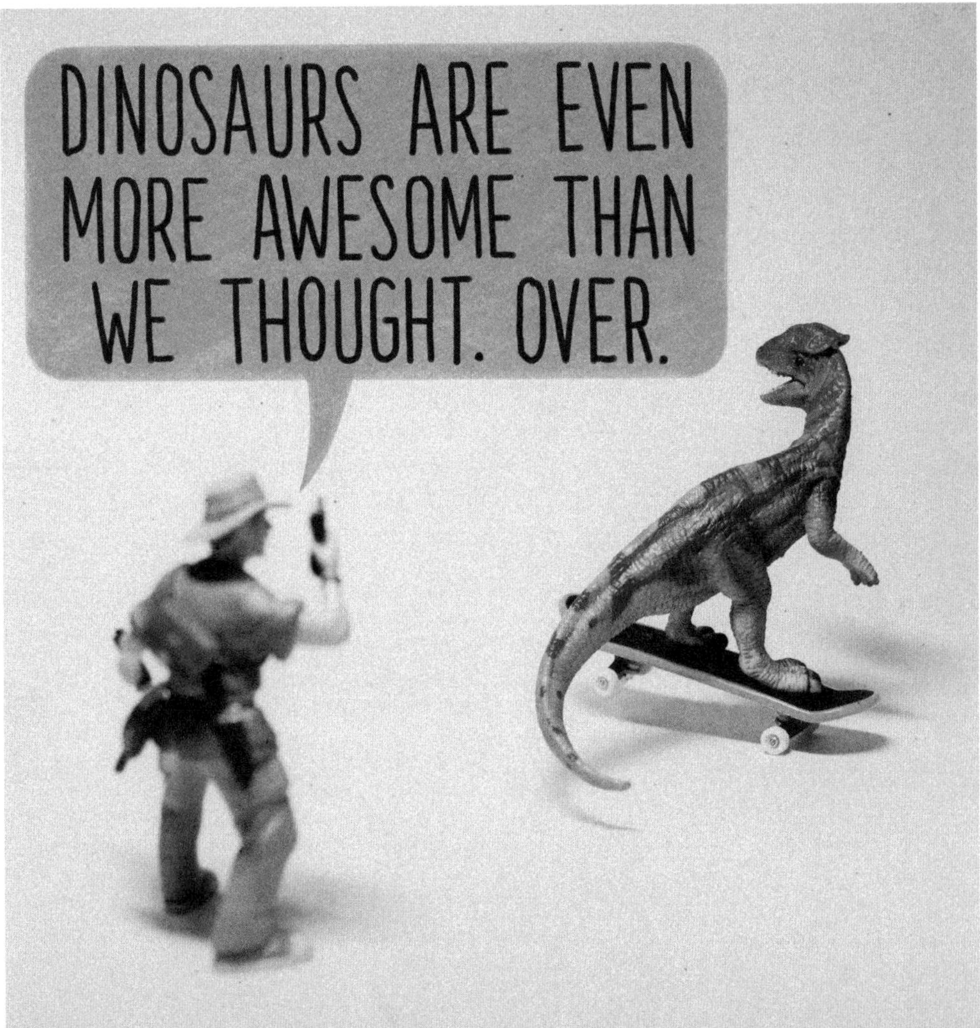
DINOSAURS ARE EVEN MORE AWESOME THAN WE THOUGHT. OVER.

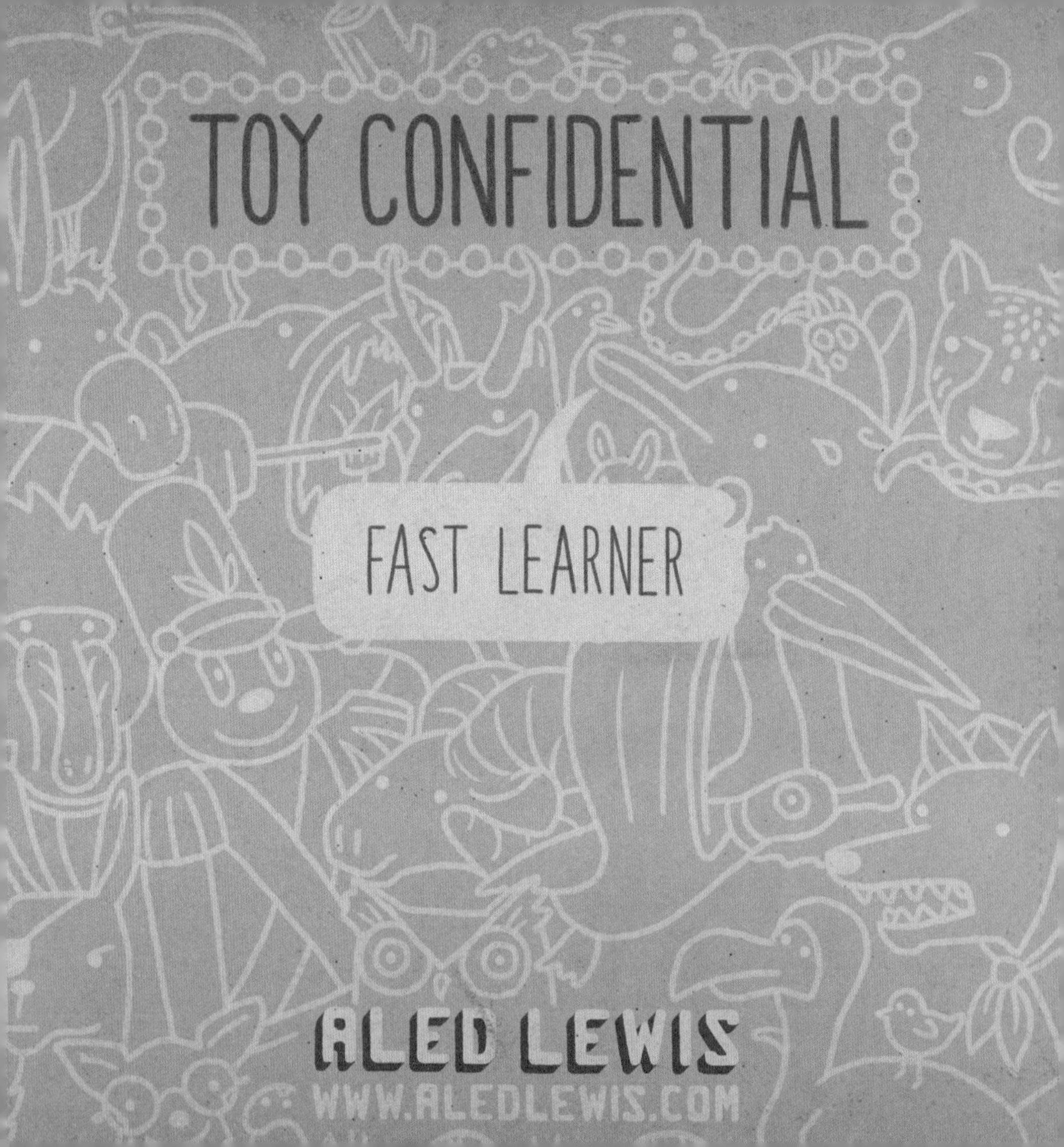
TOY CONFIDENTIAL
FAST LEARNER
ALED LEWIS
WWW.ALEDLEWIS.COM

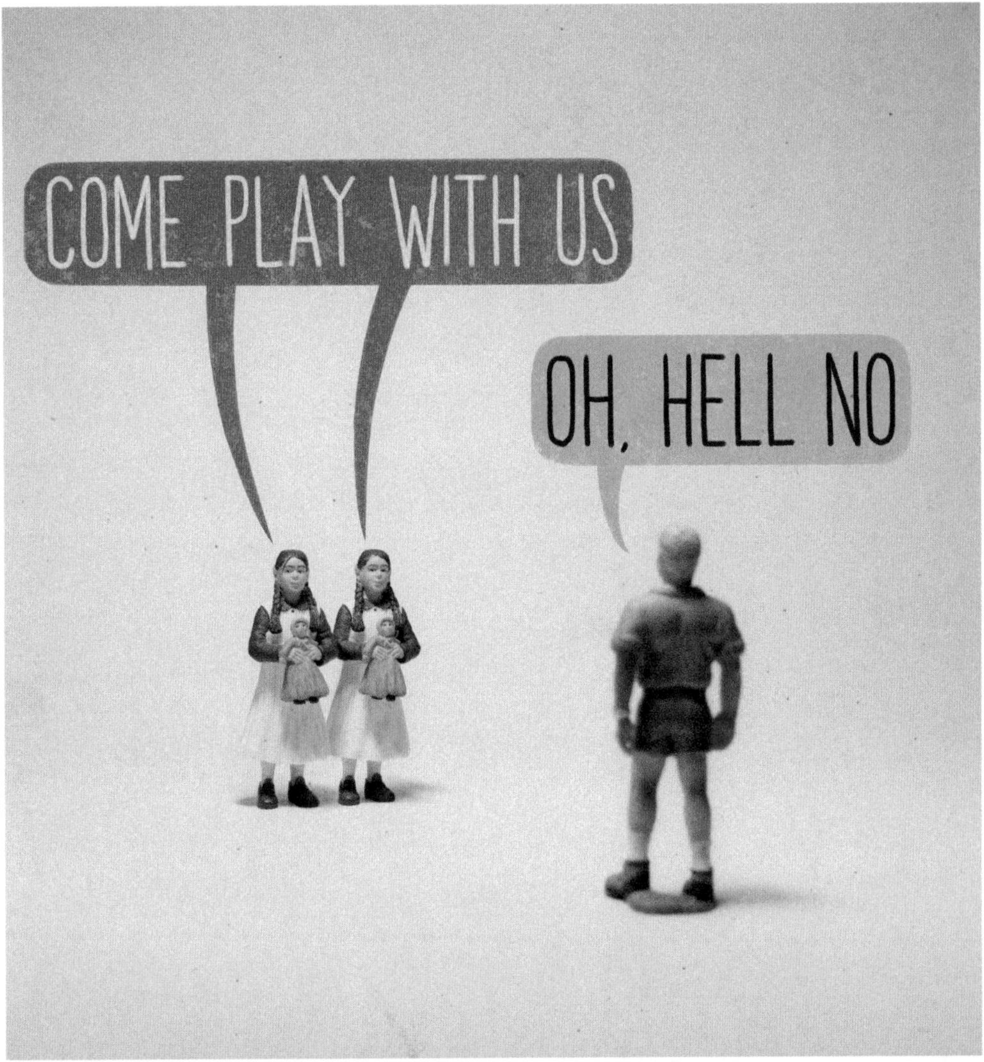
COME PLAY WITH US
OH, HELL NO

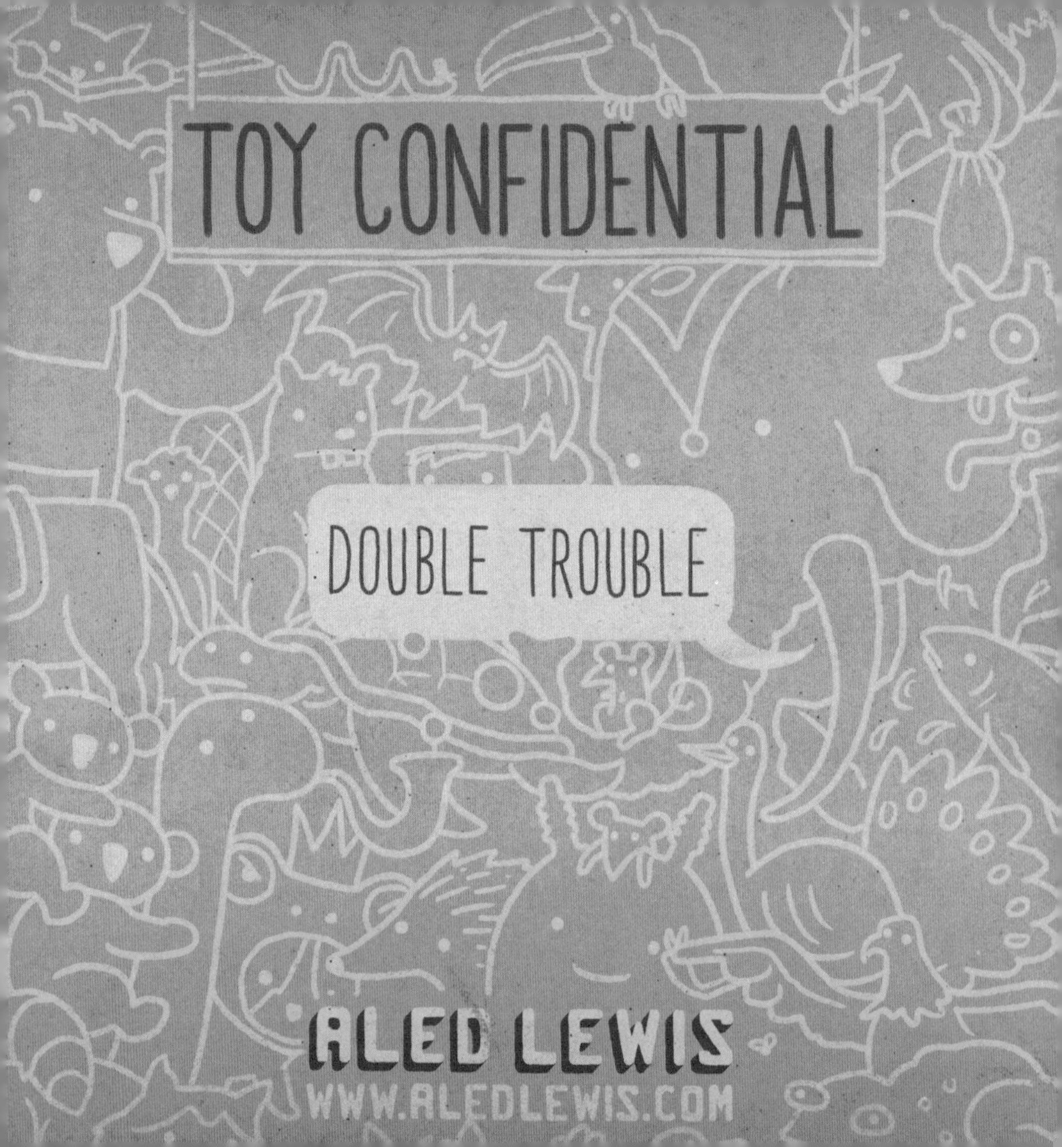
TOY CONFIDENTIAL
DOUBLE TROUBLE
ALED LEWIS
WWW.ALEDLEWIS.COM

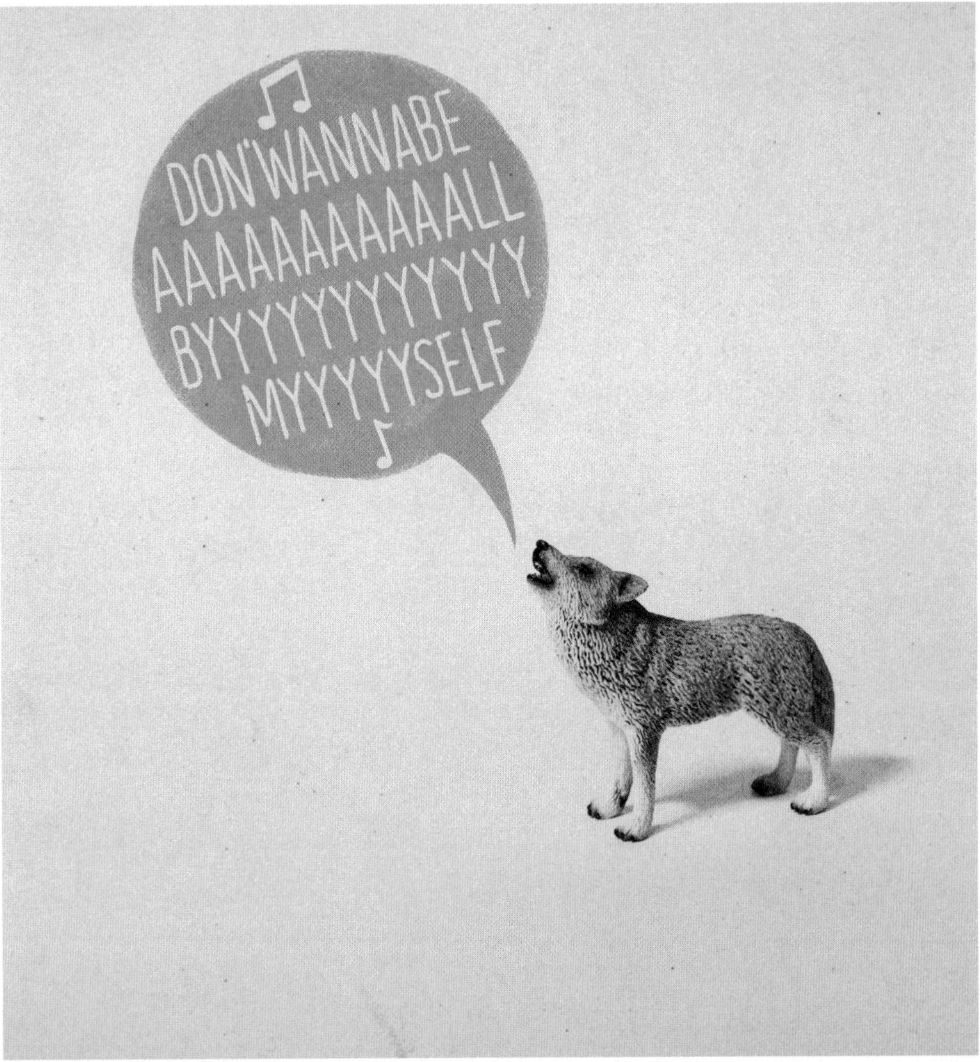
DON'WANNABE
AAAAAAAAAALL
BYYYYYYYYYYY
MYYYYYSELF

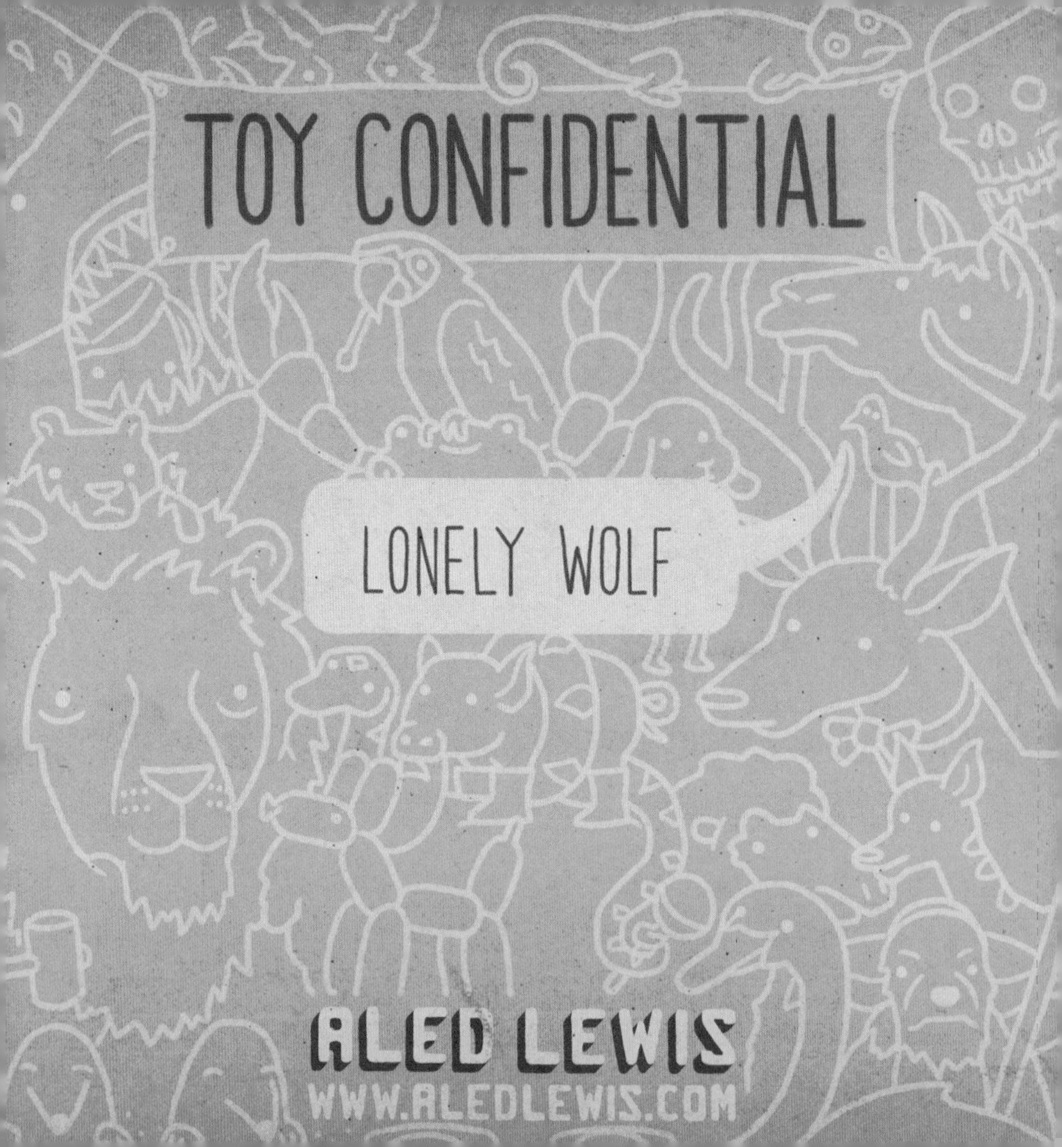
TOY CONFIDENTIAL
LONELY WOLF
ALED LEWIS
WWW.ALEDLEWIS.COM

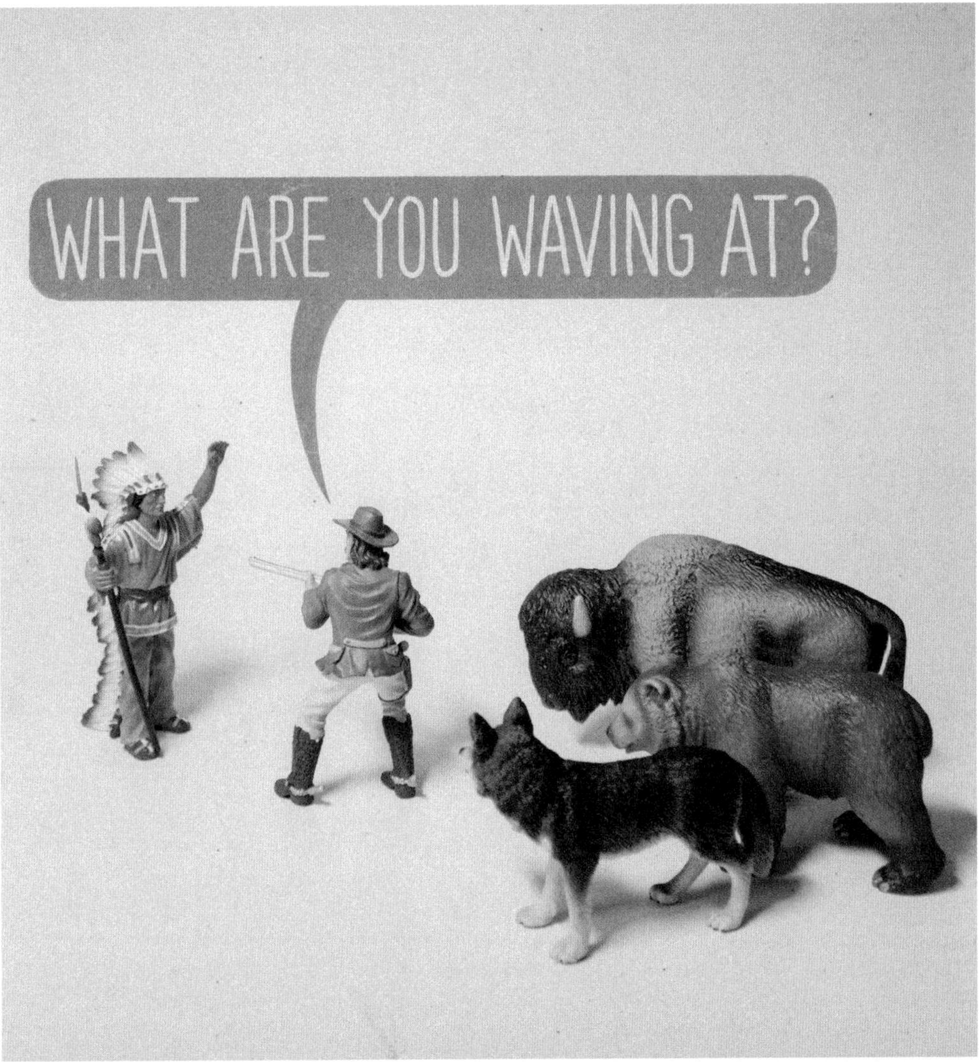
WHAT ARE YOU WAVING AT?

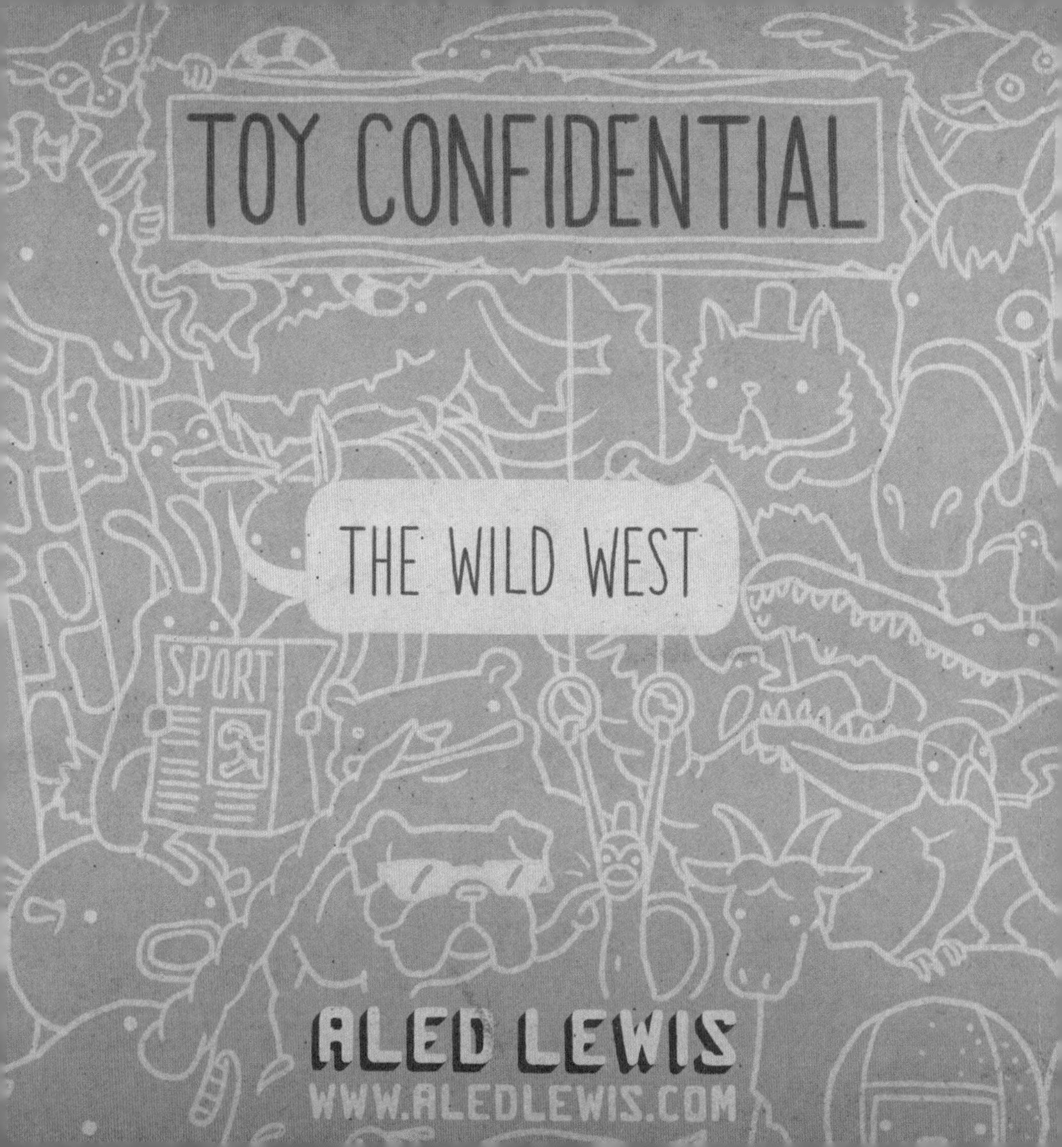
TOY CONFIDENTIAL
THE WILD WEST
SPORT
ALED LEWIS
WWW.ALEDLEWIS.COM

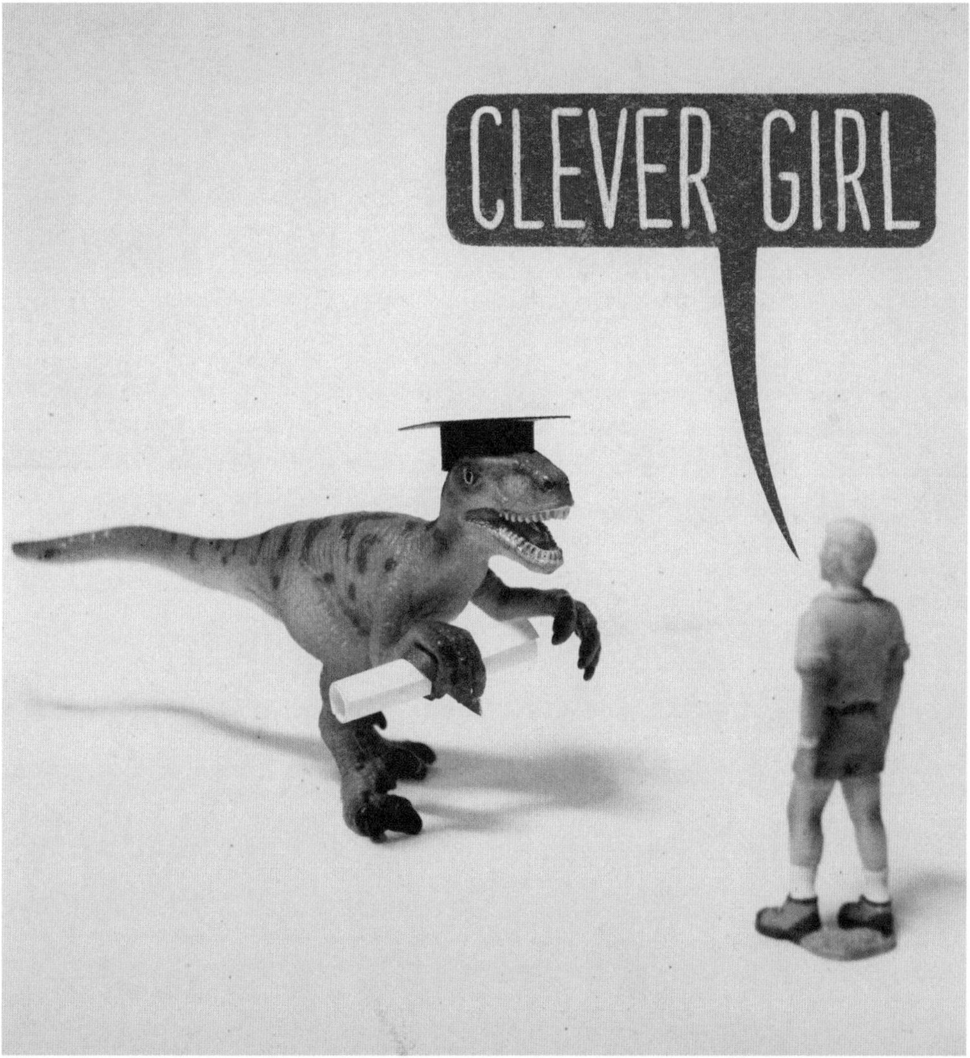
CLEVER GIRL

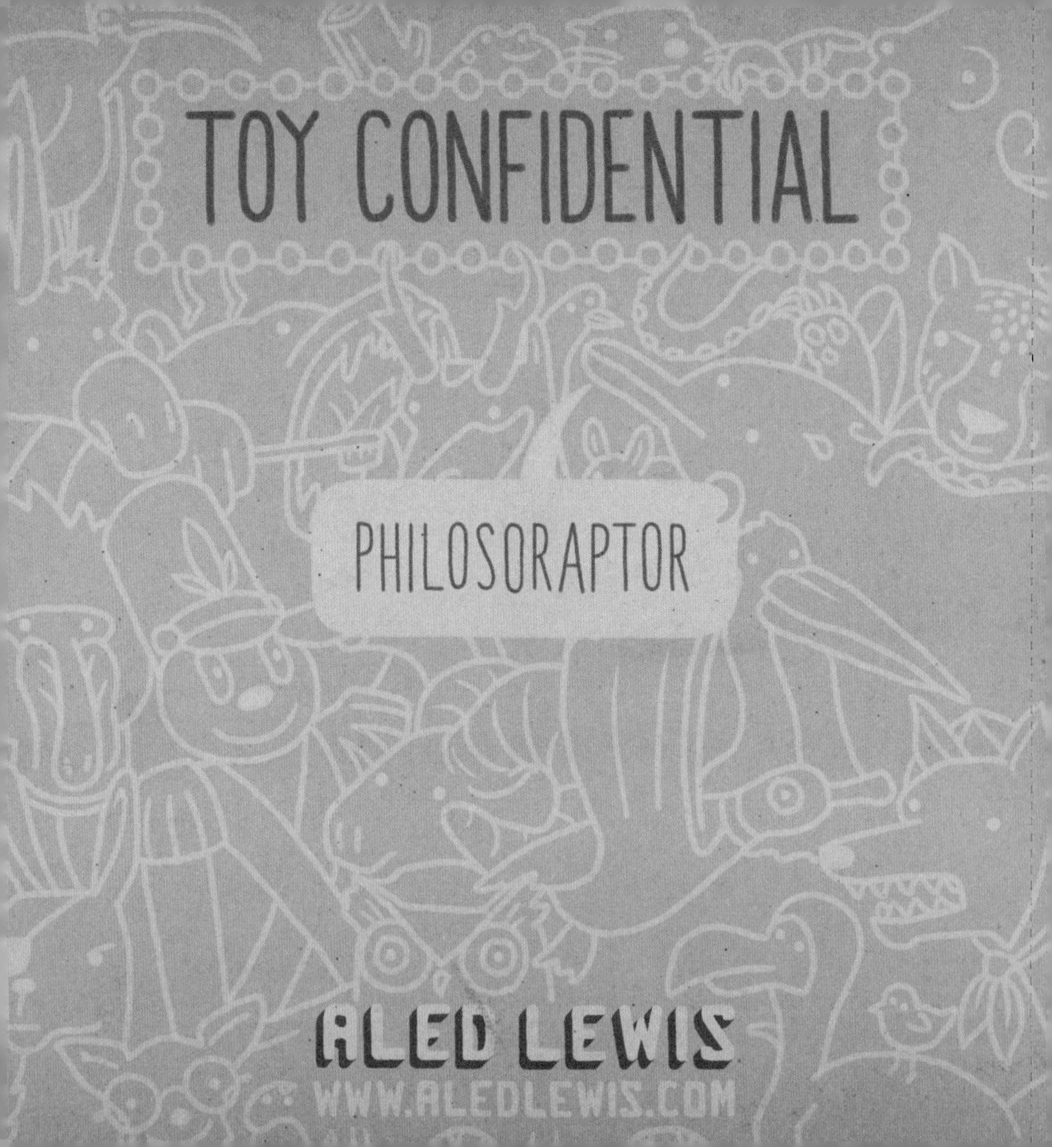
TOY CONFIDENTIAL
PHILOSORAPTOR
ALED LEWIS
WWW.ALEDLEWIS.COM

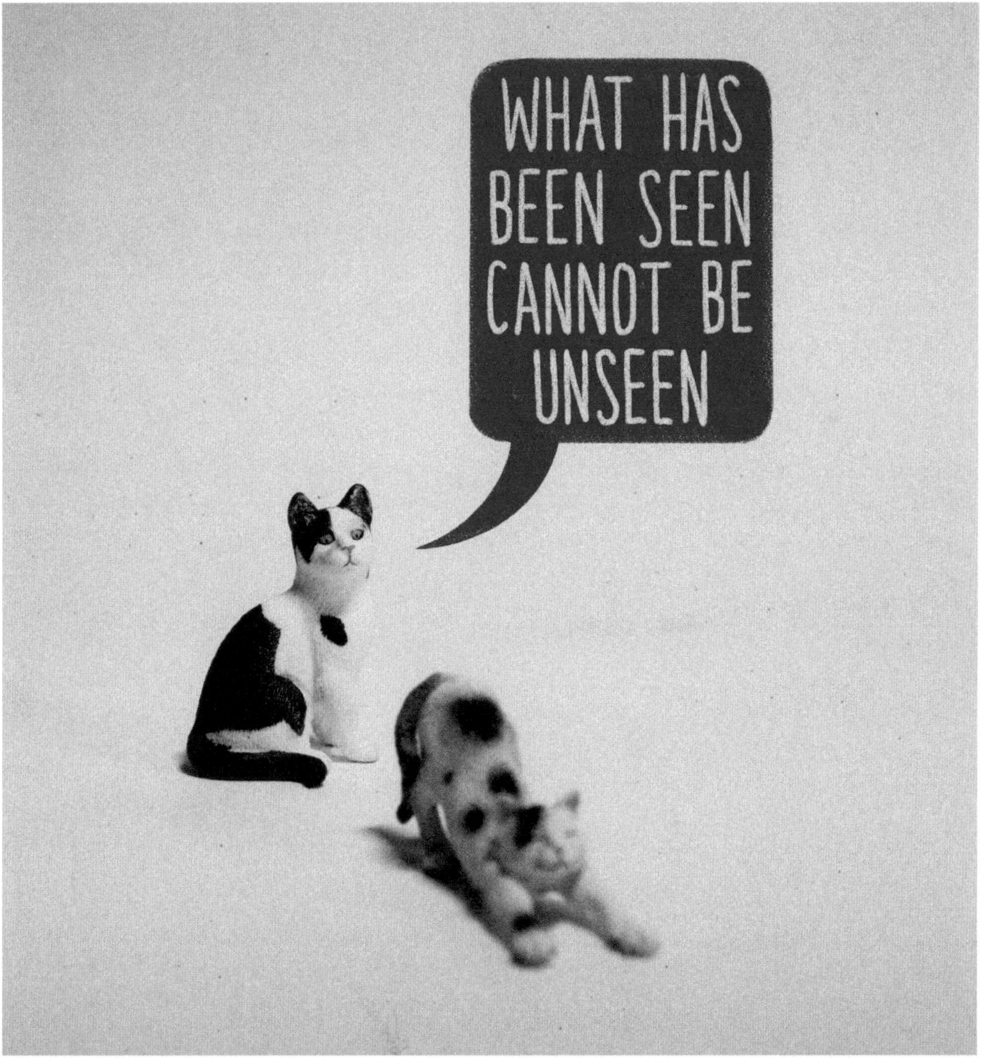
WHAT HAS BEEN SEEN CANNOT BE UNSEEN

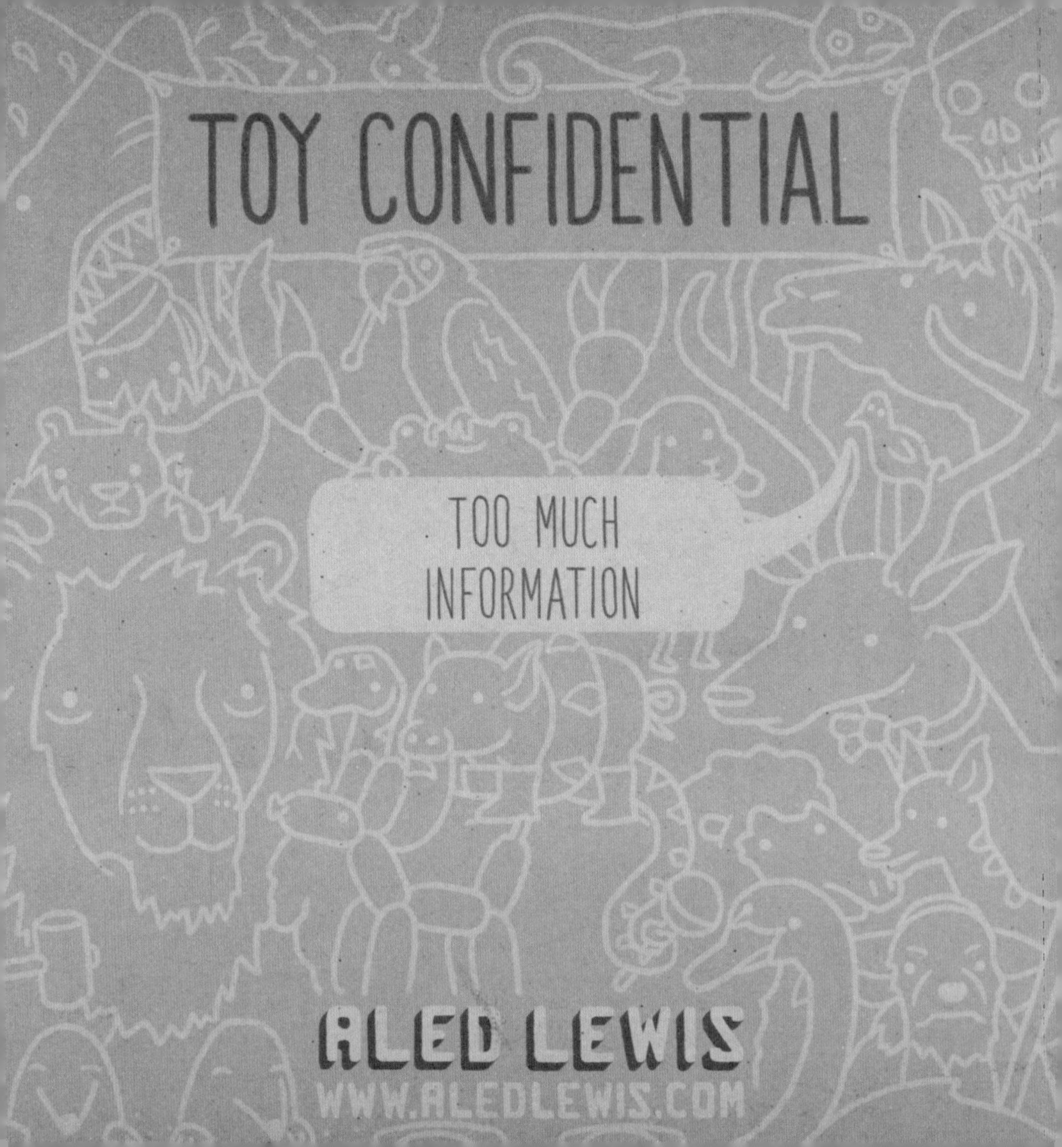
TOY CONFIDENTIAL
TOO MUCH INFORMATION
ALED LEWIS
WWW.ALEDLEWIS.COM

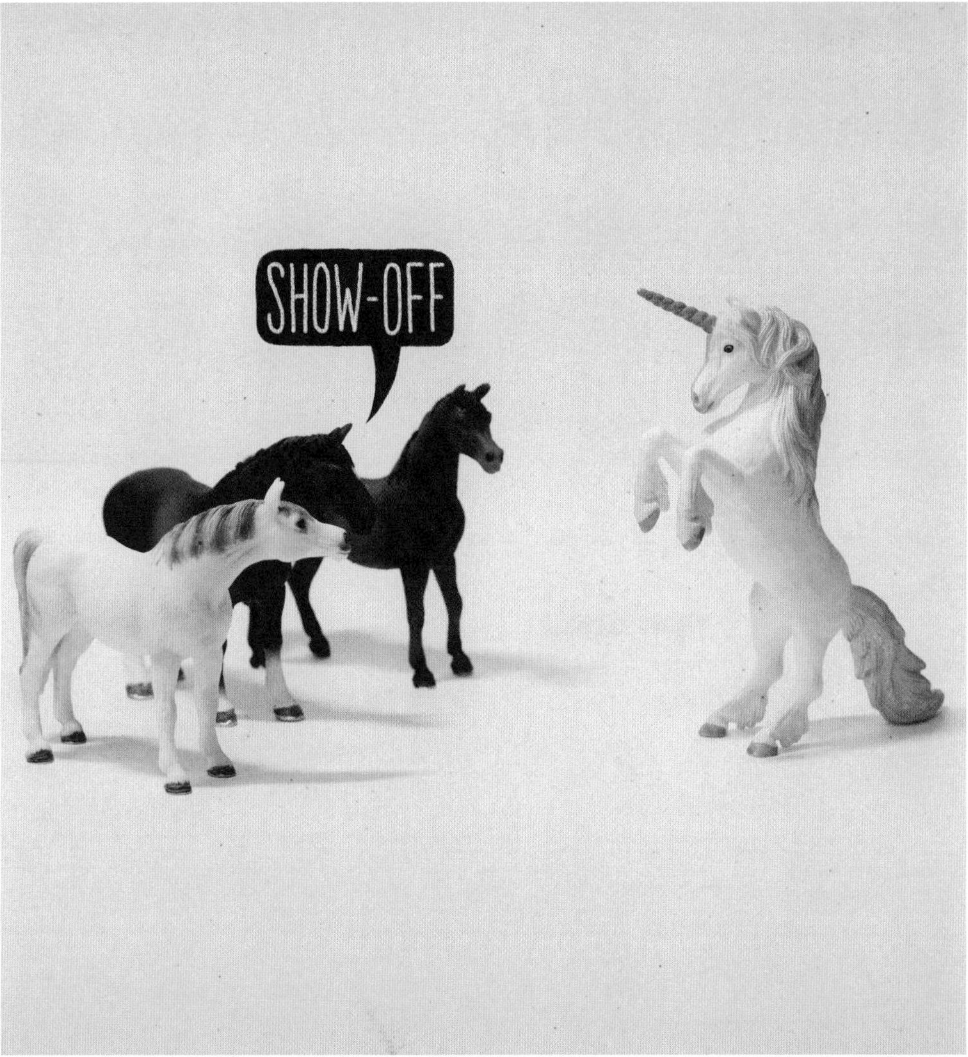
SHOW-OFF

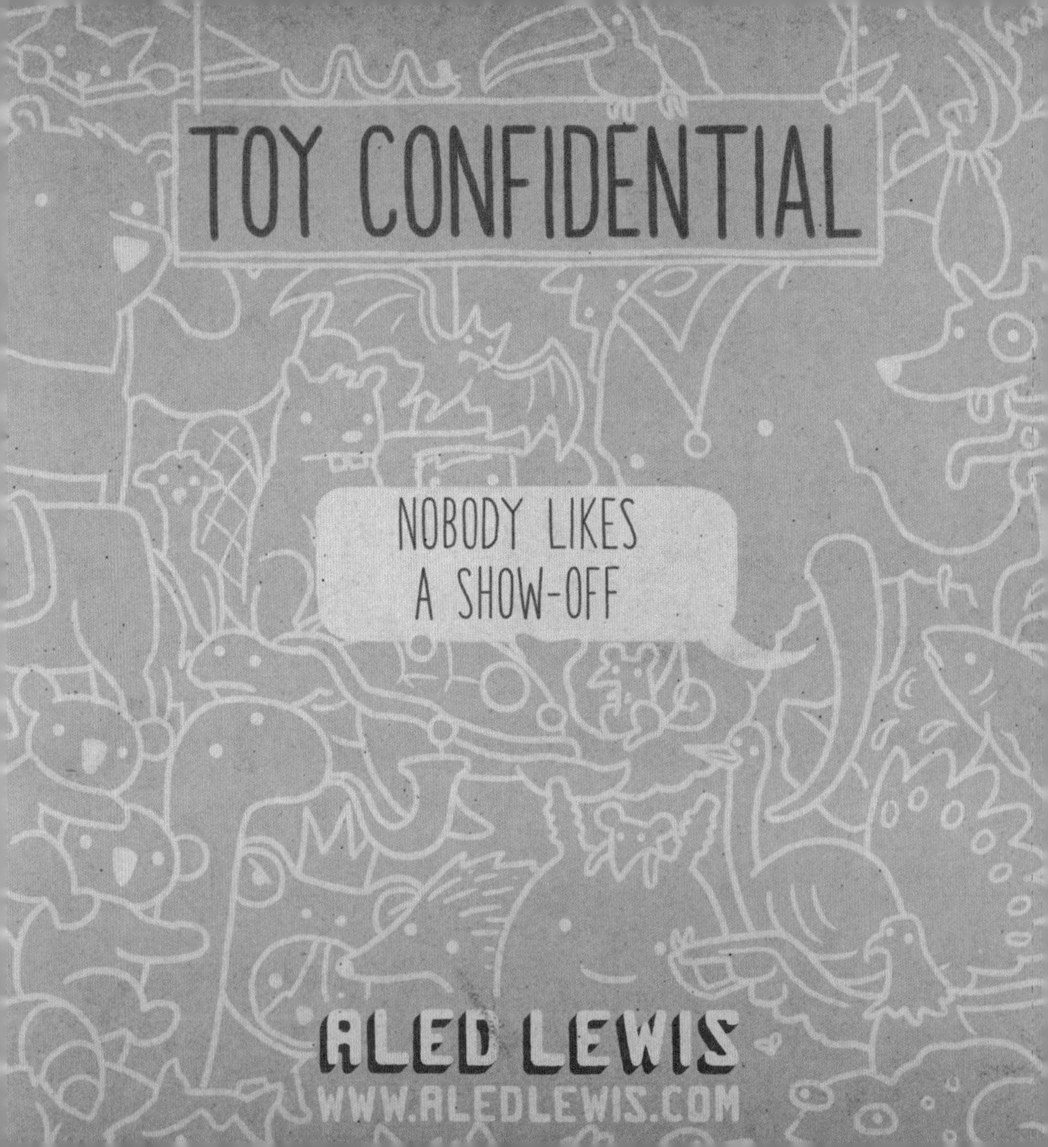
TOY CONFIDENTIAL
NOBODY LIKES A SHOW-OFF
ALED LEWIS
WWW.ALEDLEWIS.COM

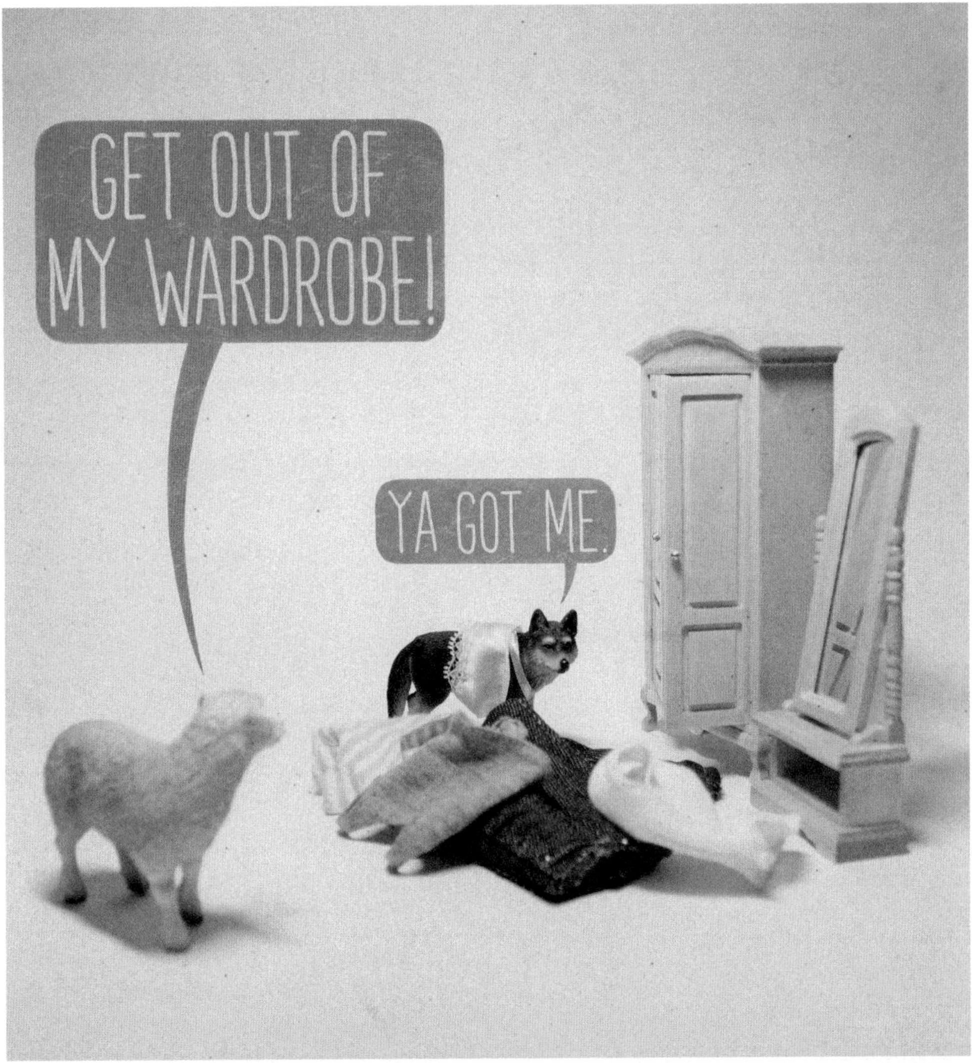
GET OUT OF MY WARDROBE!
YA GOT ME.

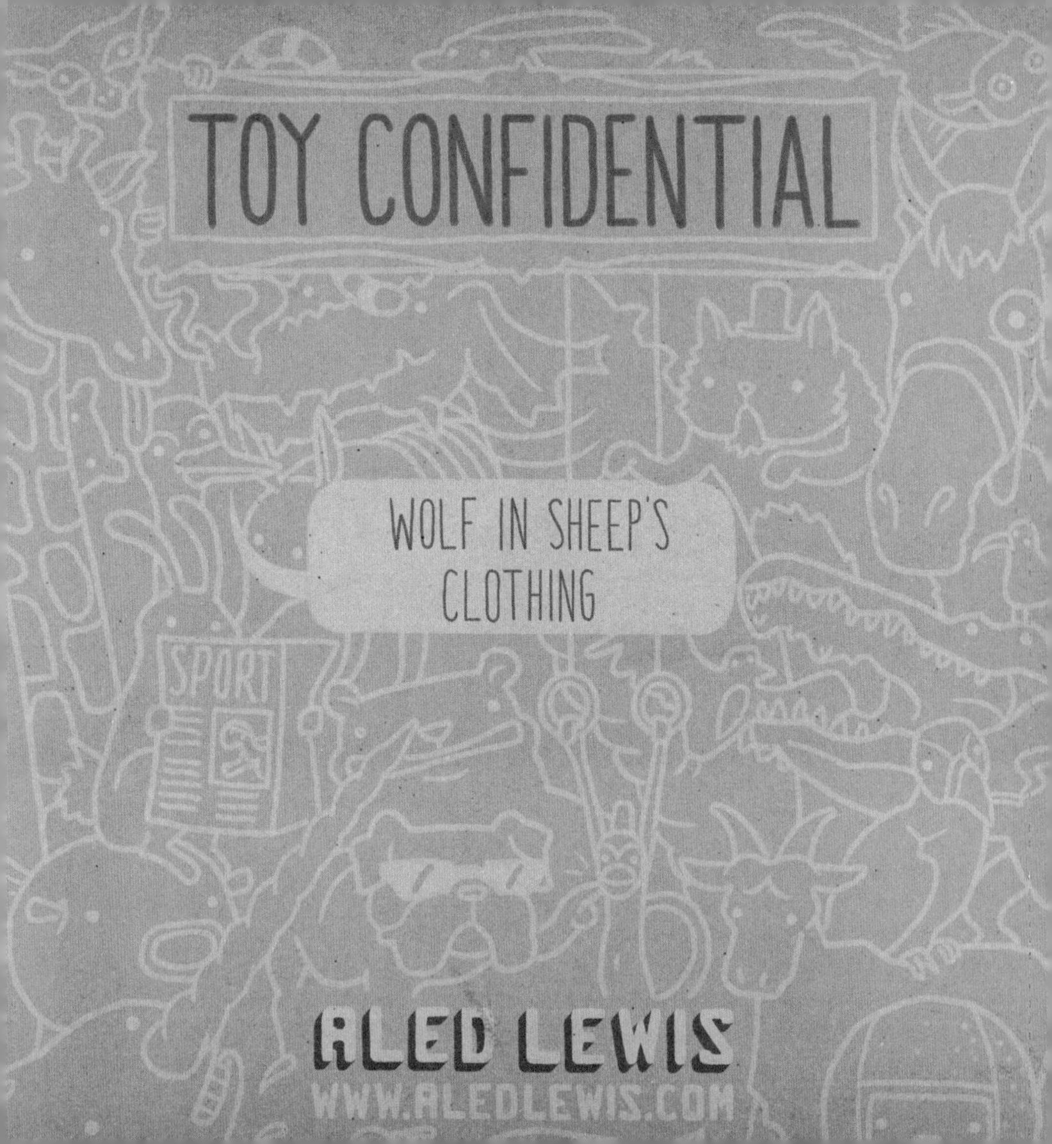
TOY CONFIDENTIAL
WOLF IN SHEEP'S CLOTHING
SPORT
ALED LEWIS
WWW.ALEDLEWIS.COM

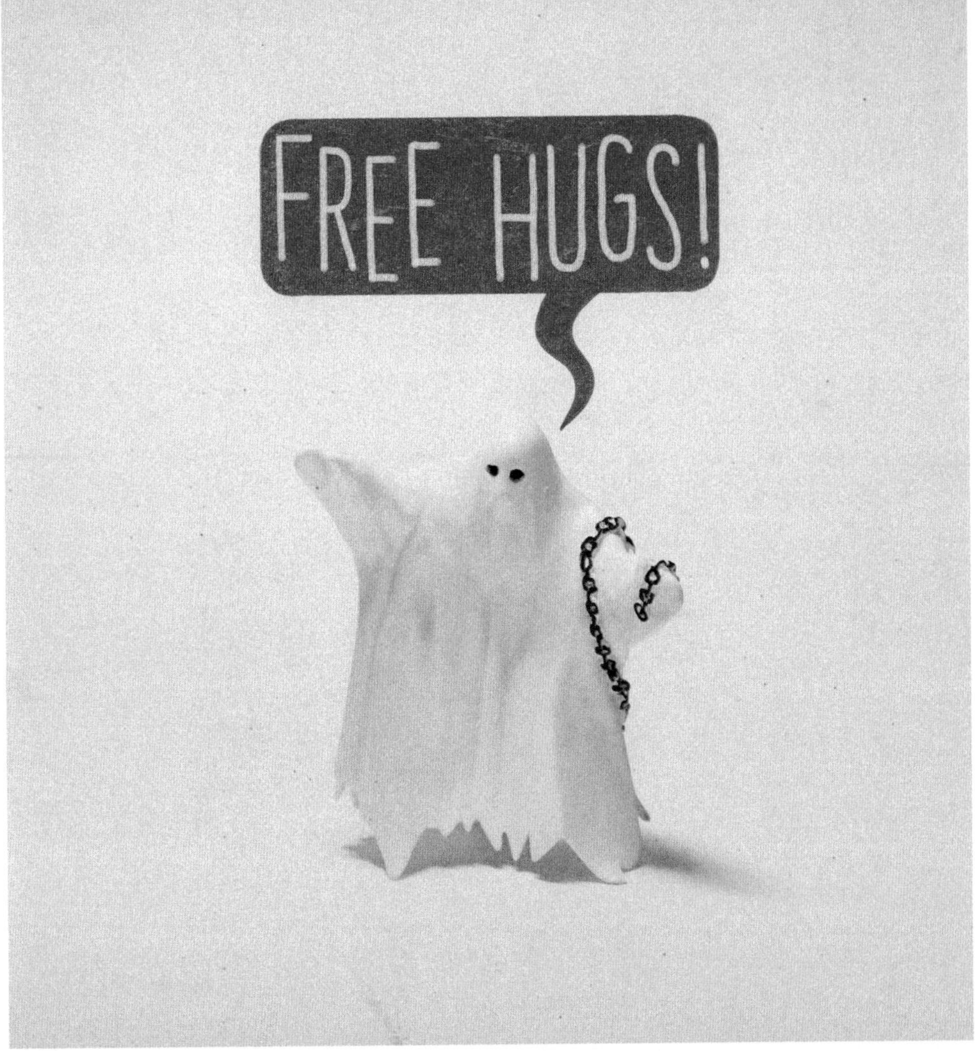
FREE HUGS!

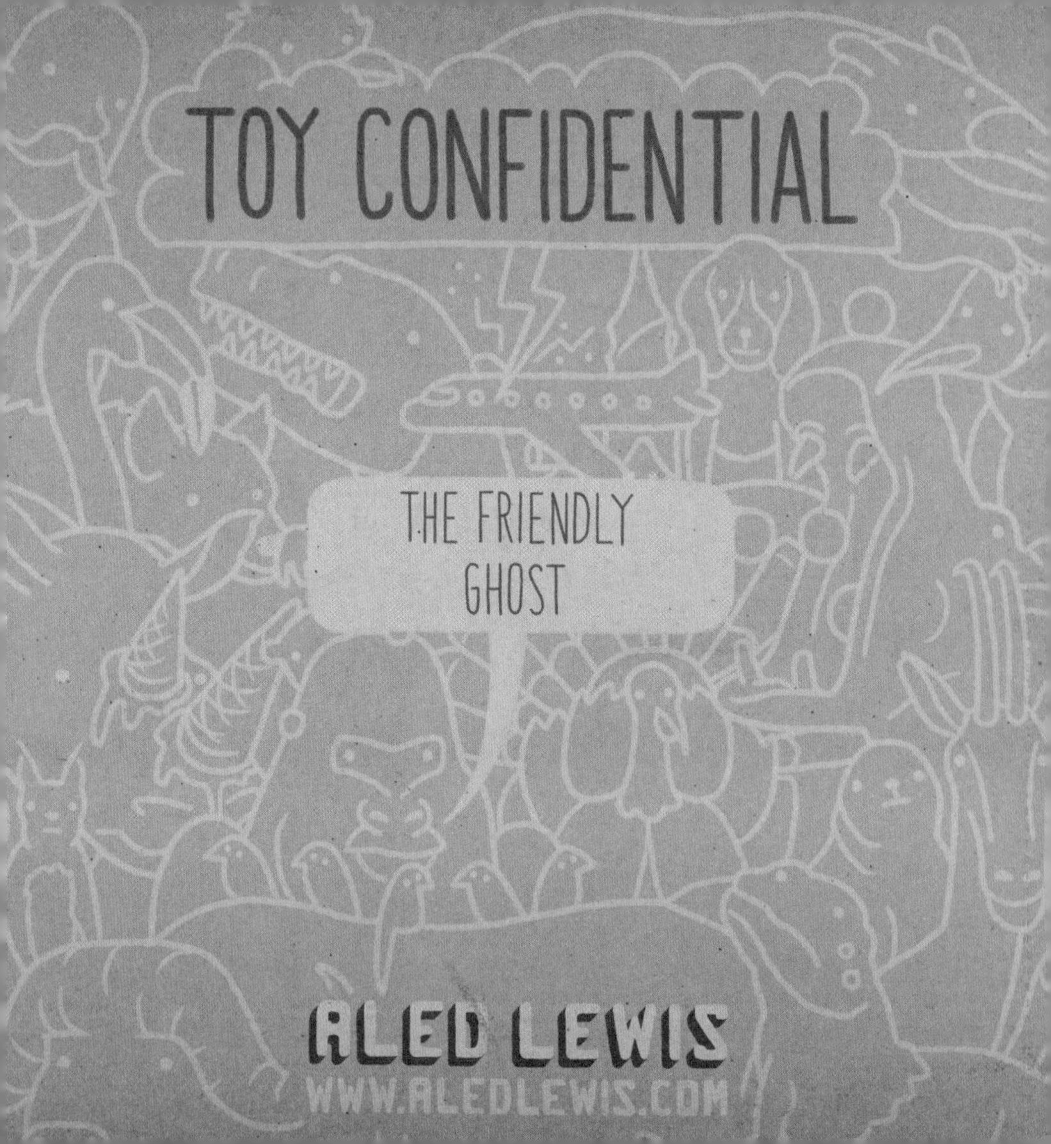
TOY CONFIDENTIAL
THE FRIENDLY GHOST
ALED LEWIS
WWW.ALEDLEWIS.COM

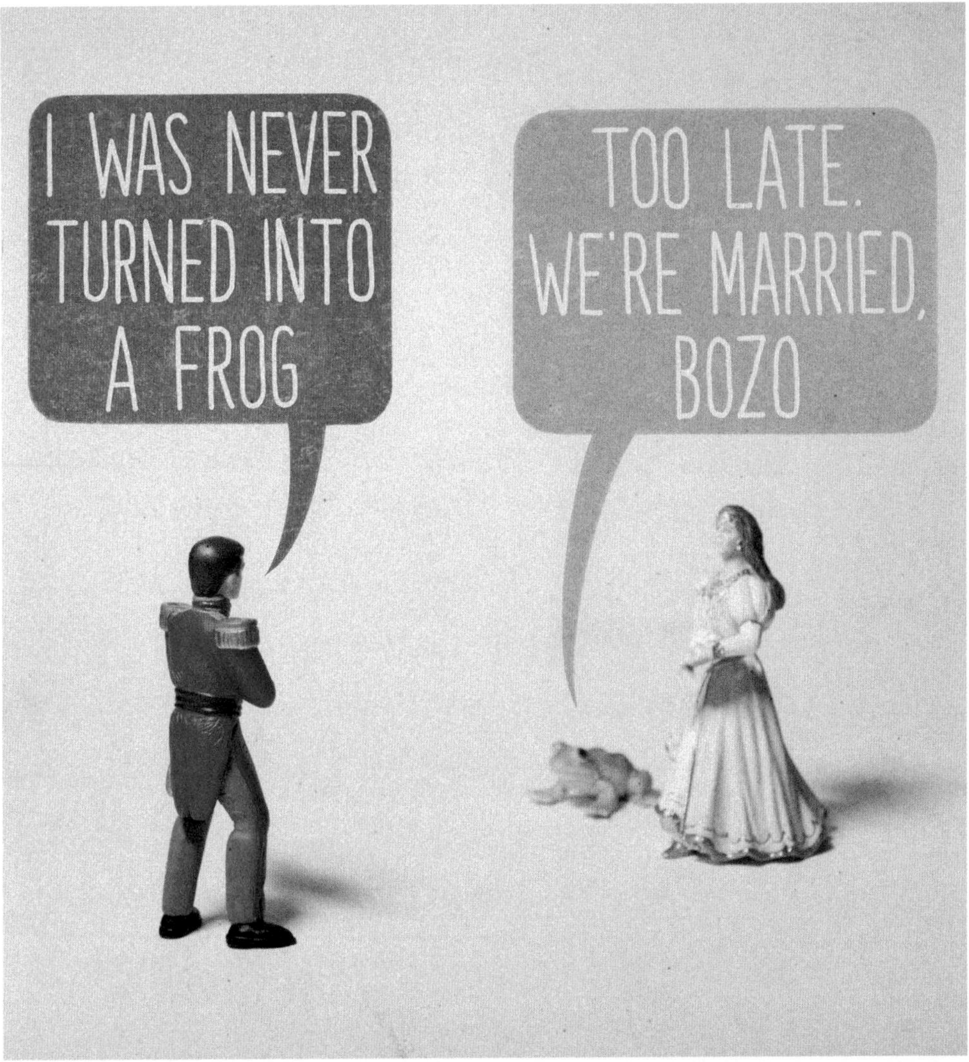
I WAS NEVER TURNED INTO A FROG
TOO LATE. WE'RE MARRIED, BOZO

TOY CONFIDENTIAL

THE FROG PRINCE

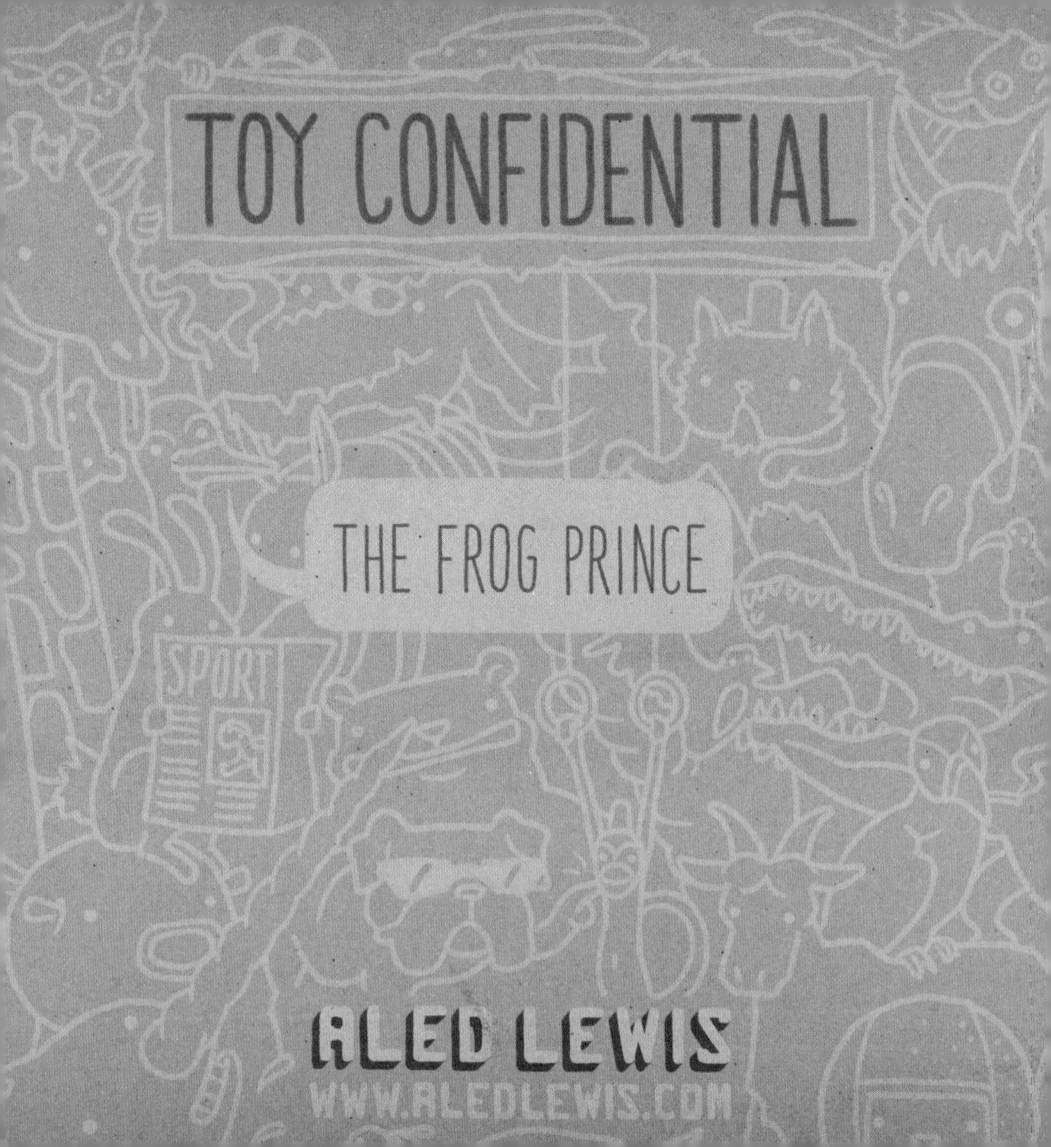
SPORT

ALED LEWIS

WWW.ALEDLEWIS.COM

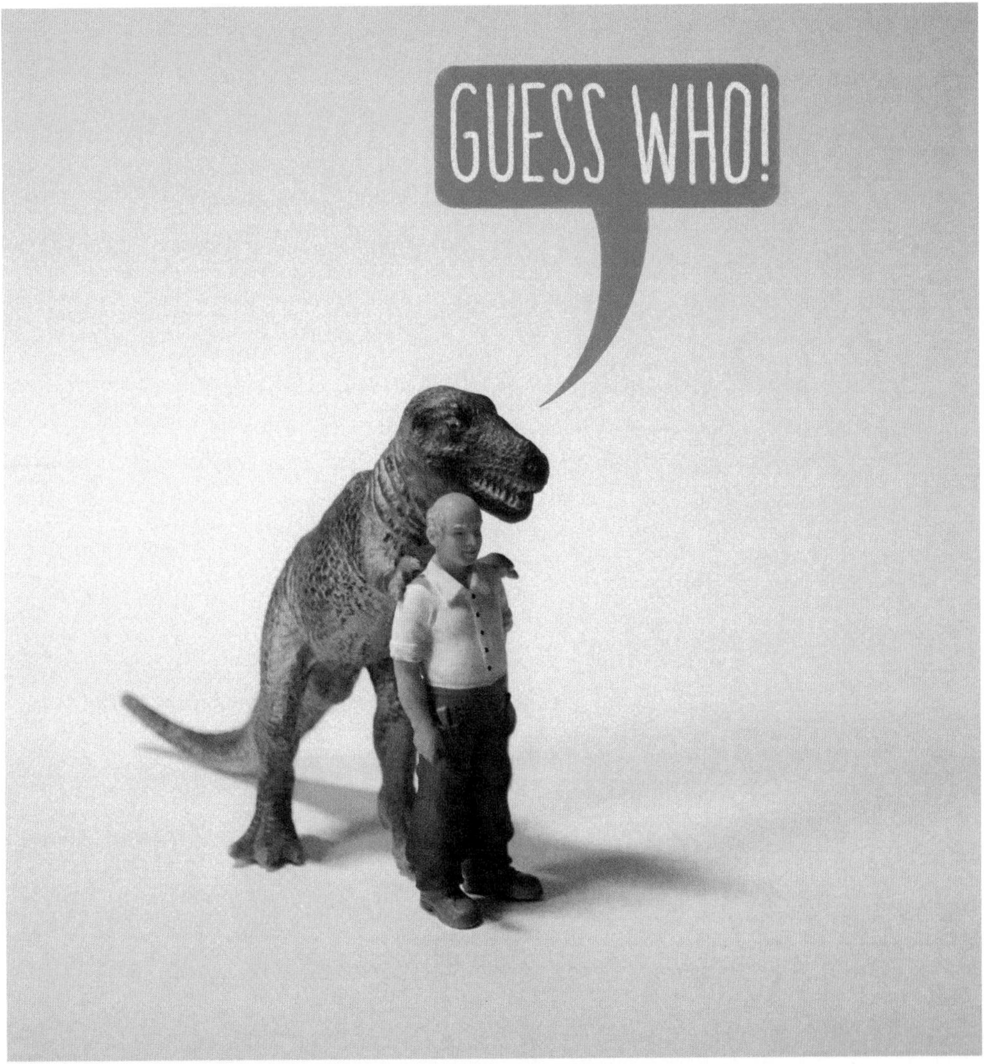
GUESS WHO!

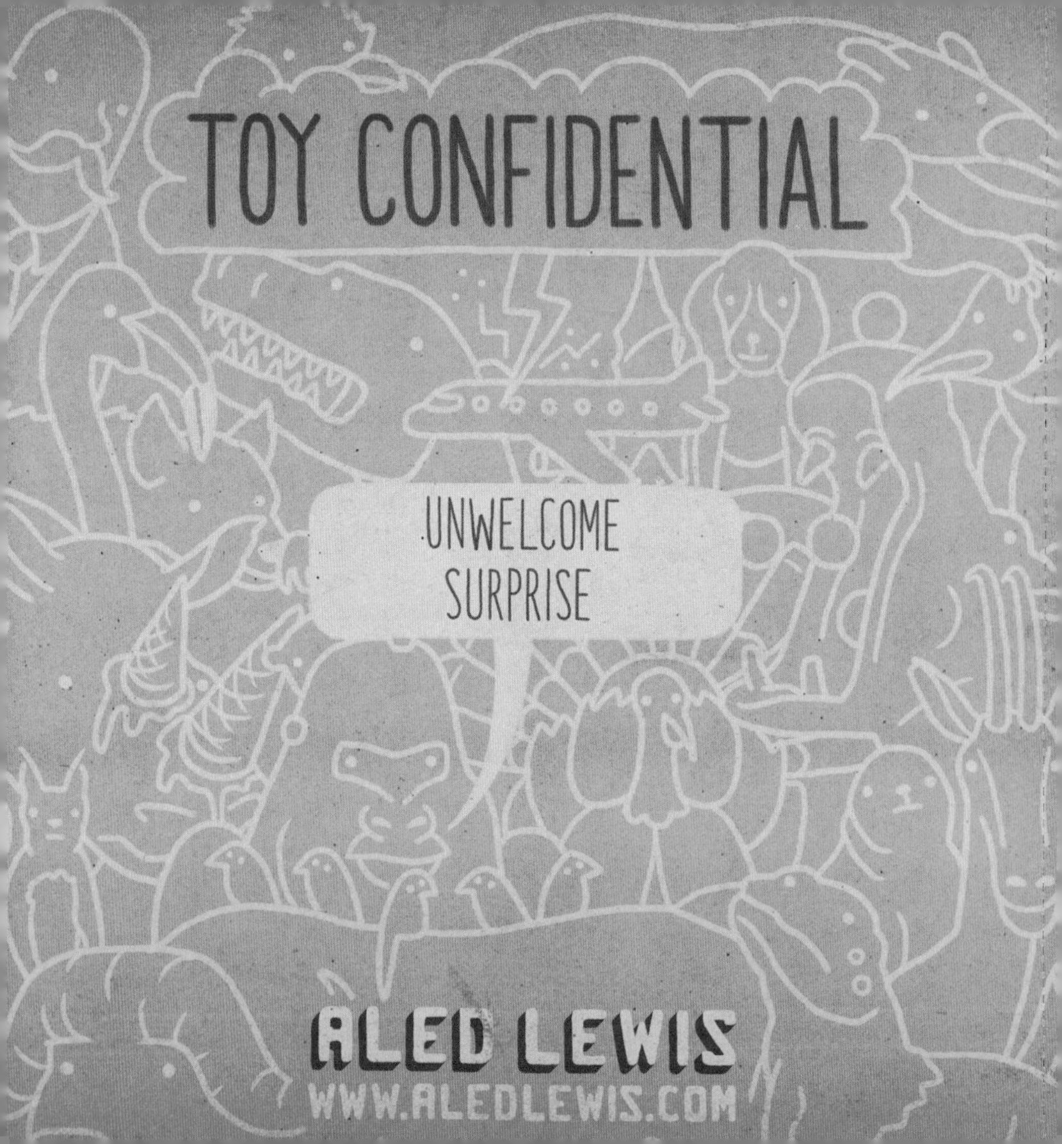
TOY CONFIDENTIAL
UNWELCOME
SURPRISE
ALED LEWIS
WWW.ALEDLEWIS.COM

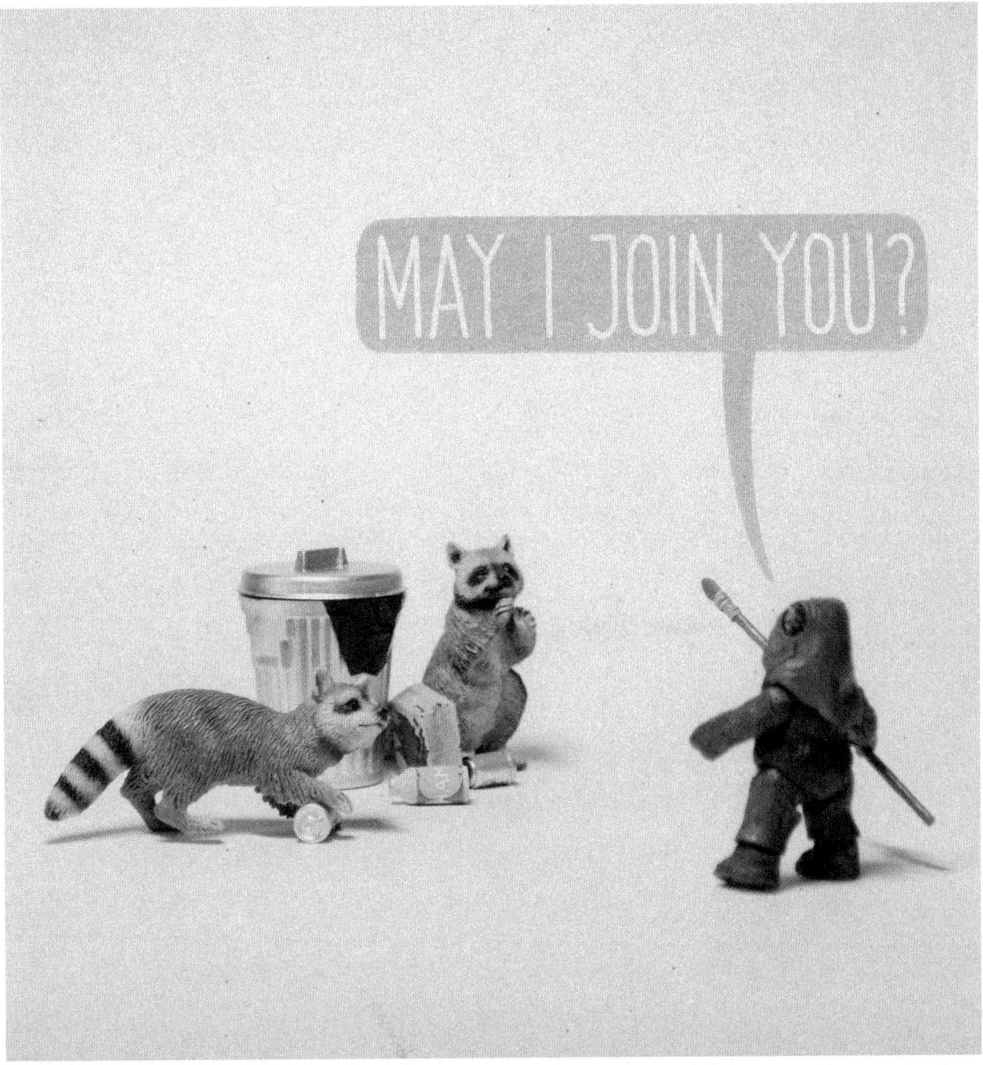
MAY I JOIN YOU?

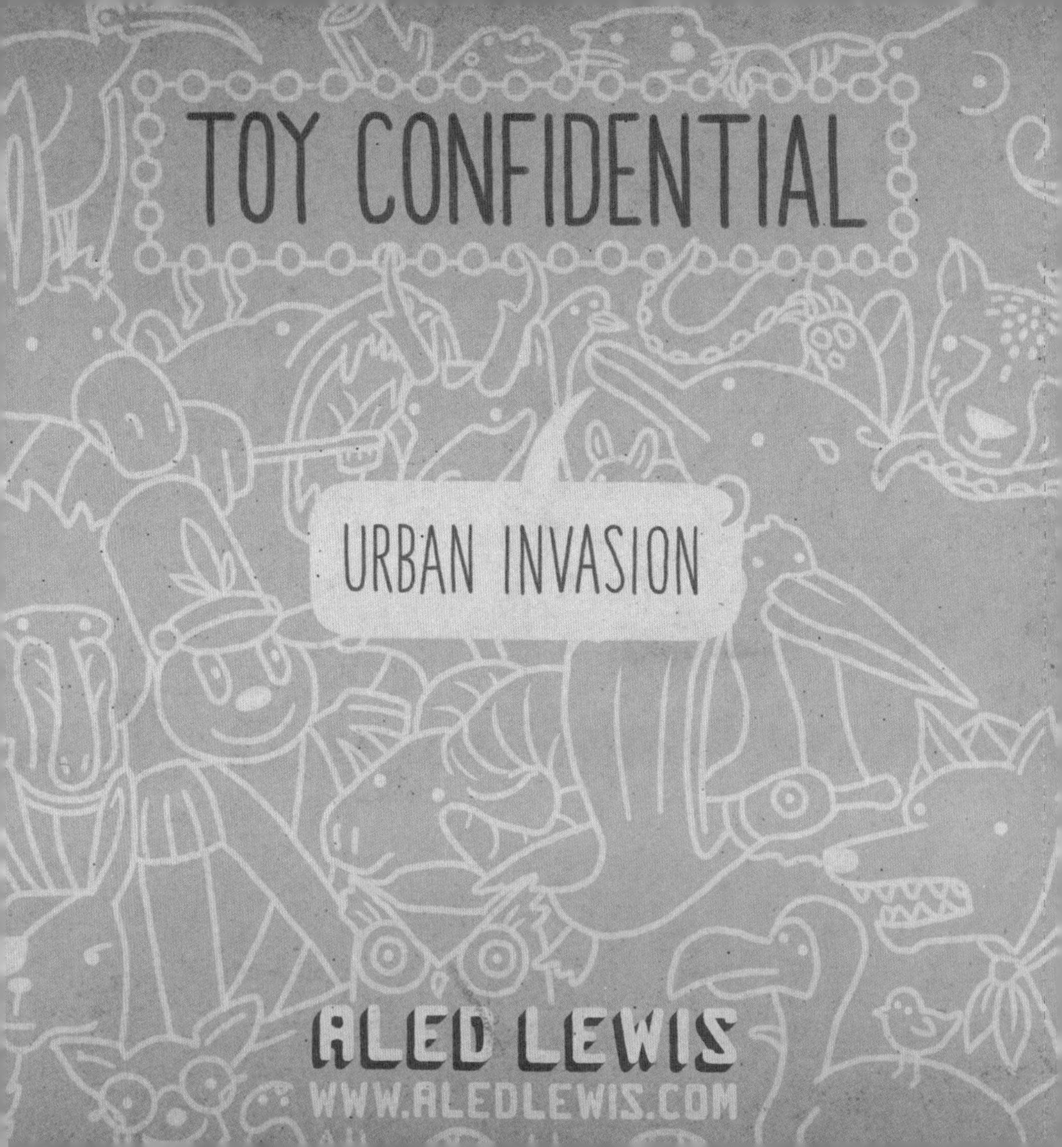
TOY CONFIDENTIAL
URBAN INVASION
ALED LEWIS
WWW.ALEDLEWIS.COM

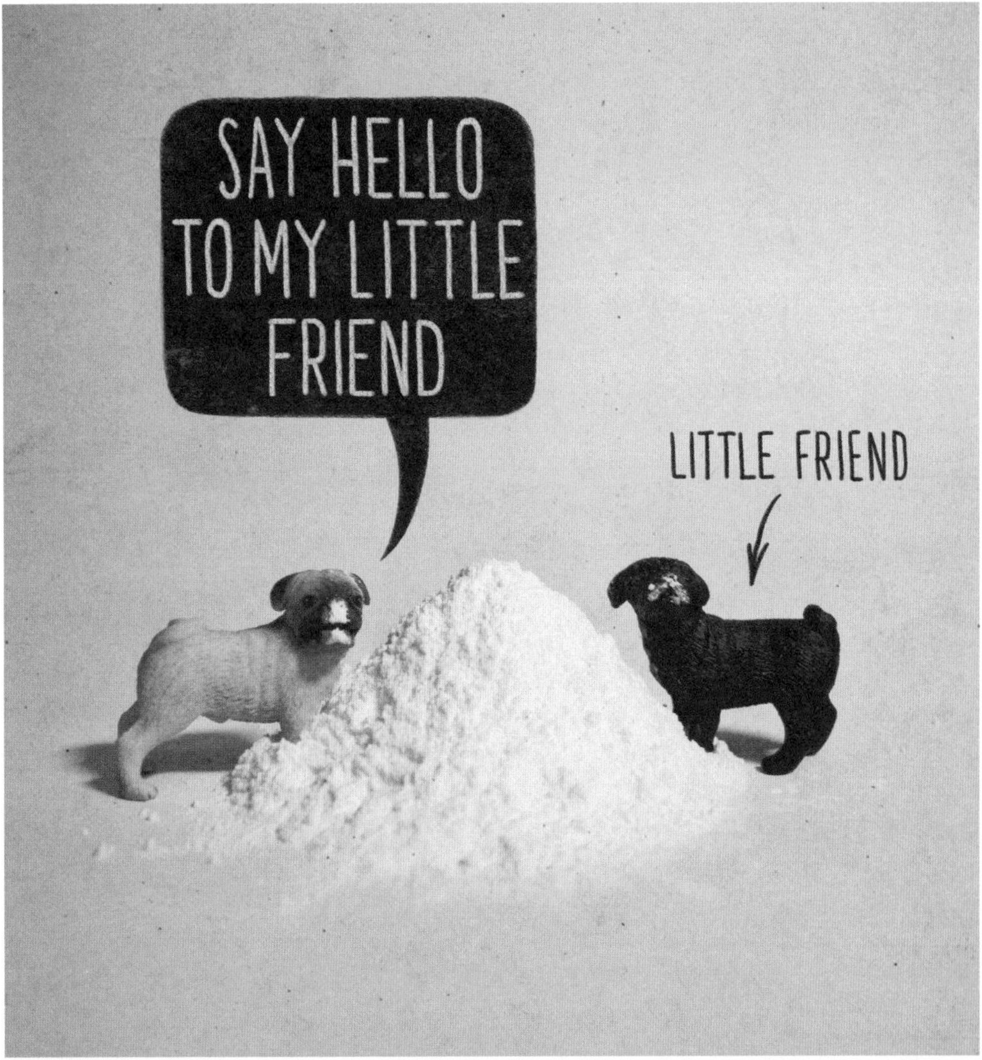
SAY HELLO TO MY LITTLE FRIEND
LITTLE FRIEND

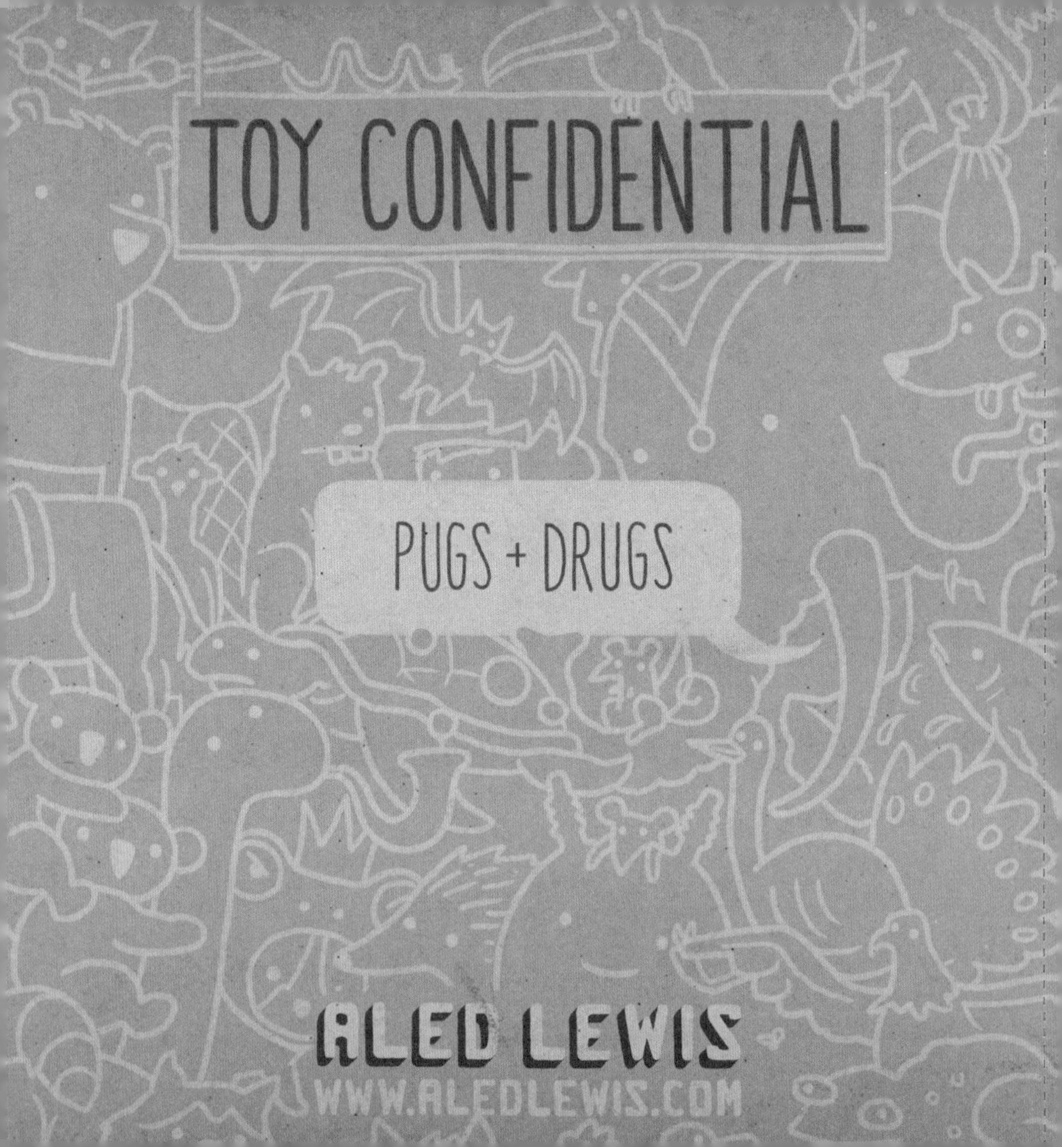
TOY CONFIDENTIAL
PUGS + DRUGS
ALED LEWIS
WWW.ALEDLEWIS.COM

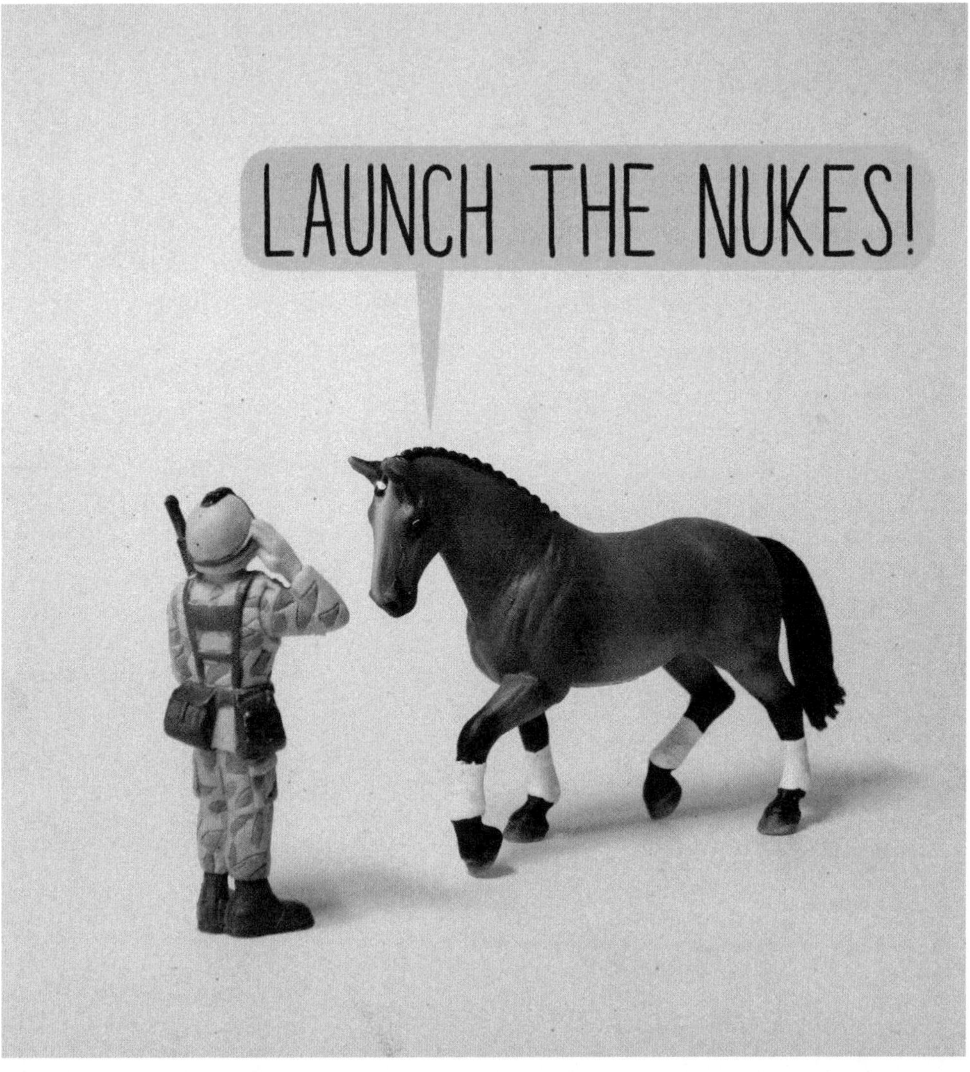
LAUNCH THE NUKES!

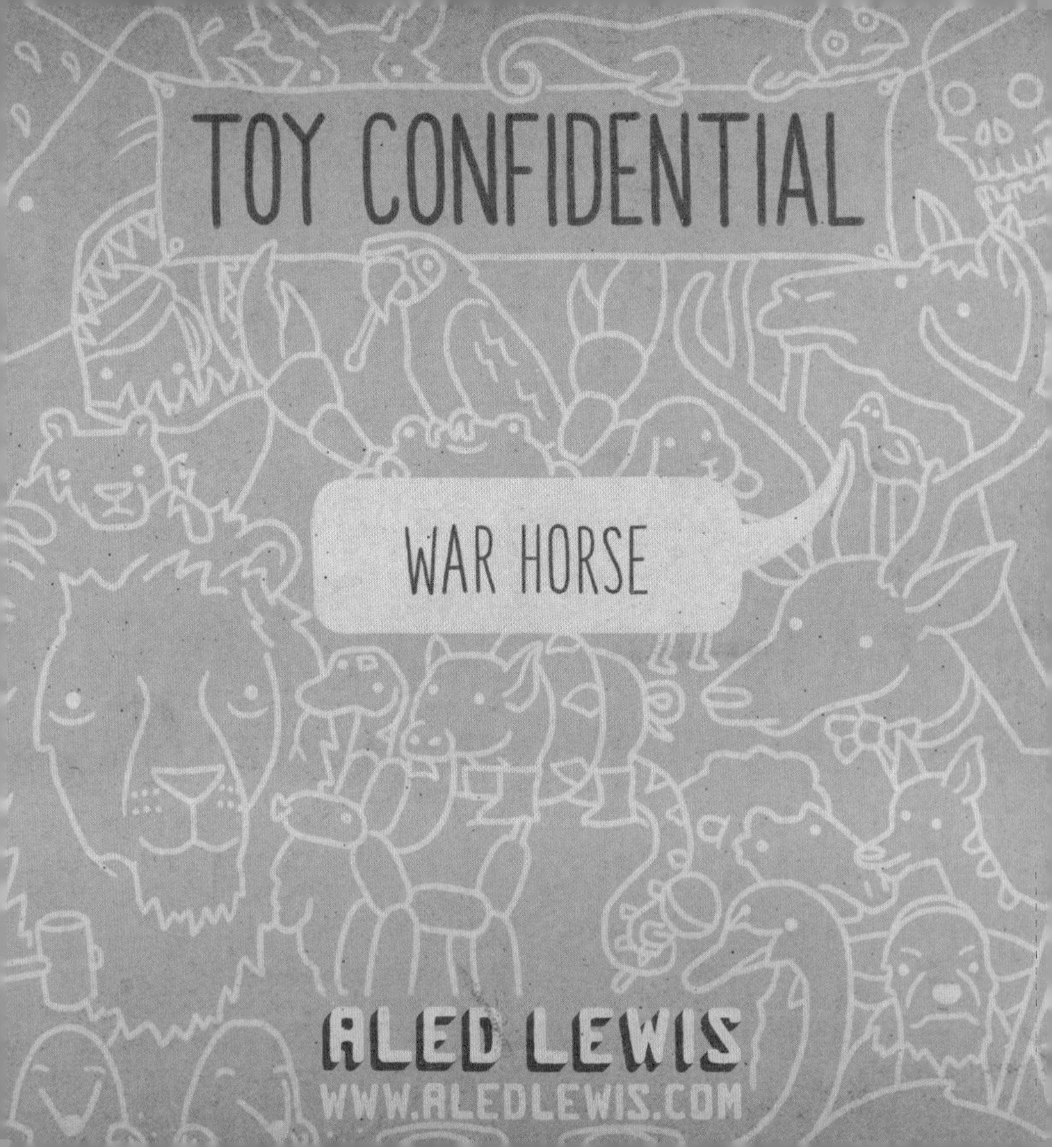
TOY CONFIDENTIAL
WAR HORSE
ALED LEWIS
WWW.ALEDLEWIS.COM

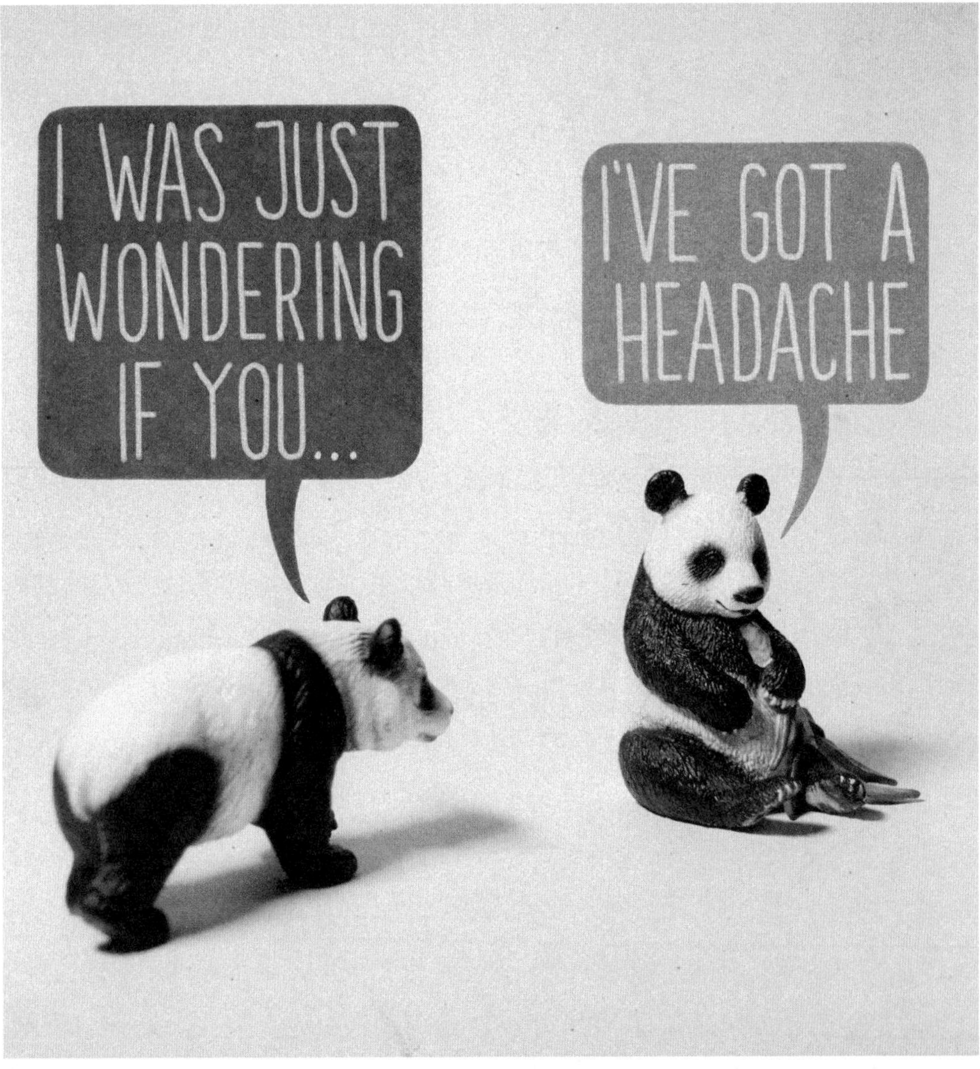
I WAS JUST WONDERING IF YOU...
I'VE GOT A HEADACHE

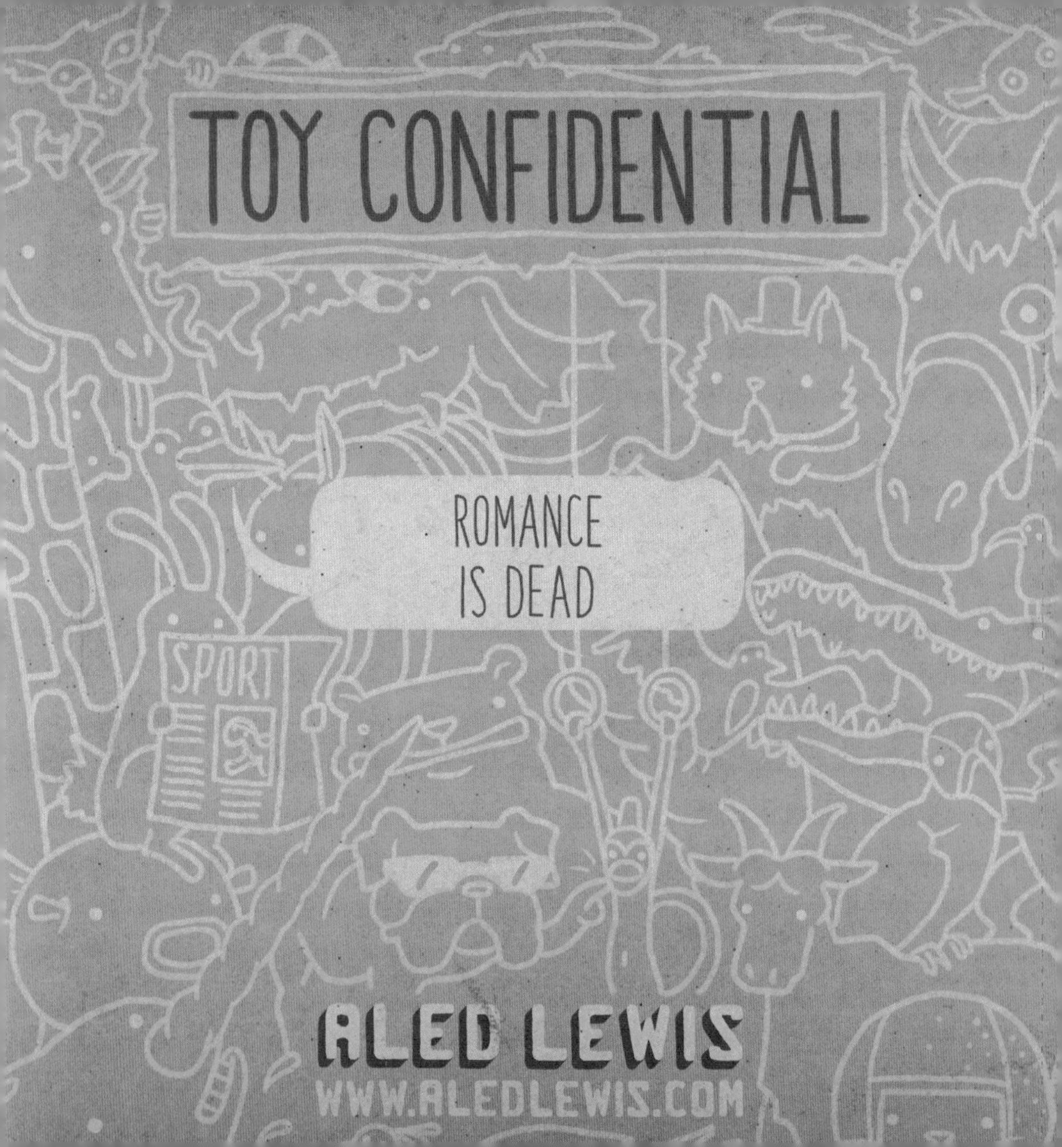
TOY CONFIDENTIAL
ROMANCE
IS DEAD
SPORT
ALED LEWIS
WWW.ALEDLEWIS.COM

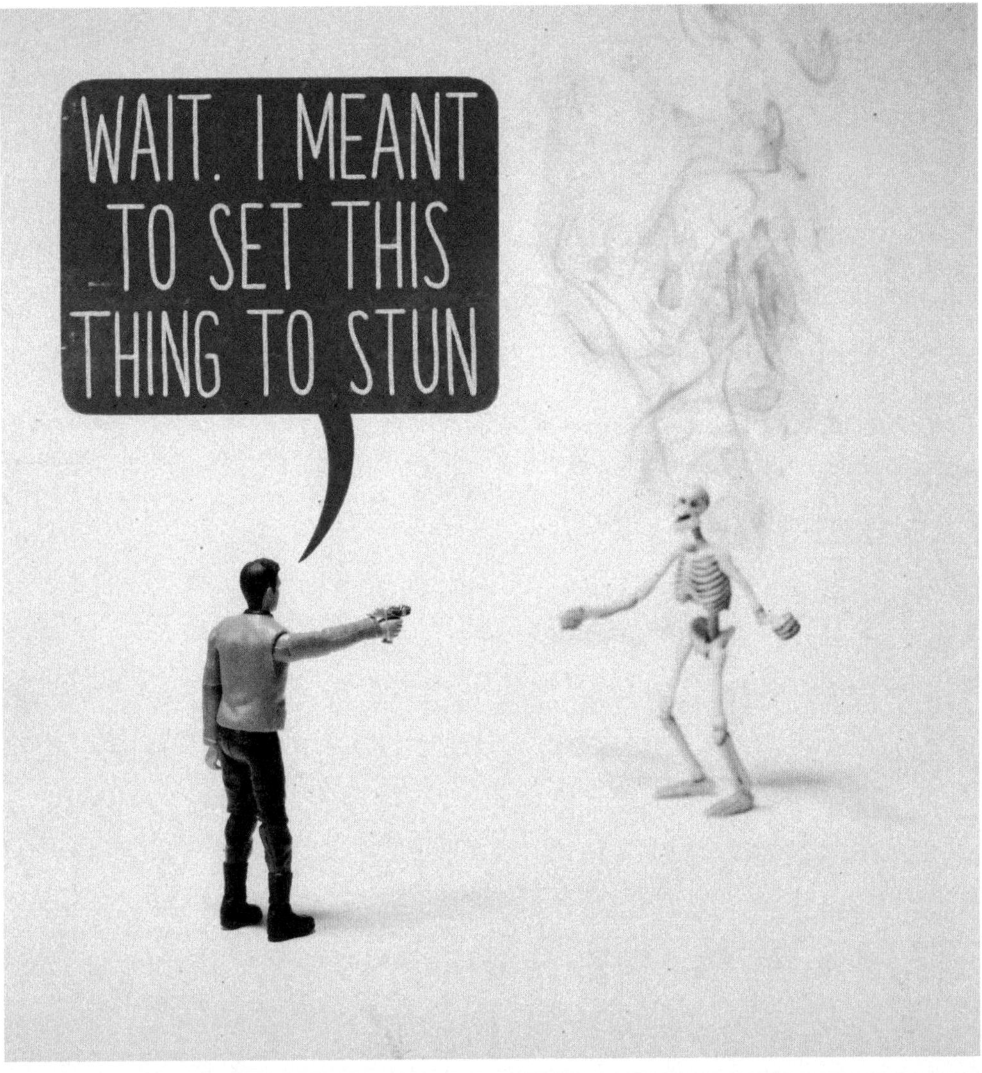
WAIT. I MEANT TO SET THIS THING TO STUN

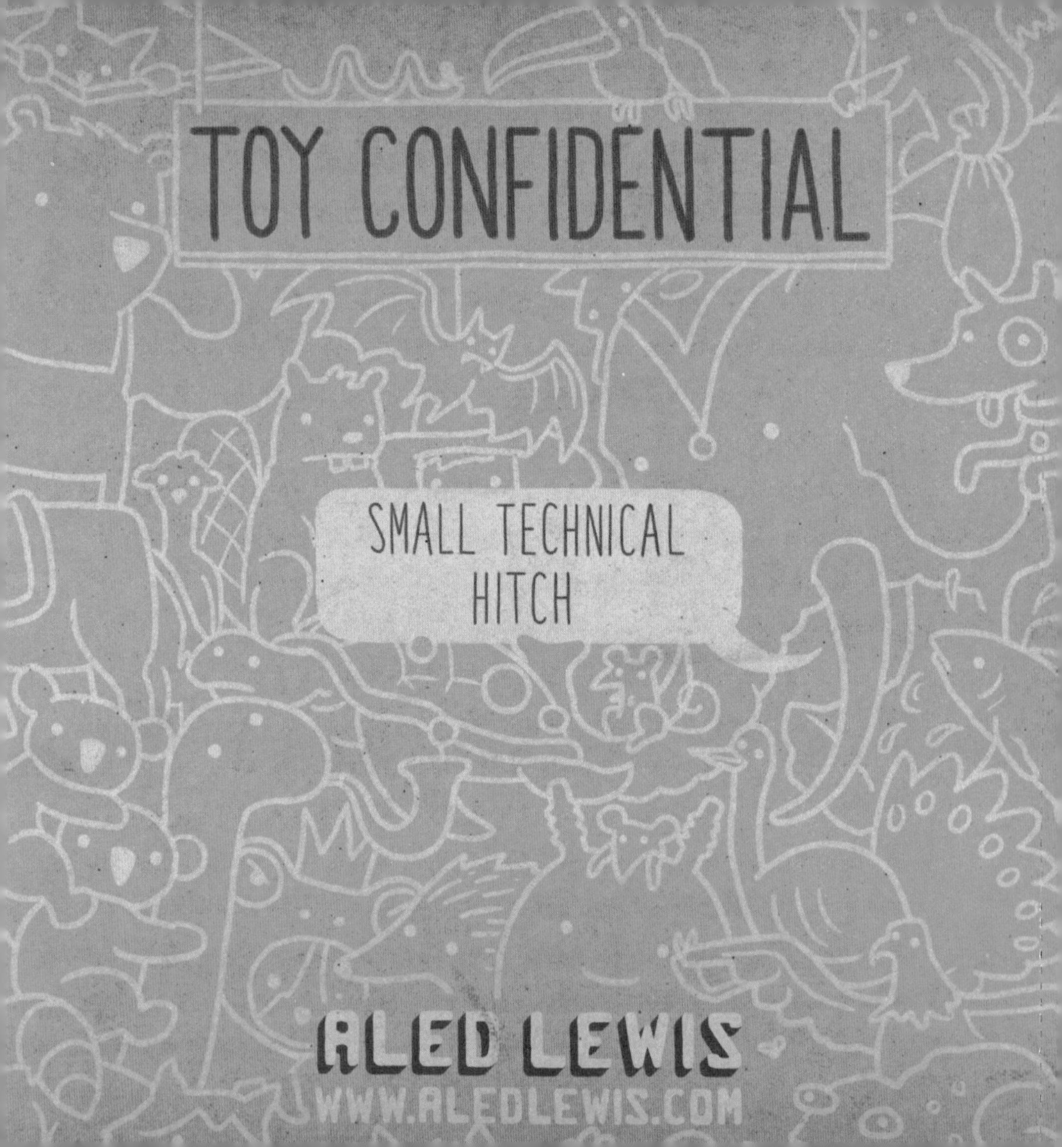
TOY CONFIDENTIAL
SMALL TECHNICAL HITCH
ALED LEWIS
WWW.ALEDLEWIS.COM

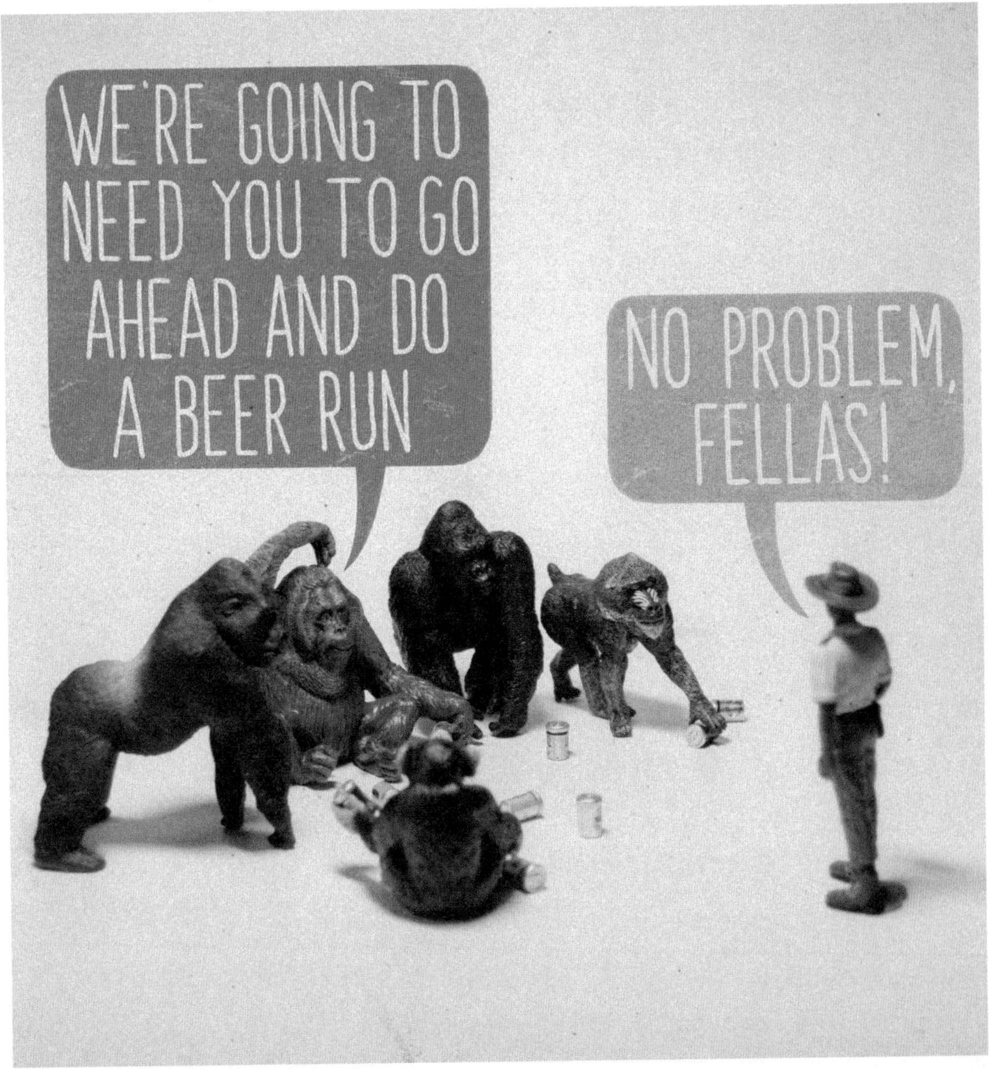
WE'RE GOING TO NEED YOU TO GO AHEAD AND DO A BEER RUN
NO PROBLEM, FELLAS!

TOY CONFIDENTIAL

RISE OF
THE APES

ALED LEWIS
WWW.ALEDLEWIS.COM

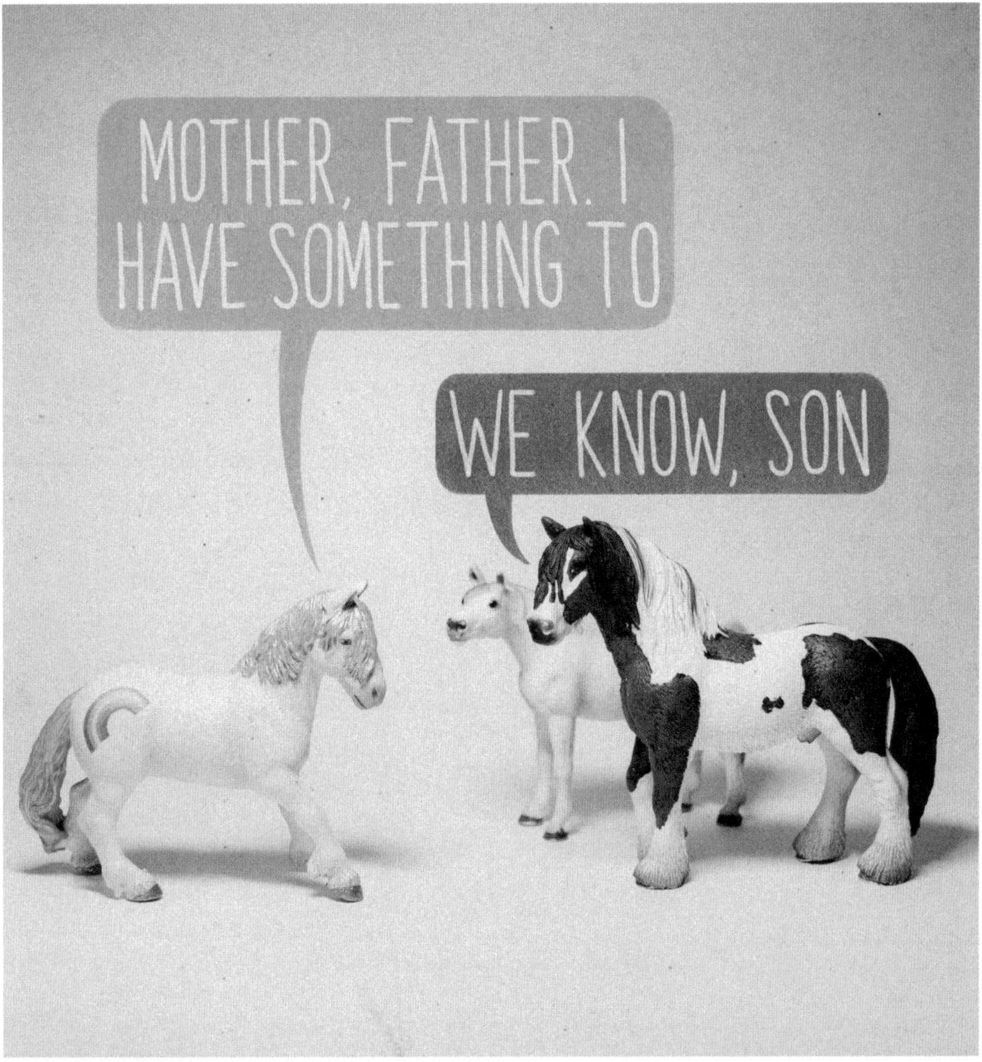
MOTHER, FATHER. I HAVE SOMETHING TO
WE KNOW, SON

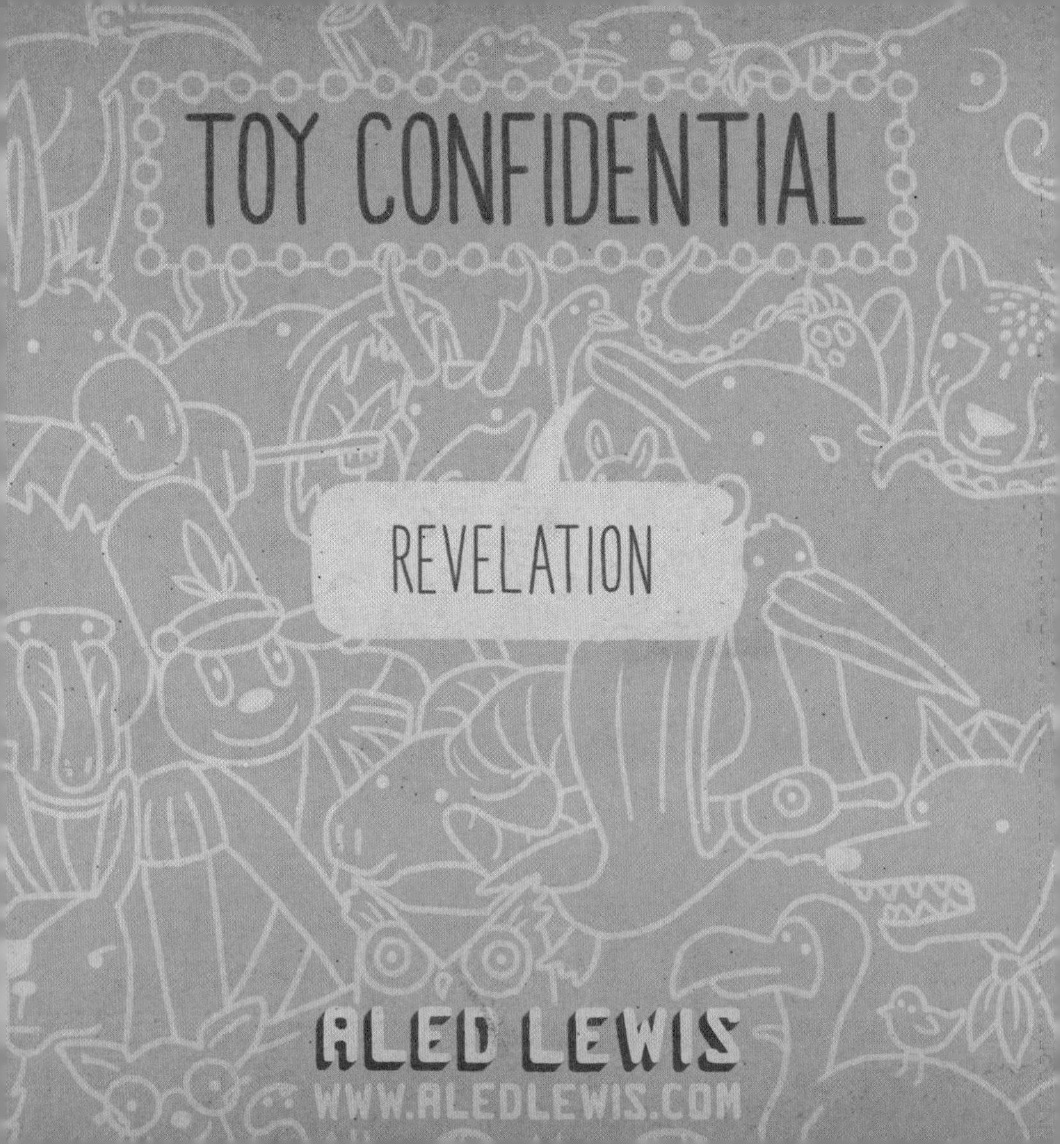
TOY CONFIDENTIAL
REVELATION
ALED LEWIS
WWW.ALEDLEWIS.COM

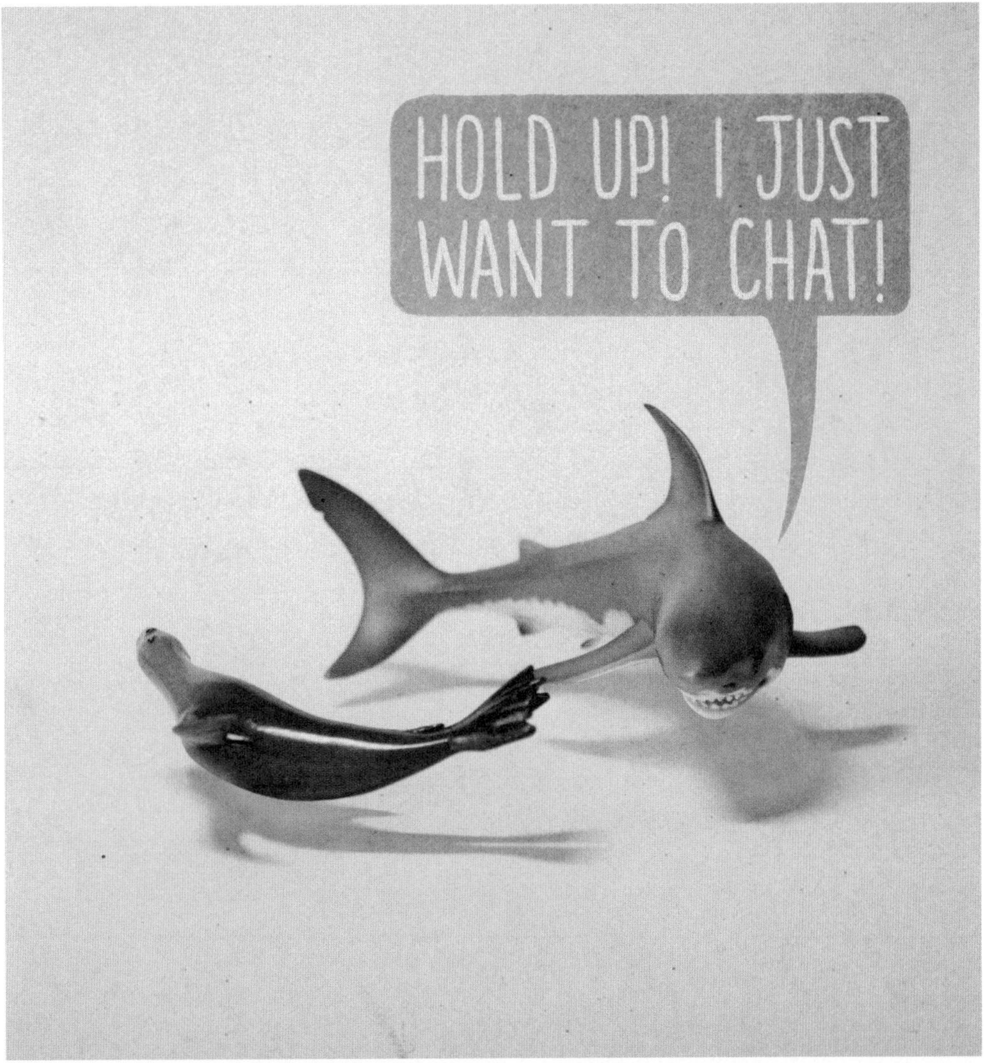
HOLD UP! I JUST WANT TO CHAT!

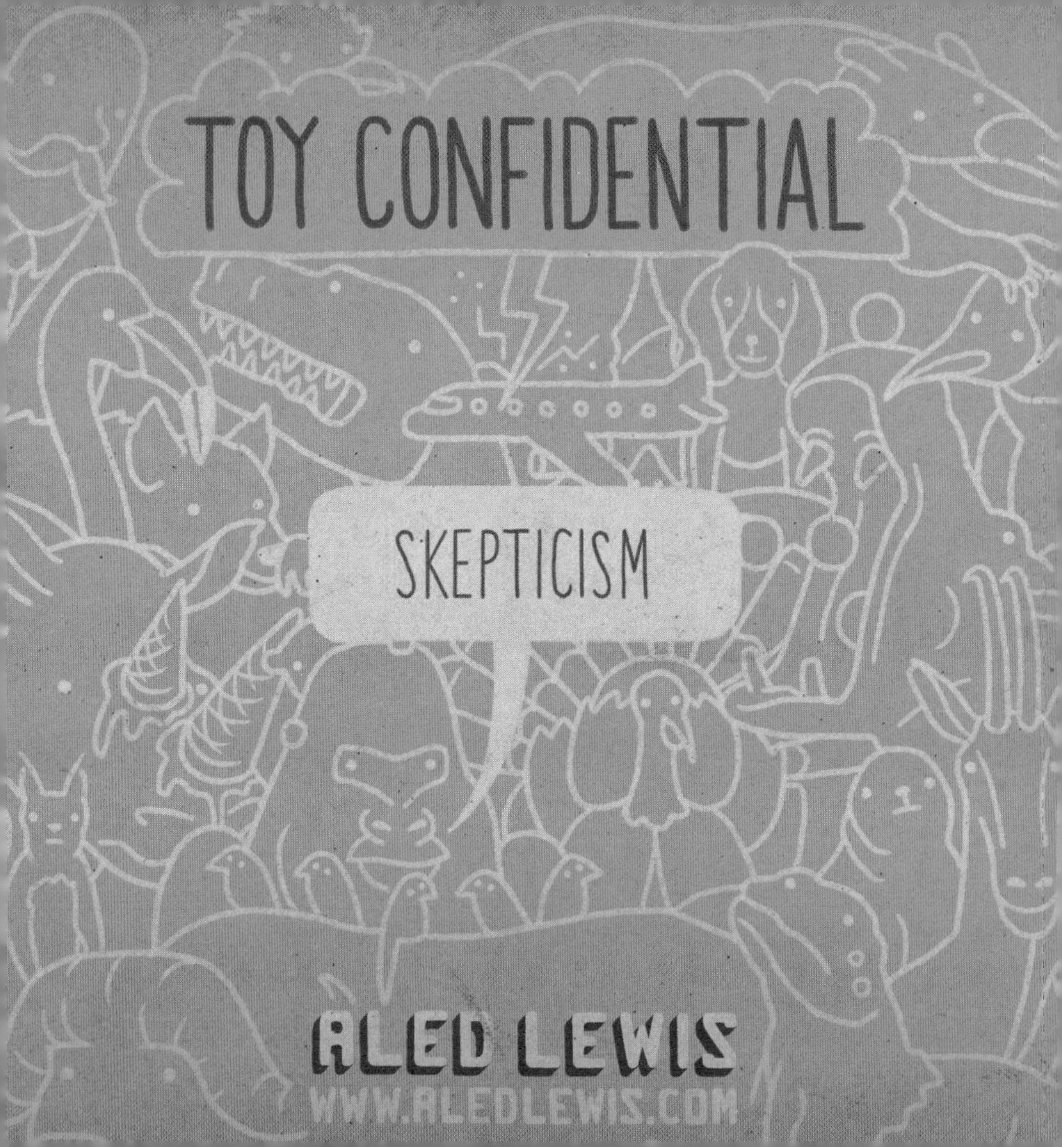
TOY CONFIDENTIAL
SKEPTICISM
ALED LEWIS
WWW.ALEDLEWIS.COM

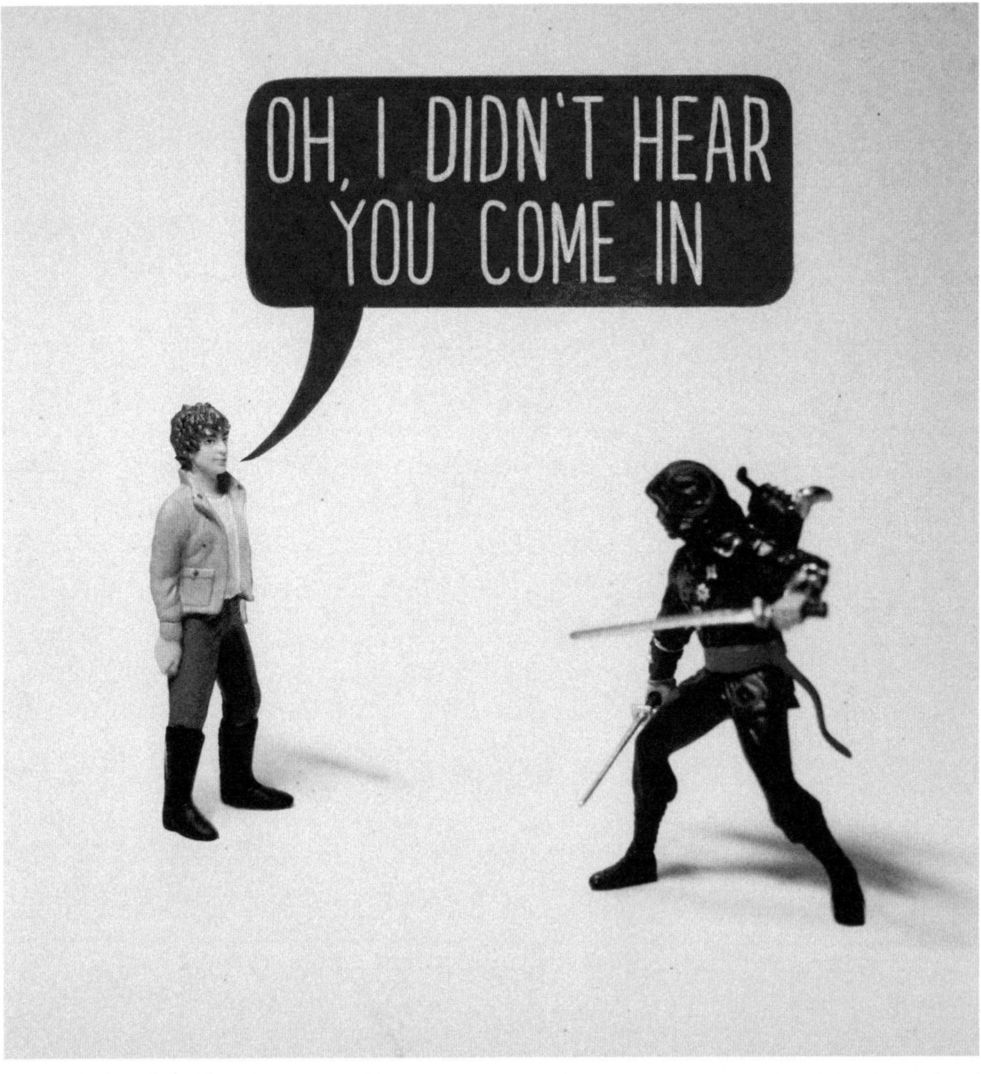
OH, I DIDN'T HEAR YOU COME IN

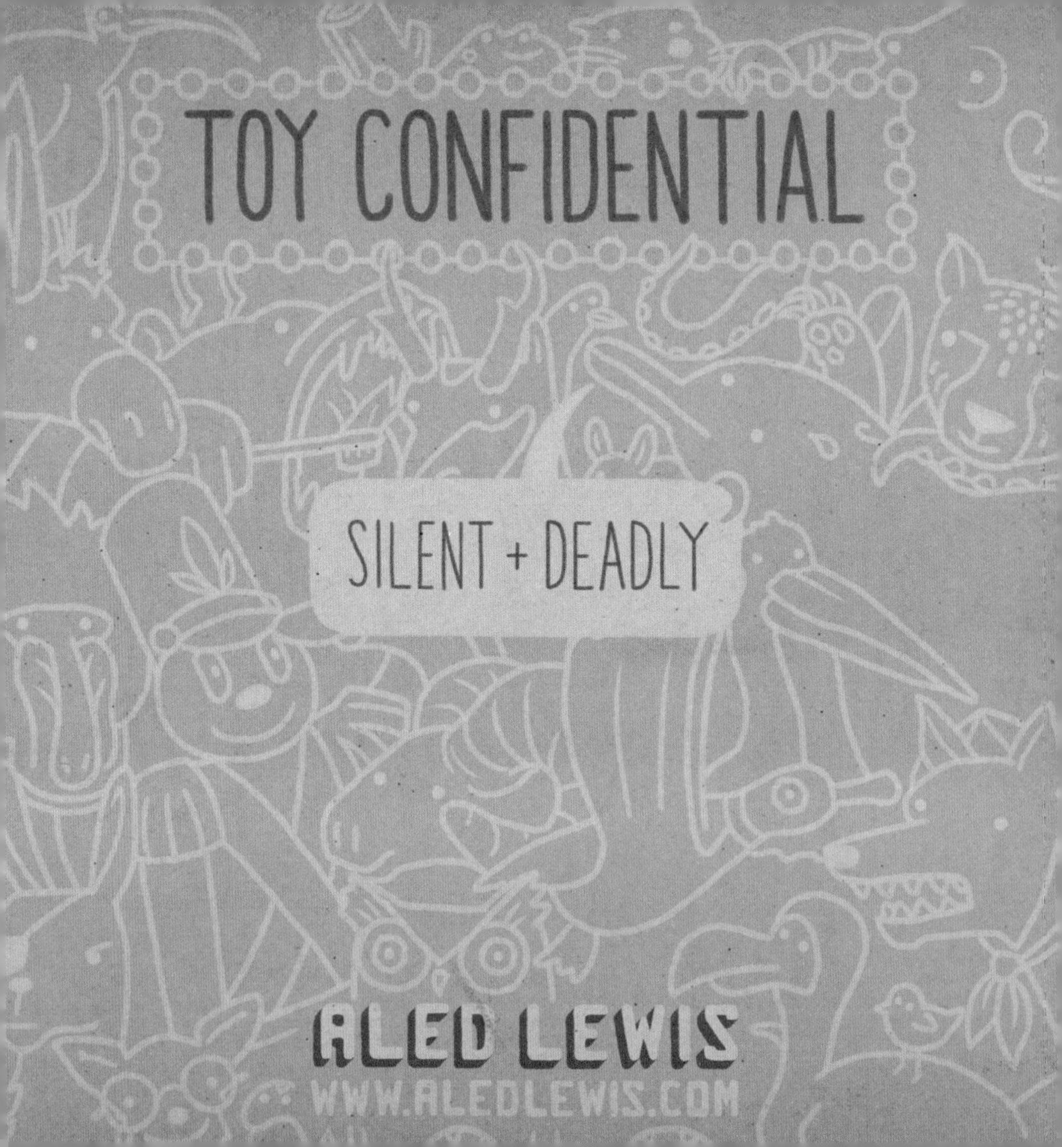
TOY CONFIDENTIAL
SILENT + DEADLY
ALED LEWIS
WWW.ALEDLEWIS.COM

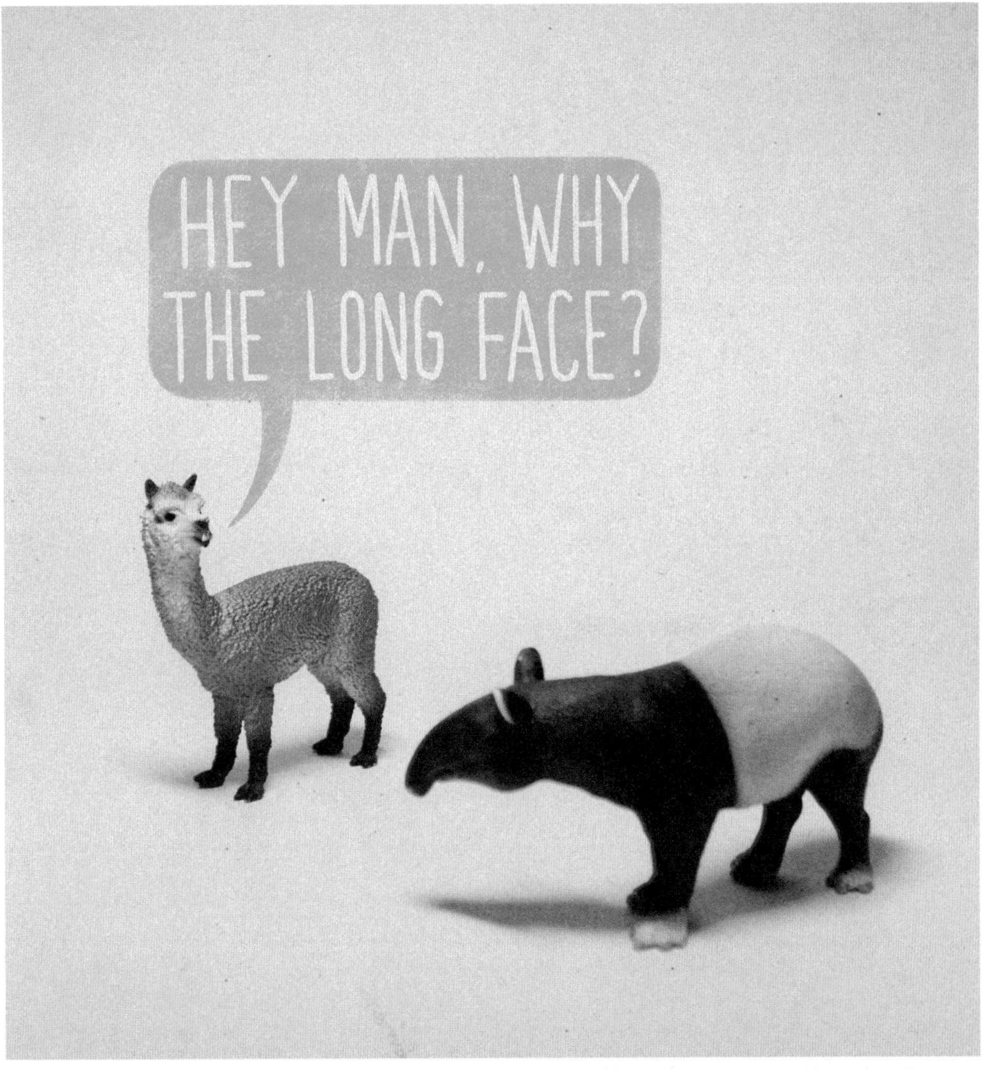
HEY MAN, WHY THE LONG FACE?

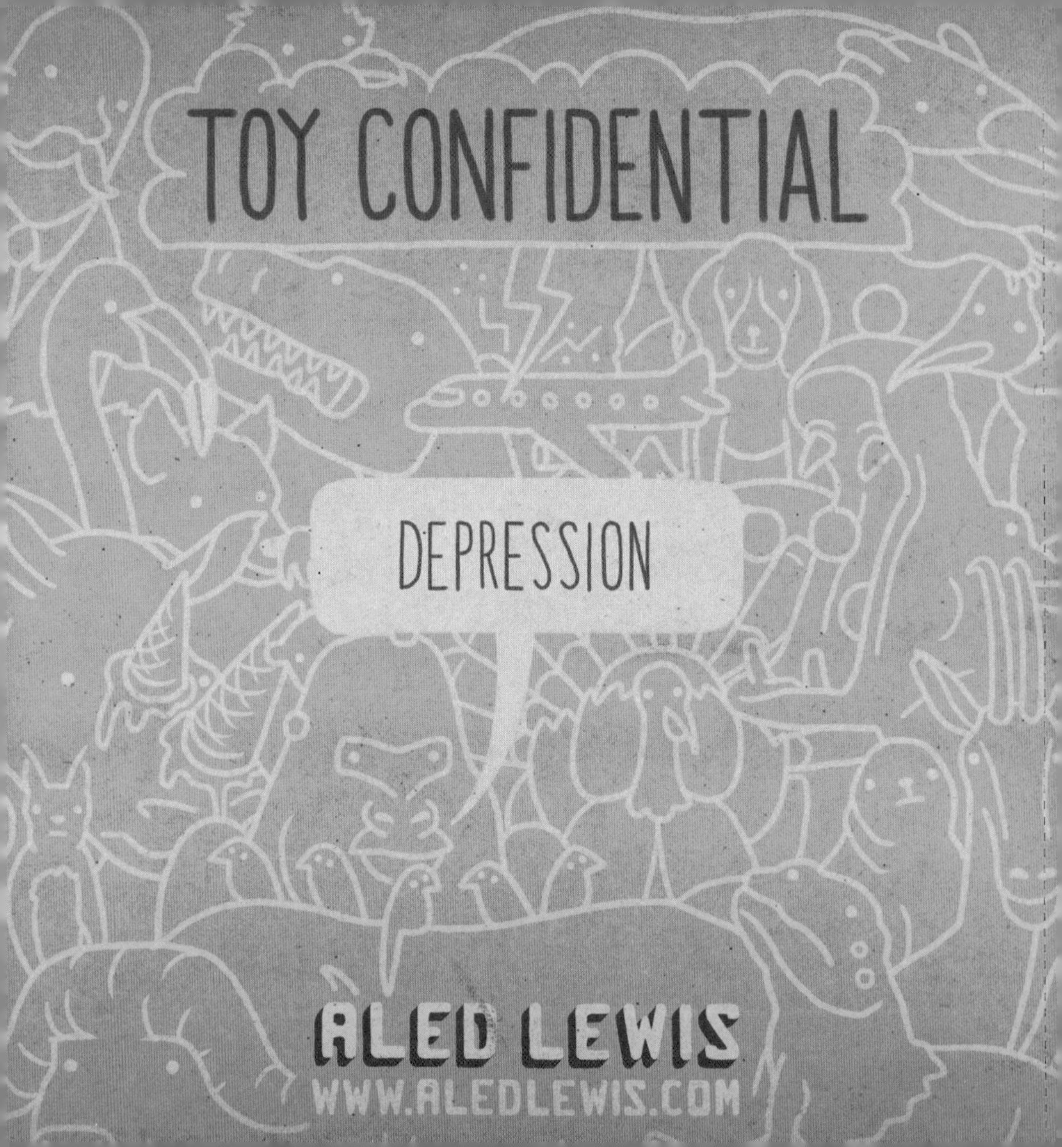
TOY CONFIDENTIAL
DEPRESSION
ALED LEWIS
WWW.ALEDLEWIS.COM

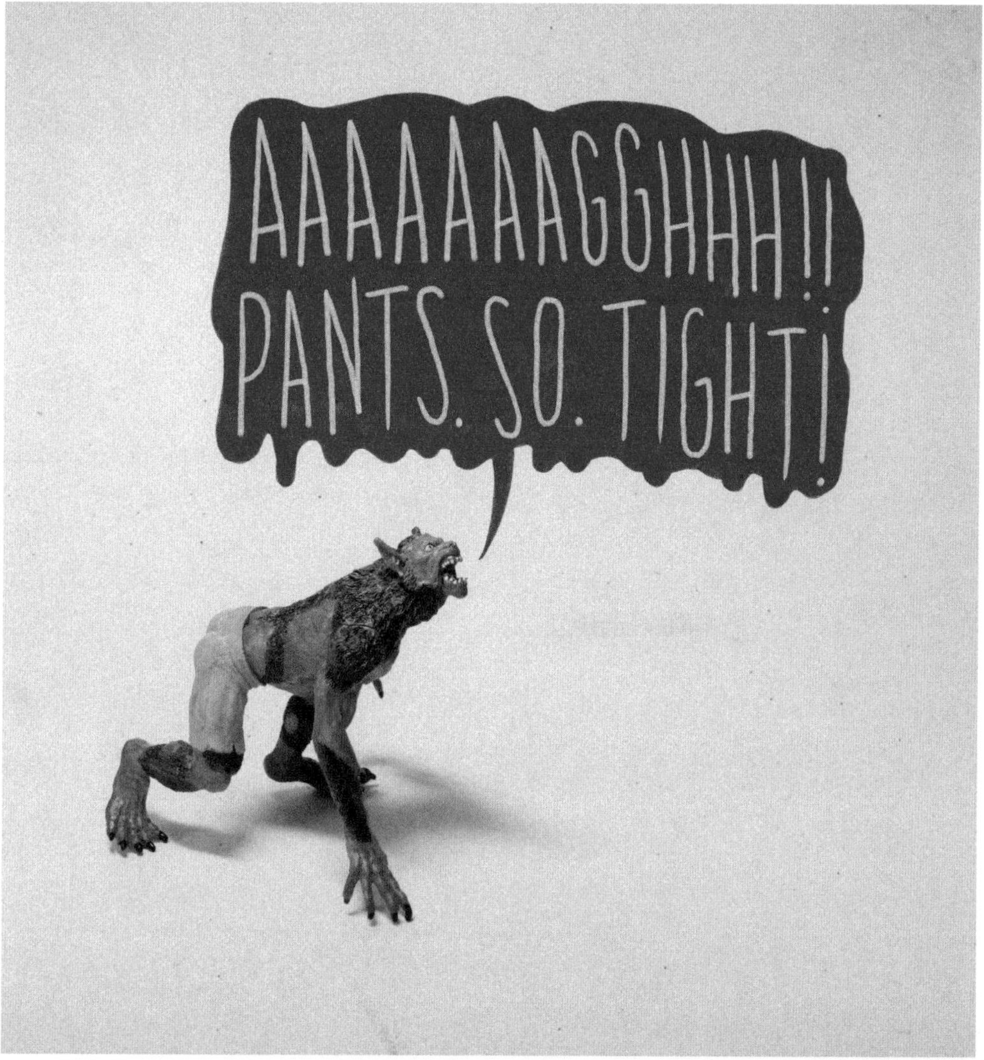
AAAAAAGGHHH!!
PANTS. SO. TIGHT!

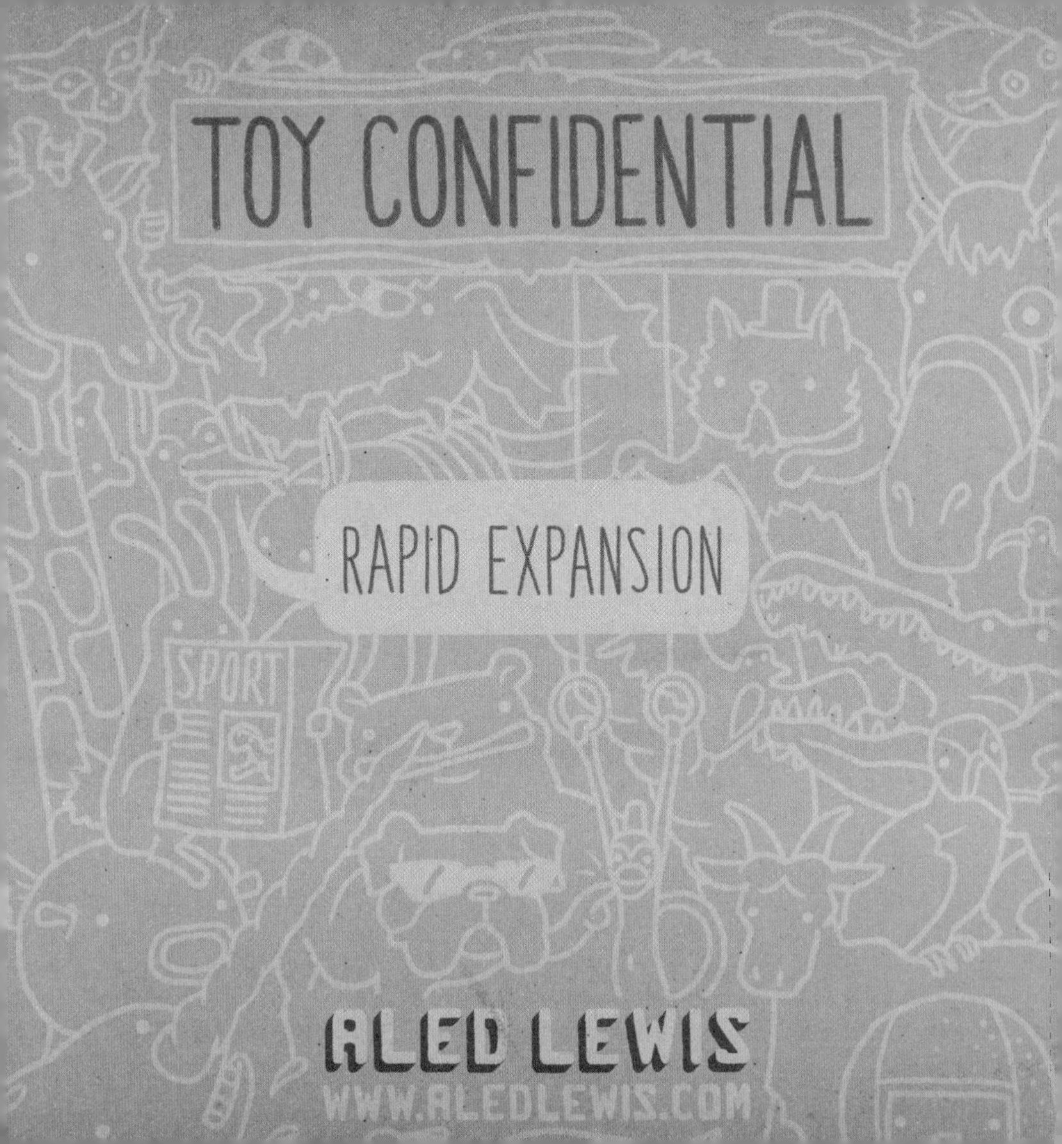
TOY CONFIDENTIAL
RAPID EXPANSION
SPORT
ALED LEWIS
WWW.ALEDLEWIS.COM

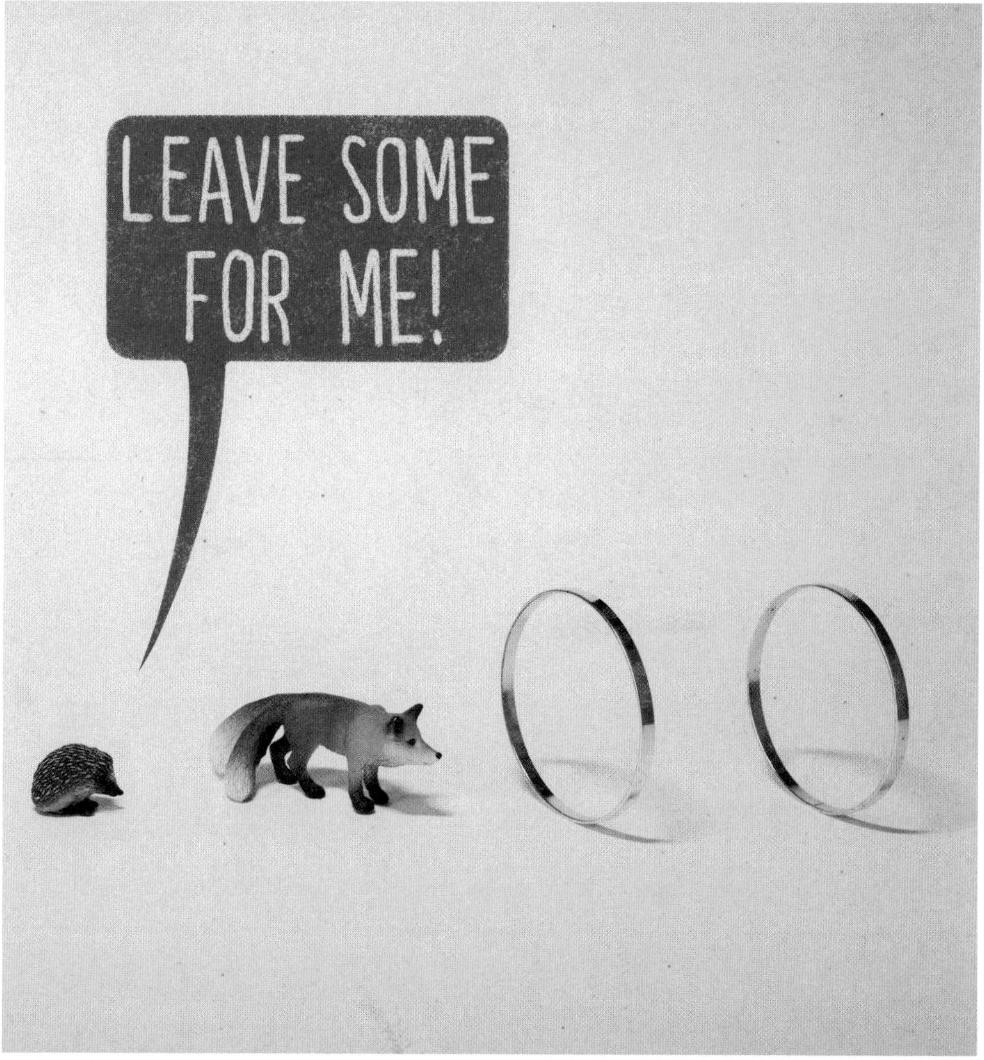
LEAVE SOME FOR ME!

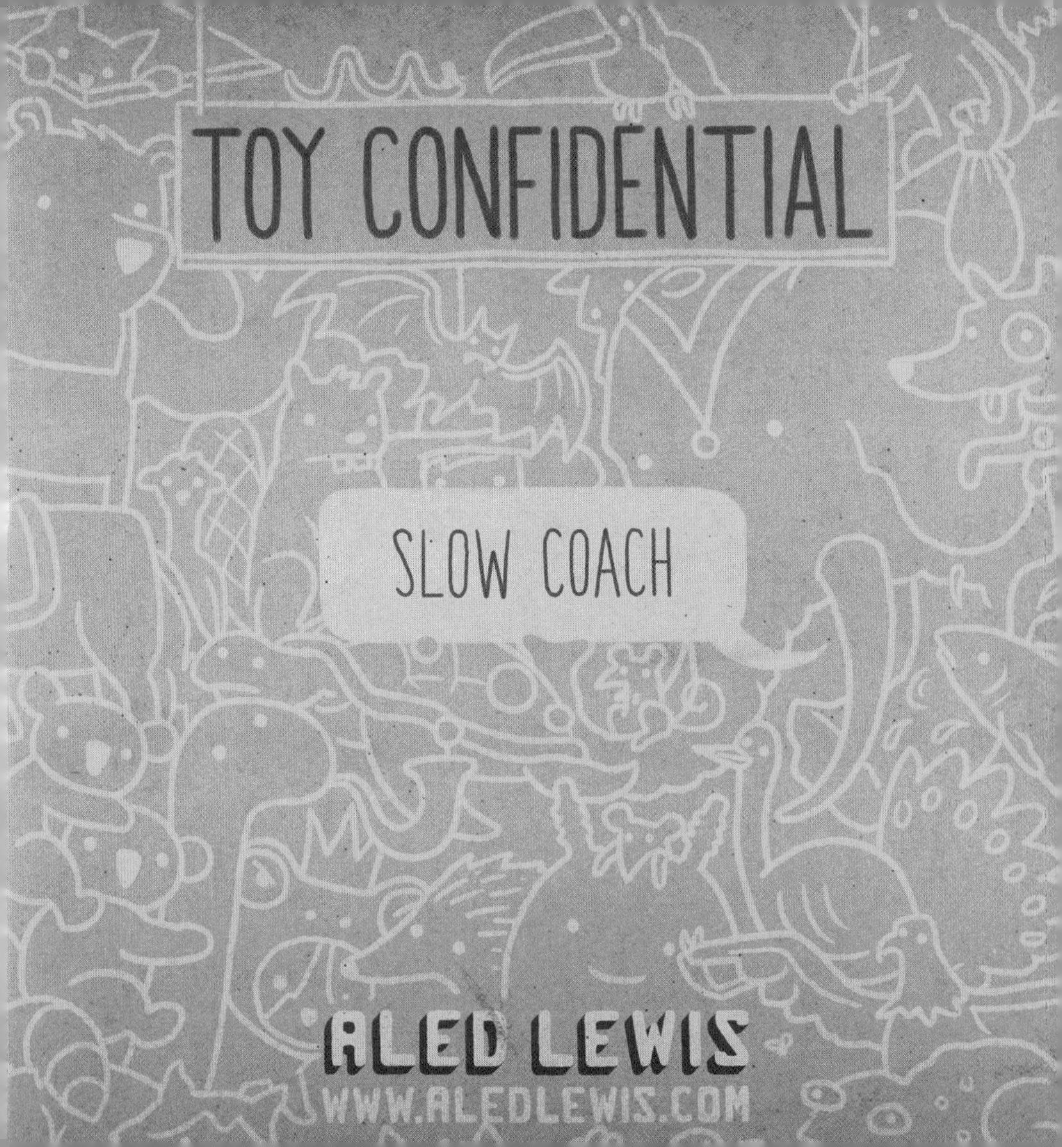
TOY CONFIDENTIAL
SLOW COACH
ALED LEWIS
WWW.ALEDLEWIS.COM

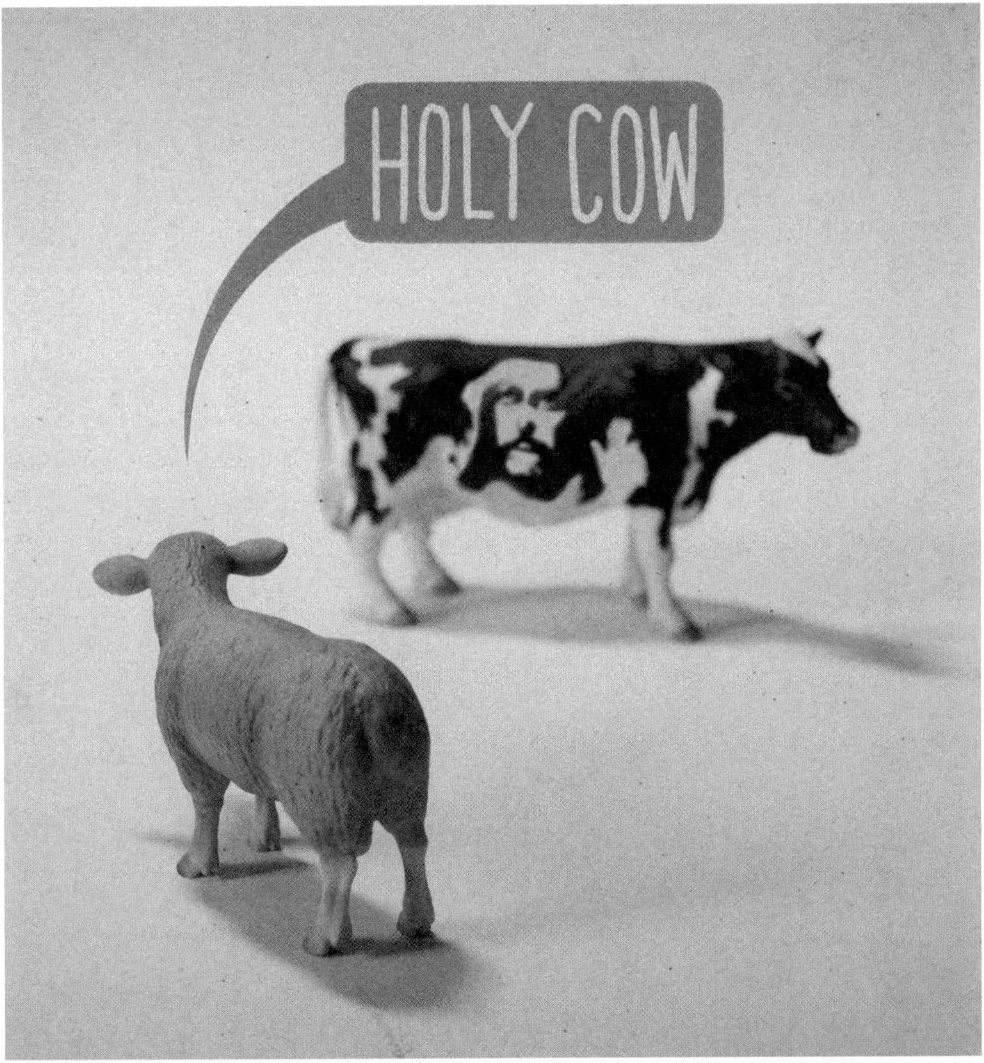
HOLY COW

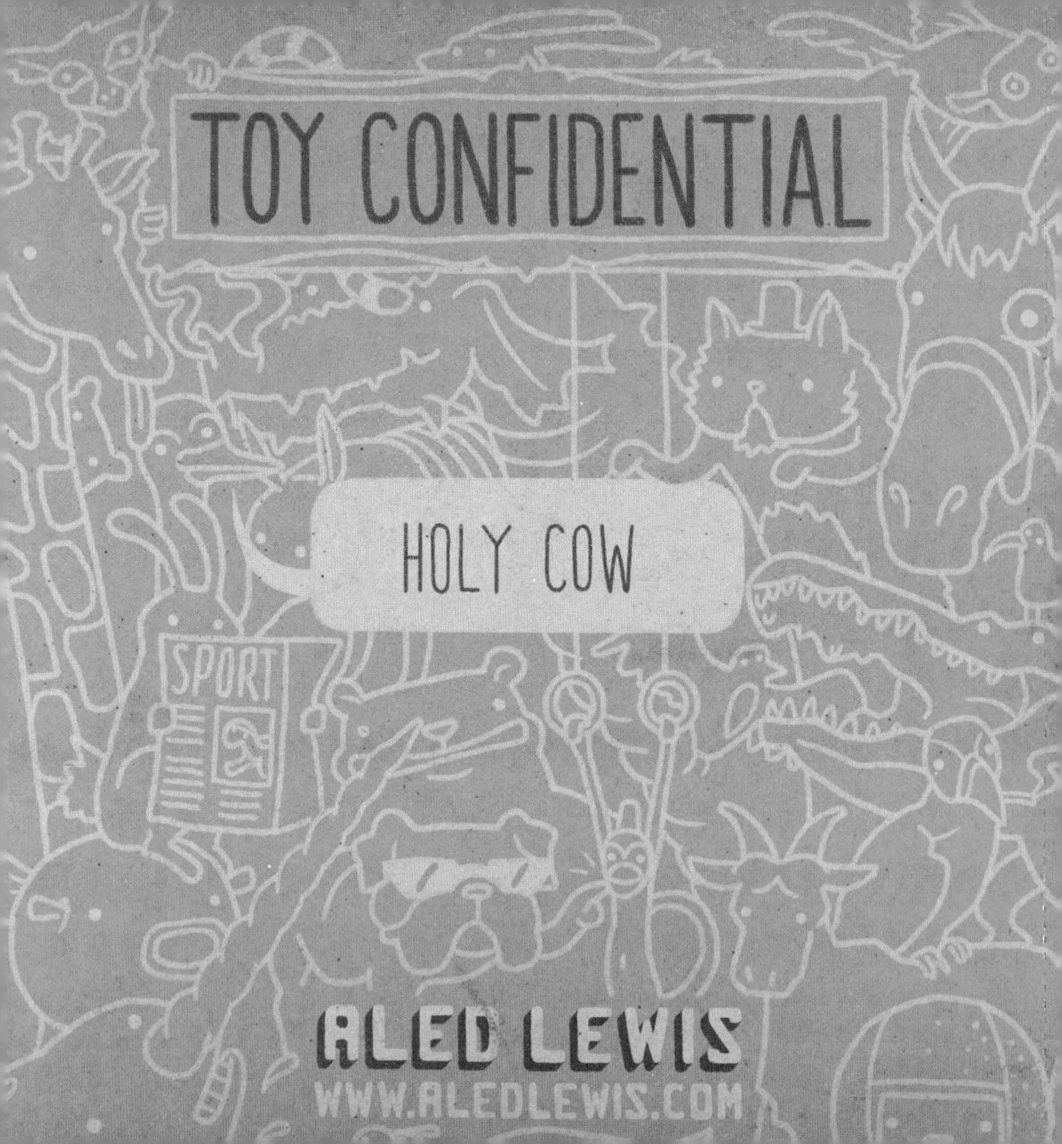
TOY CONFIDENTIAL
HOLY COW
SPORT
ALED LEWIS
WWW.ALEDLEWIS.COM

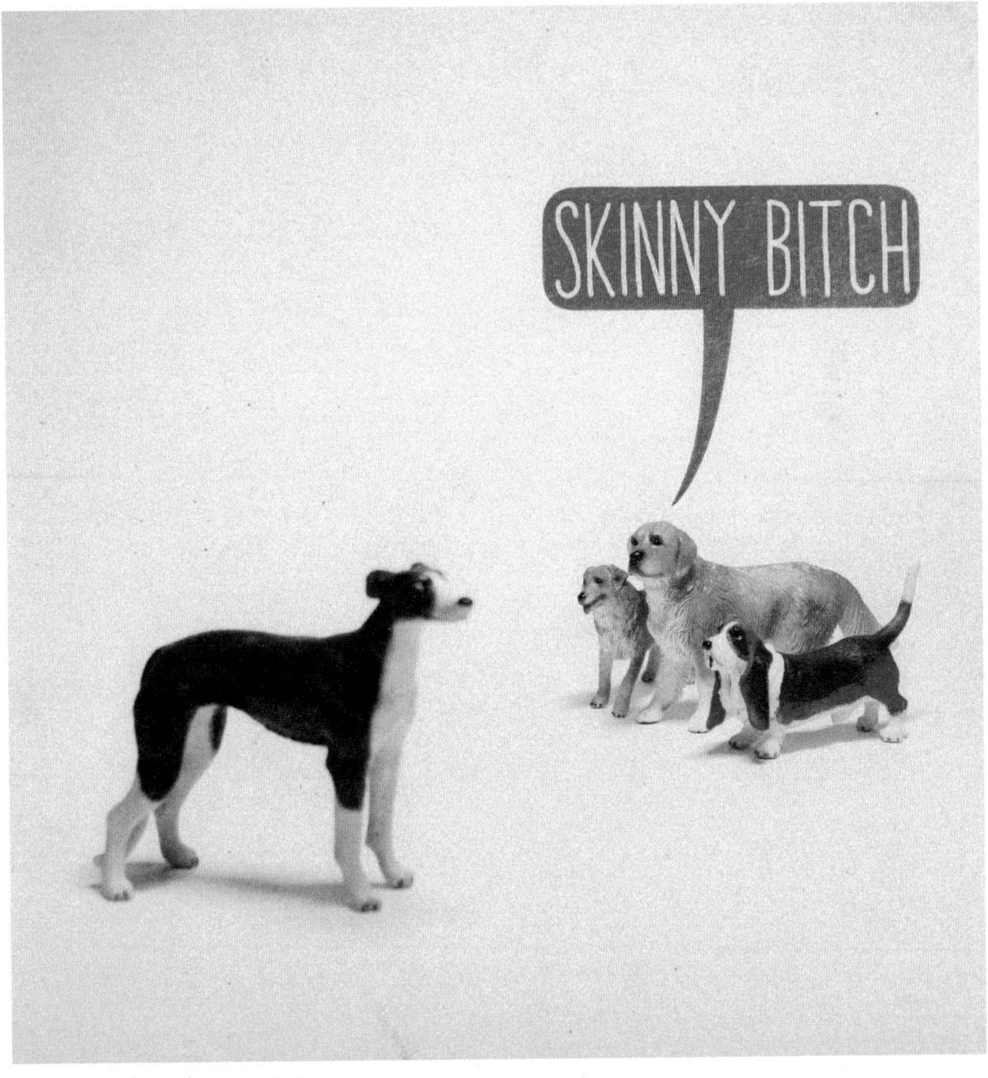
SKINNY BITCH

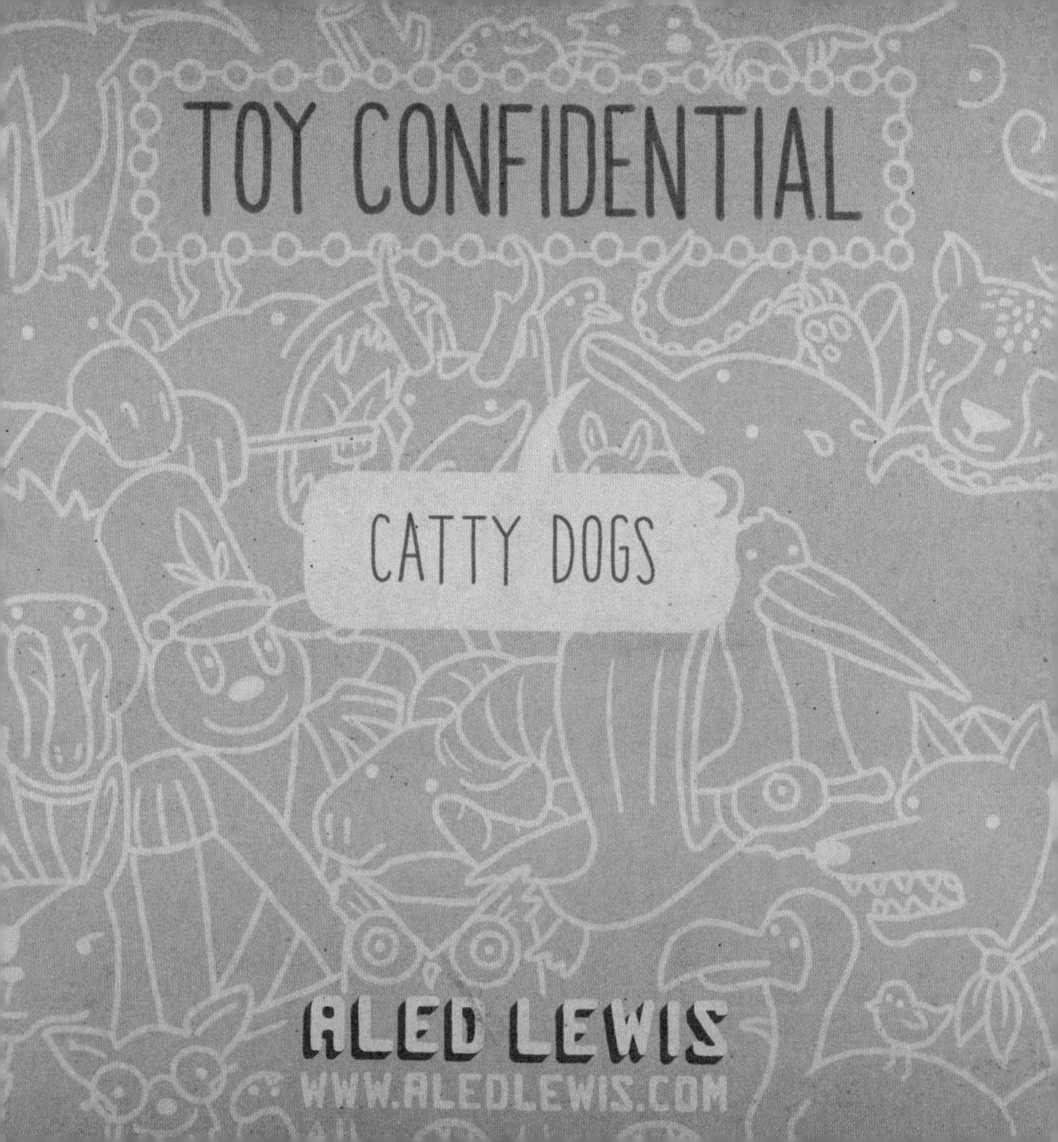
TOY CONFIDENTIAL
CATTY DOGS
ALED LEWIS
WWW.ALEDLEWIS.COM

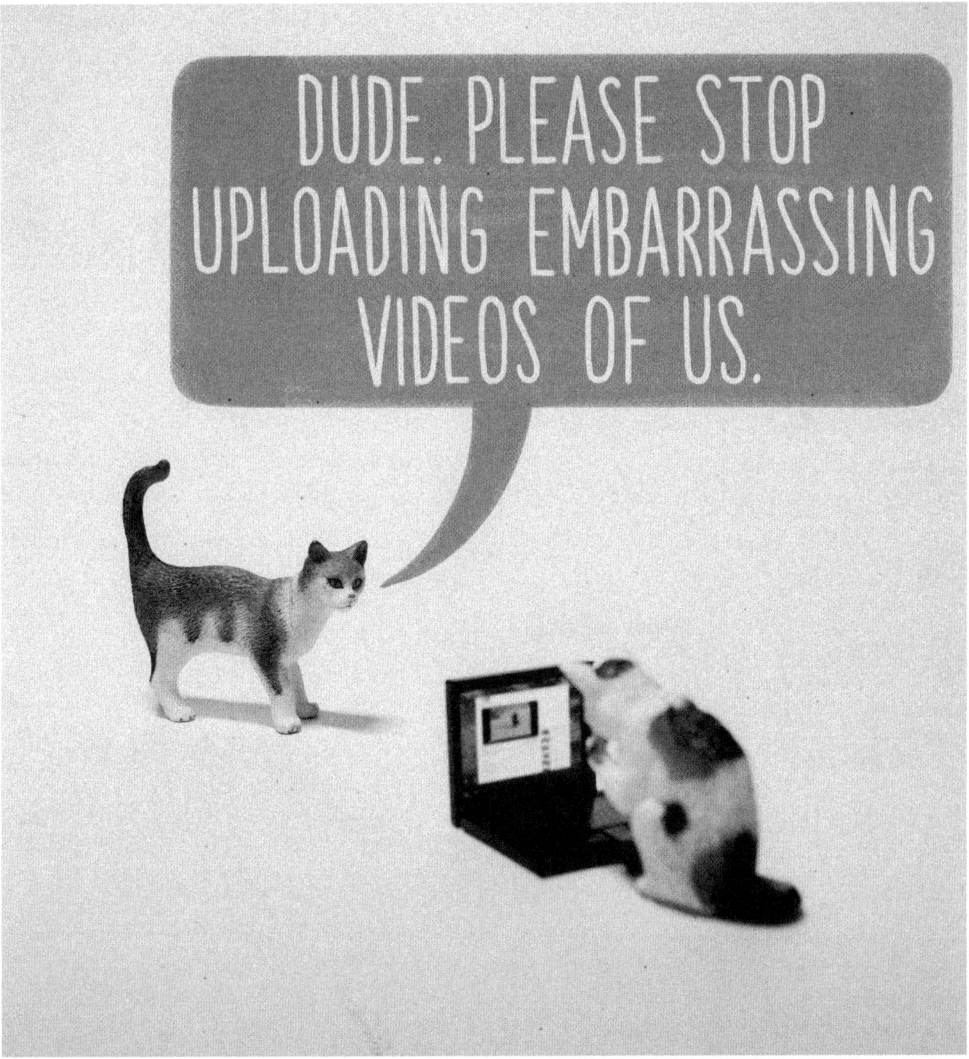
DUDE. PLEASE STOP UPLOADING EMBARRASSING VIDEOS OF US.

TOY CONFIDENTIAL

LOL CATS

ALED LEWIS

WWW.ALEDLEWIS.COM

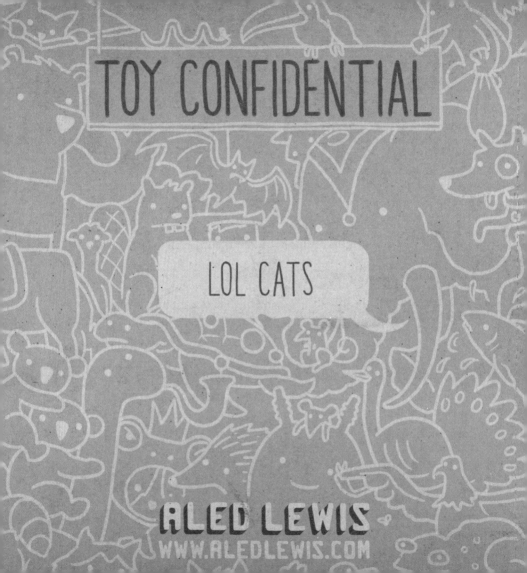

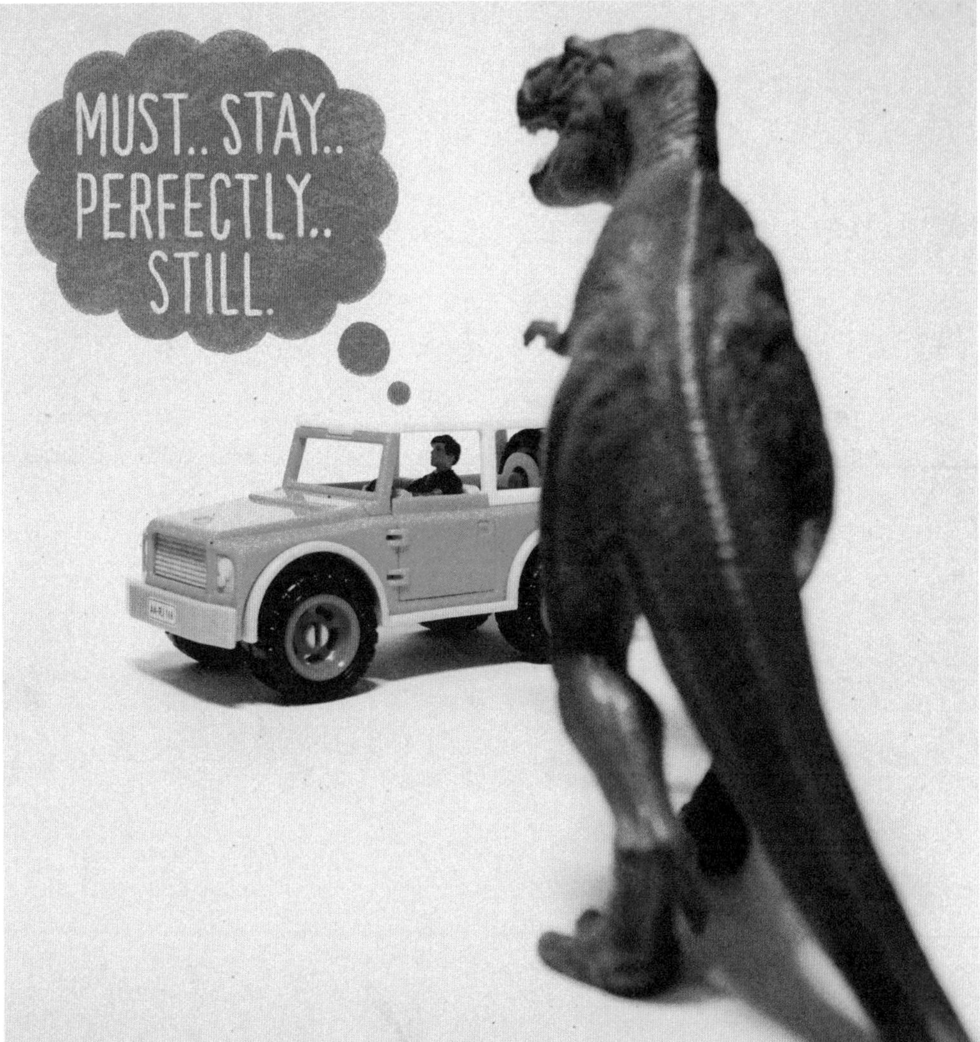
MUST.. STAY.. PERFECTLY.. STILL.

TOY CONFIDENTIAL

BENEFITS OF BEING INANIMATE

ALED LEWIS

WWW.ALEDLEWIS.COM

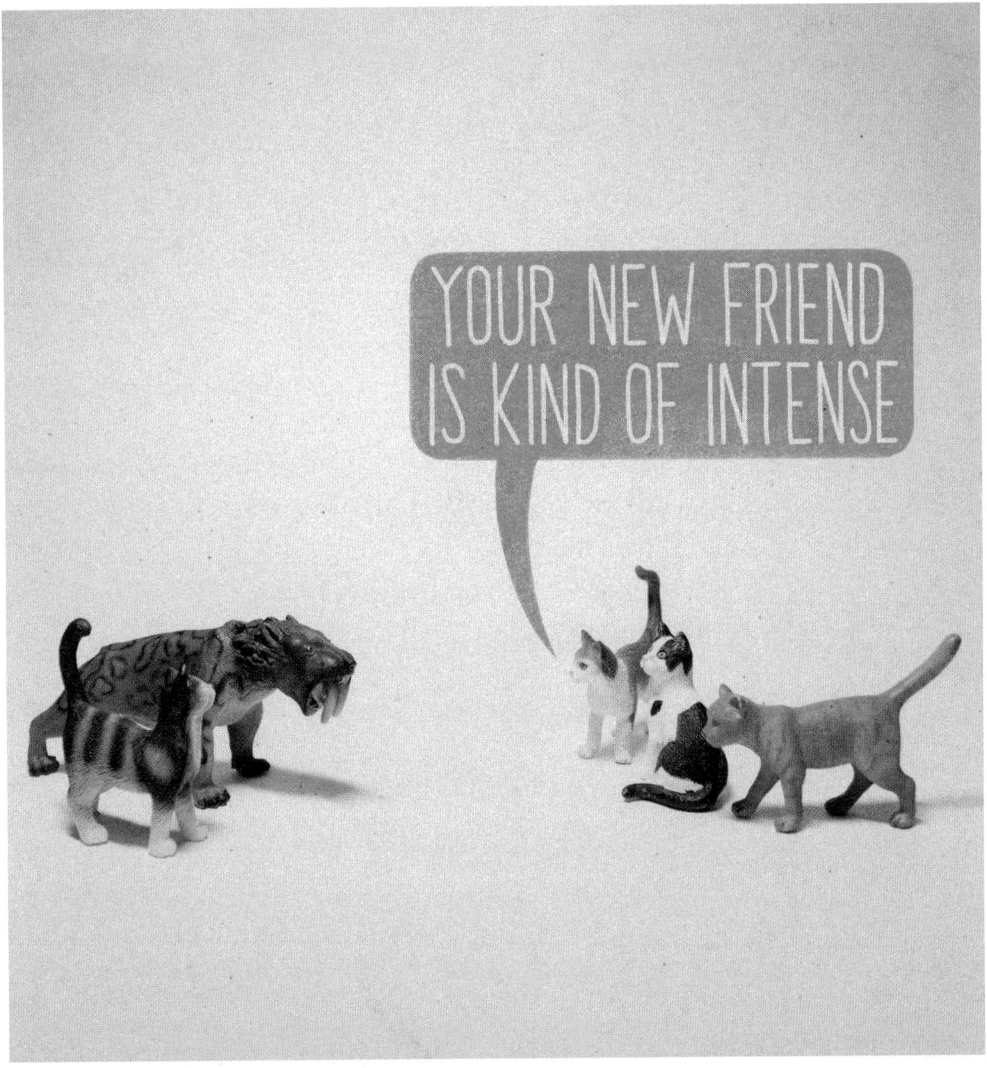
YOUR NEW FRIEND IS KIND OF INTENSE

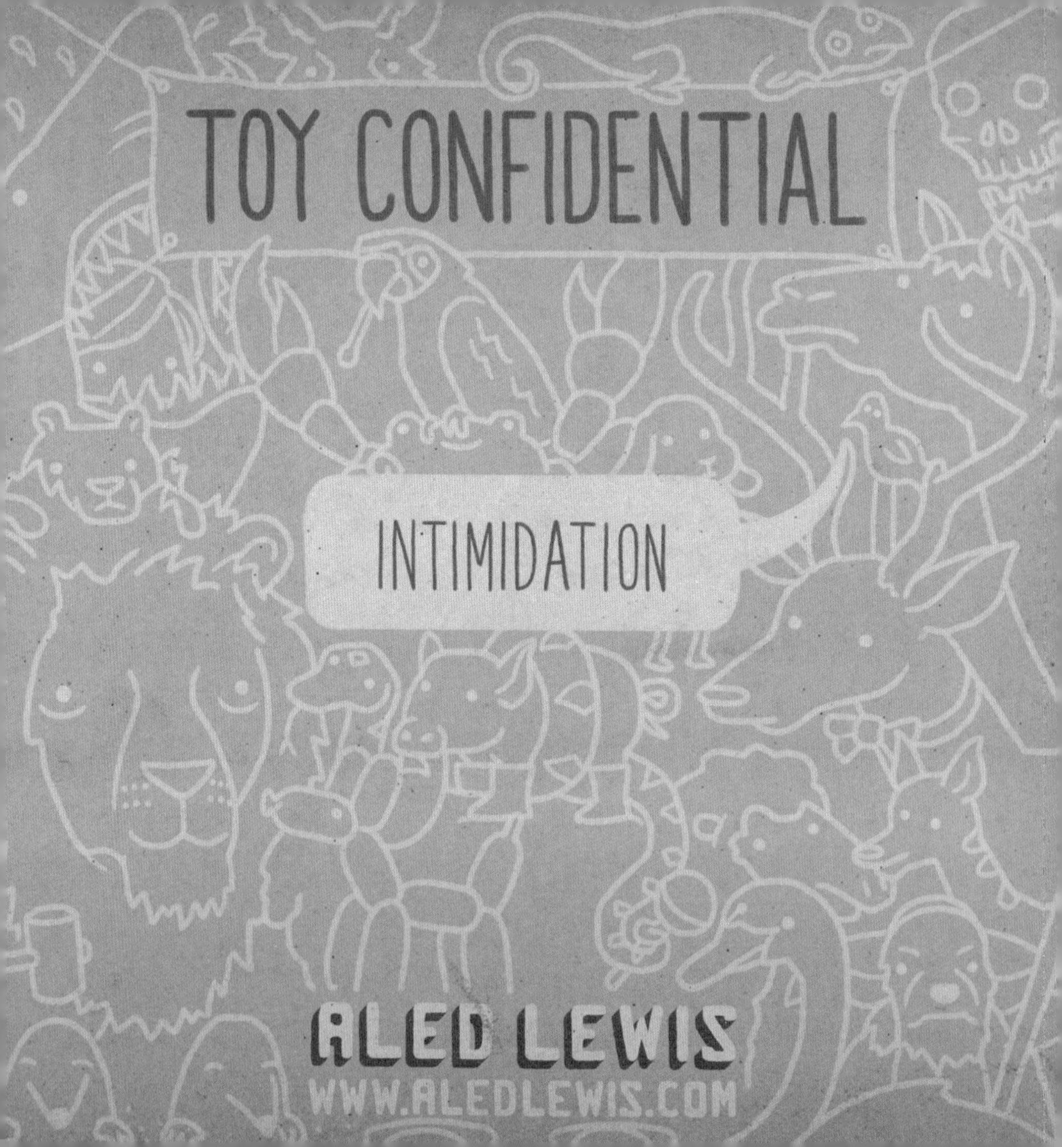
TOY CONFIDENTIAL
INTIMIDATION
ALED LEWIS
WWW.ALEDLEWIS.COM

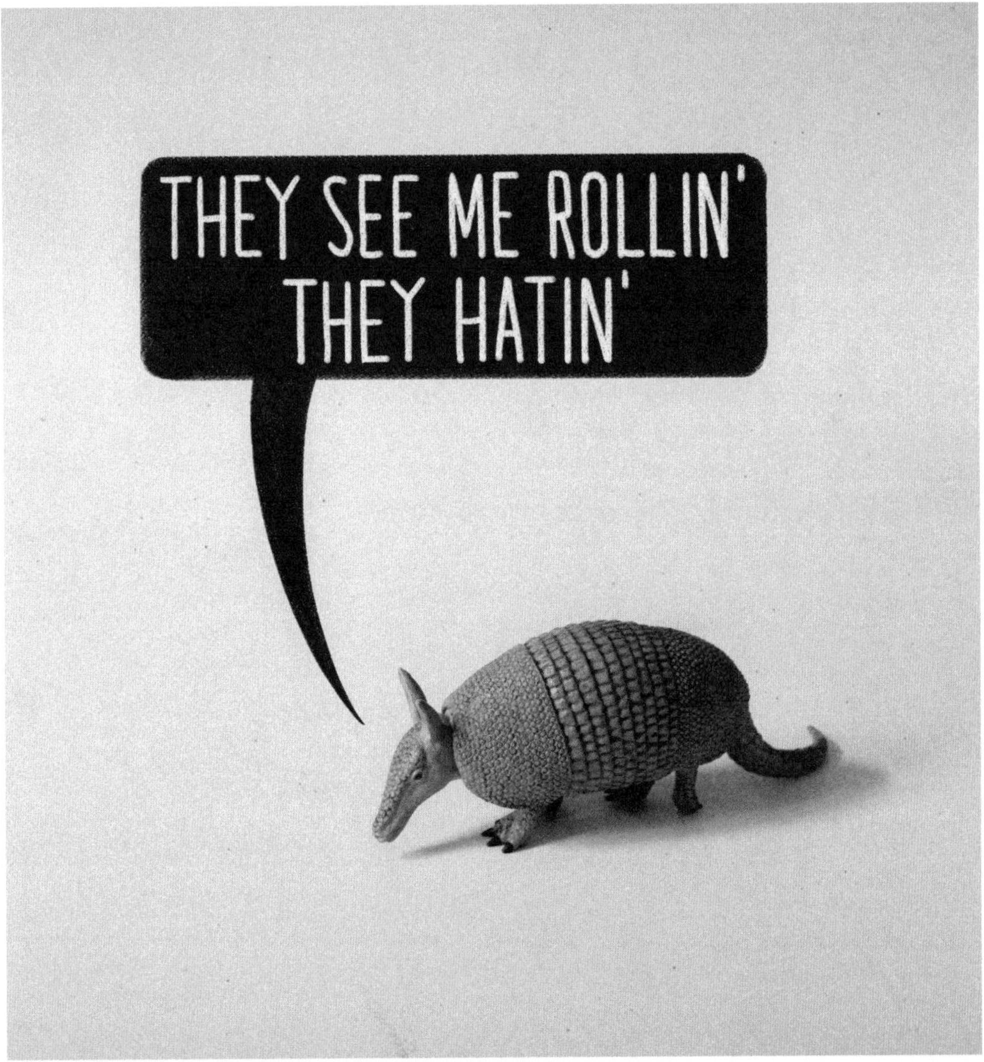
THEY SEE ME ROLLIN'
THEY HATIN'

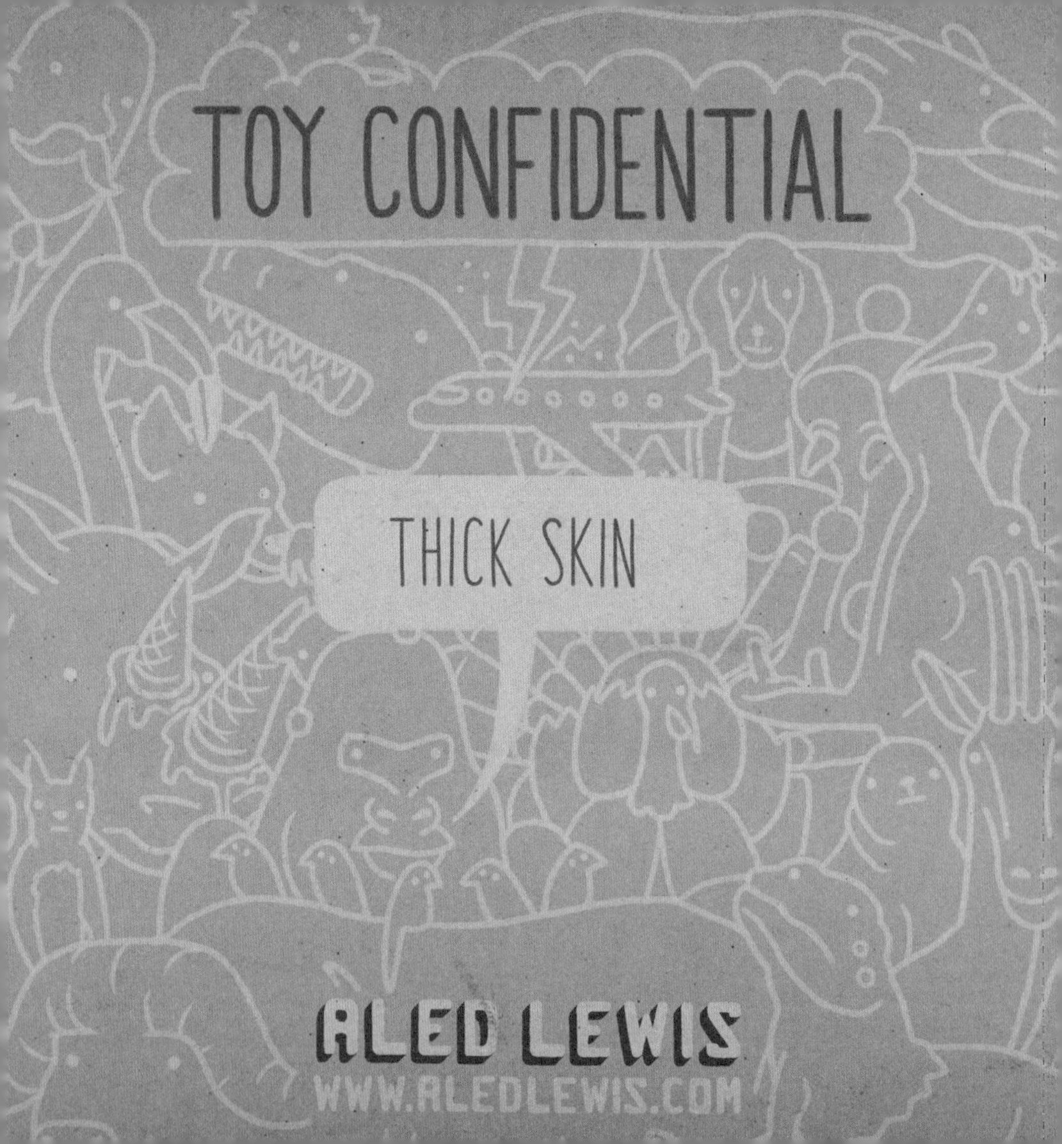
TOY CONFIDENTIAL
THICK SKIN
ALED LEWIS
WWW.ALEDLEWIS.COM

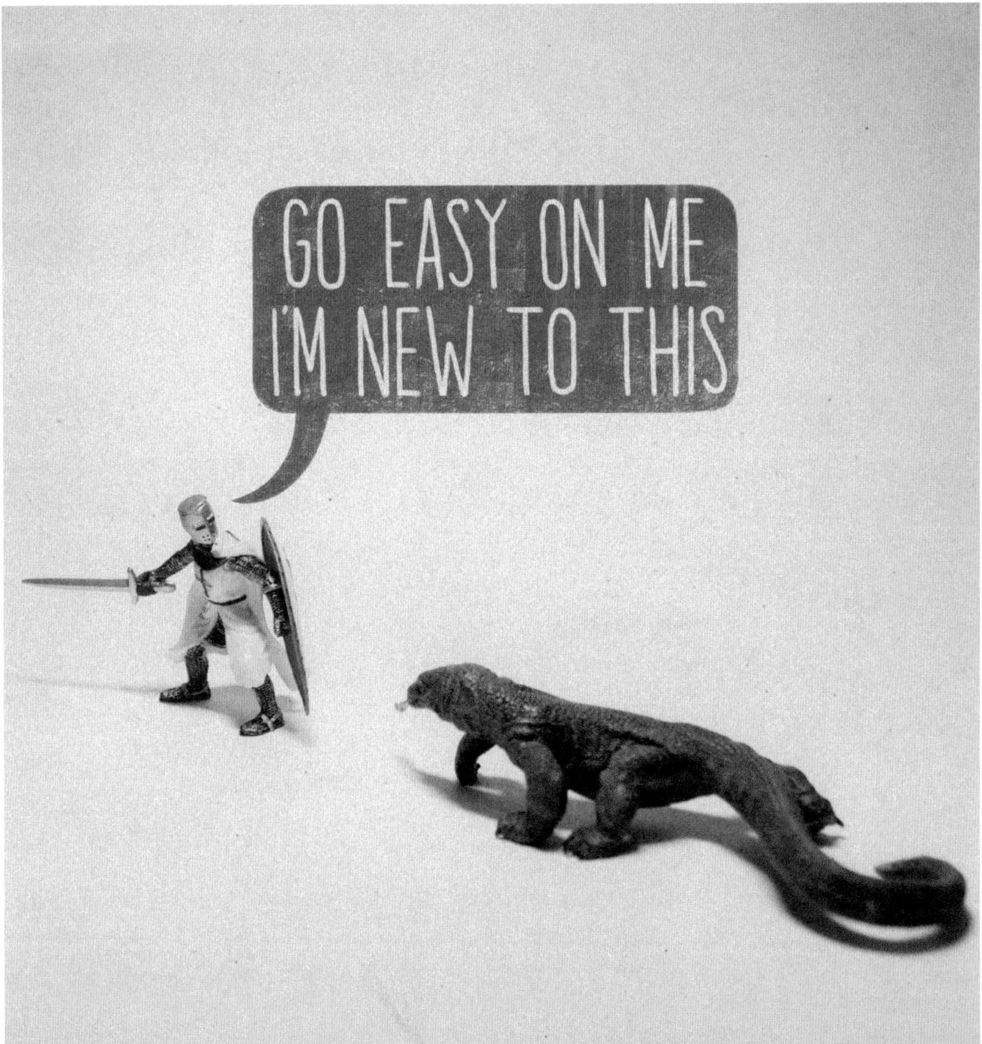
GO EASY ON ME I'M NEW TO THIS

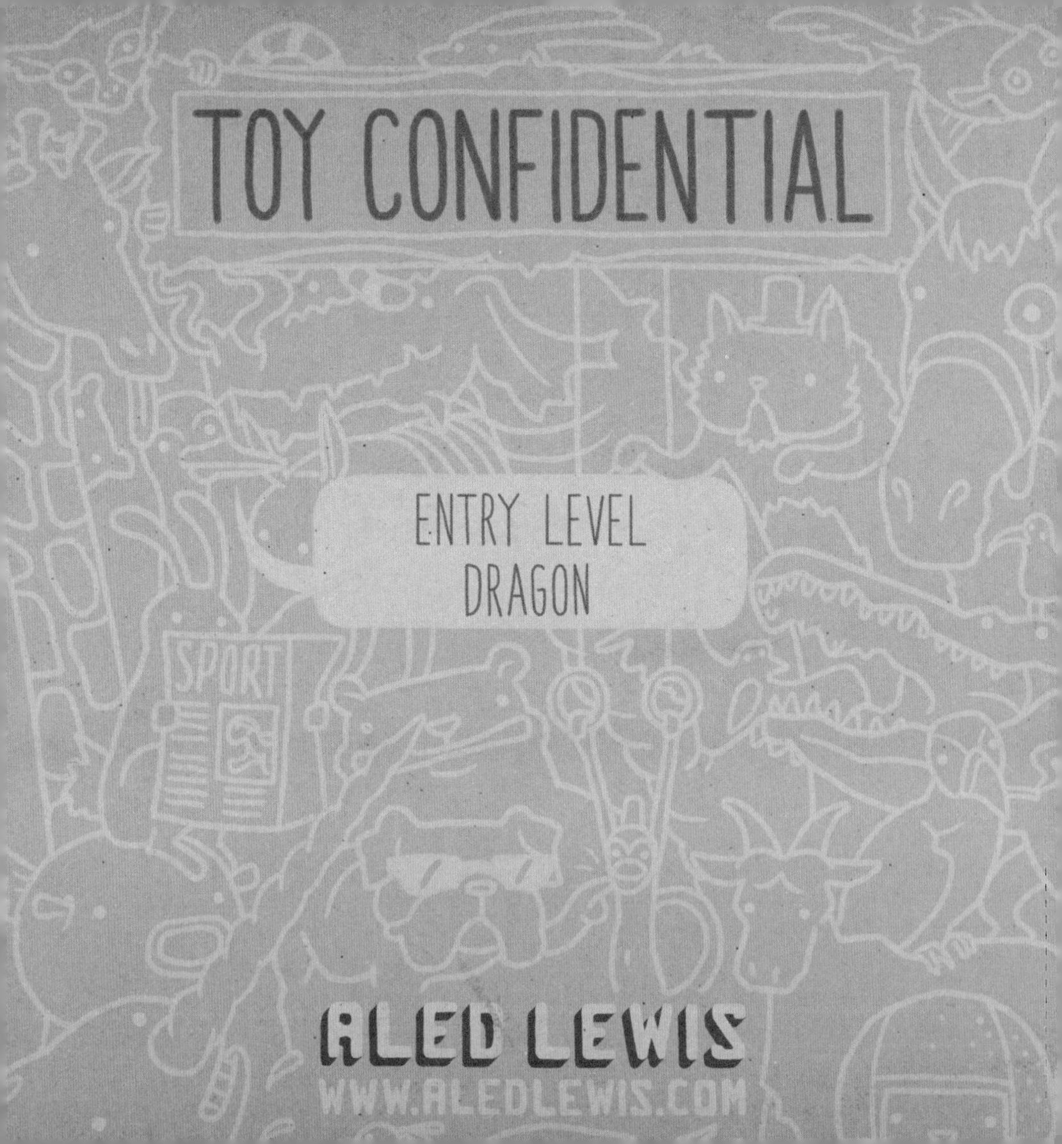
TOY CONFIDENTIAL
ENTRY LEVEL
DRAGON
SPORT
ALED LEWIS
WWW.ALEDLEWIS.COM

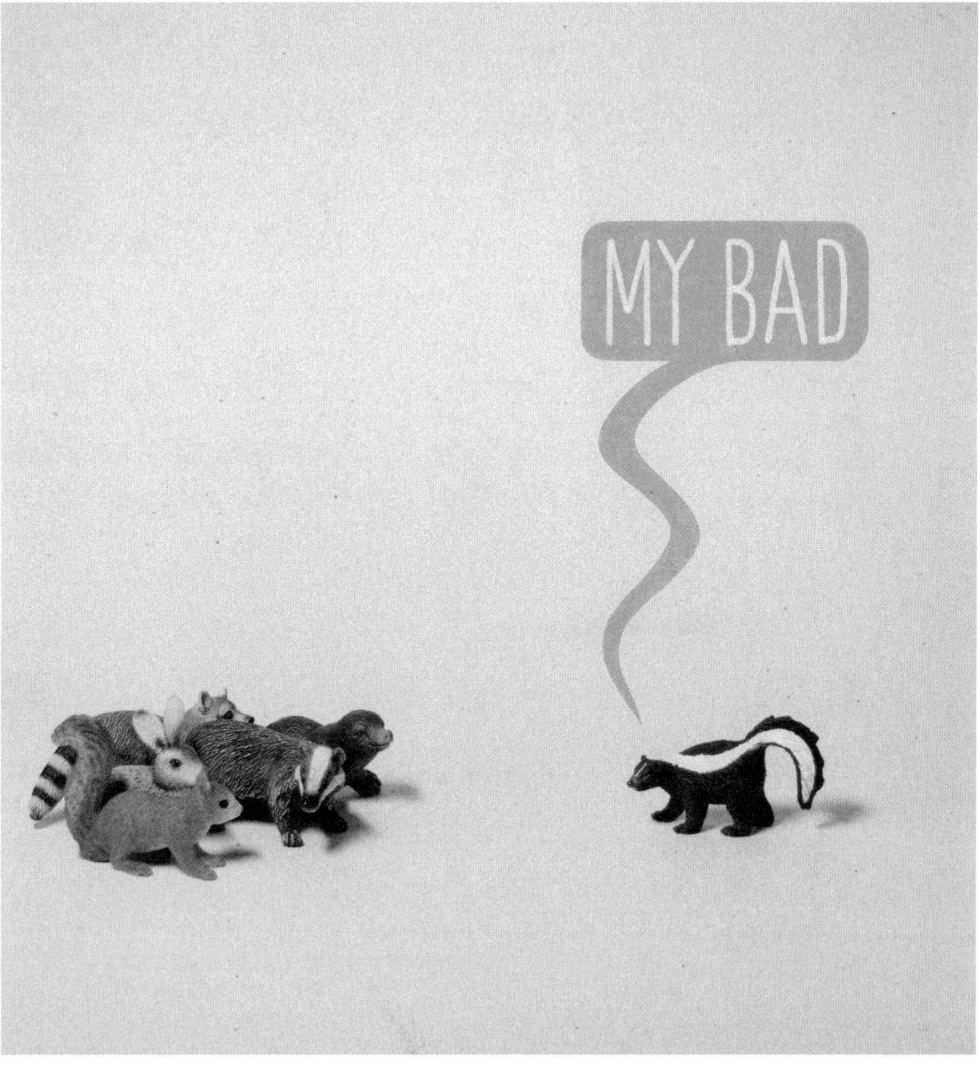
MY BAD

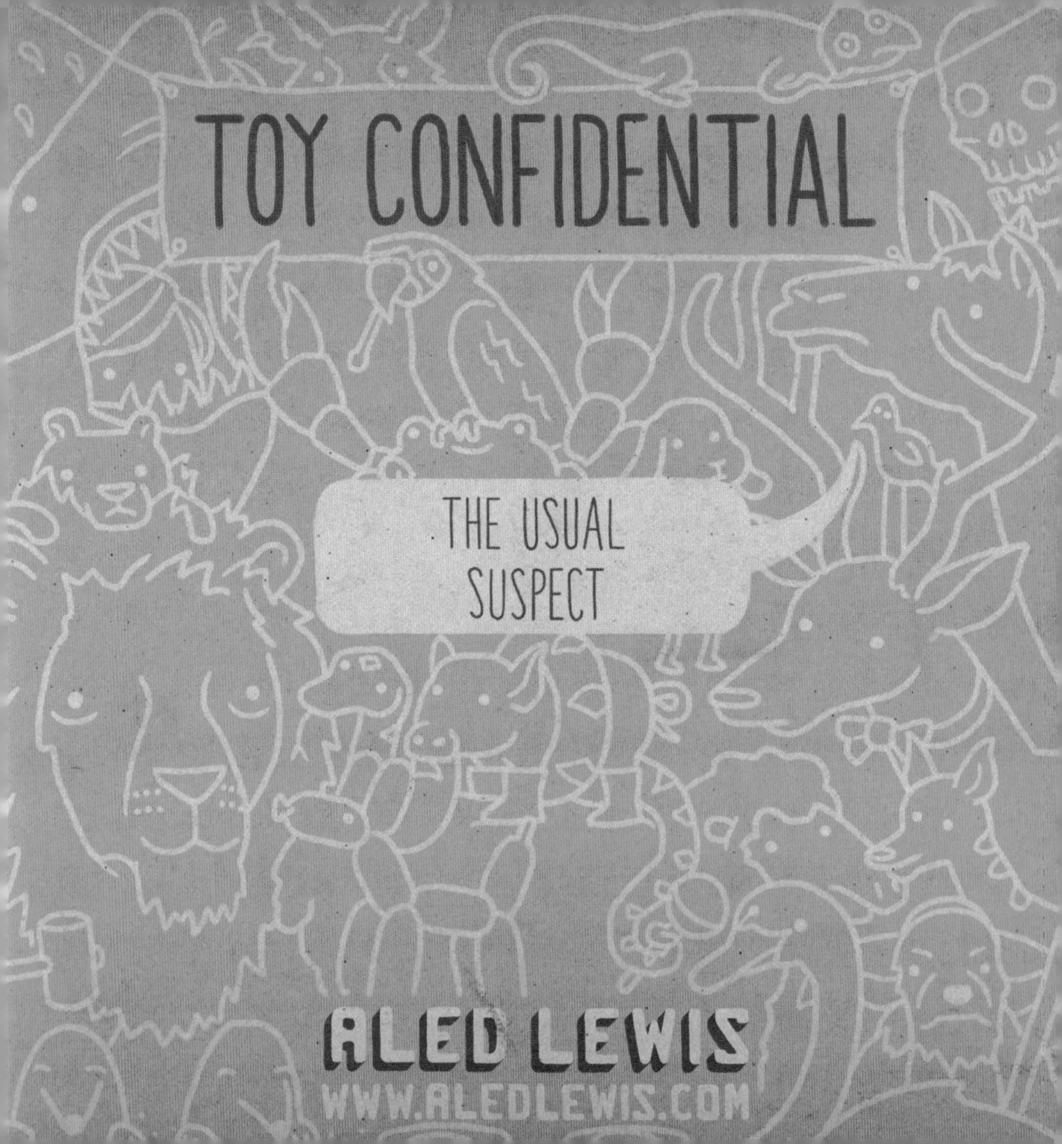
TOY CONFIDENTIAL
THE USUAL SUSPECT
ALED LEWIS
WWW.ALEDLEWIS.COM

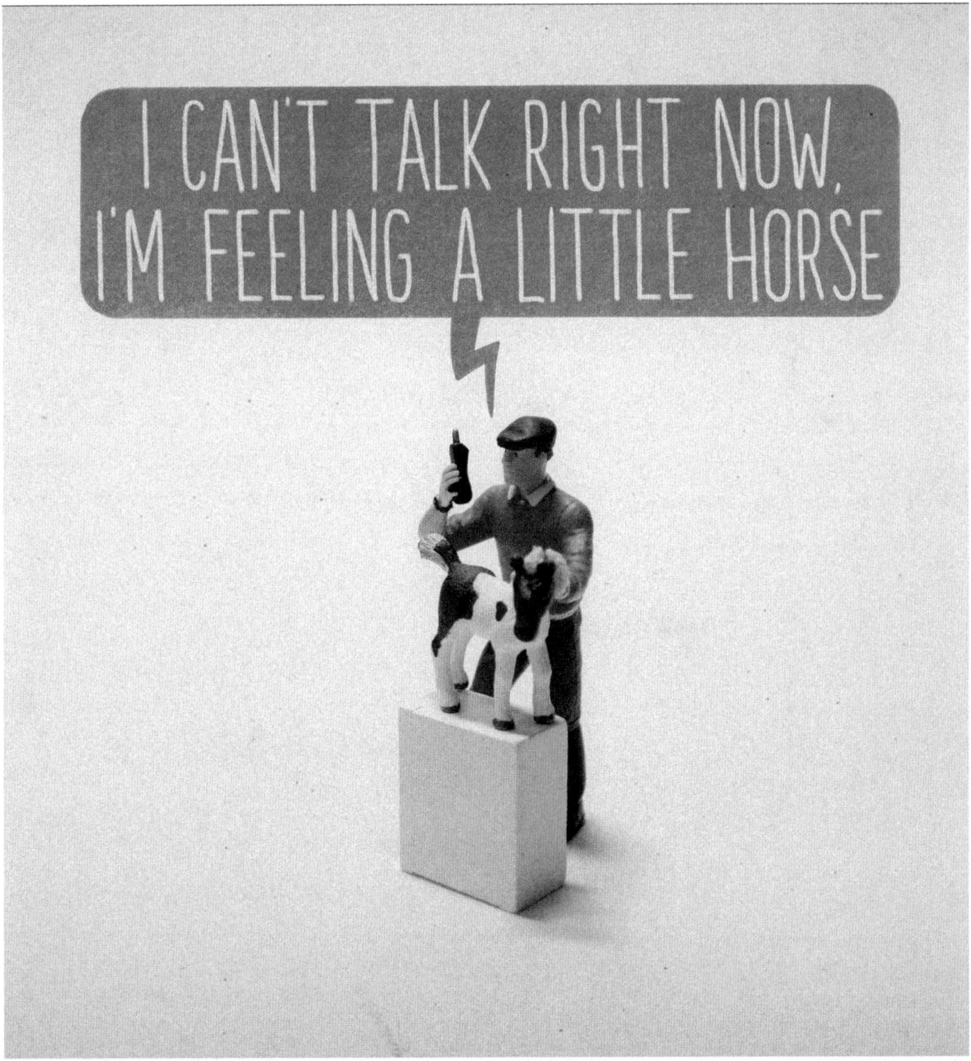
I CAN'T TALK RIGHT NOW, I'M FEELING A LITTLE HORSE

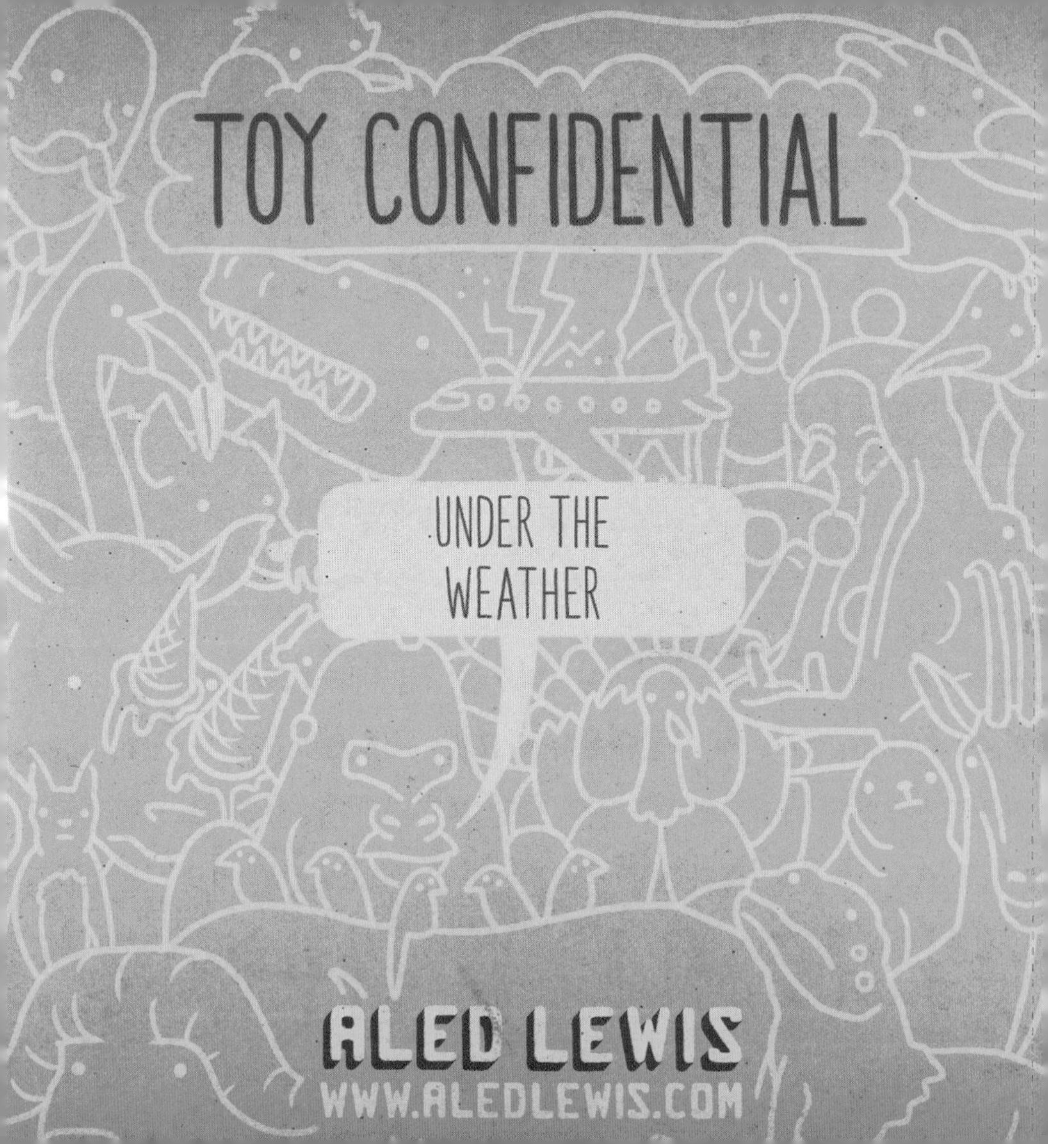
TOY CONFIDENTIAL
UNDER THE WEATHER
ALED LEWIS
WWW.ALEDLEWIS.COM

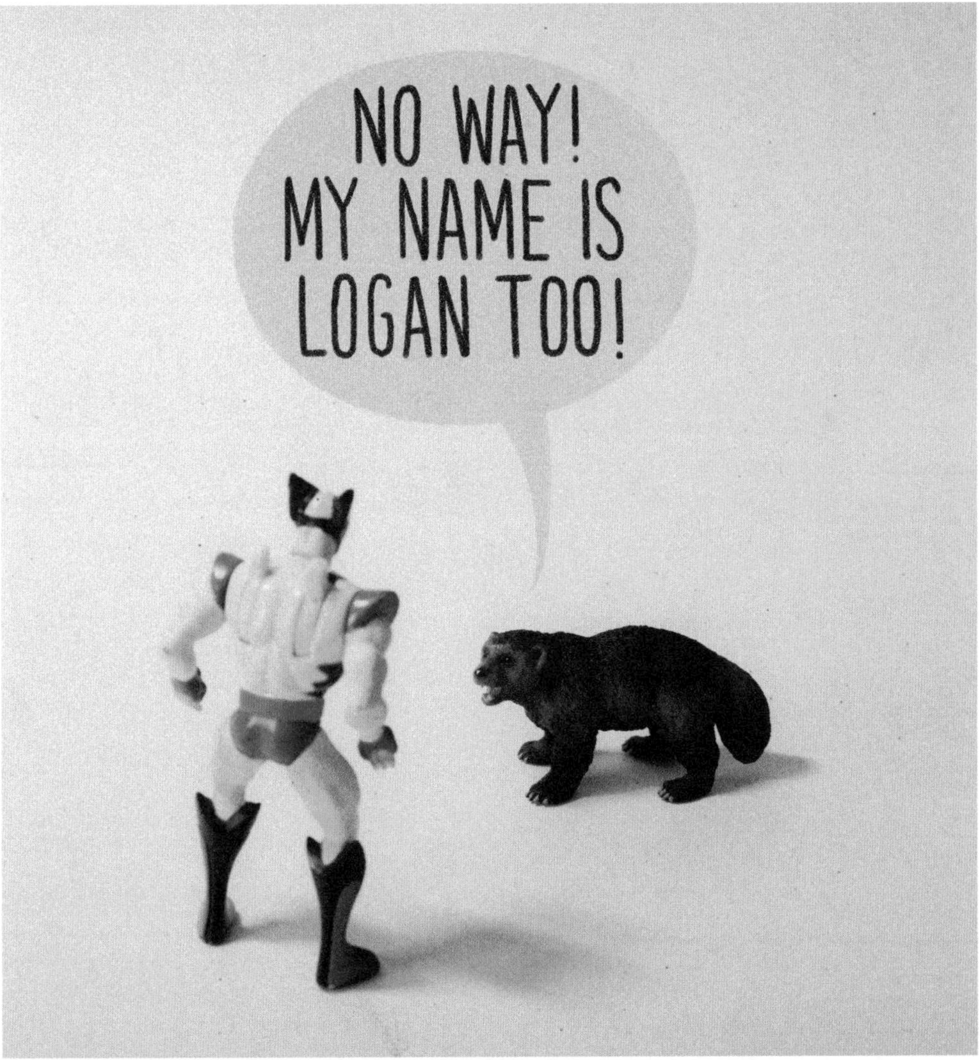
NO WAY!
MY NAME IS
LOGAN TOO!

TOY CONFIDENTIAL

WOLVERINE

ALED LEWIS
WWW.ALEDLEWIS.COM

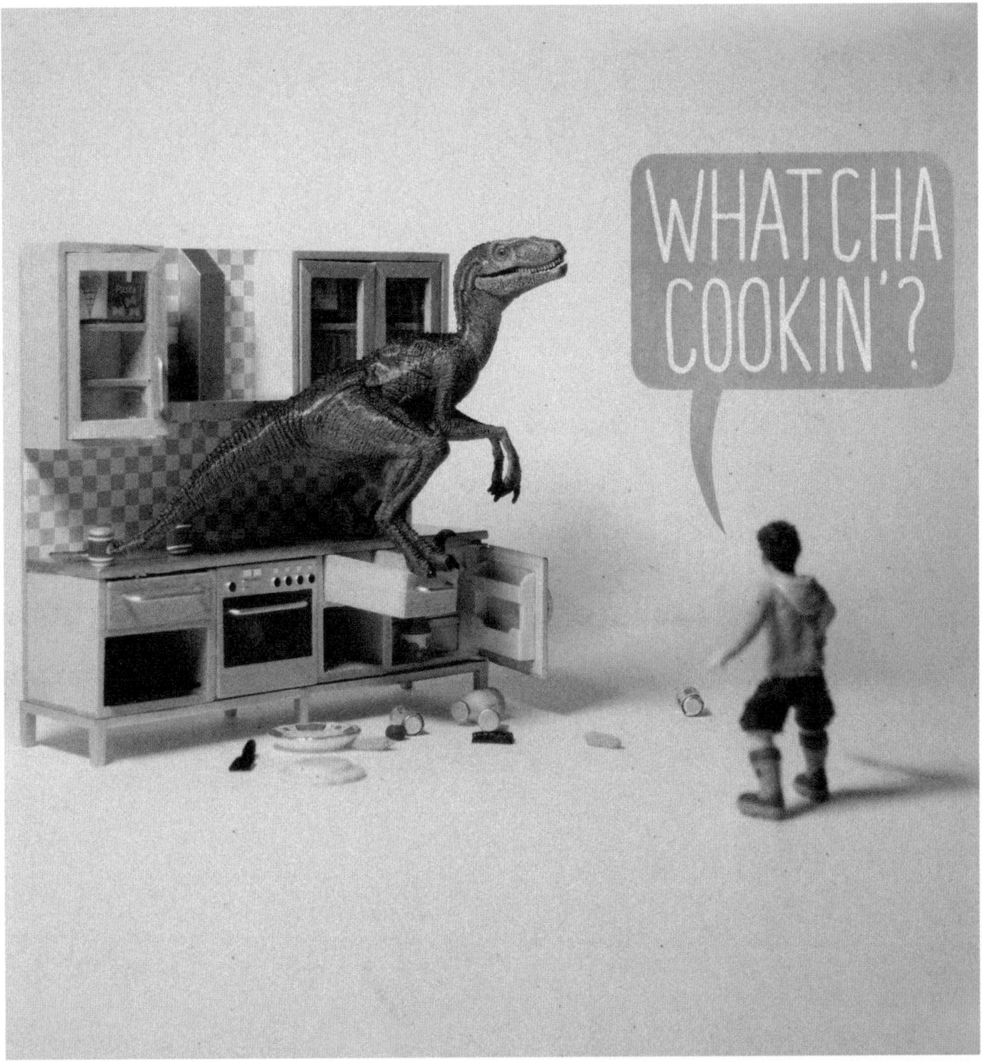
WHATCHA COOKIN'?

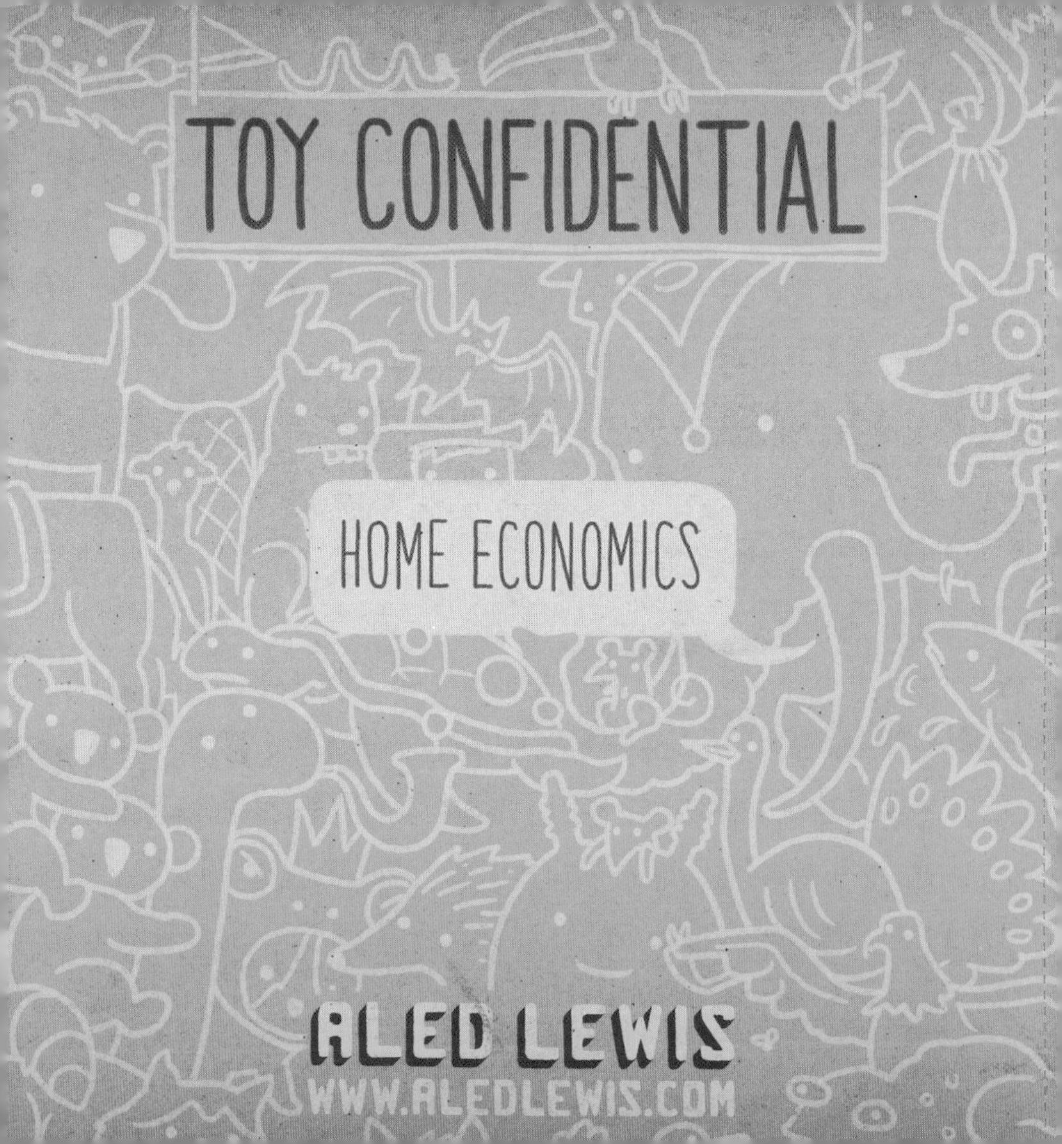
TOY CONFIDENTIAL
HOME ECONOMICS
ALED LEWIS
WWW.ALEDLEWIS.COM

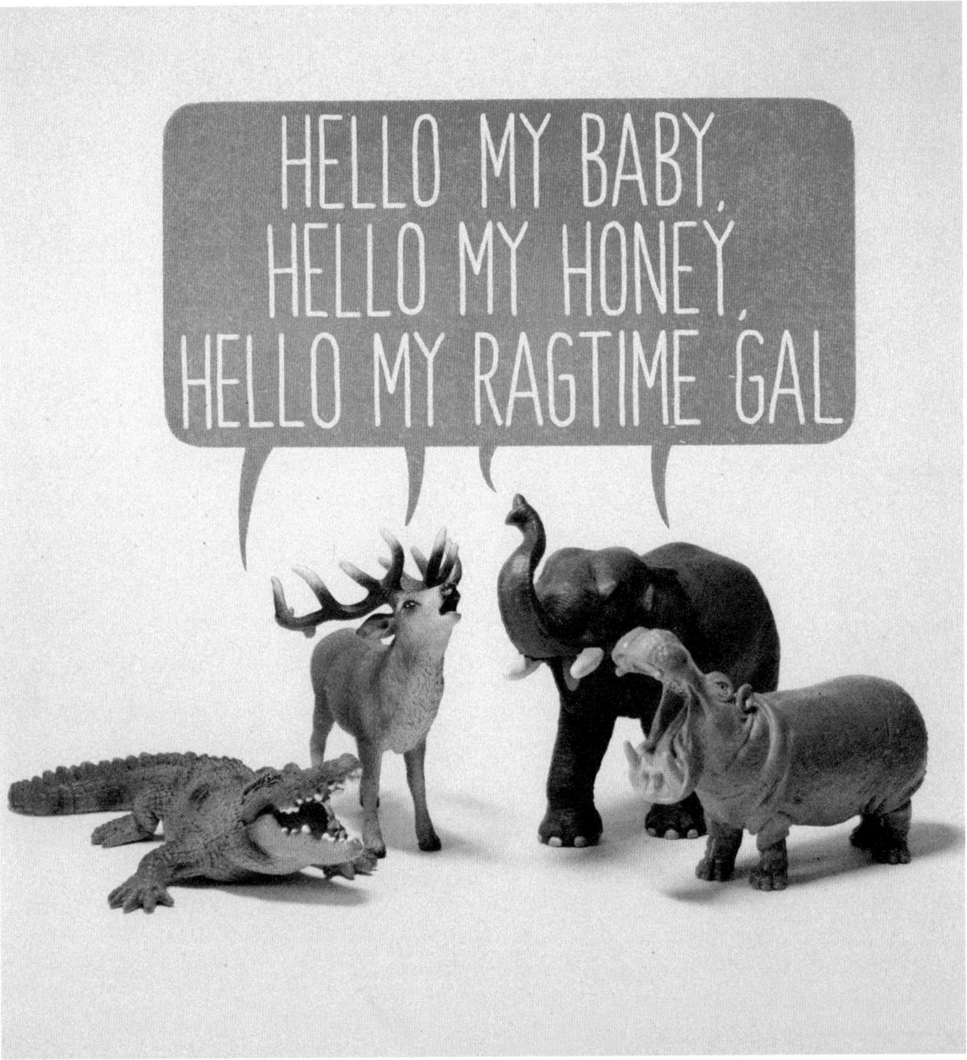
HELLO MY BABY,
HELLO MY HONEY,
HELLO MY RAGTIME GAL

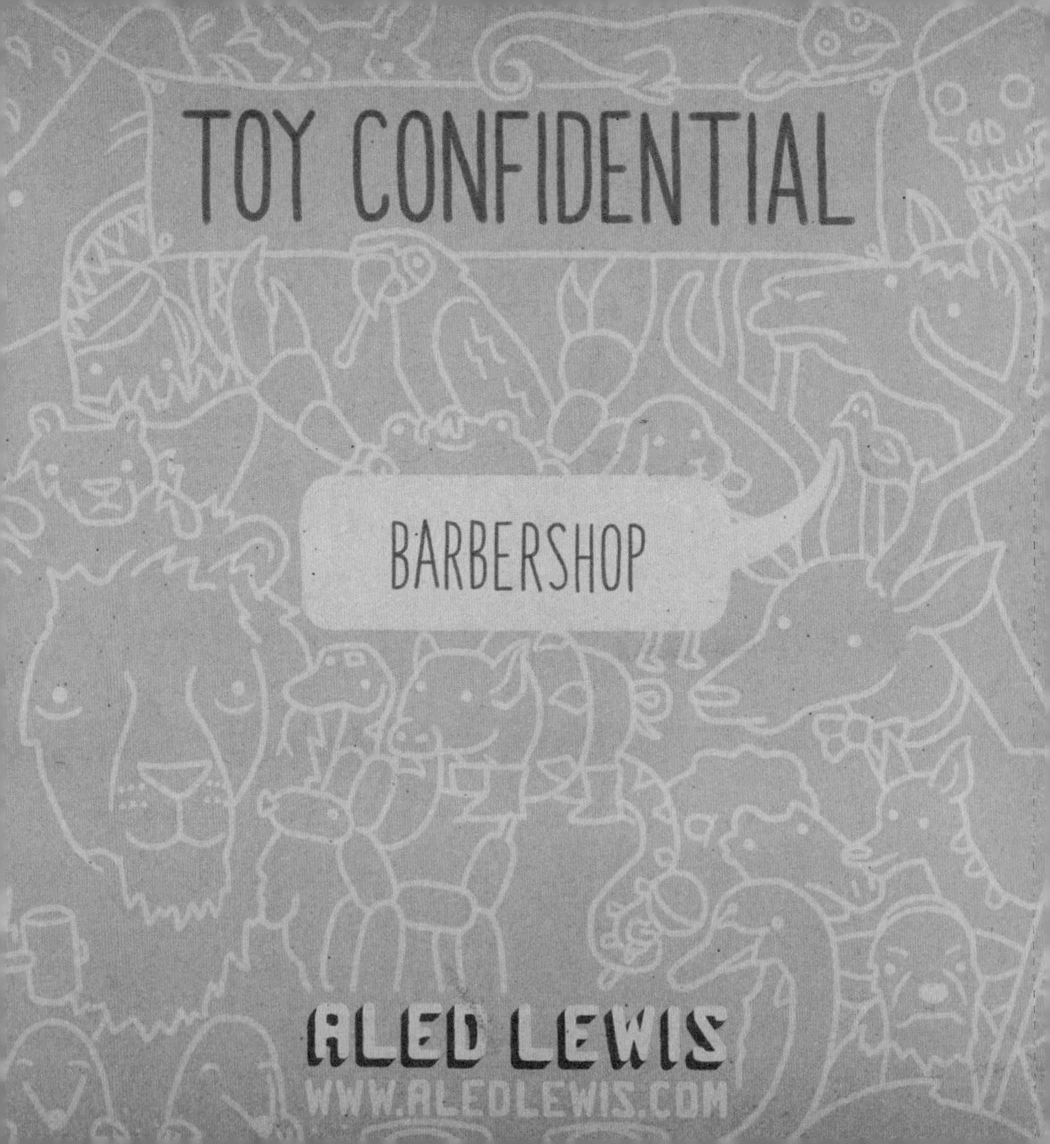
TOY CONFIDENTIAL
BARBERSHOP
ALED LEWIS
WWW.ALEDLEWIS.COM

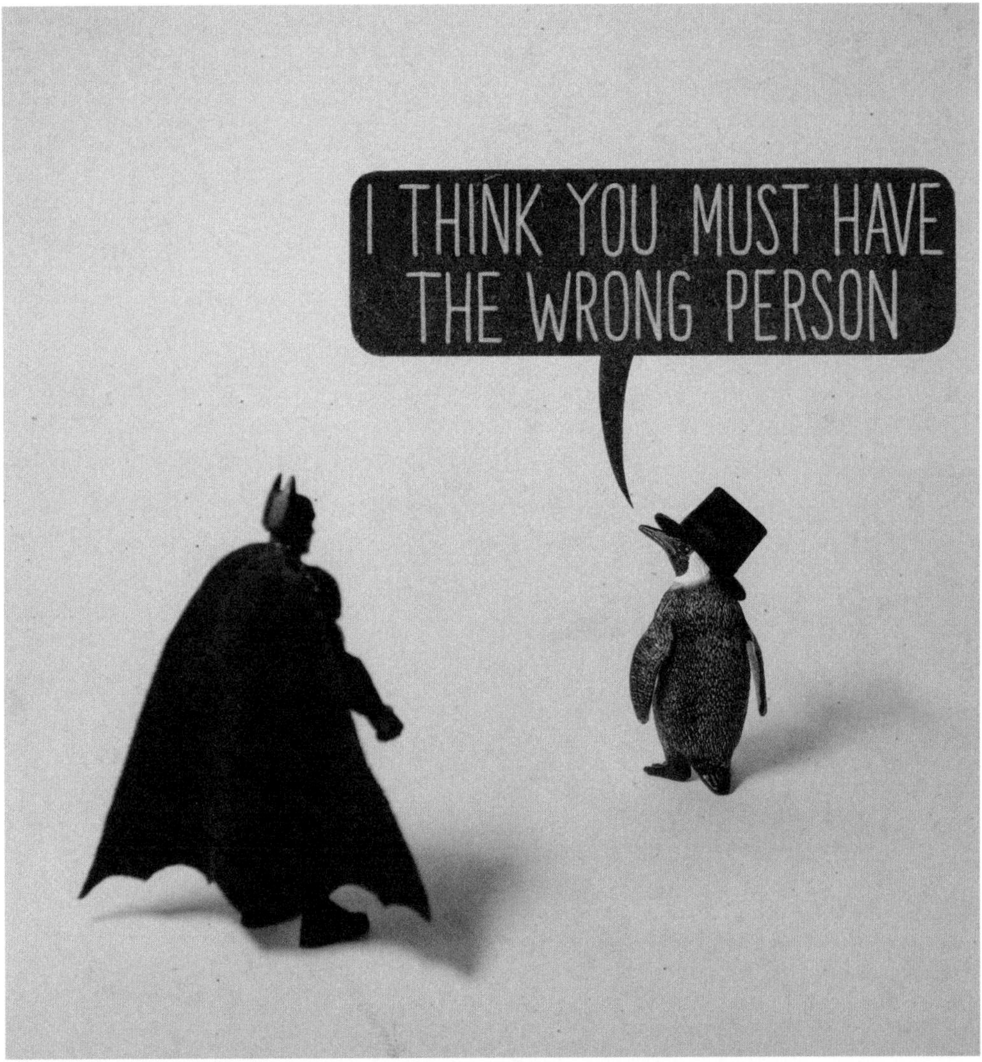
I THINK YOU MUST HAVE THE WRONG PERSON

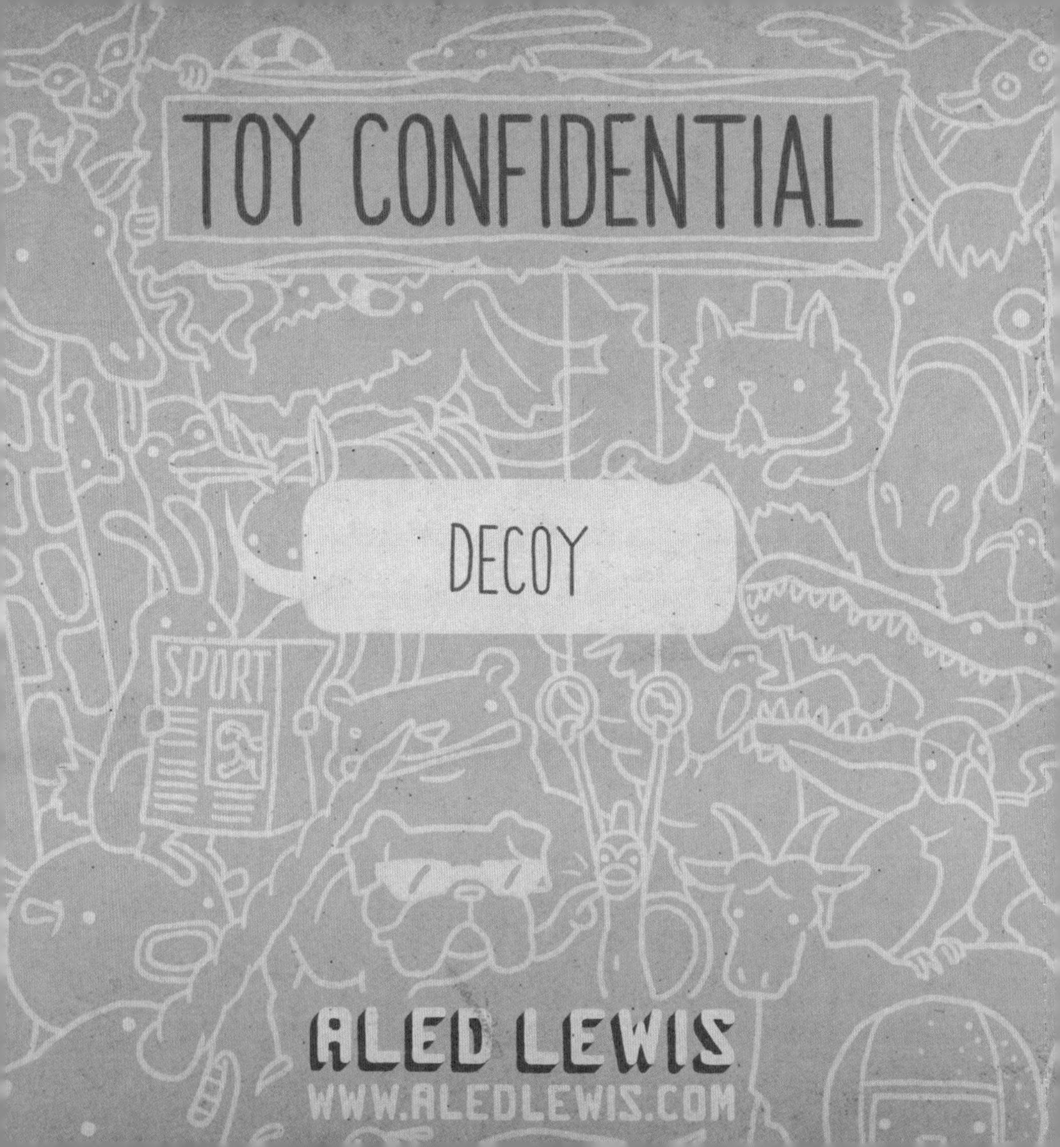
TOY CONFIDENTIAL
DECOY
SPORT
ALED LEWIS
WWW.ALEDLEWIS.COM

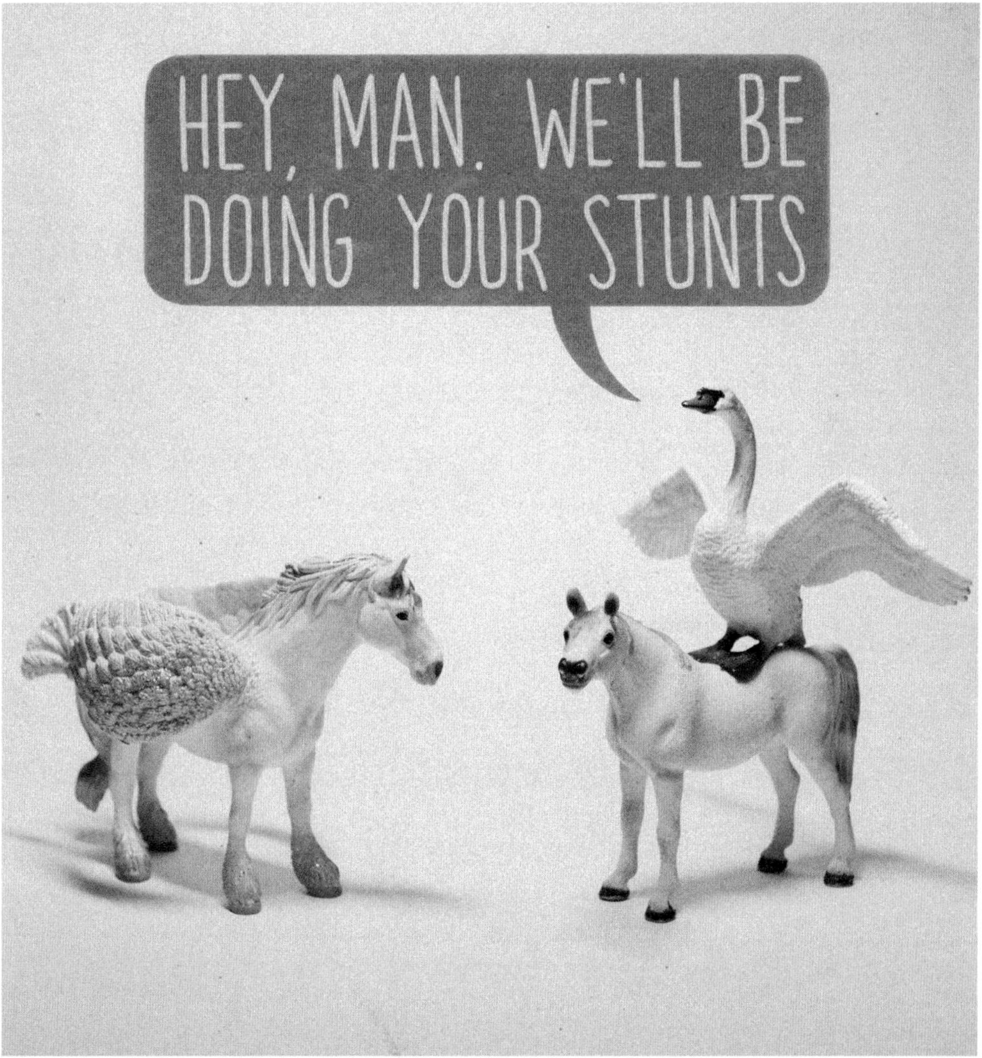
HEY, MAN. WE'LL BE DOING YOUR STUNTS

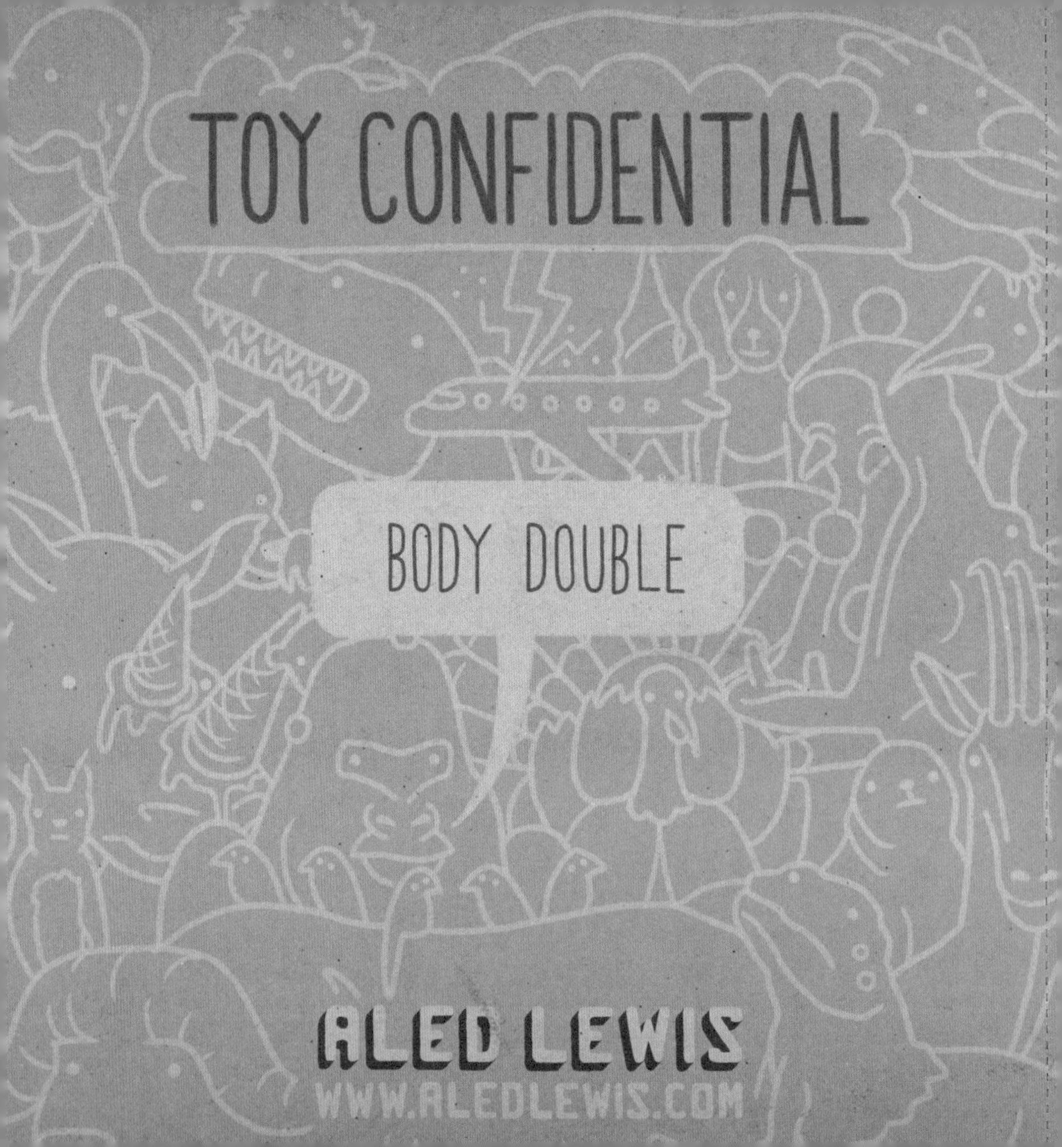
TOY CONFIDENTIAL
BODY DOUBLE
ALED LEWIS
WWW.ALEDLEWIS.COM

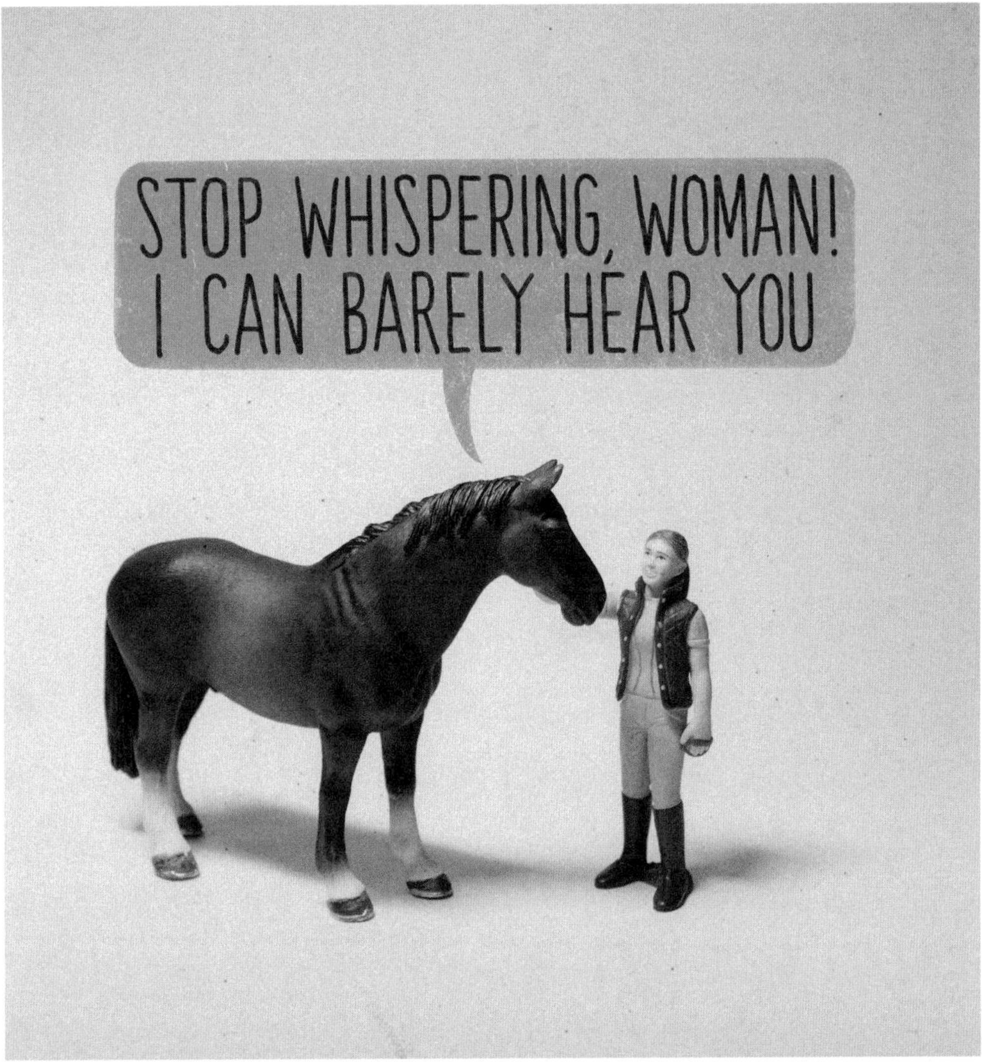
STOP WHISPERING, WOMAN!
I CAN BARELY HEAR YOU

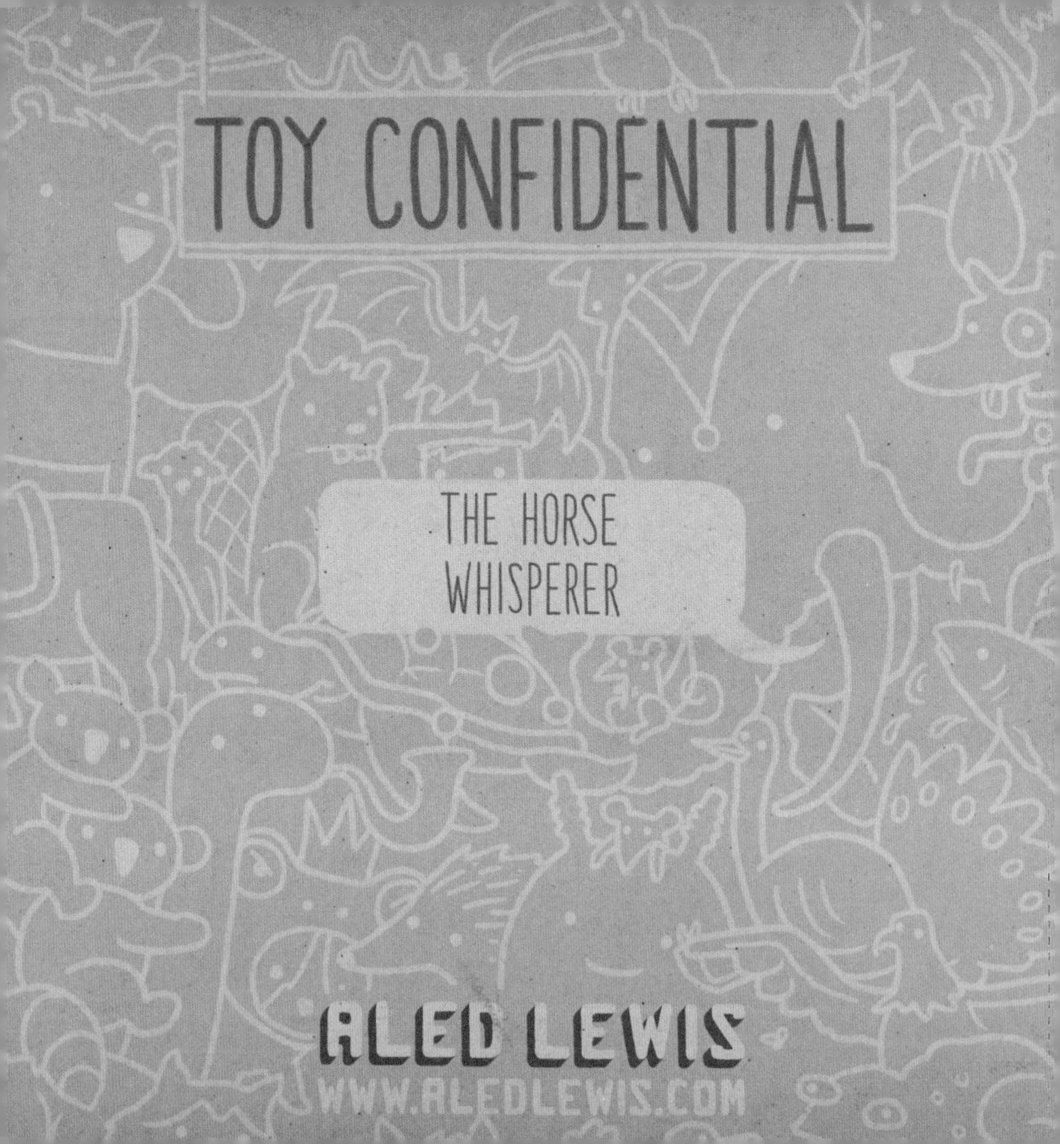
TOY CONFIDENTIAL
THE HORSE WHISPERER
ALED LEWIS
WWW.ALEDLEWIS.COM

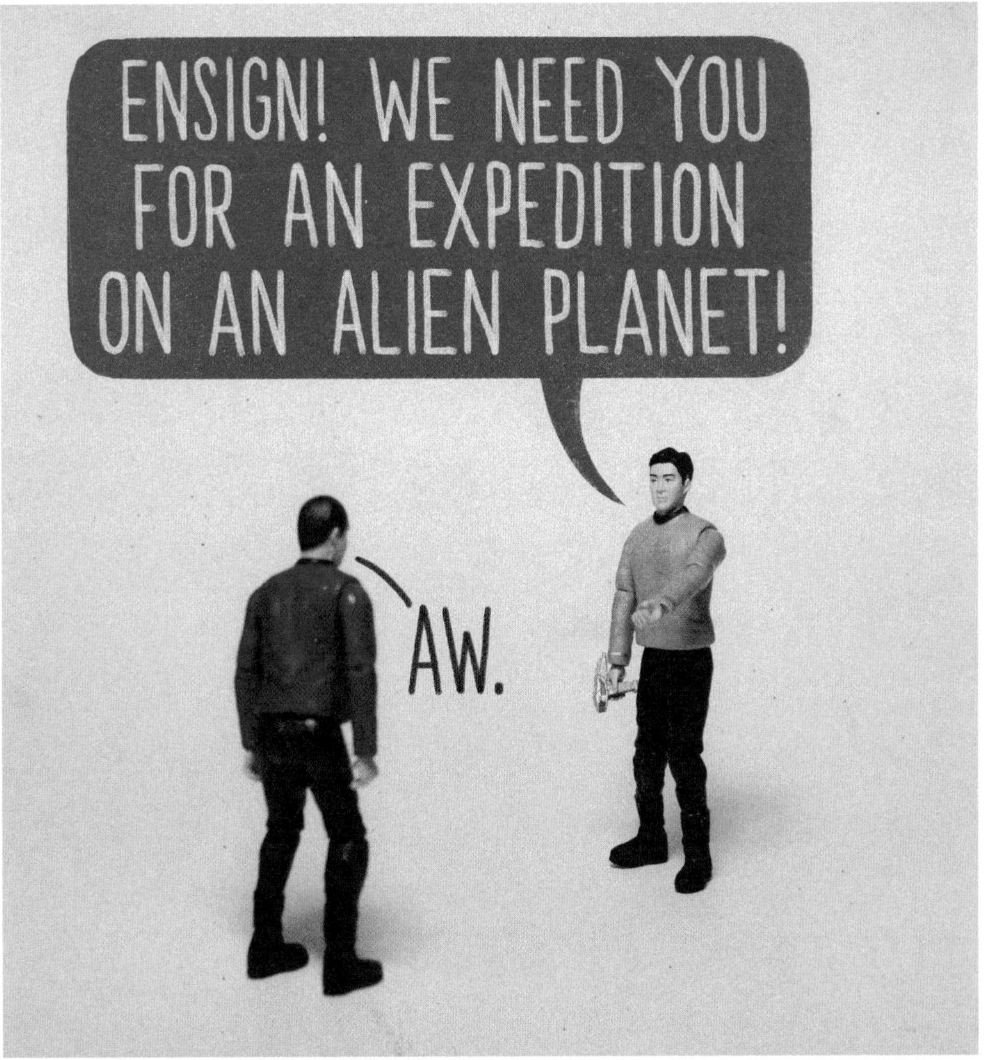
ENSIGN! WE NEED YOU FOR AN EXPEDITION ON AN ALIEN PLANET!
AW.

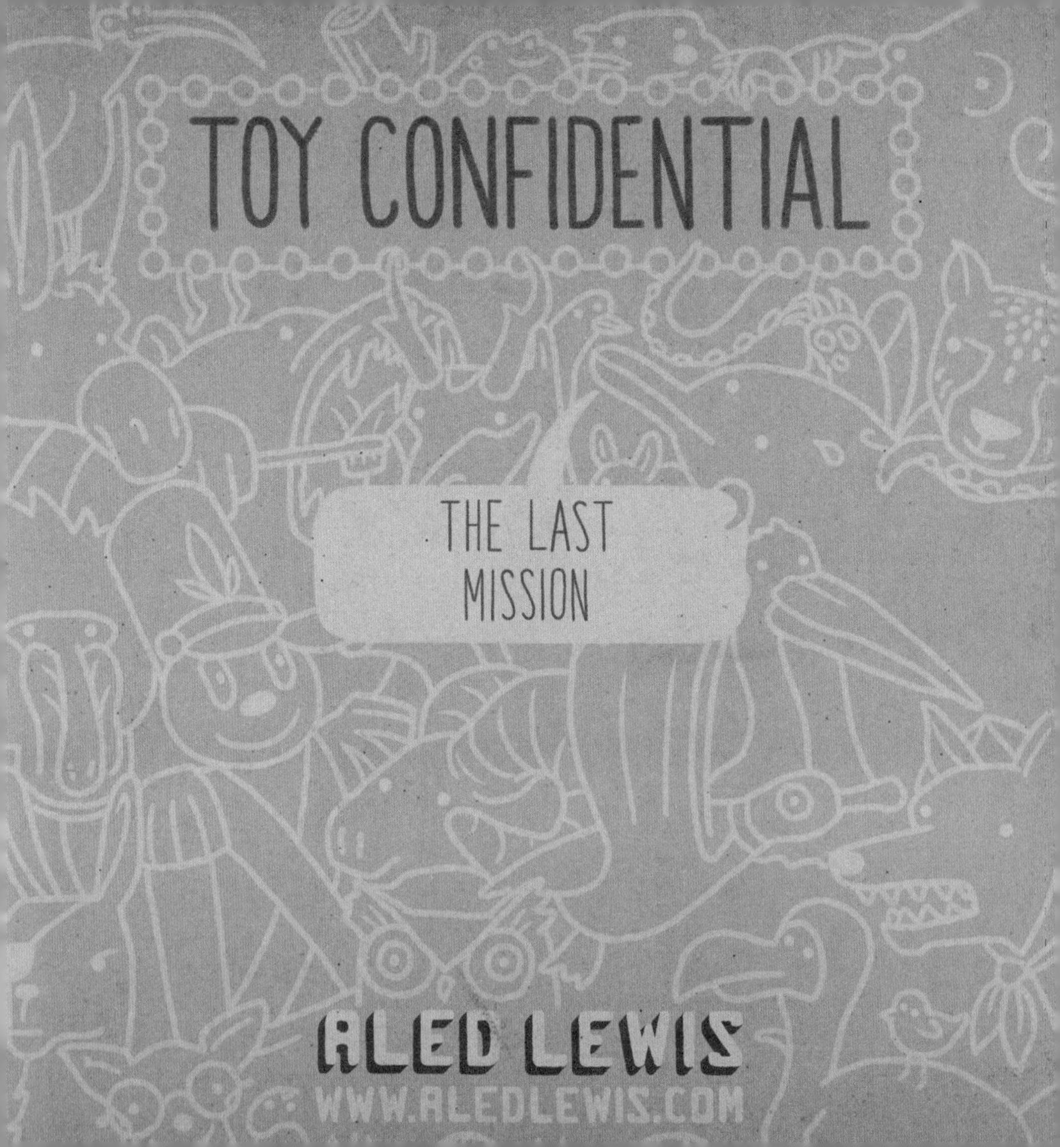
TOY CONFIDENTIAL
THE LAST MISSION
ALED LEWIS
WWW.ALEDLEWIS.COM

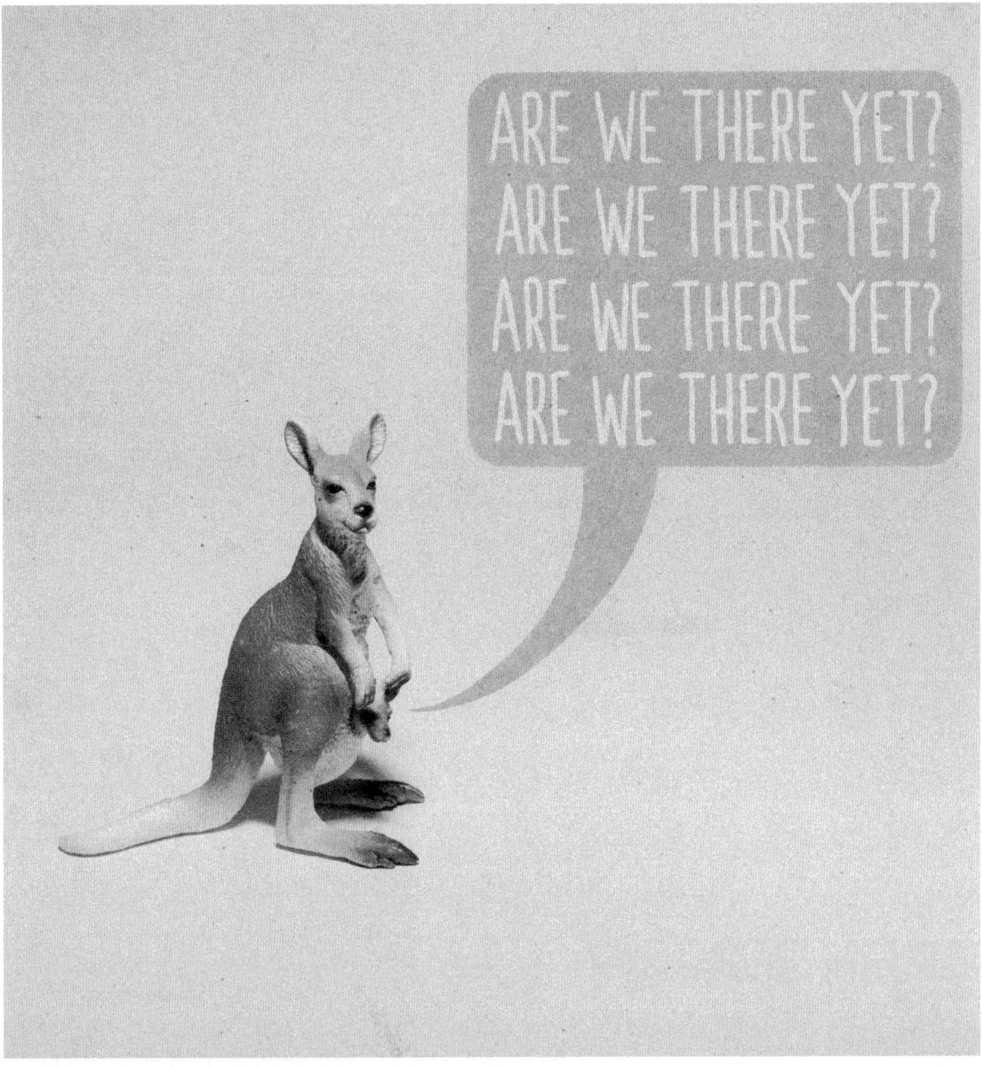
ARE WE THERE YET?
ARE WE THERE YET?
ARE WE THERE YET?
ARE WE THERE YET?

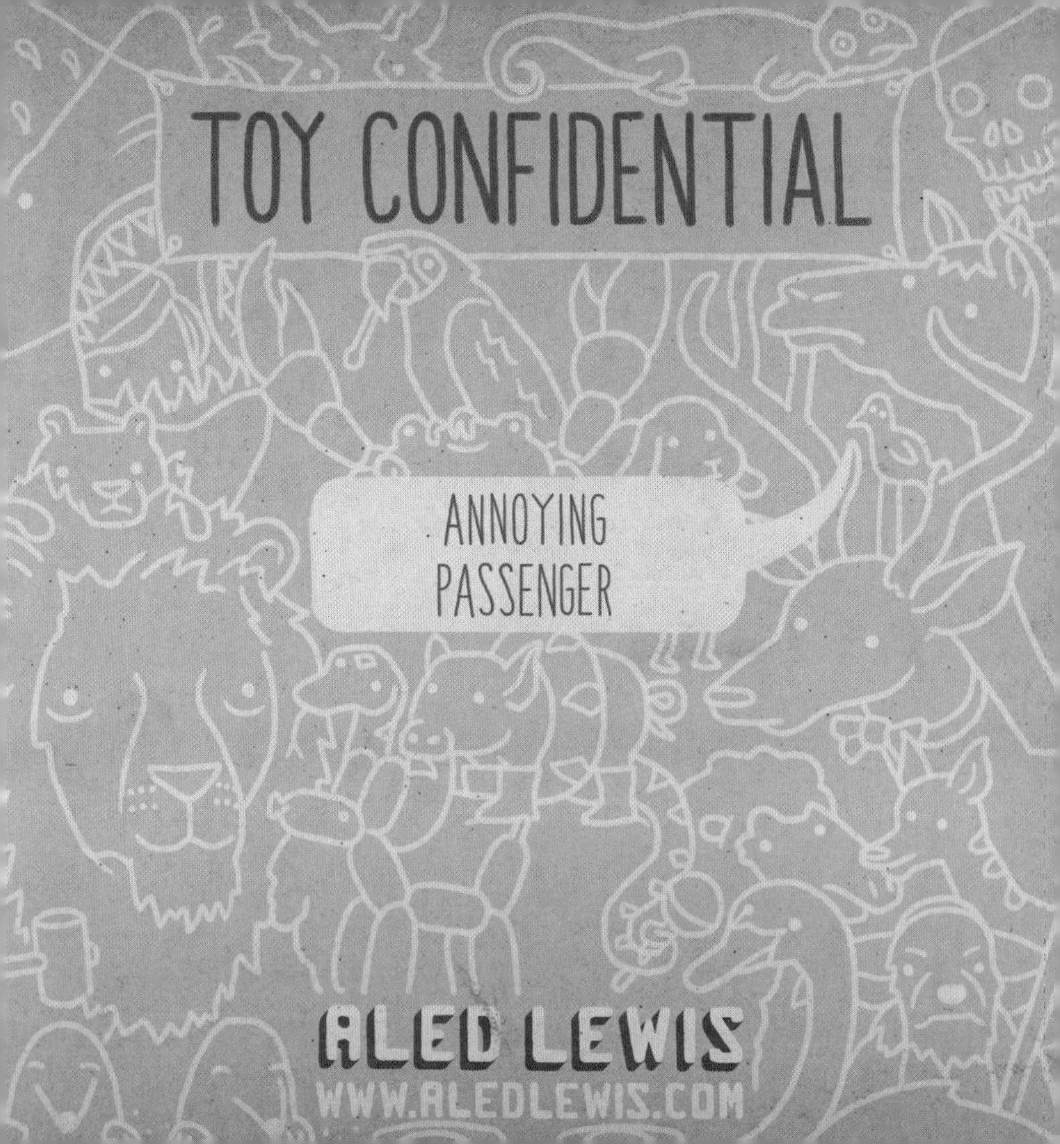
TOY CONFIDENTIAL
ANNOYING PASSENGER
ALED LEWIS
WWW.ALEDLEWIS.COM

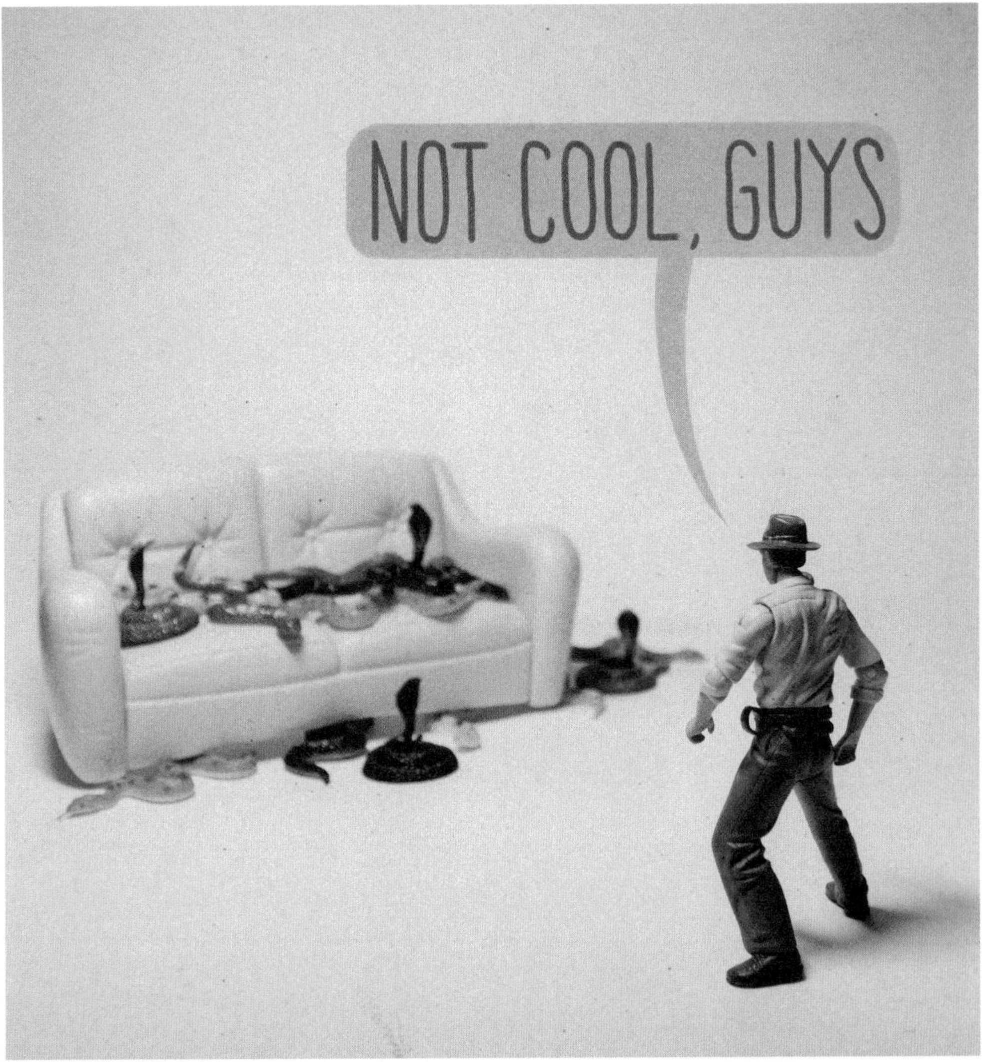
NOT COOL, GUYS

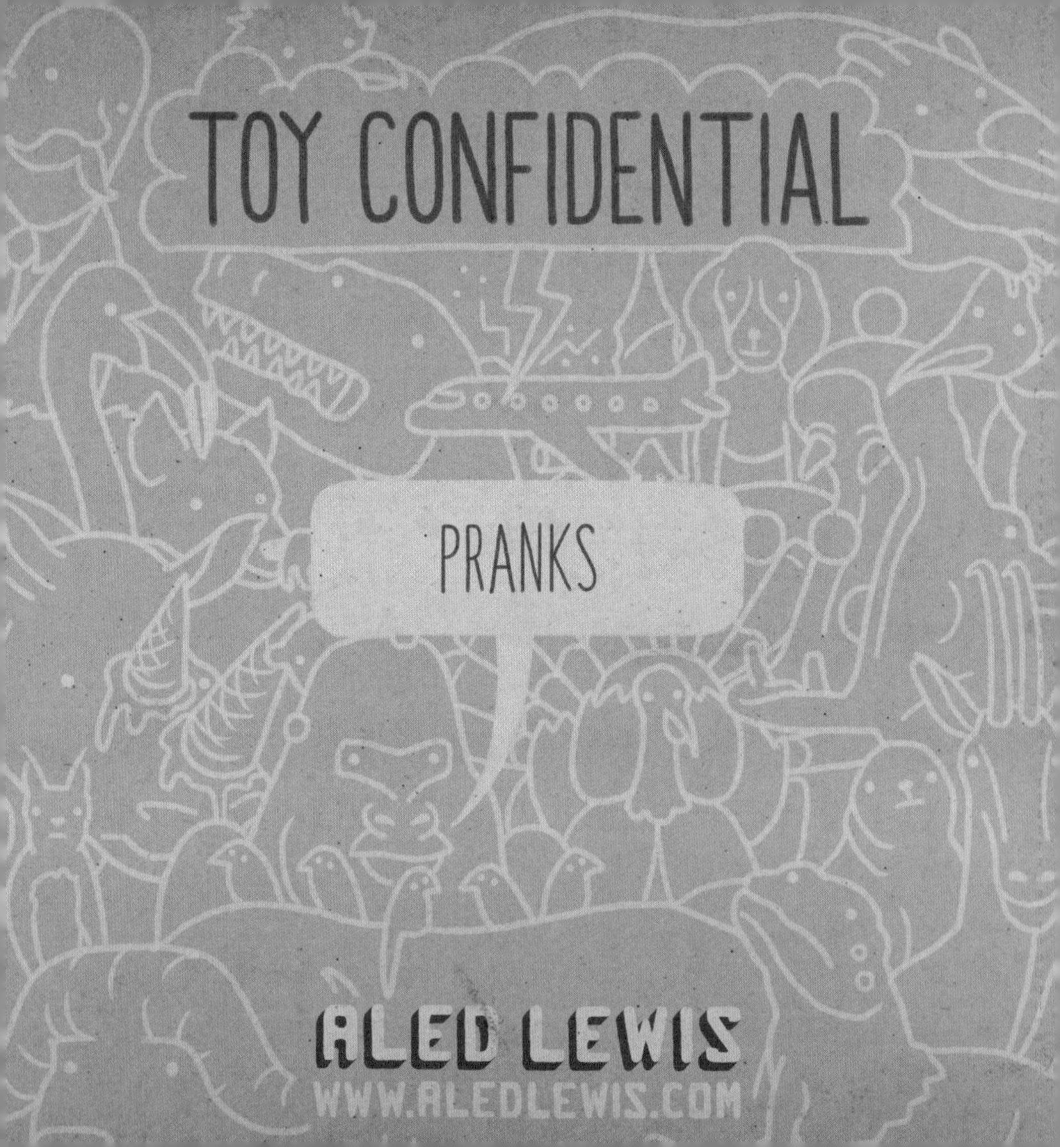
TOY CONFIDENTIAL
PRANKS
ALED LEWIS
WWW.ALEDLEWIS.COM

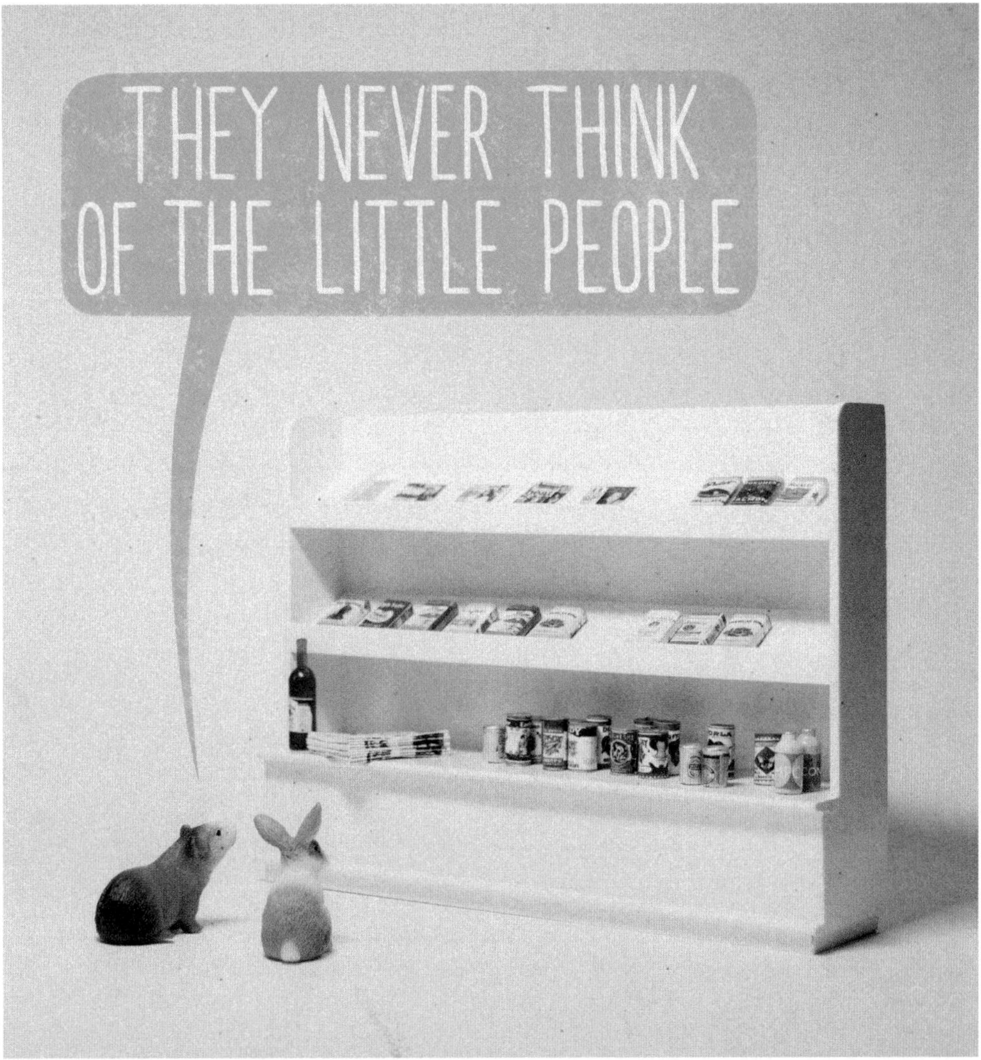
THEY NEVER THINK
OF THE LITTLE PEOPLE

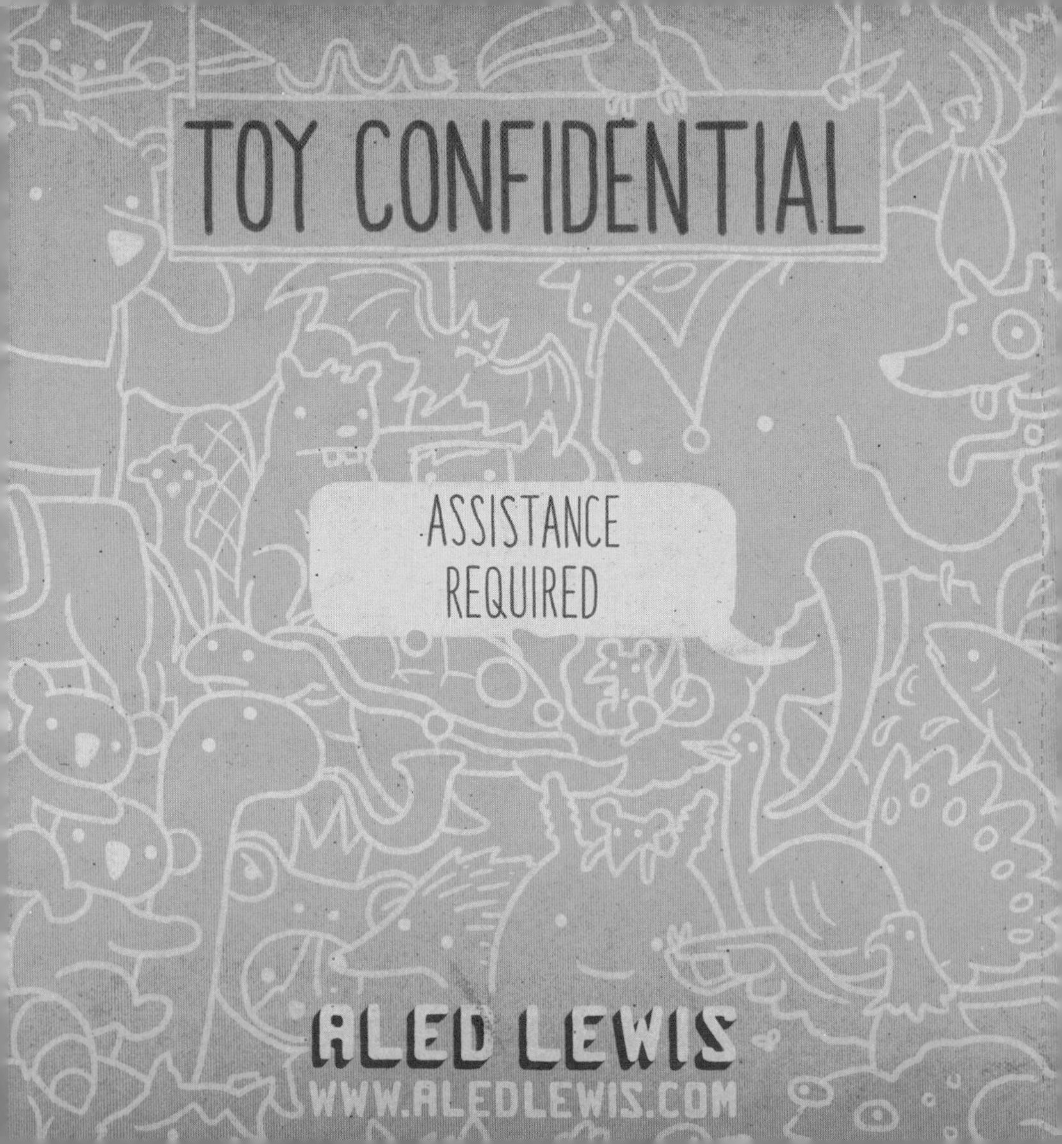
TOY CONFIDENTIAL
ASSISTANCE
REQUIRED
ALED LEWIS
WWW.ALEDLEWIS.COM

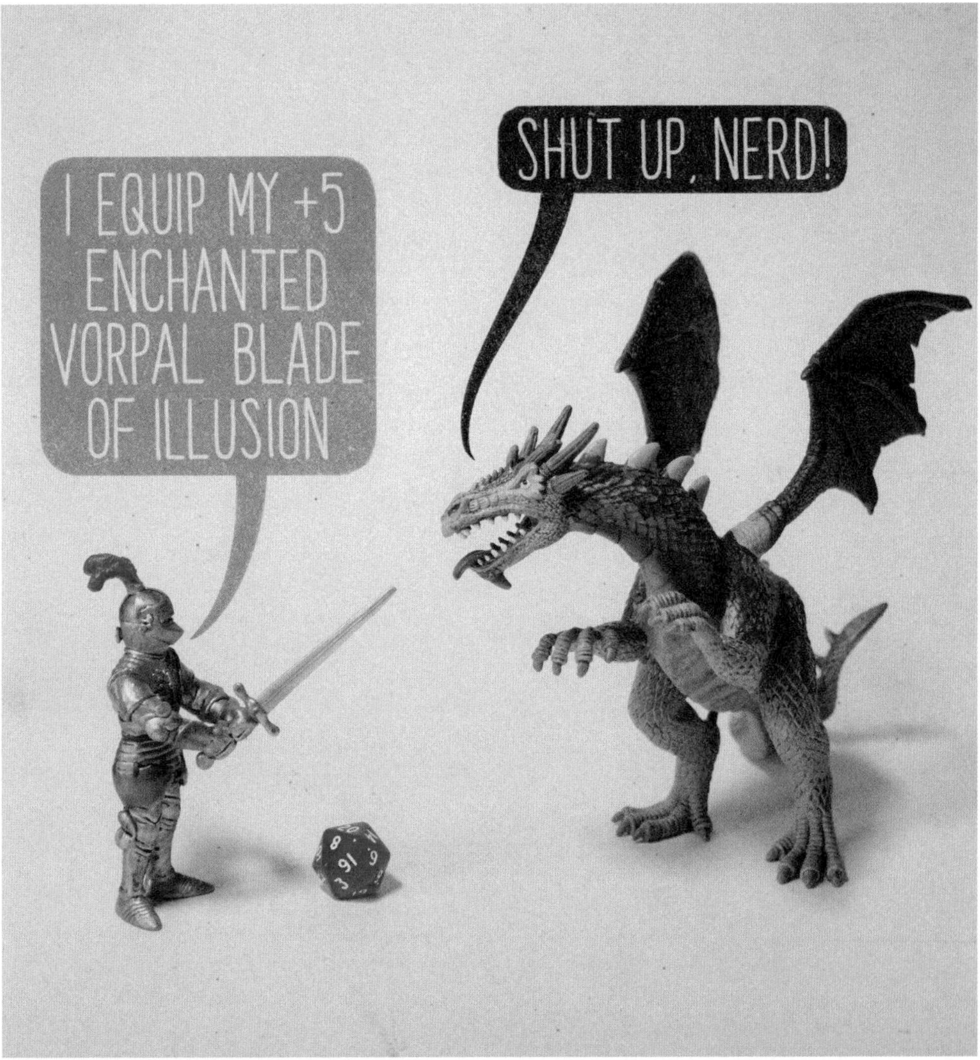
I EQUIP MY +5 ENCHANTED VORPAL BLADE OF ILLUSION
SHUT UP, NERD!

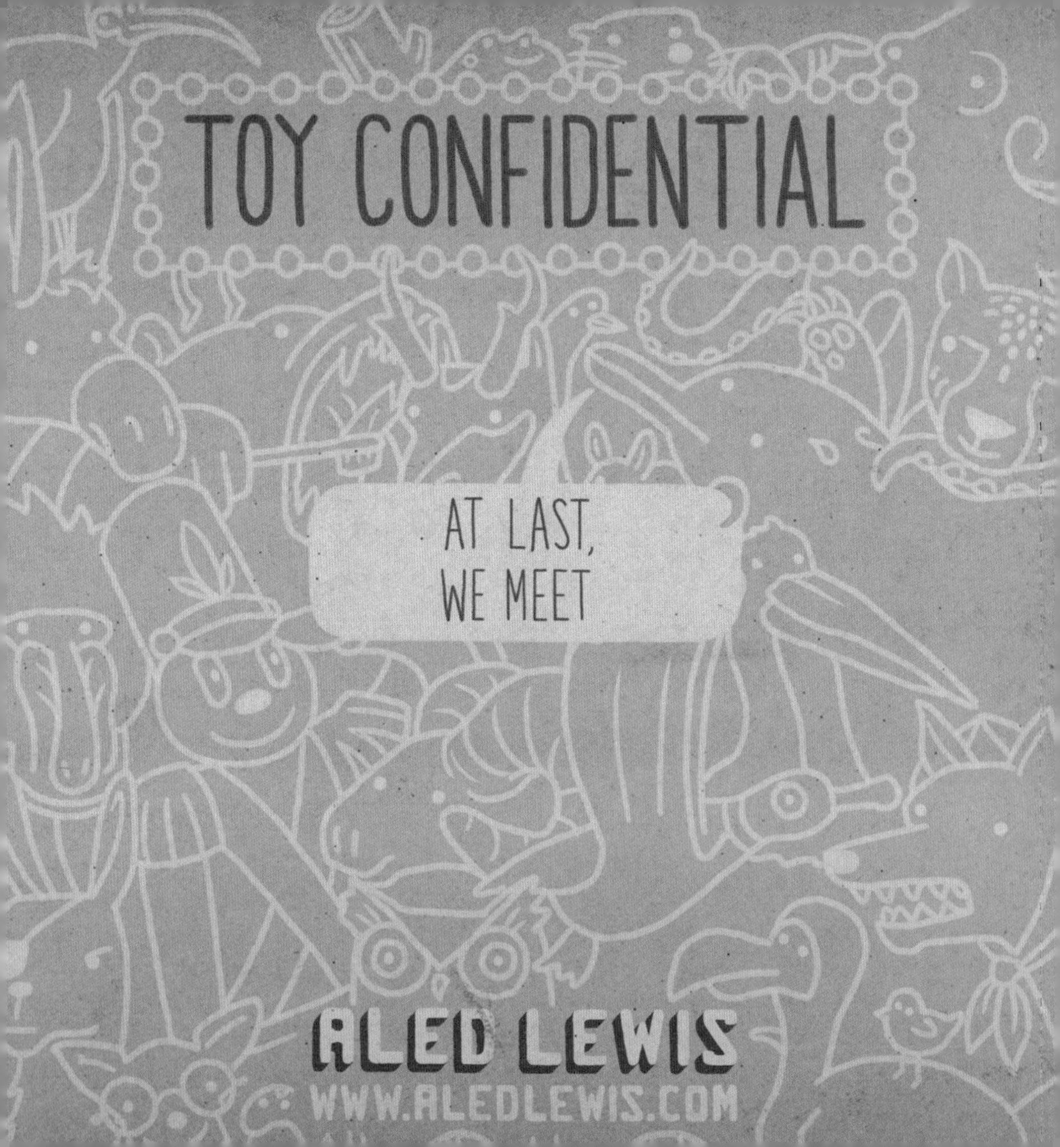
TOY CONFIDENTIAL
AT LAST, WE MEET
ALED LEWIS
WWW.ALEDLEWIS.COM

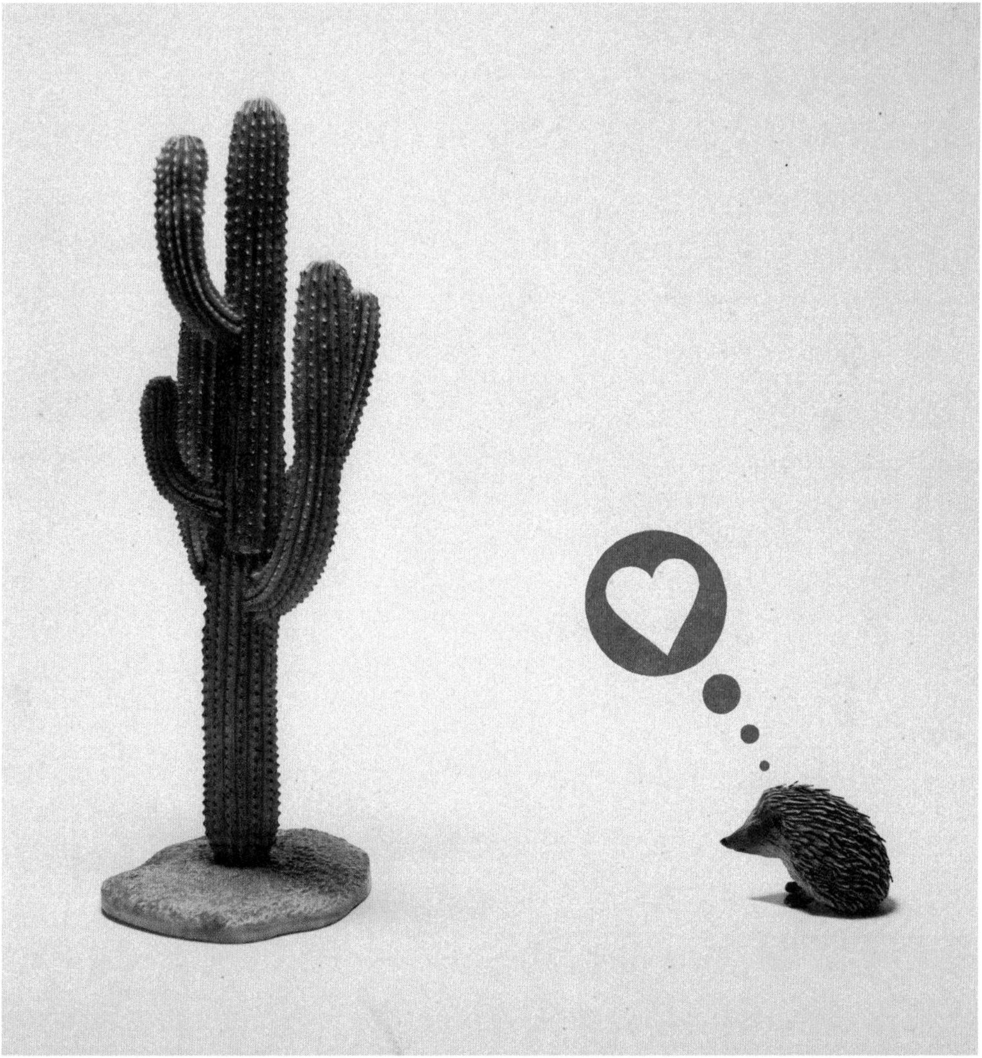

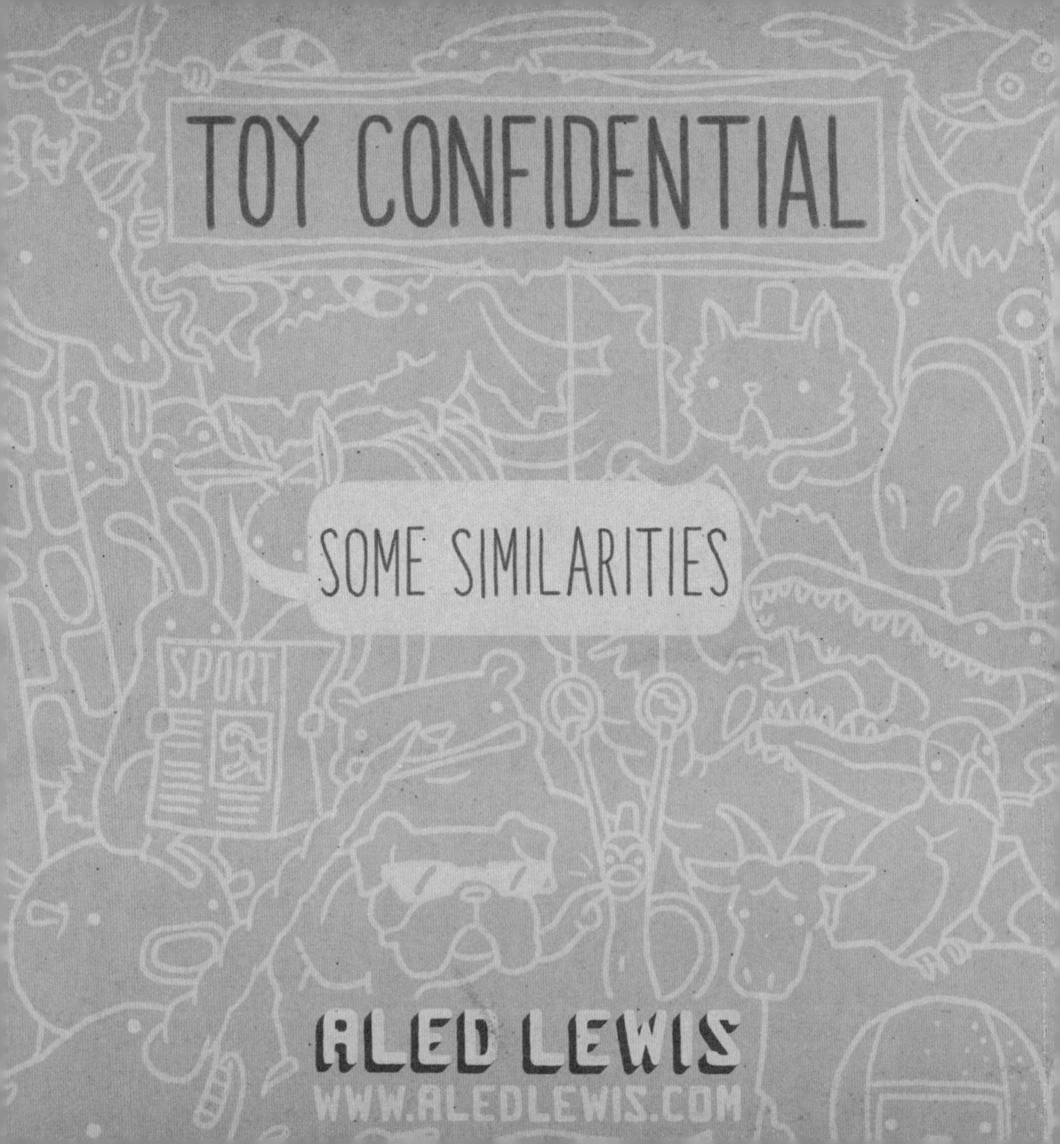
TOY CONFIDENTIAL
SOME SIMILARITIES
SPORT
ALED LEWIS
WWW.ALEDLEWIS.COM

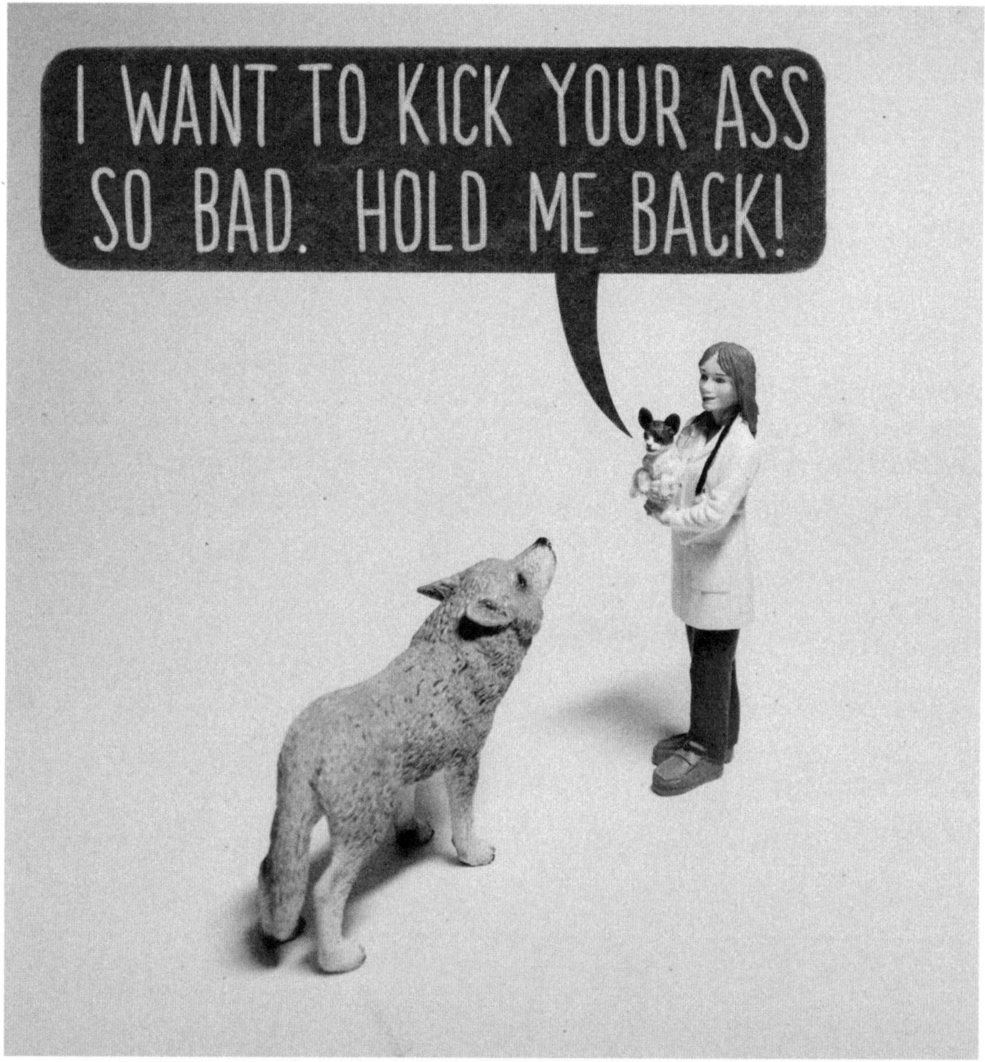
I WANT TO KICK YOUR ASS SO BAD. HOLD ME BACK!

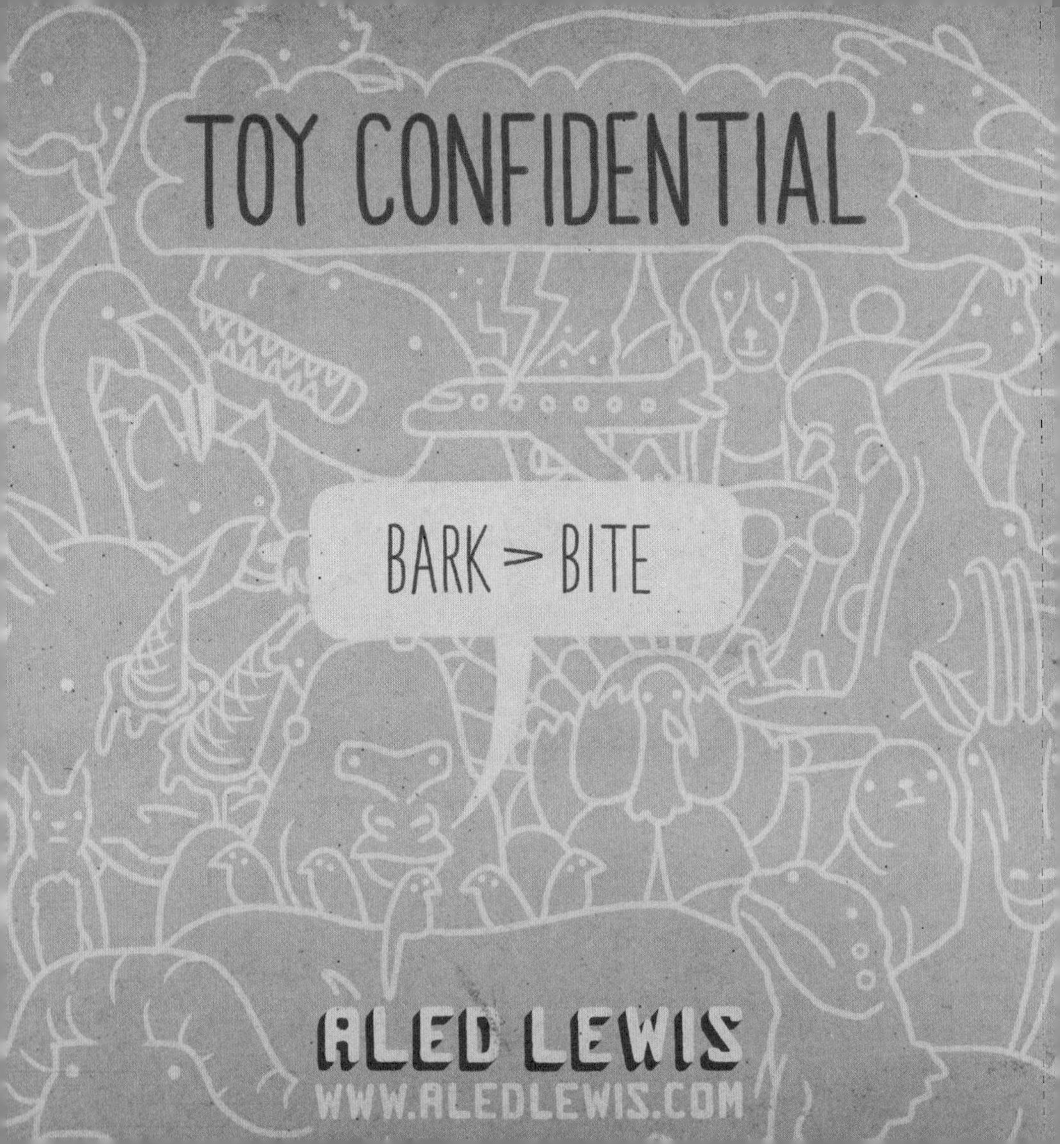
TOY CONFIDENTIAL
BARK > BITE
ALED LEWIS
WWW.ALEDLEWIS.COM

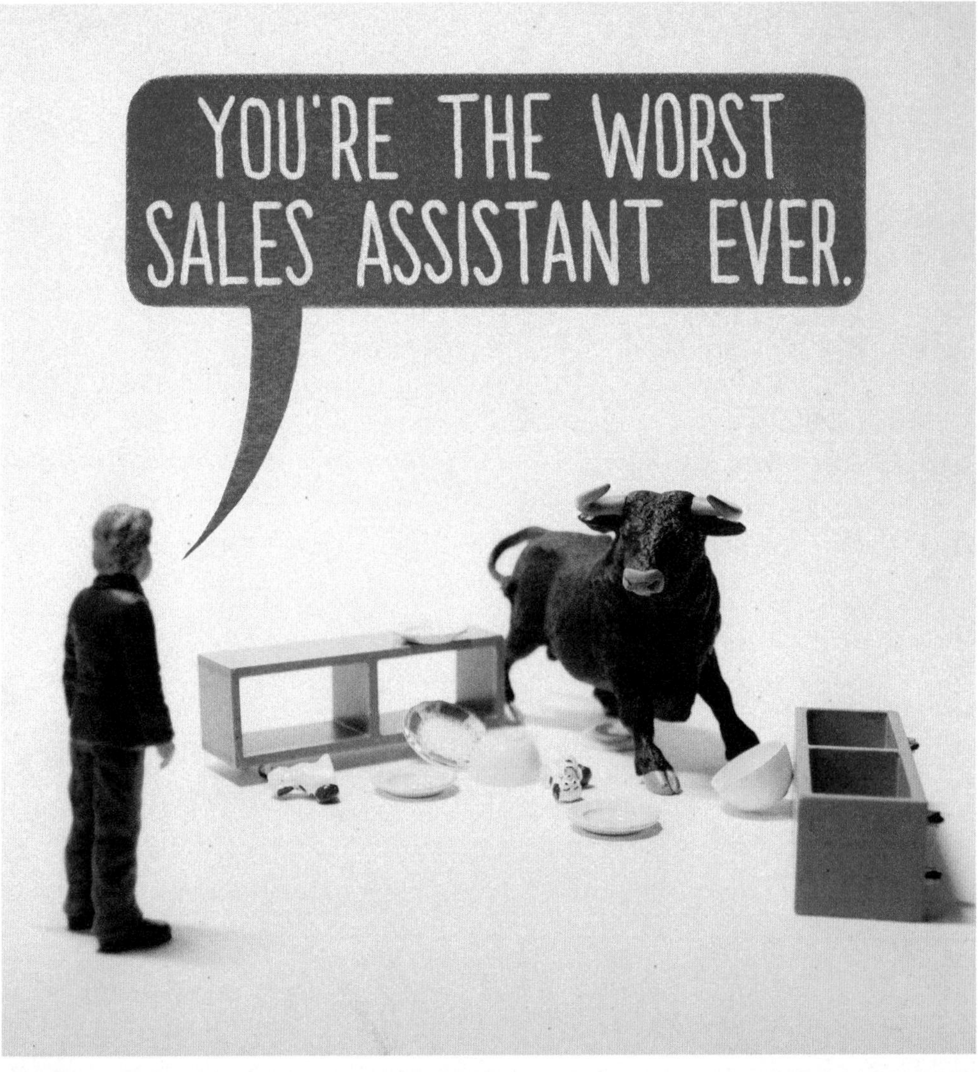
YOU'RE THE WORST SALES ASSISTANT EVER.

TOY CONFIDENTIAL

BULL IN A
CHINA SHOP

ALED LEWIS
WWW.ALEDLEWIS.COM

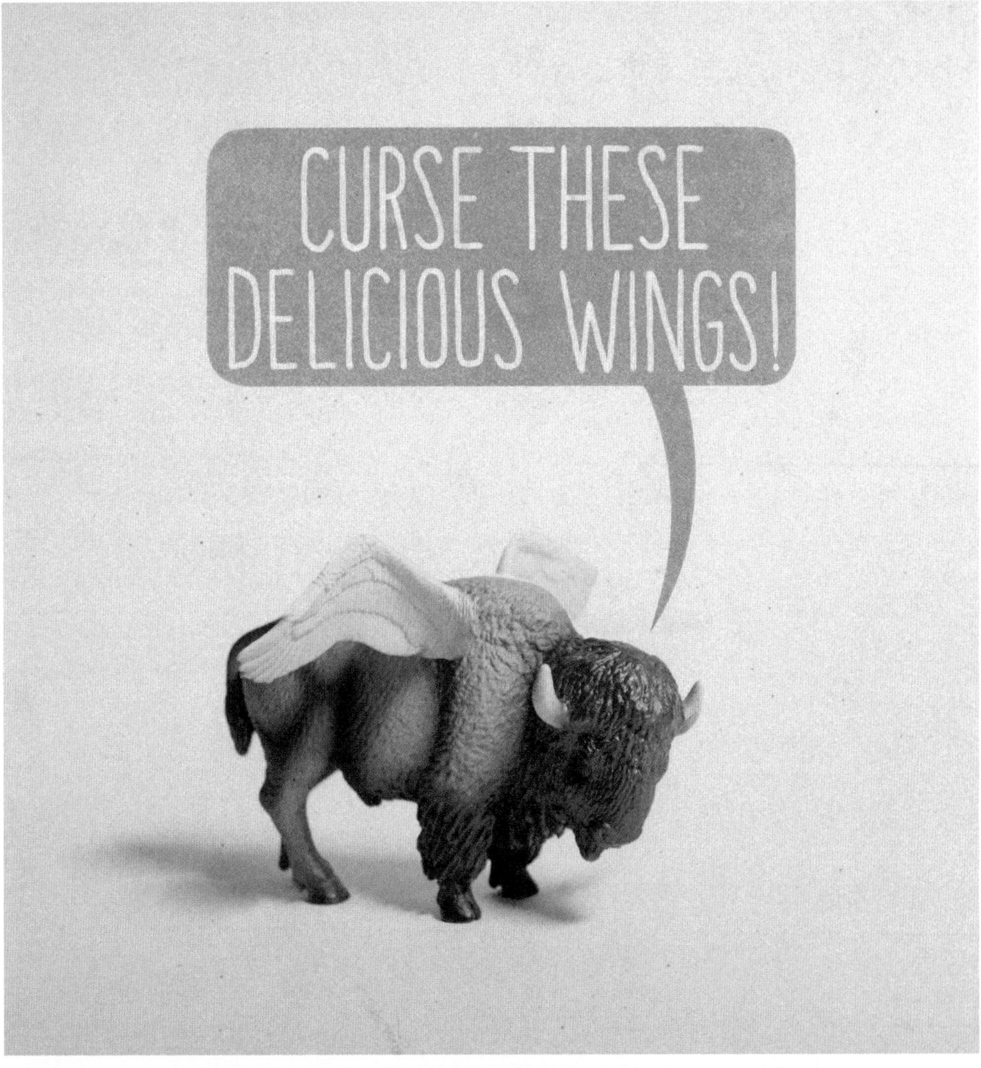
CURSE THESE DELICIOUS WINGS!

TOY CONFIDENTIAL

BURDEN

ALED LEWIS
WWW.ALEDLEWIS.COM

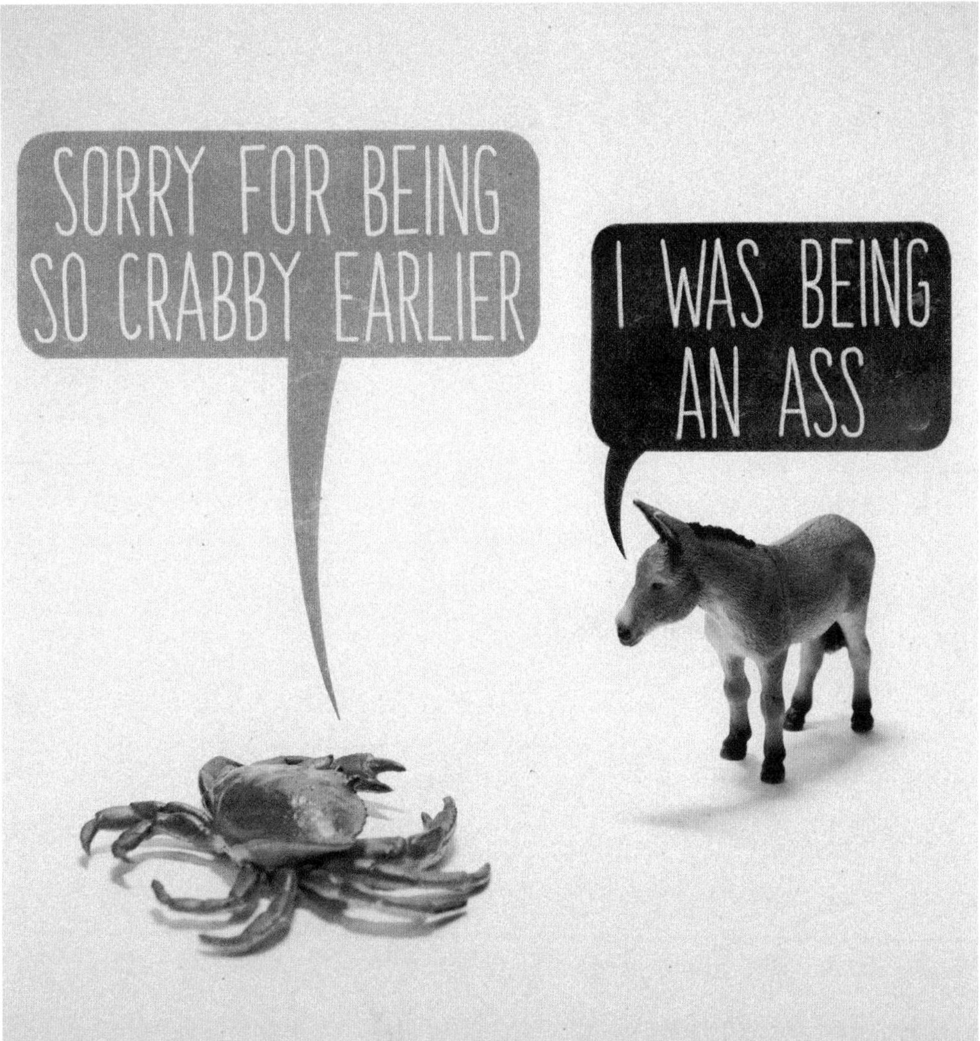
SORRY FOR BEING SO CRABBY EARLIER
I WAS BEING AN ASS

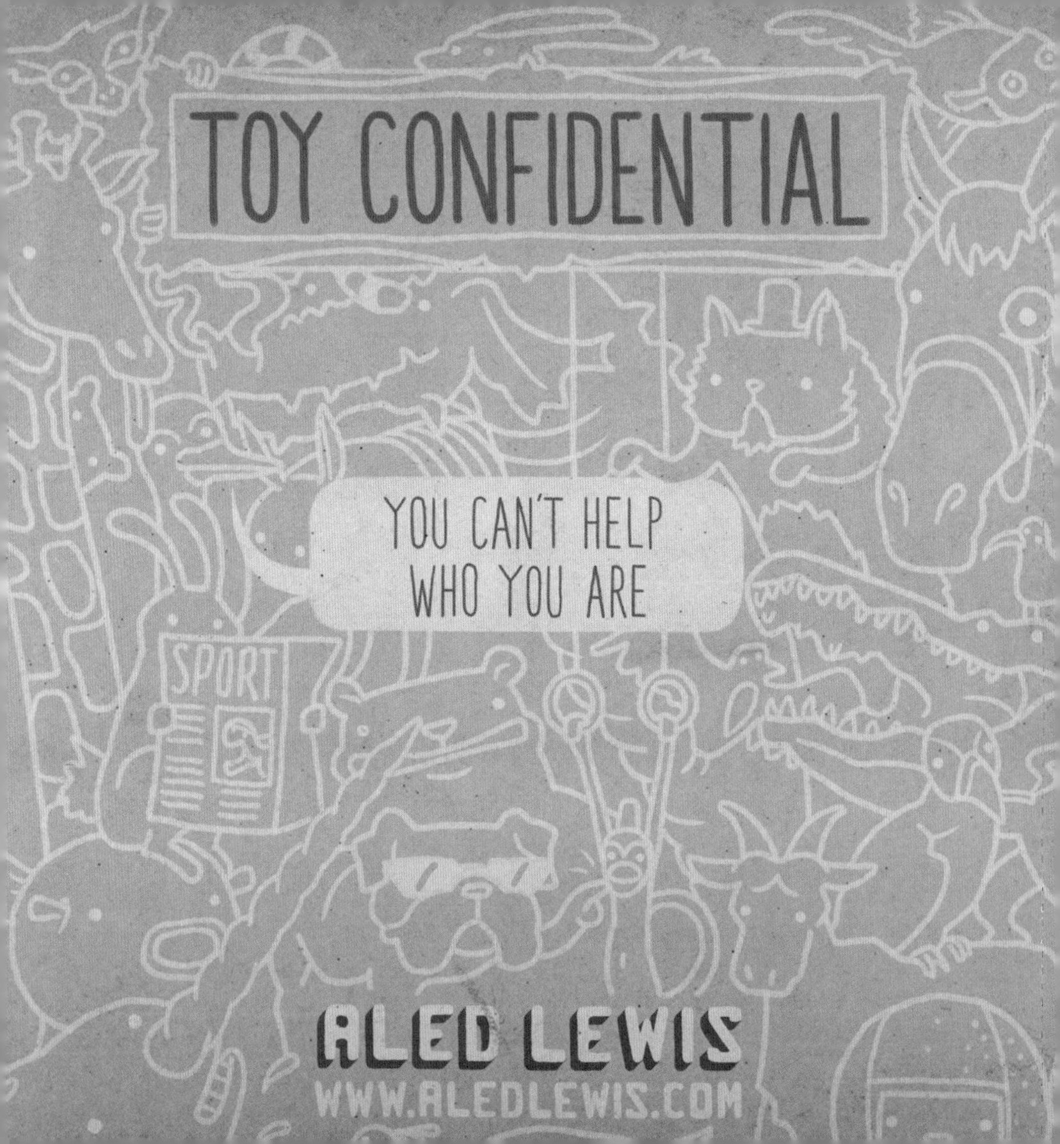
TOY CONFIDENTIAL
YOU CAN'T HELP WHO YOU ARE
SPORT
ALED LEWIS
WWW.ALEDLEWIS.COM

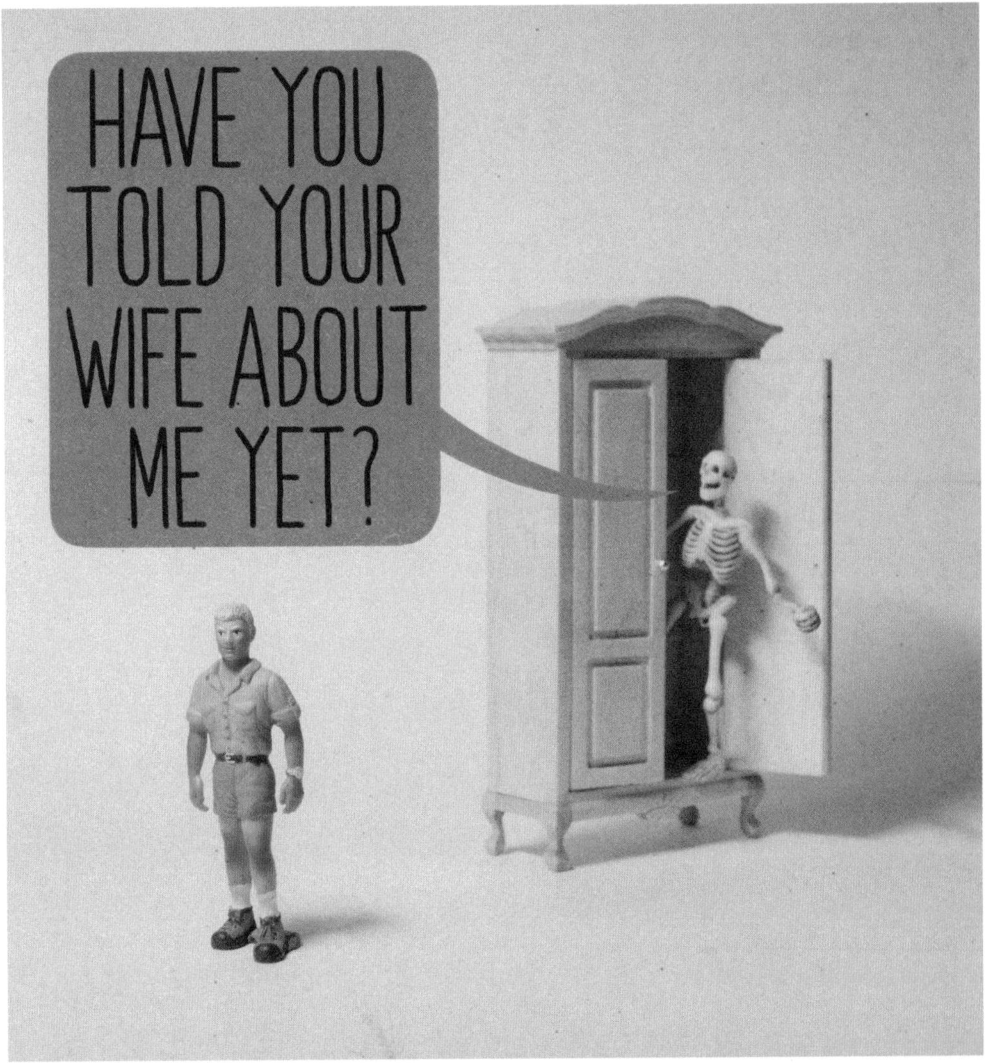
HAVE YOU TOLD YOUR WIFE ABOUT ME YET?

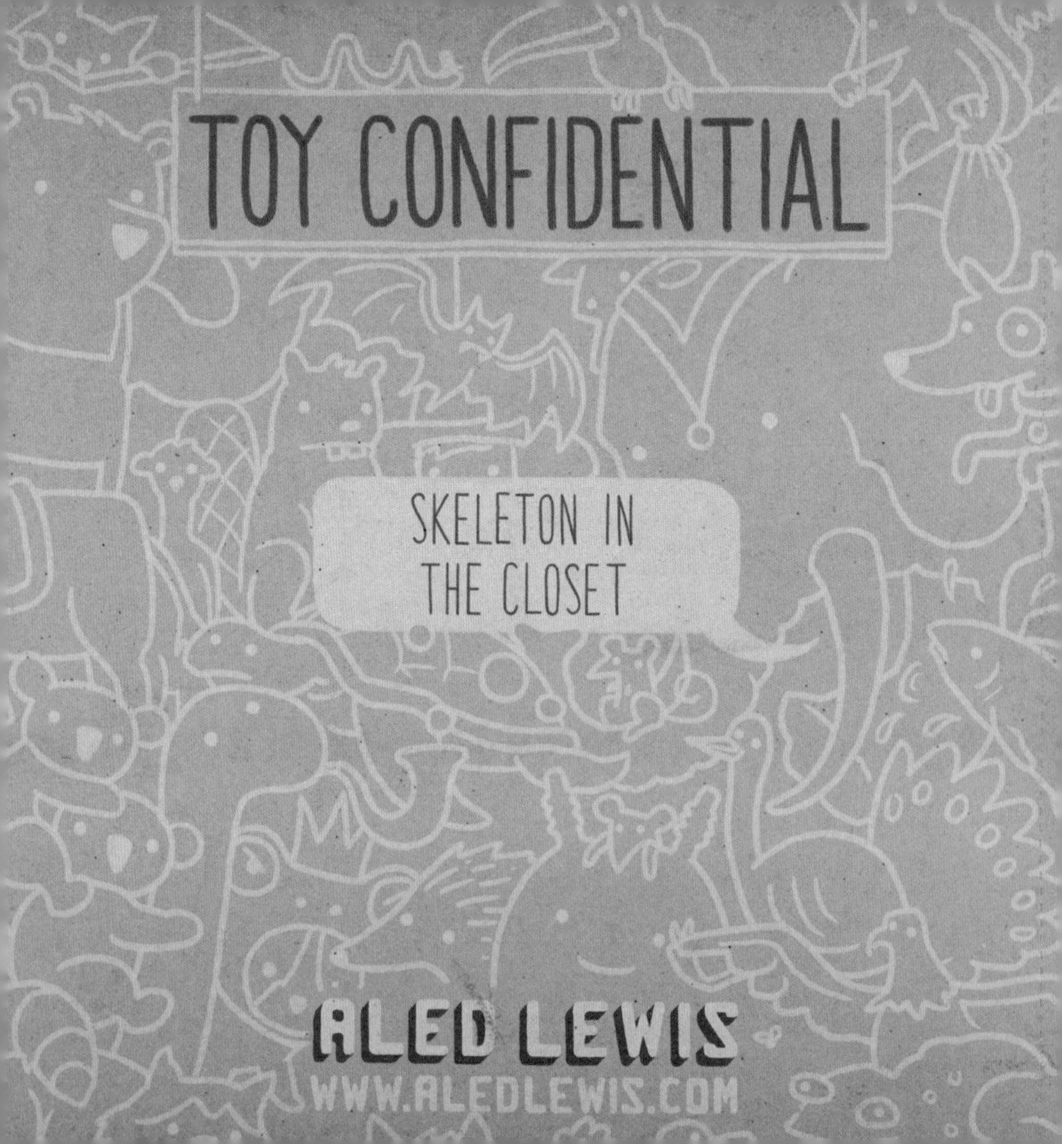
TOY CONFIDENTIAL
SKELETON IN THE CLOSET
ALED LEWIS
WWW.ALEDLEWIS.COM

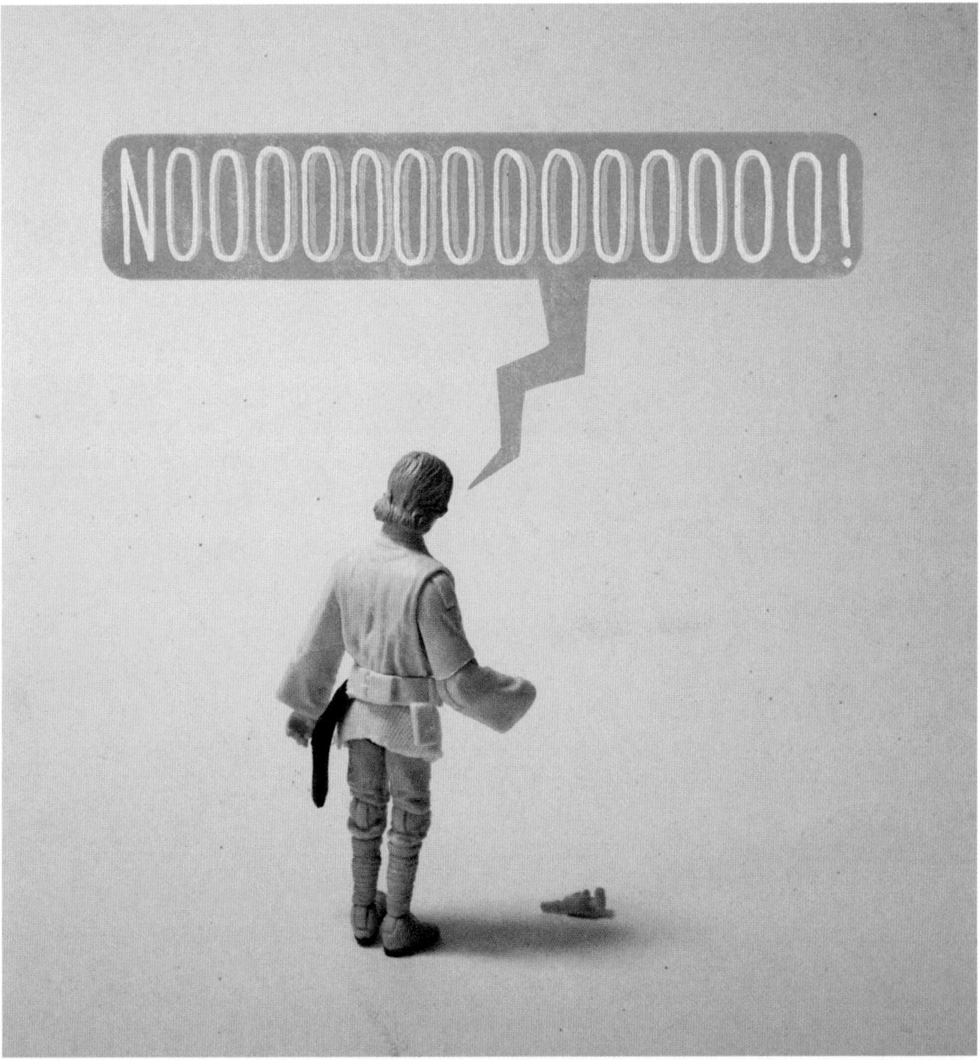
NOOOOOOOOOOOOOO!

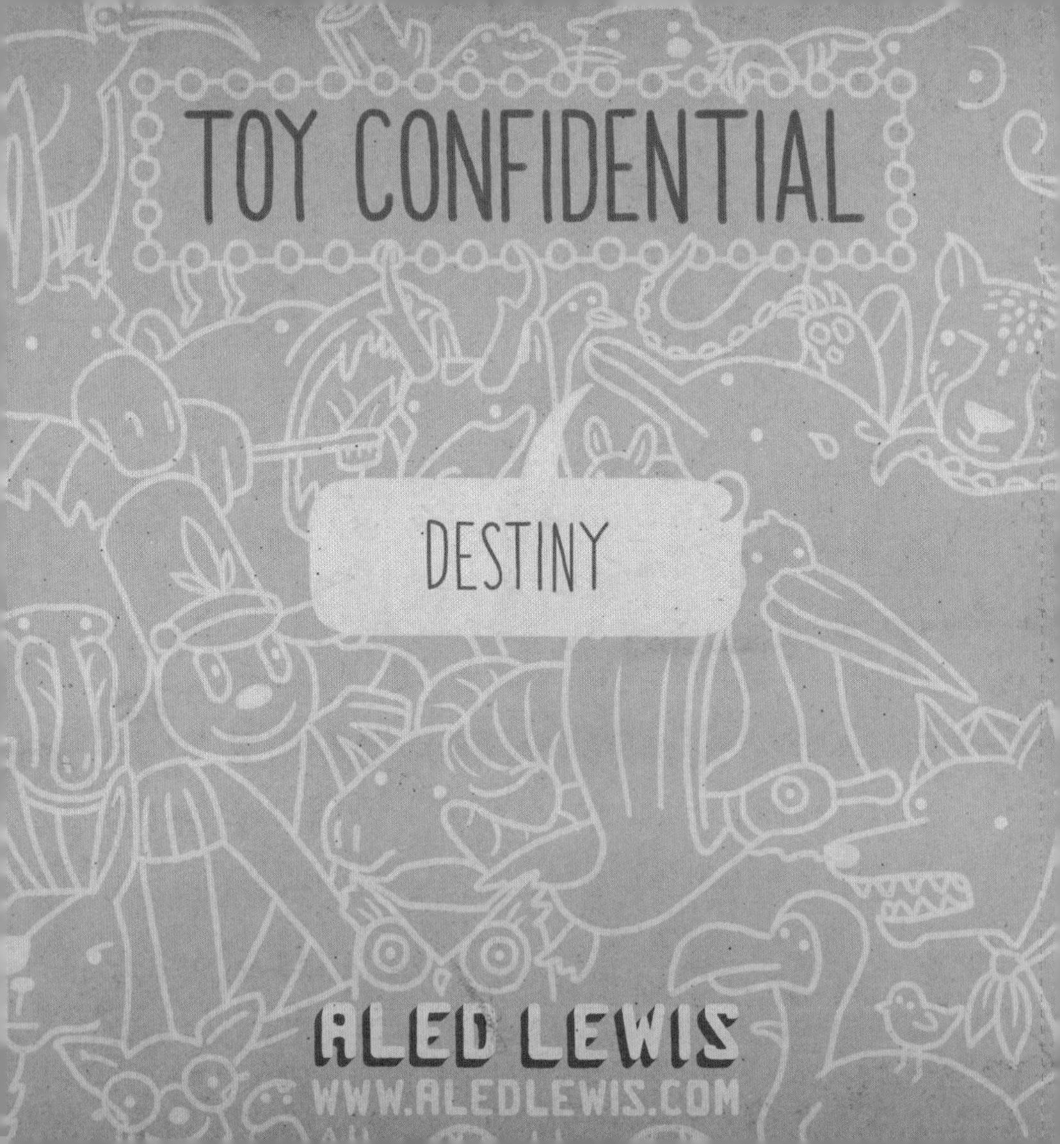
TOY CONFIDENTIAL
DESTINY
ALED LEWIS
WWW.ALEDLEWIS.COM

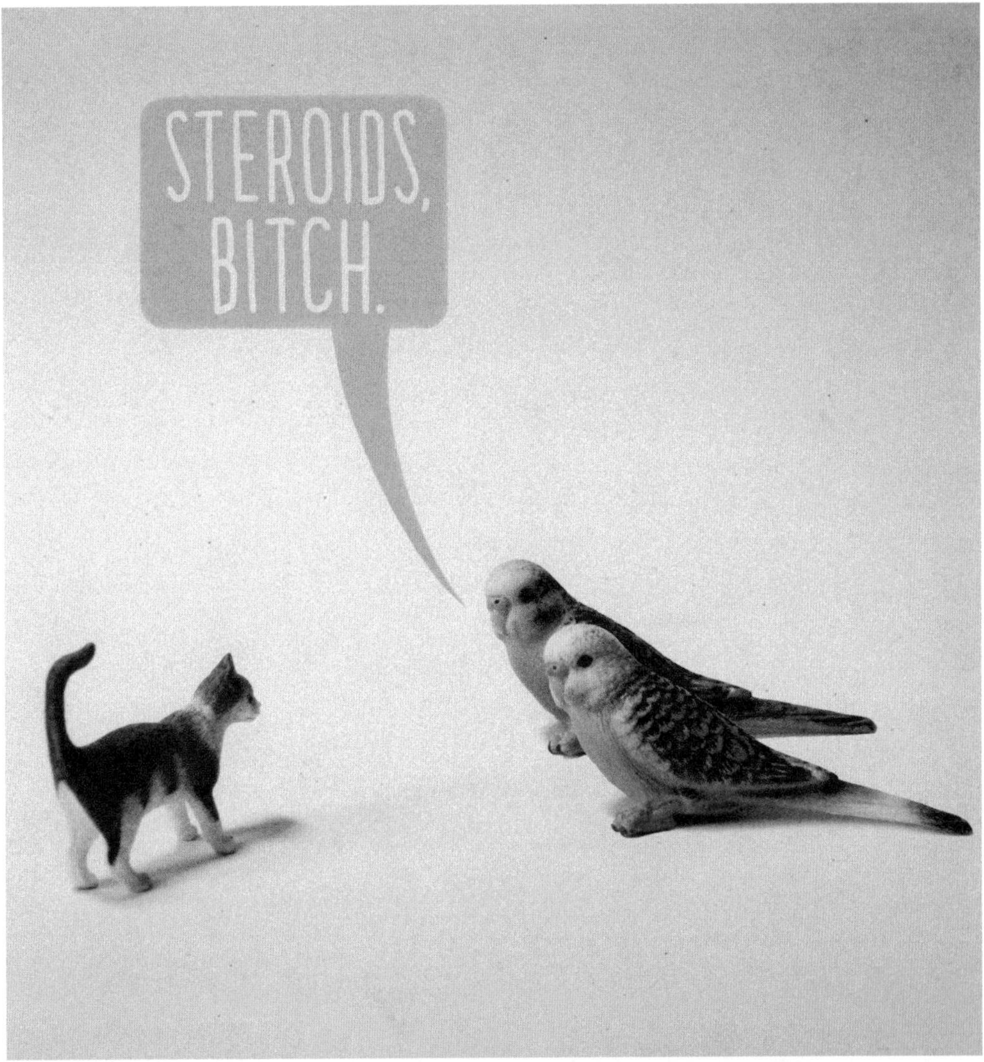
STEROIDS,
BITCH.

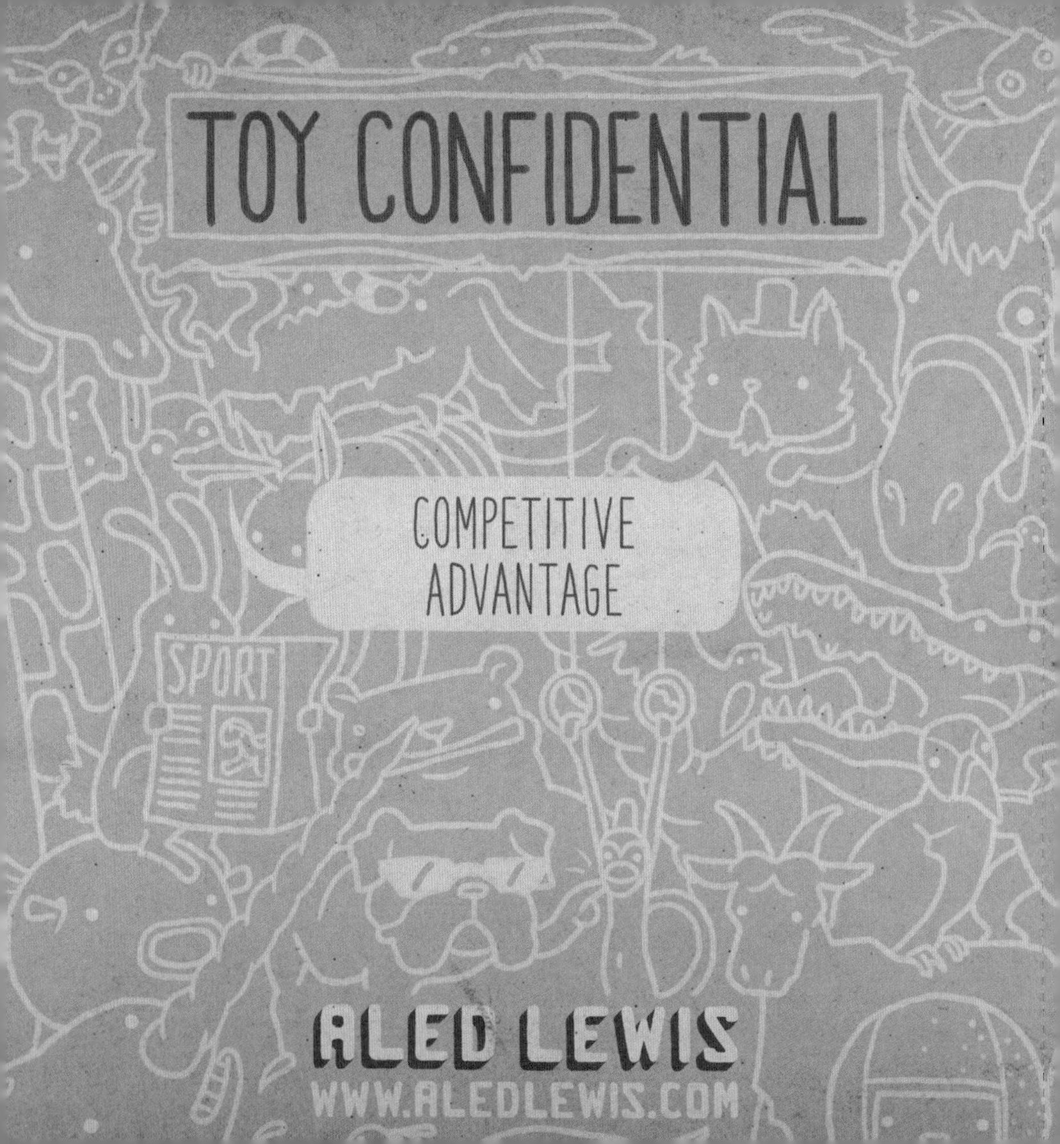
TOY CONFIDENTIAL
COMPETITIVE ADVANTAGE
SPORT
ALED LEWIS
WWW.ALEDLEWIS.COM

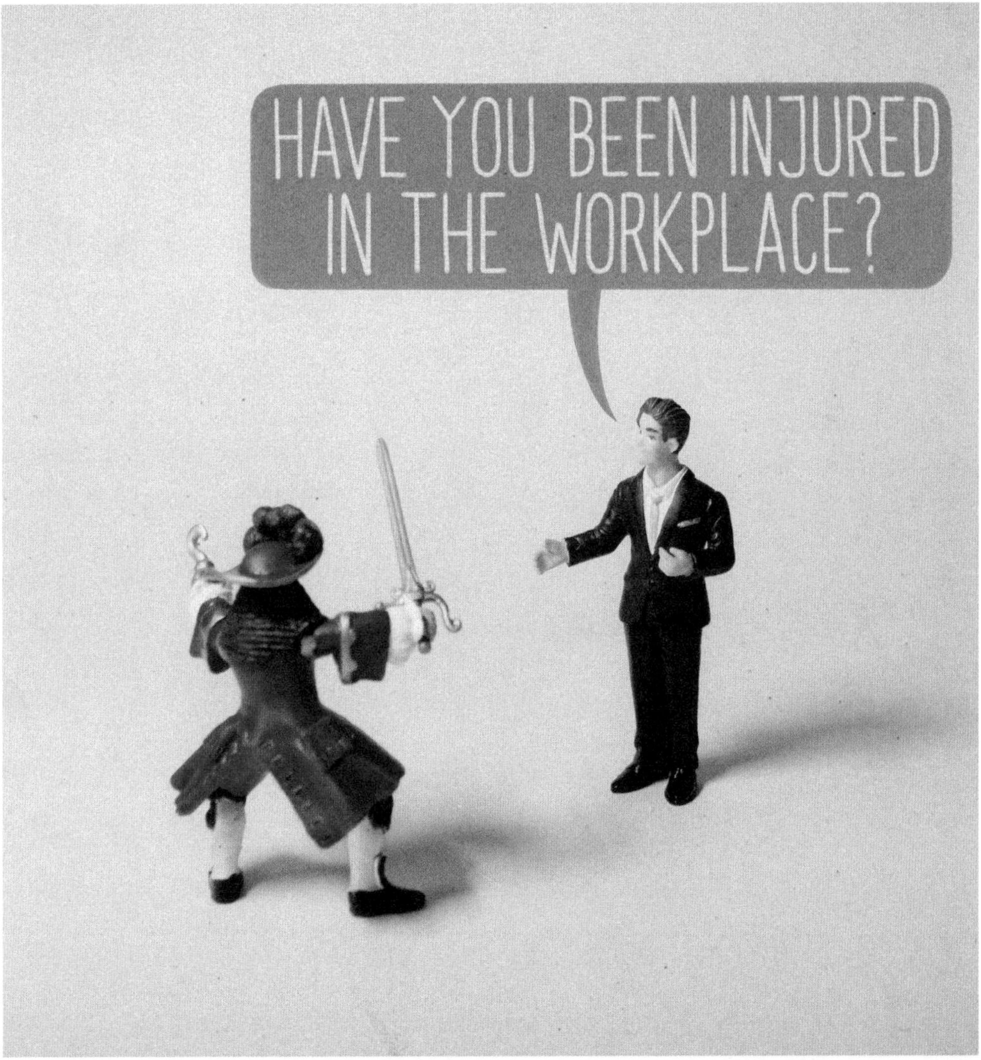
HAVE YOU BEEN INJURED IN THE WORKPLACE?

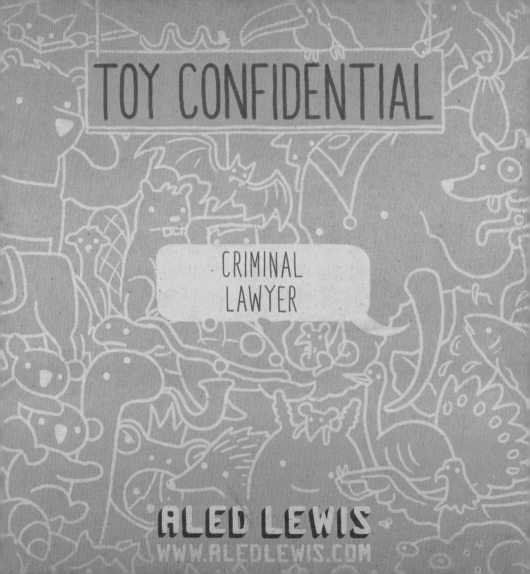

TOY CONFIDENTIAL

CRIMINAL
LAWYER

ALED LEWIS
WWW.ALEDLEWIS.COM

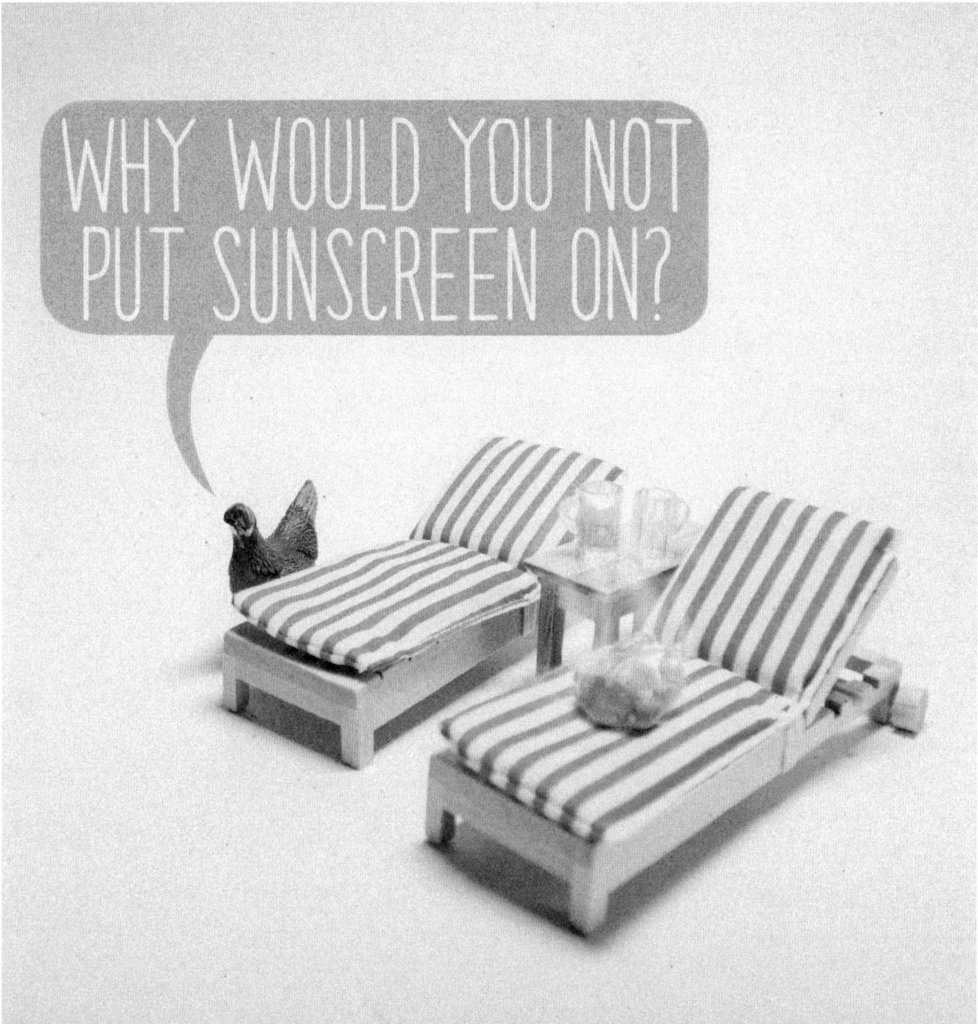
WHY WOULD YOU NOT PUT SUNSCREEN ON?

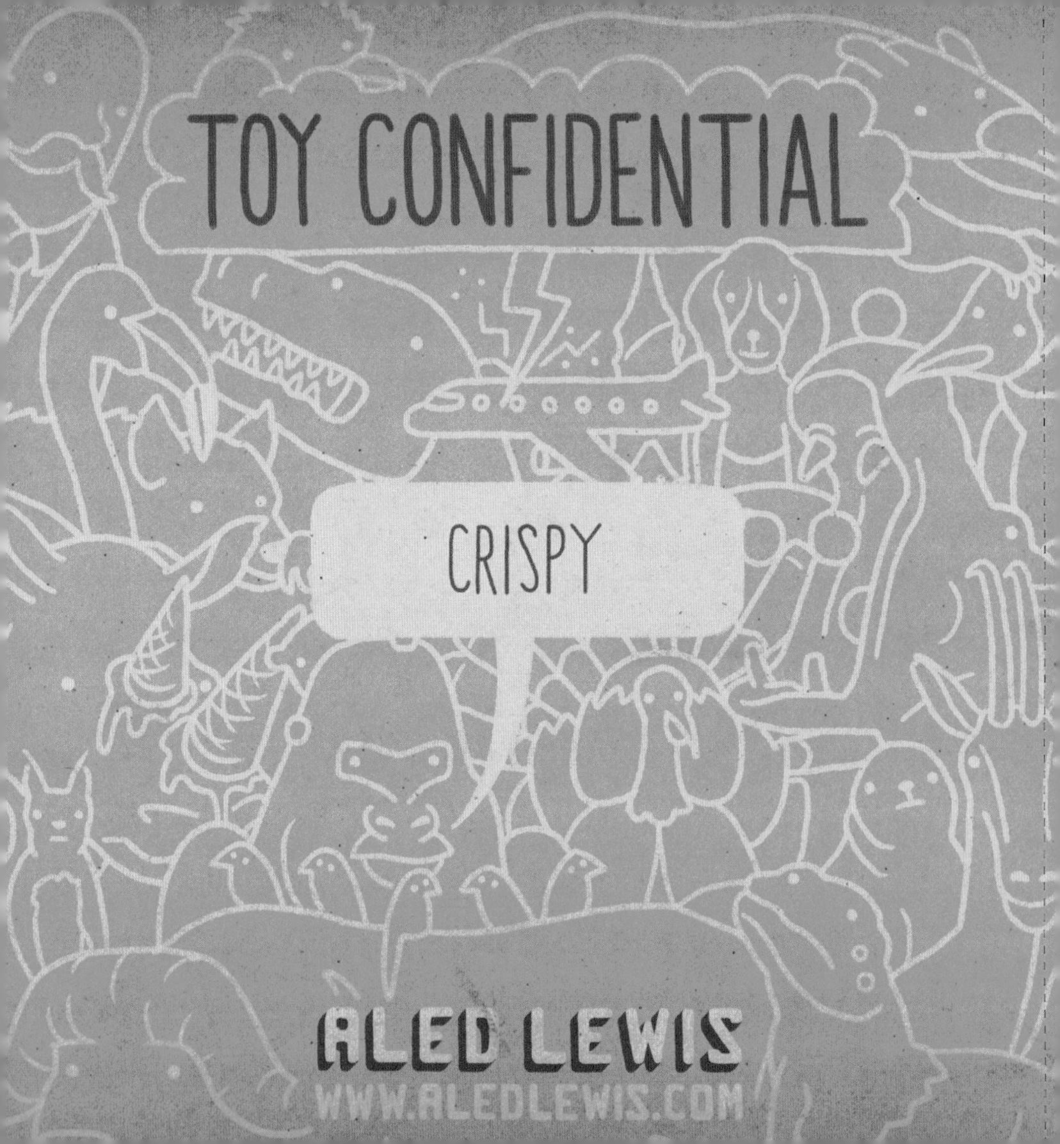
TOY CONFIDENTIAL
CRISPY
ALED LEWIS
WWW.ALEDLEWIS.COM

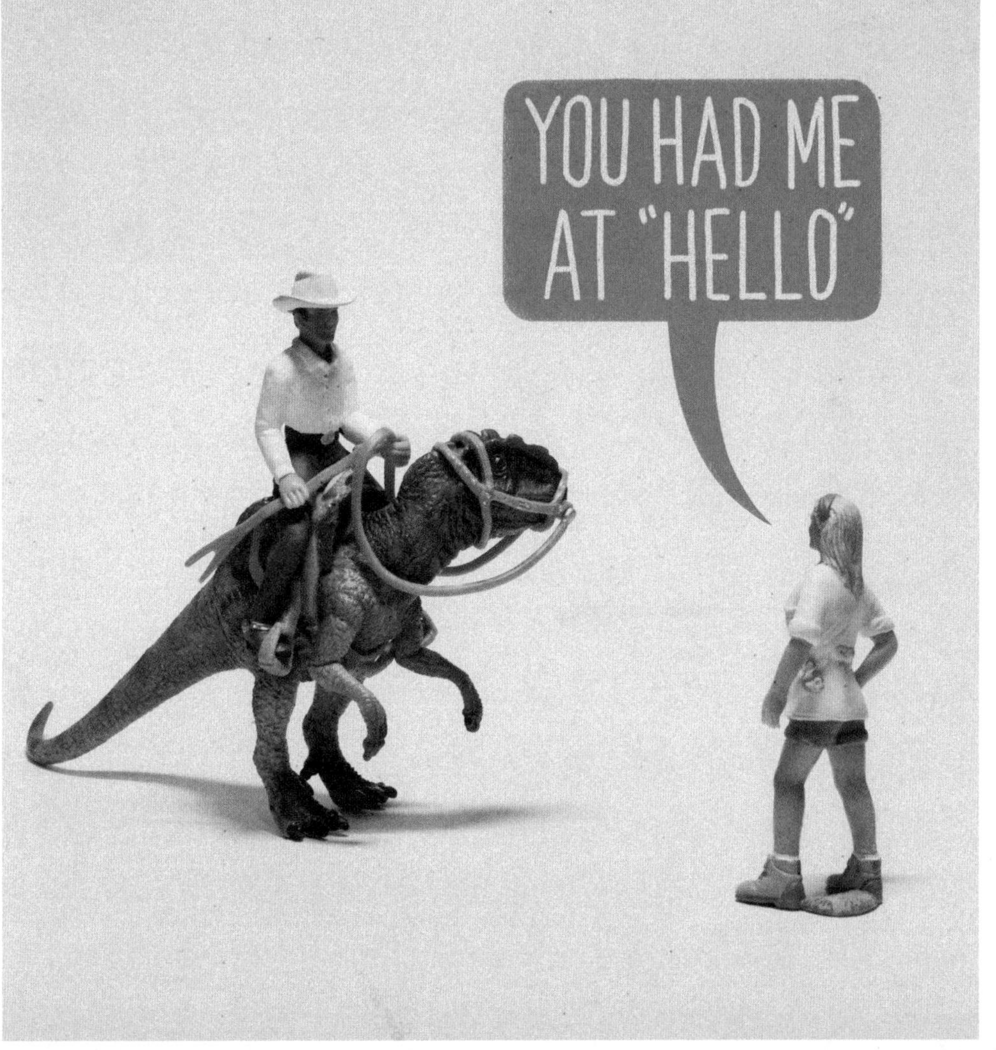
YOU HAD ME AT "HELLO"

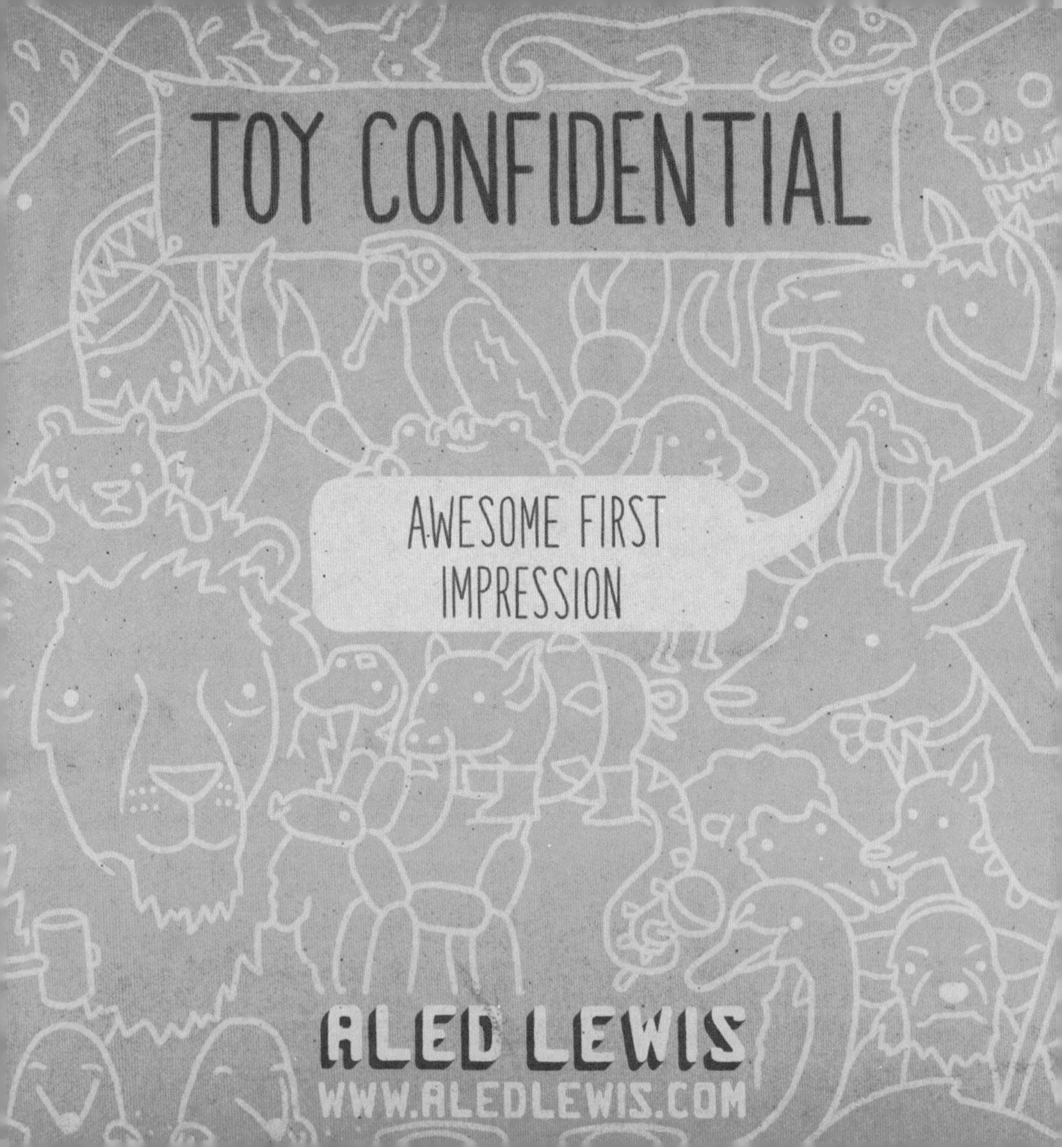
TOY CONFIDENTIAL
AWESOME FIRST IMPRESSION
ALED LEWIS
WWW.ALEDLEWIS.COM

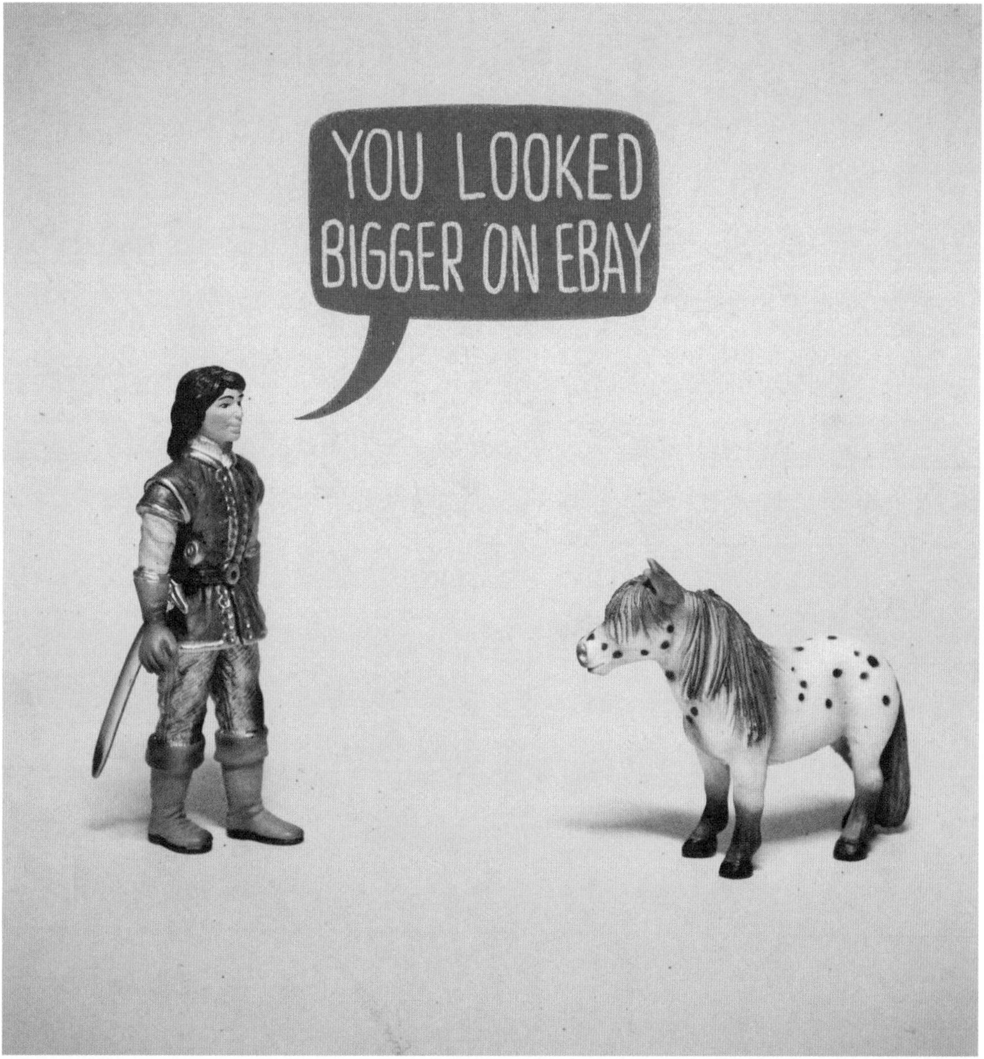
YOU LOOKED BIGGER ON EBAY

TOY CONFIDENTIAL

DECEPTION

ALED LEWIS
WWW.ALEDLEWIS.COM

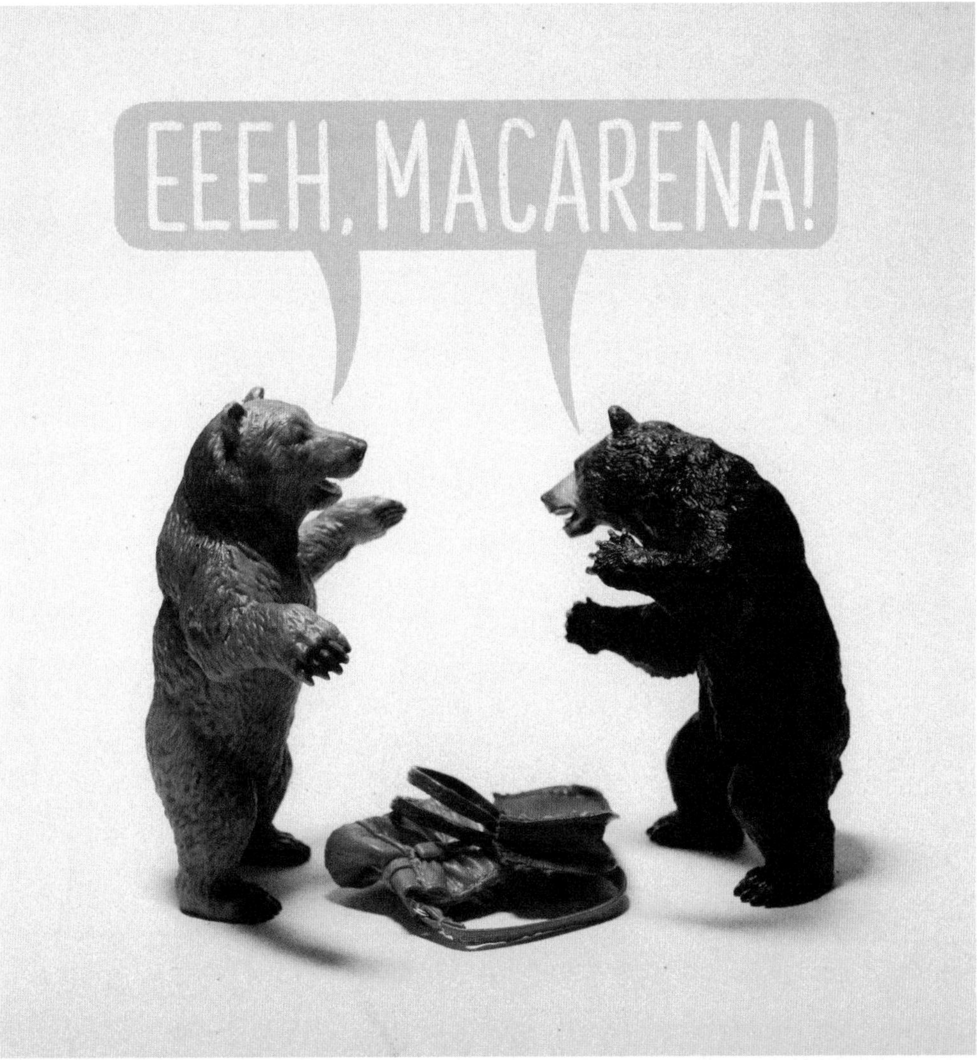
EEEH, MACARENA!

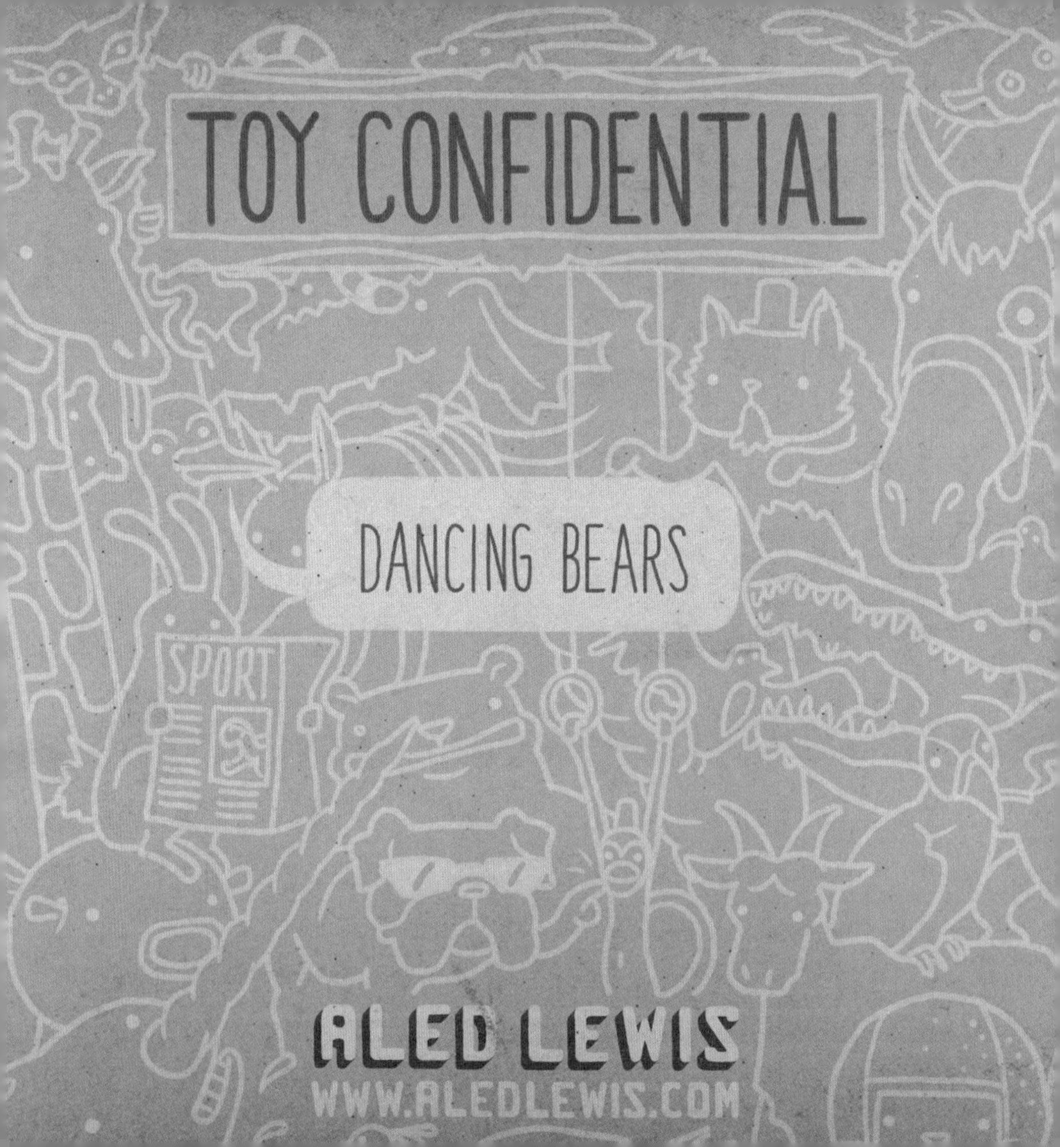
TOY CONFIDENTIAL
DANCING BEARS
SPORT
ALED LEWIS
WWW.ALEDLEWIS.COM

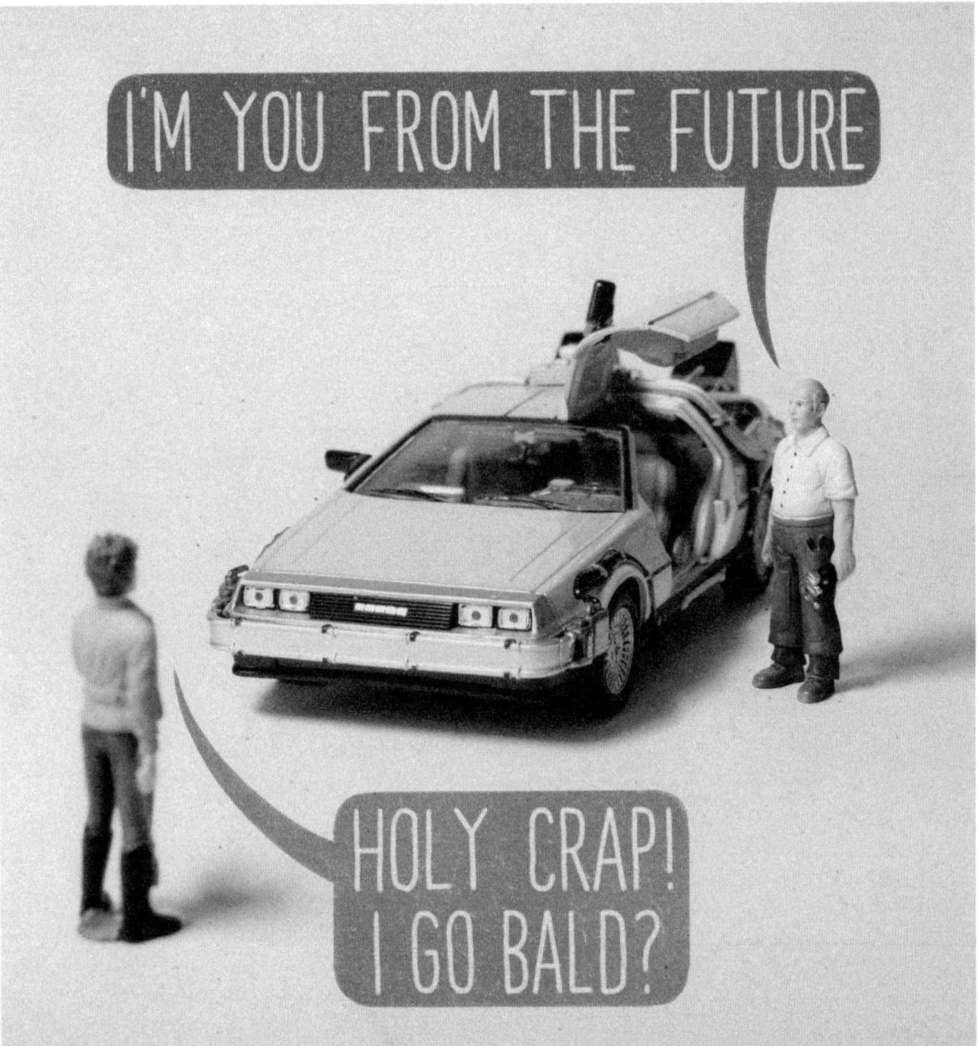
I'M YOU FROM THE FUTURE
HOLY CRAP! I GO BALD?

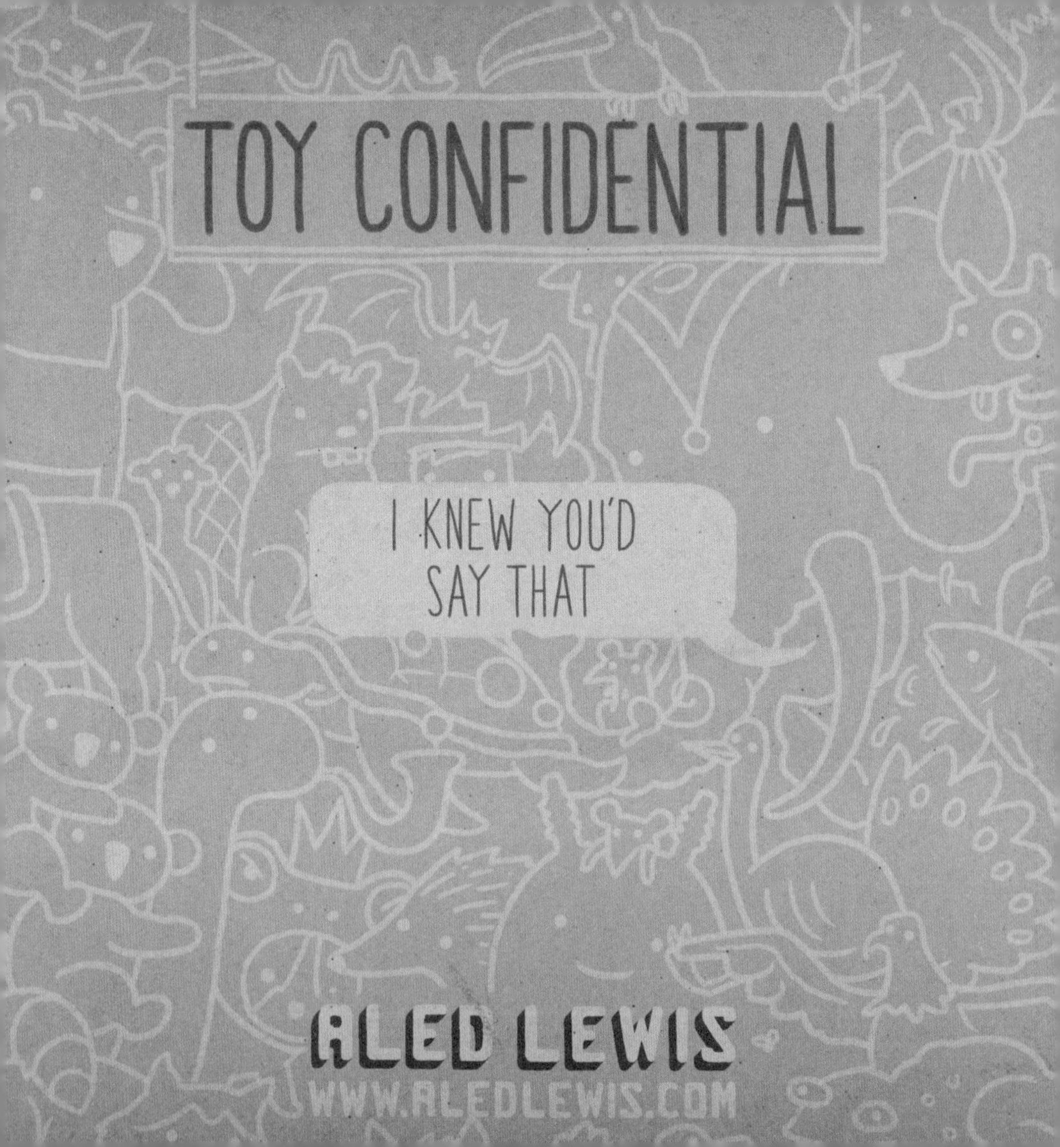
TOY CONFIDENTIAL
I KNEW YOU'D SAY THAT
ALED LEWIS
WWW.ALEDLEWIS.COM

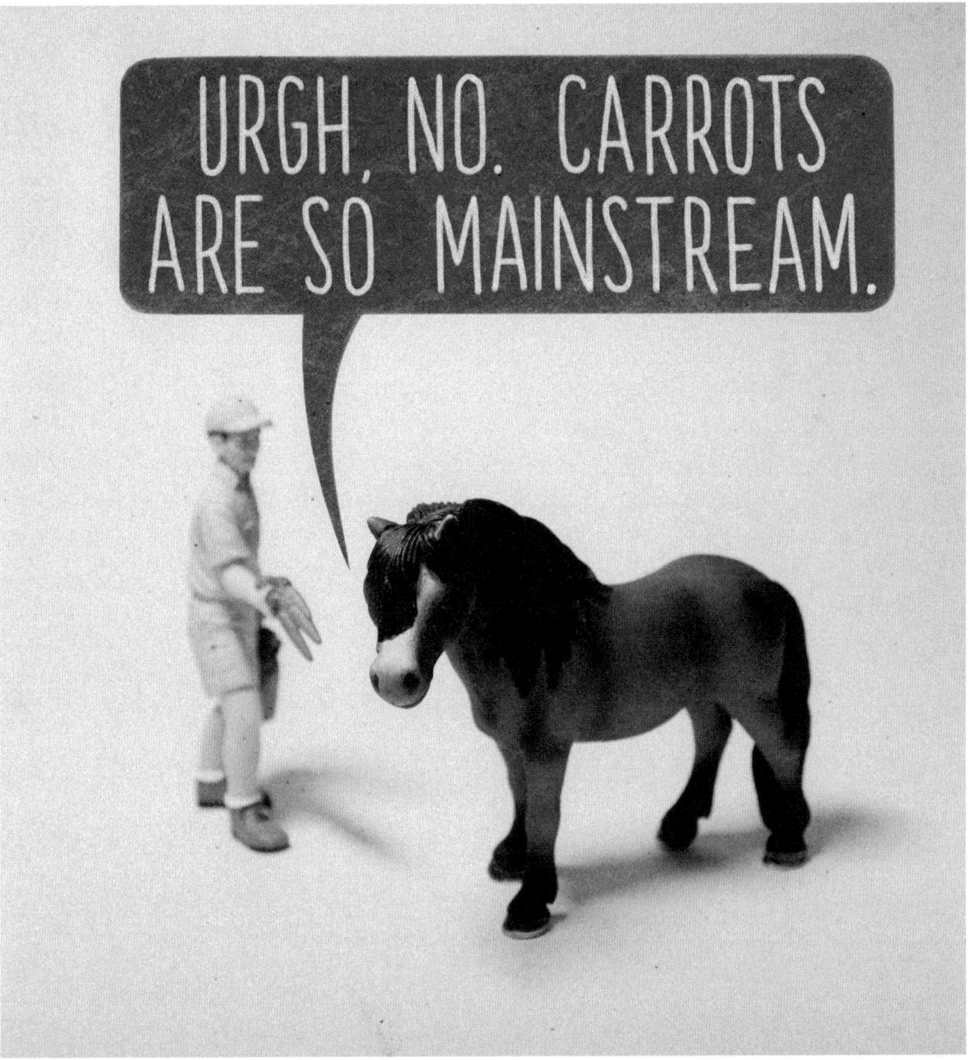
URGH, NO. CARROTS ARE SO MAINSTREAM.

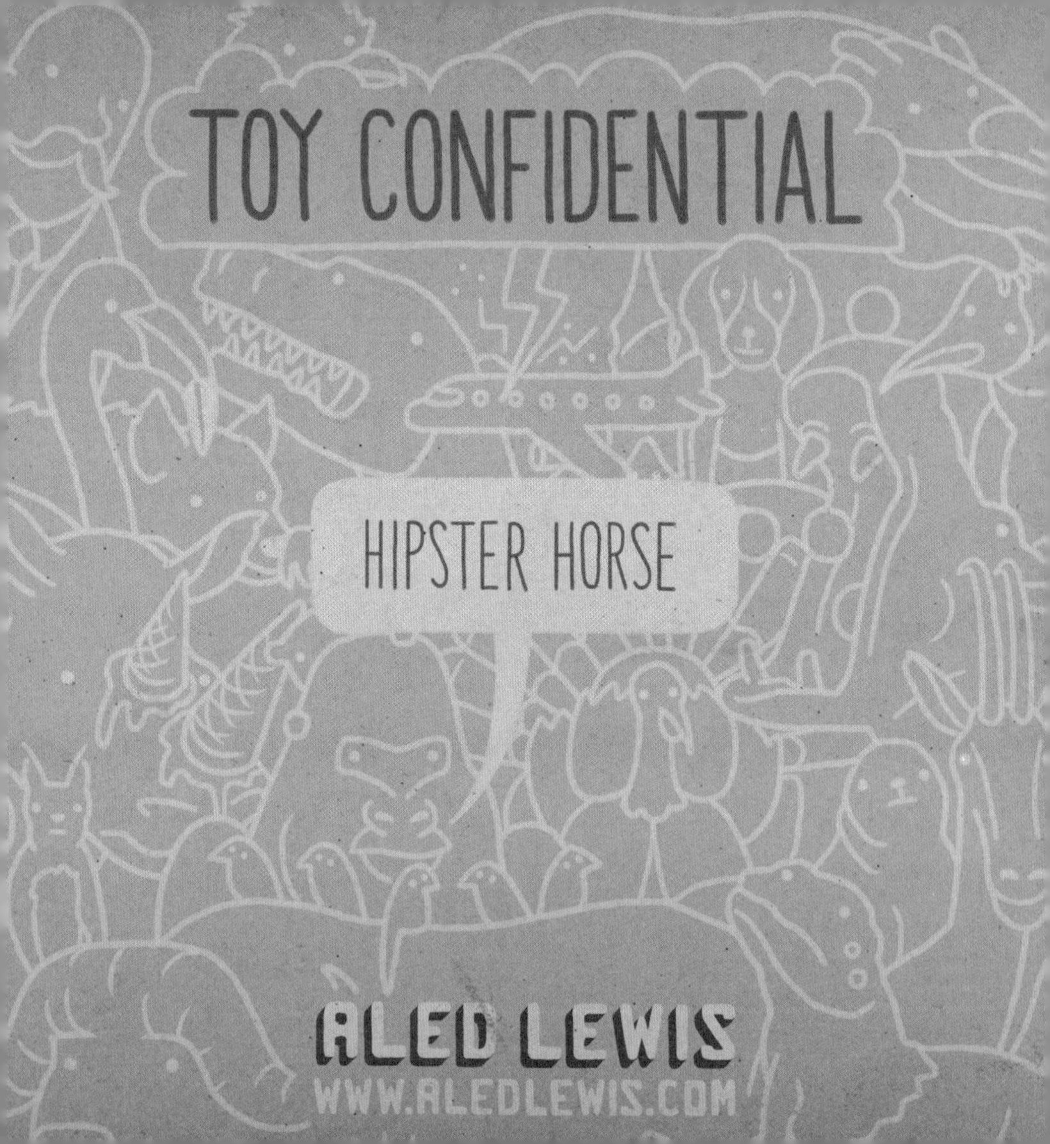
TOY CONFIDENTIAL
HIPSTER HORSE
ALED LEWIS
WWW.ALEDLEWIS.COM

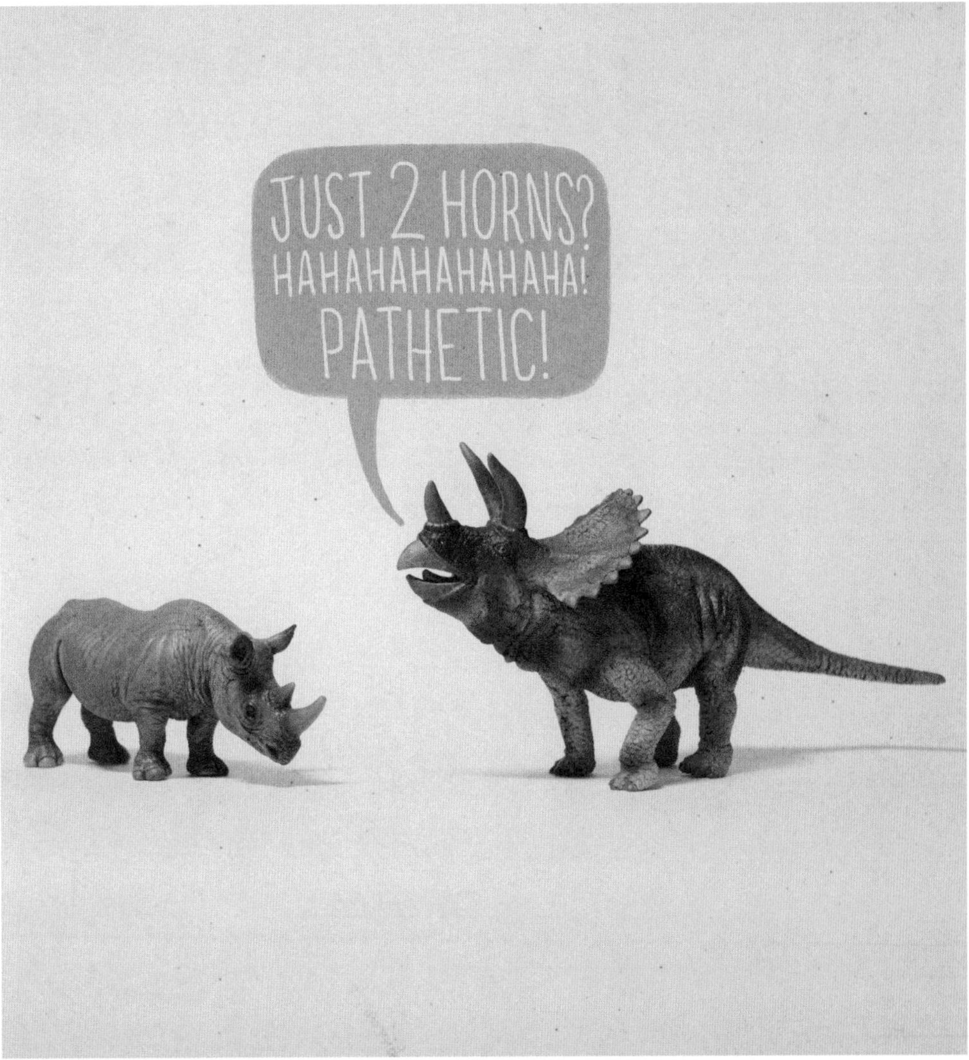
JUST 2 HORNS? HAHAHAHAHAHAHA! PATHETIC!

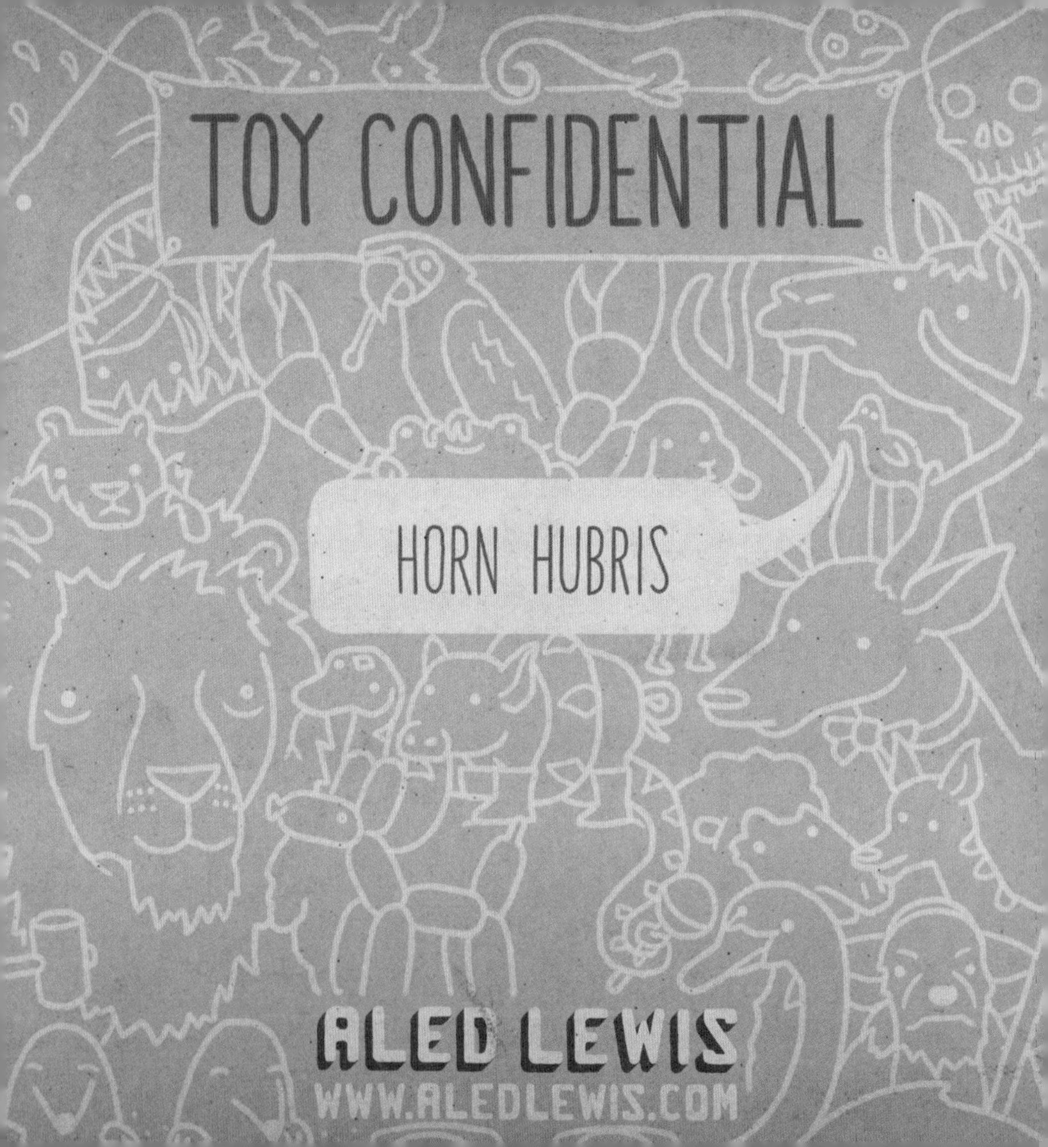
TOY CONFIDENTIAL
HORN HUBRIS
ALED LEWIS
WWW.ALEDLEWIS.COM

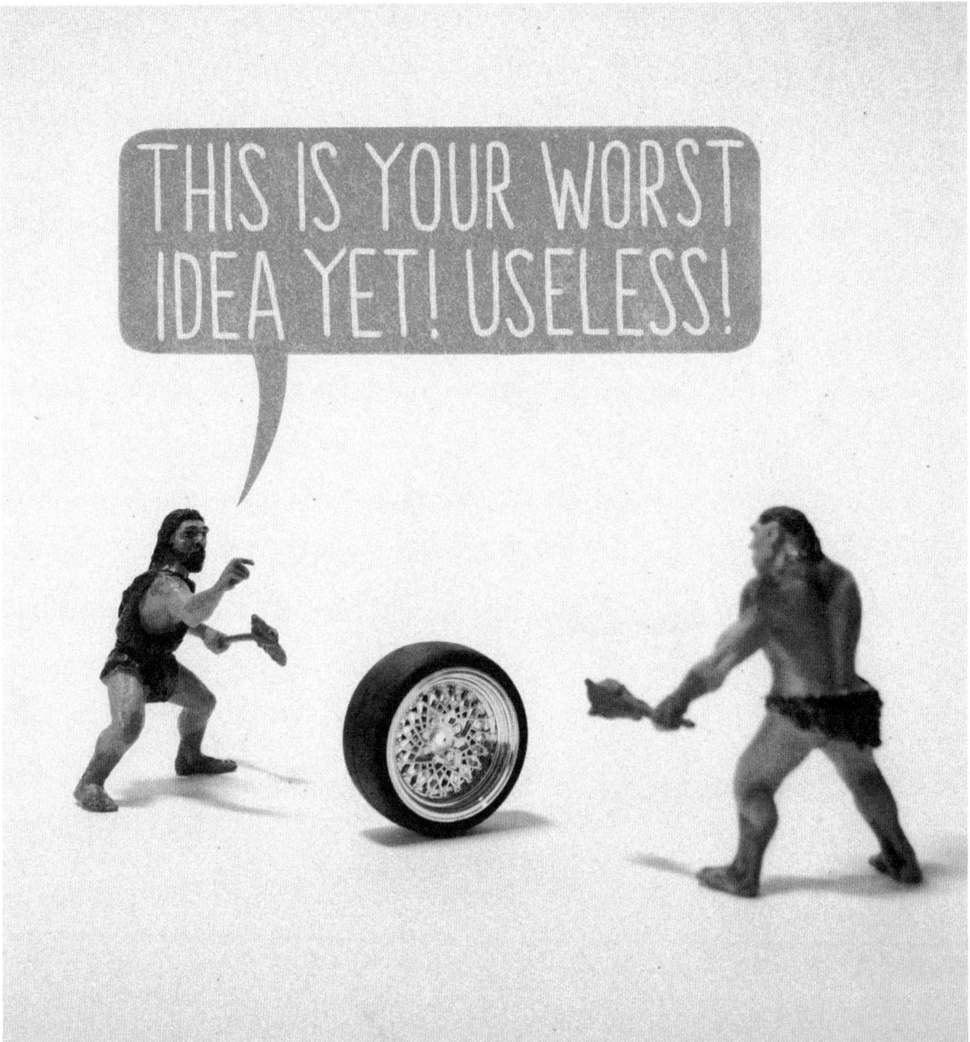
THIS IS YOUR WORST IDEA YET! USELESS!

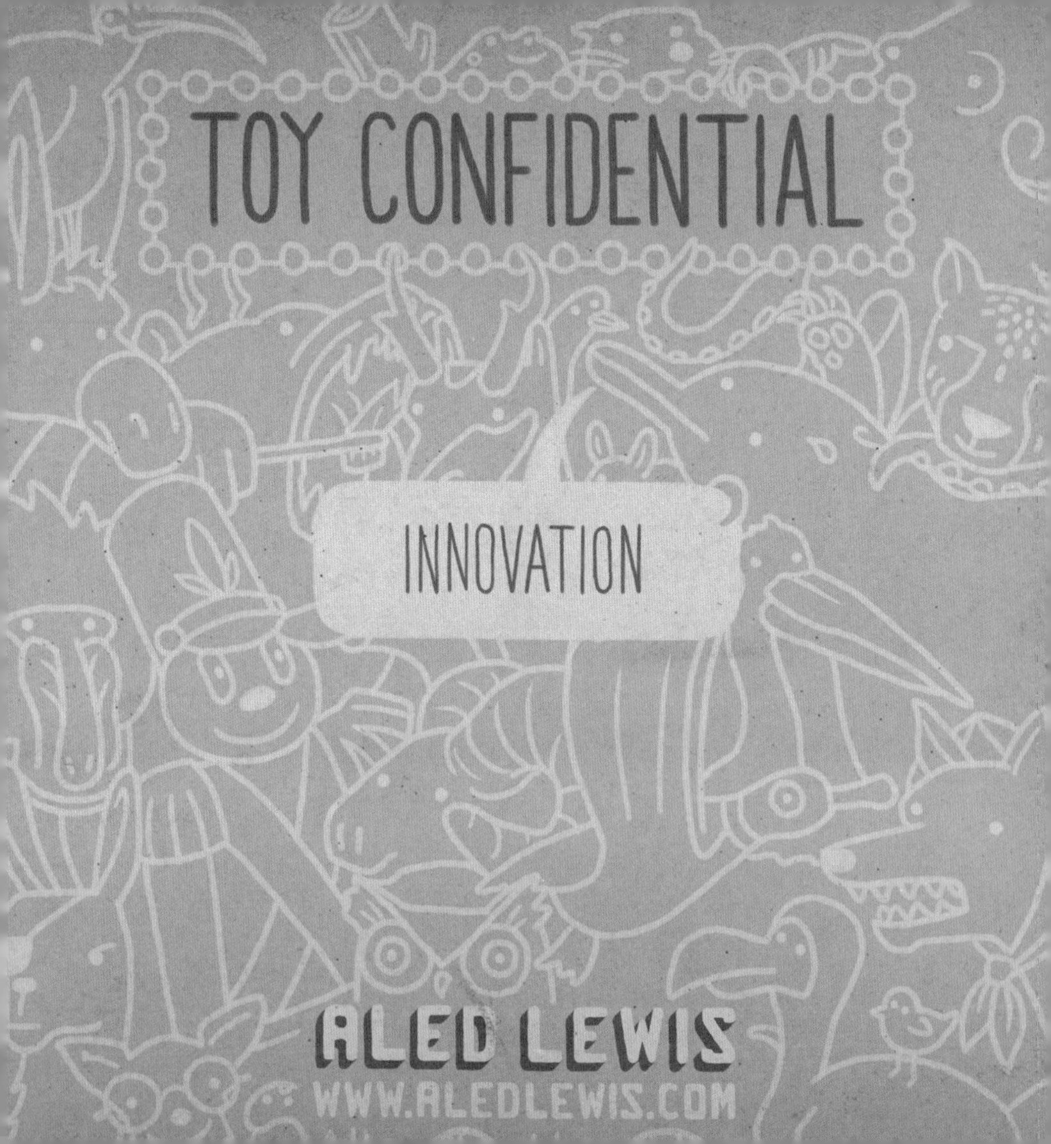
TOY CONFIDENTIAL
INNOVATION
ALED LEWIS
WWW.ALEDLEWIS.COM

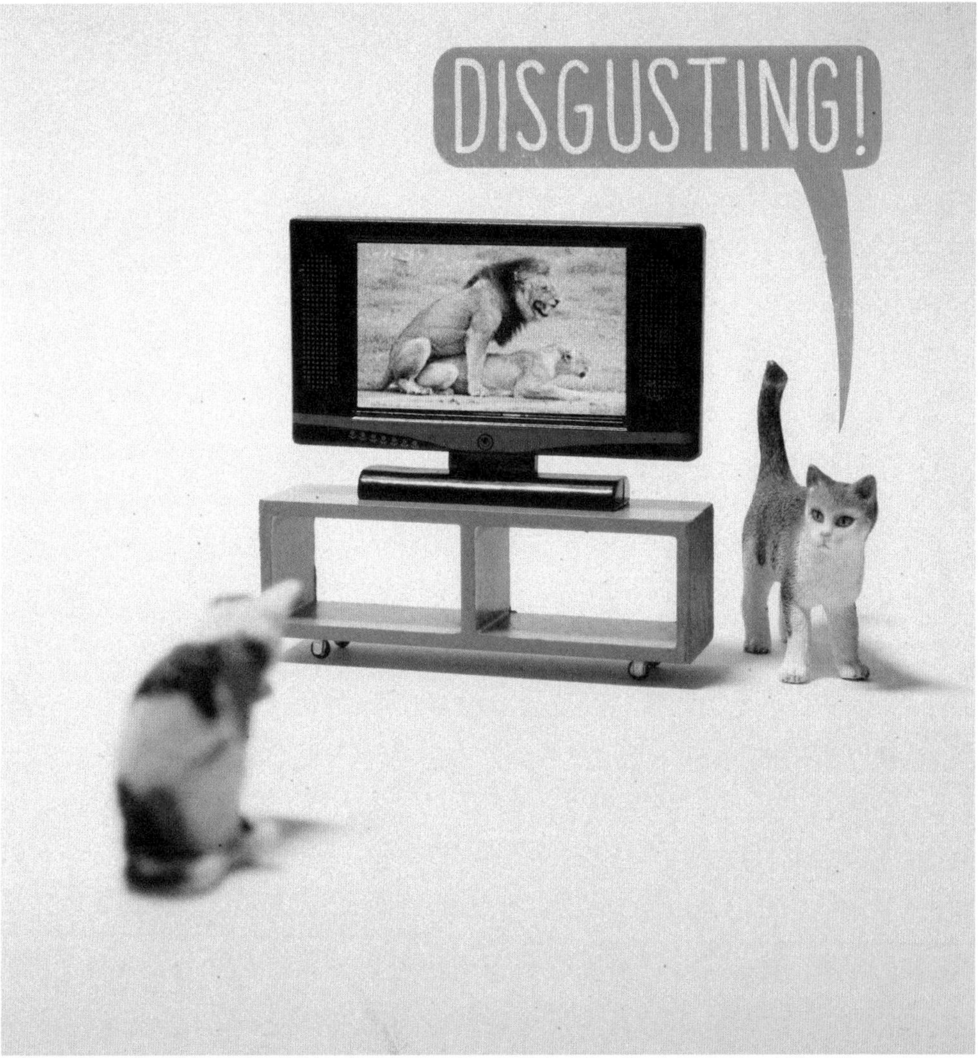
DISGUSTING!

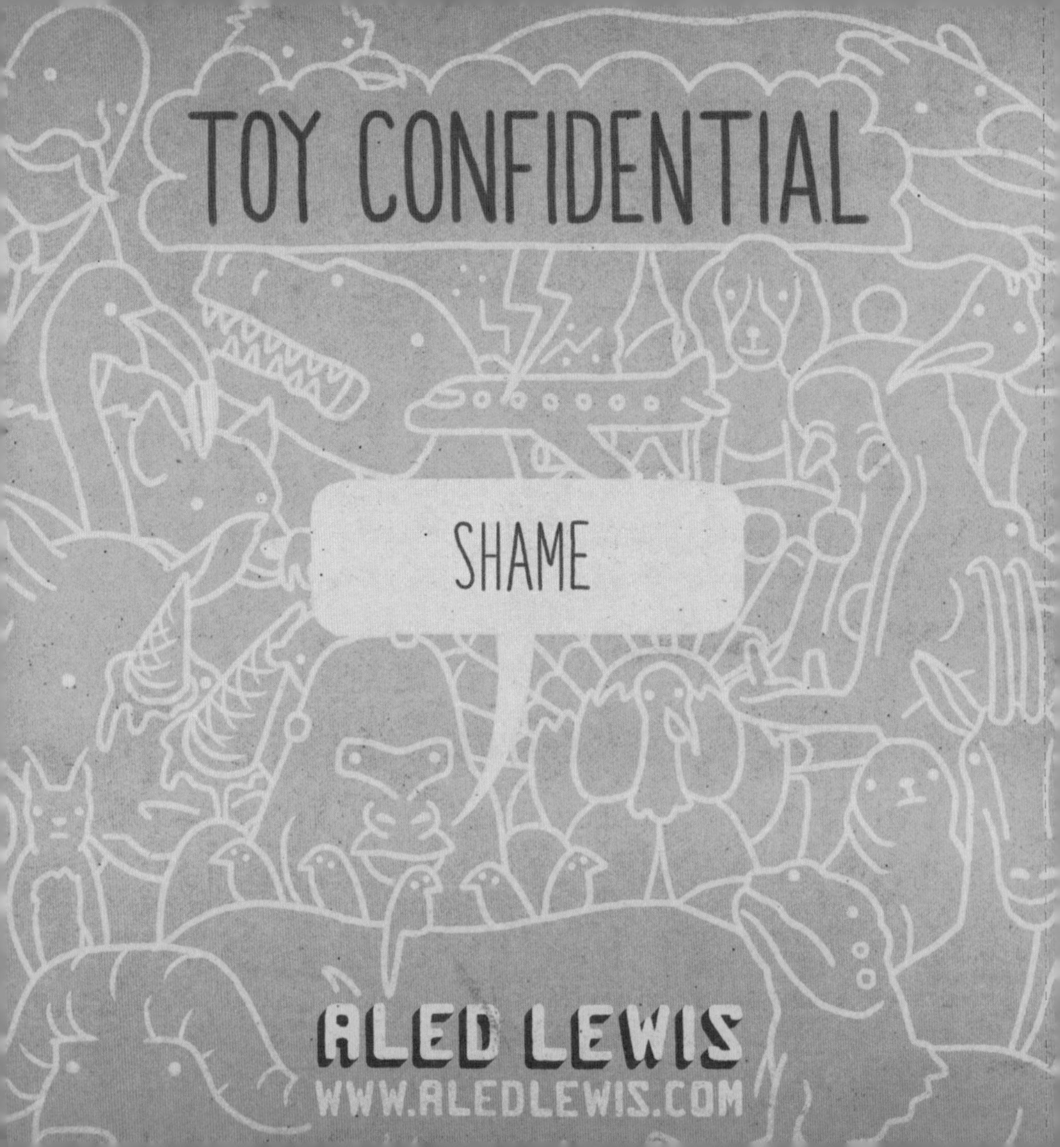
TOY CONFIDENTIAL
SHAME
ALED LEWIS
WWW.ALEDLEWIS.COM

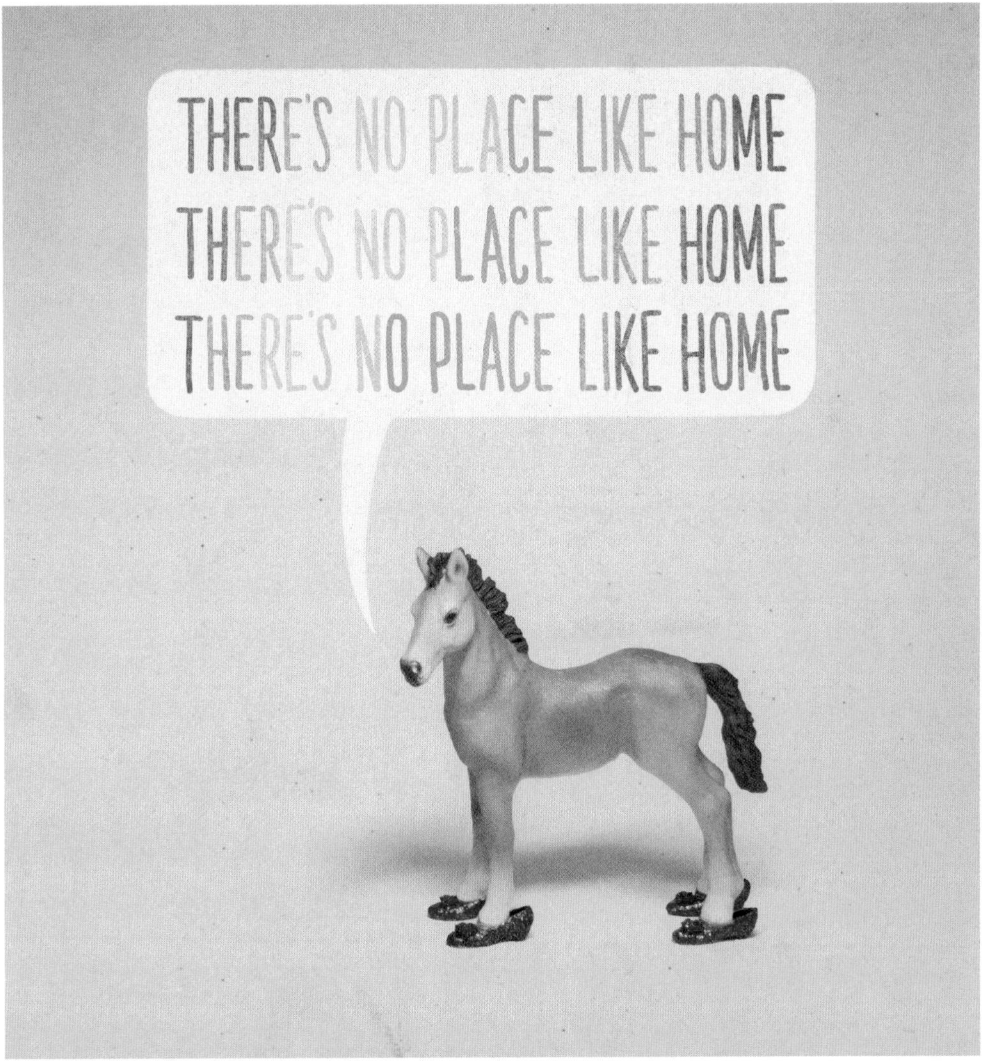
THERE'S NO PLACE LIKE HOME
THERE'S NO PLACE LIKE HOME
THERE'S NO PLACE LIKE HOME

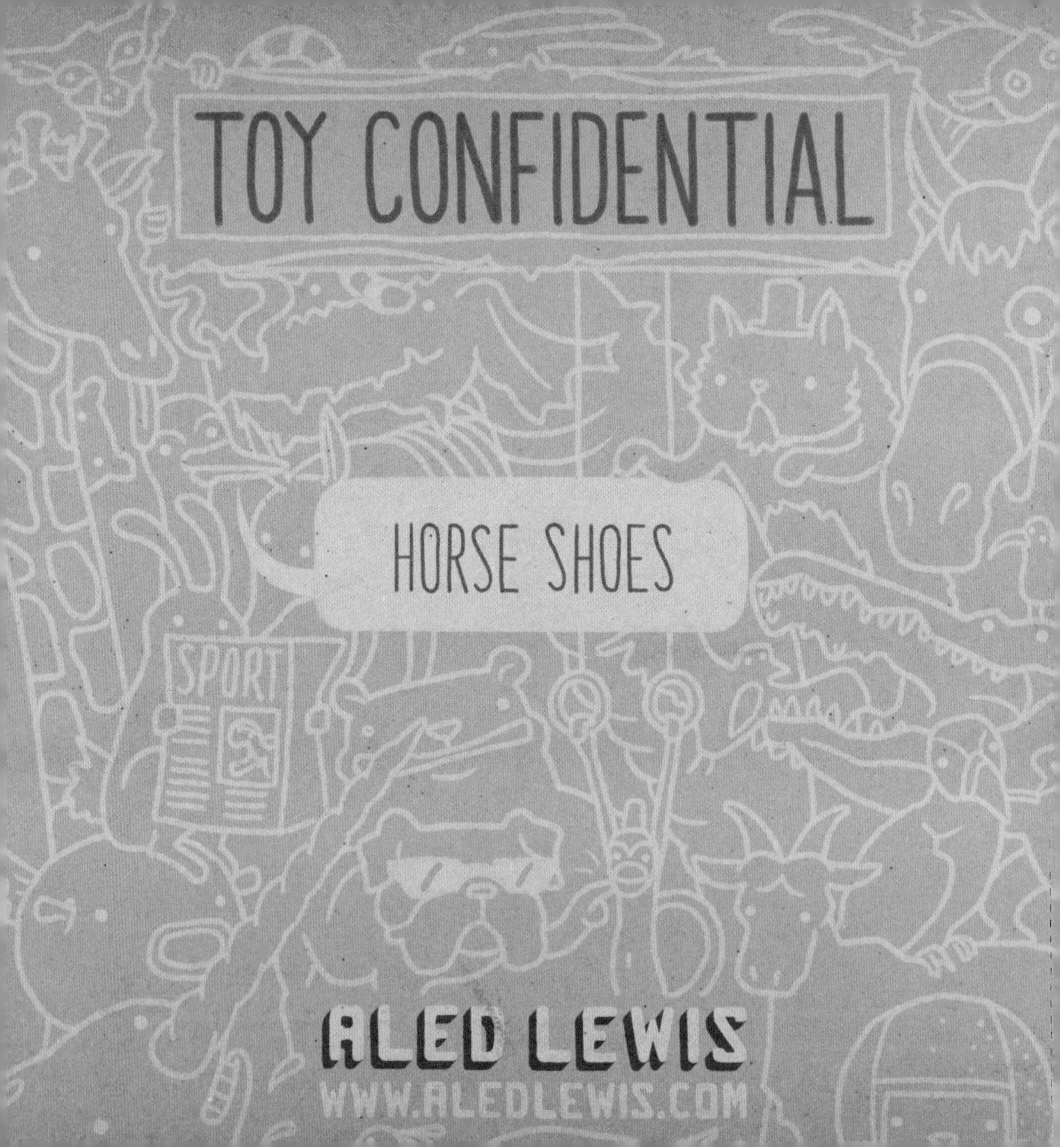
TOY CONFIDENTIAL
HORSE SHOES
SPORT
ALED LEWIS
WWW.ALEDLEWIS.COM

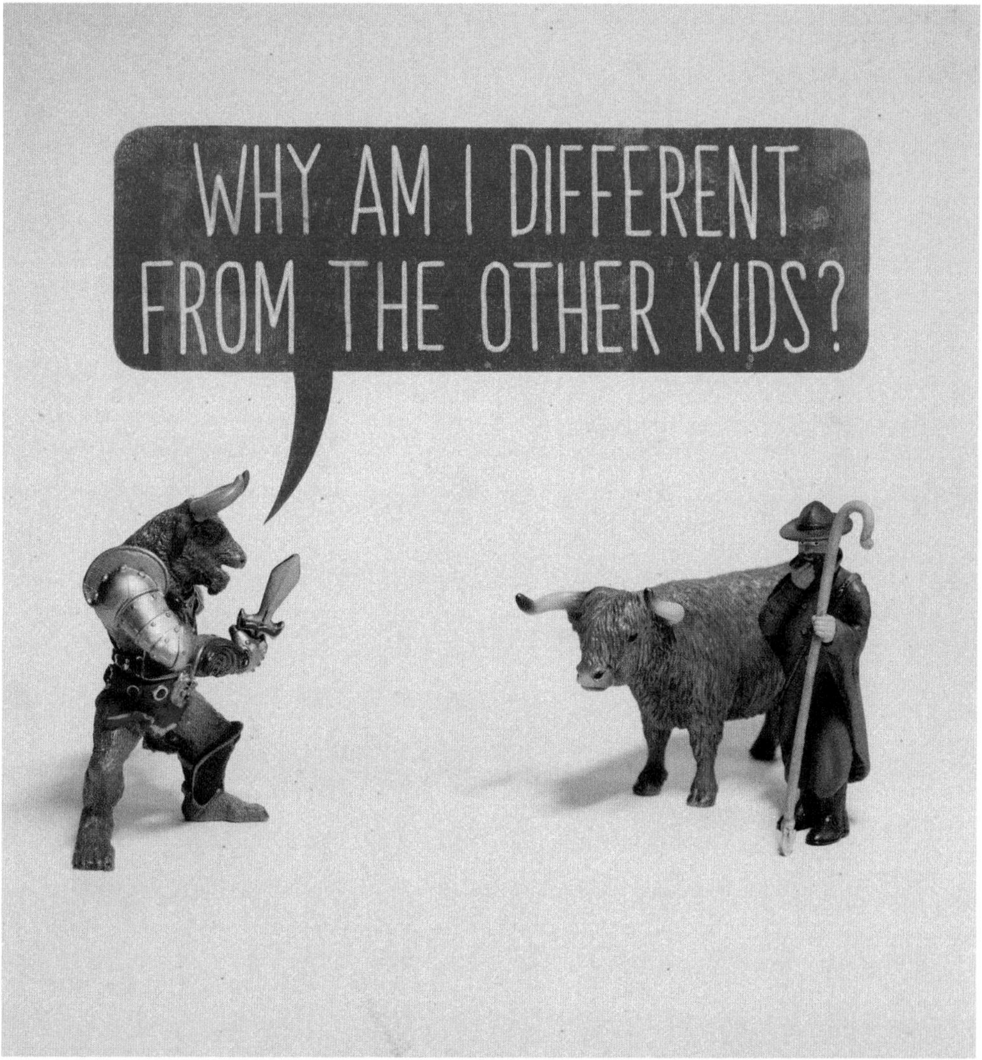
WHY AM I DIFFERENT FROM THE OTHER KIDS?

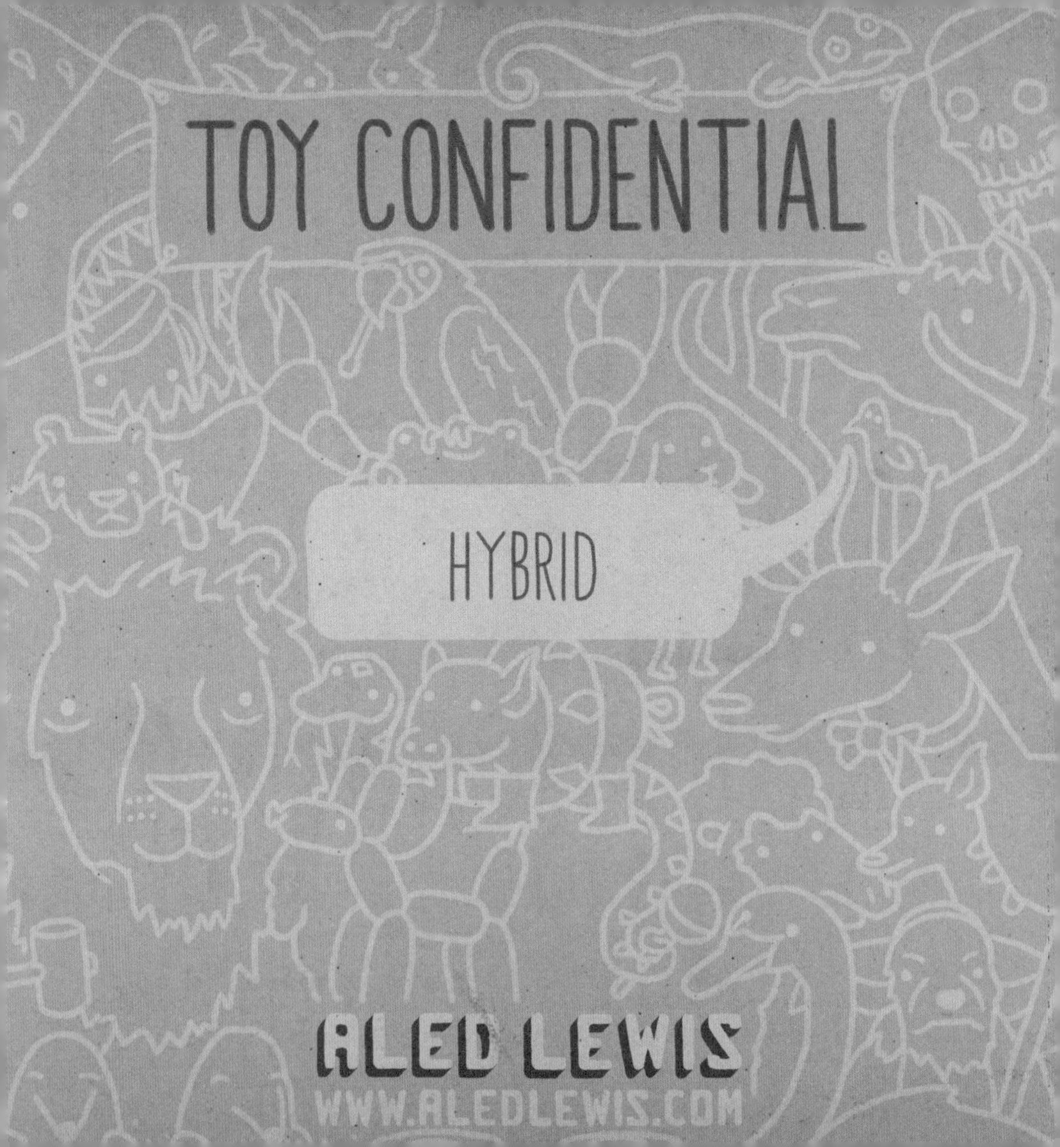

TOY CONFIDENTIAL

HYBRID

ALED LEWIS

WWW.ALEDLEWIS.COM

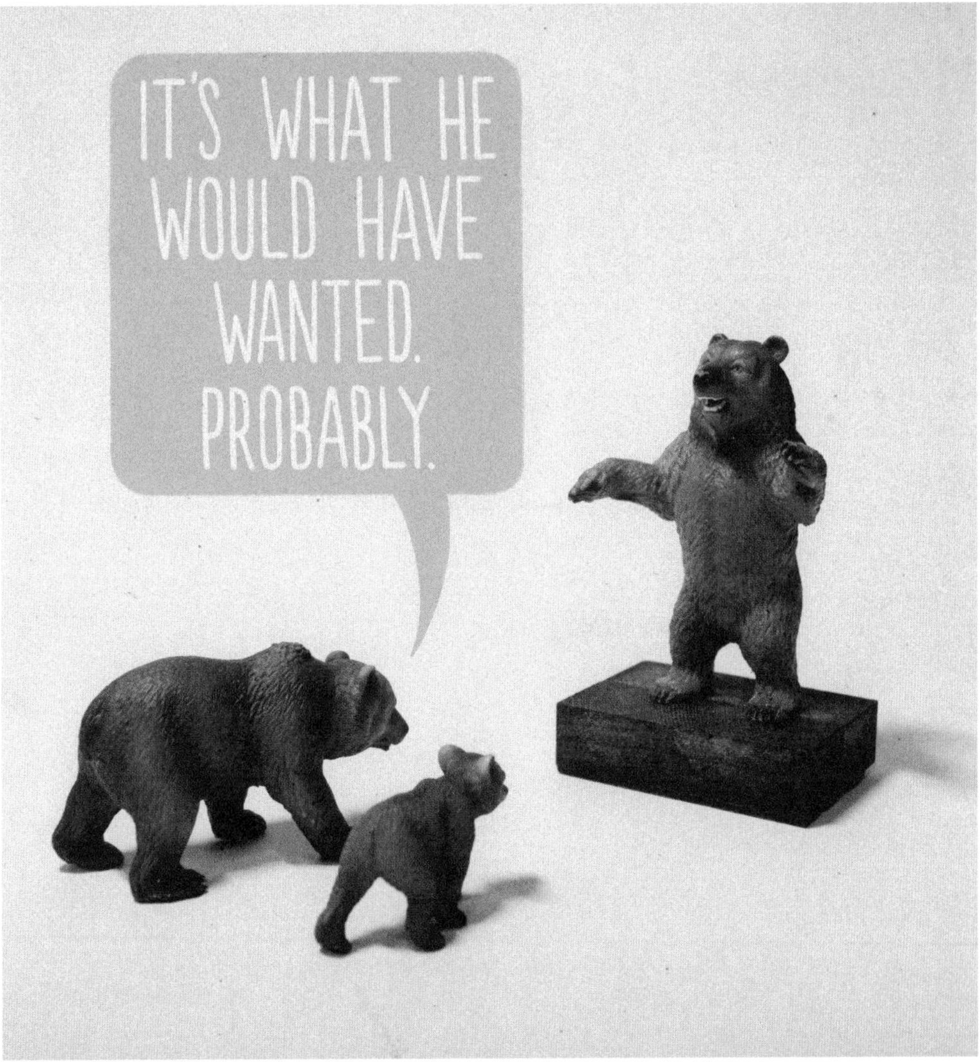
IT'S WHAT HE
WOULD HAVE
WANTED.
PROBABLY.

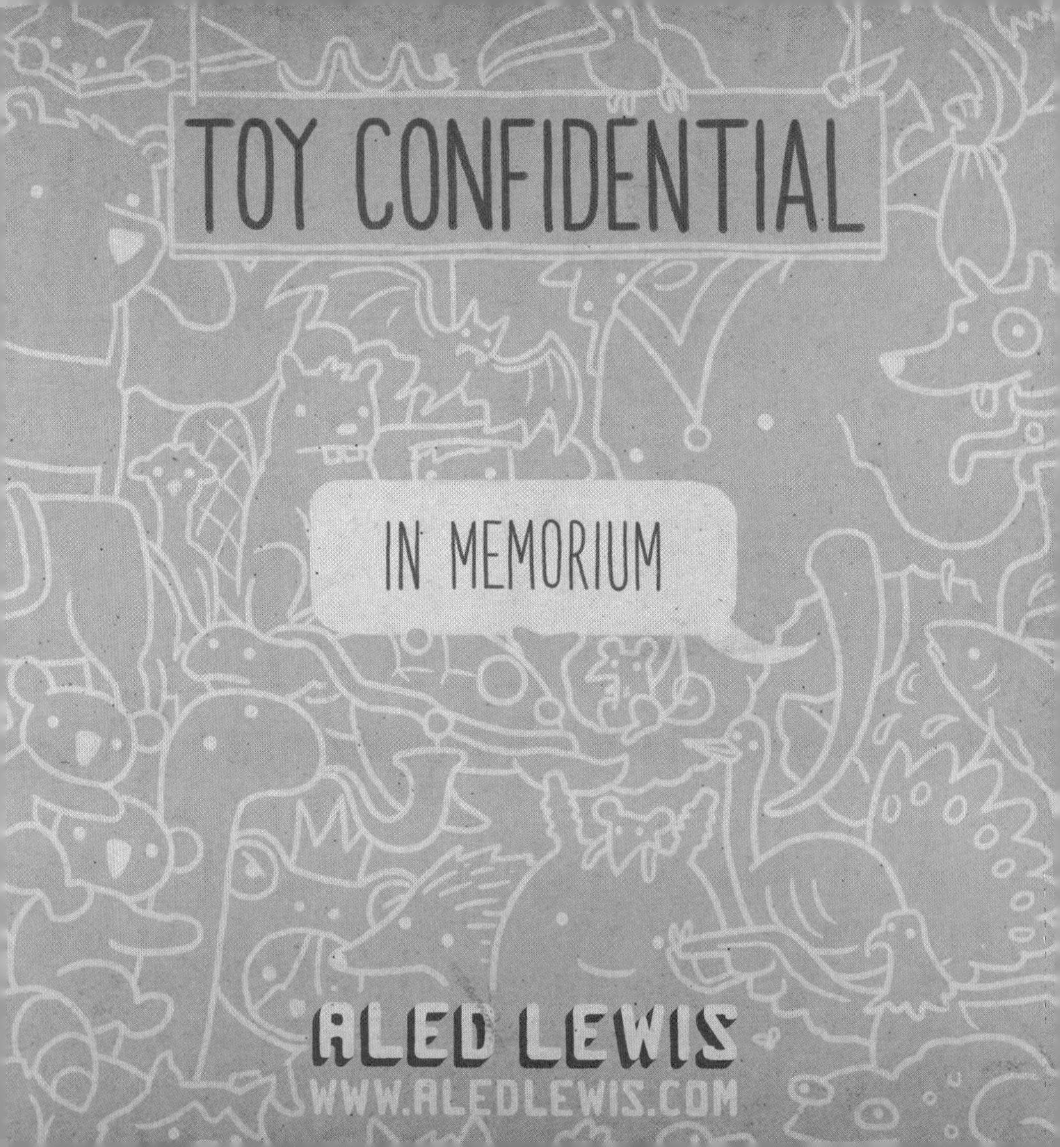
TOY CONFIDENTIAL
IN MEMORIUM
ALED LEWIS
WWW.ALEDLEWIS.COM

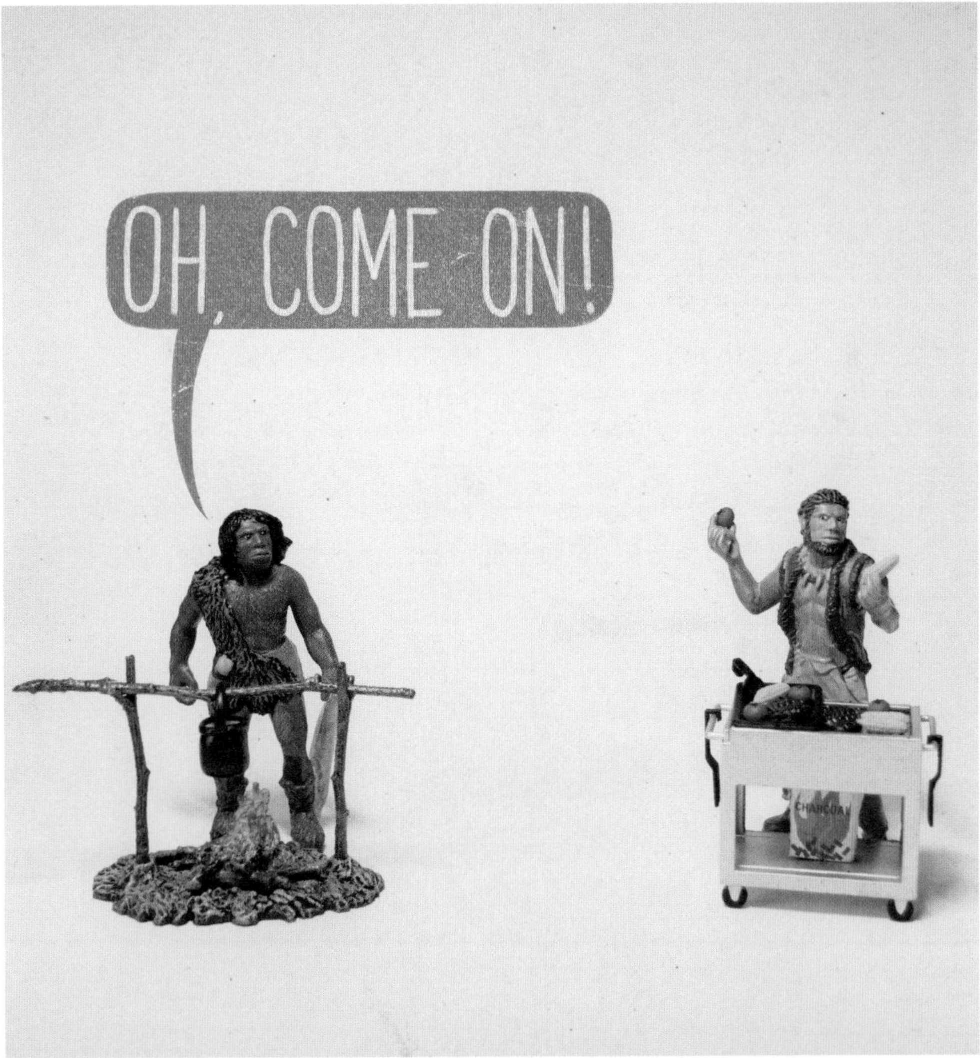
OH, COME ON!

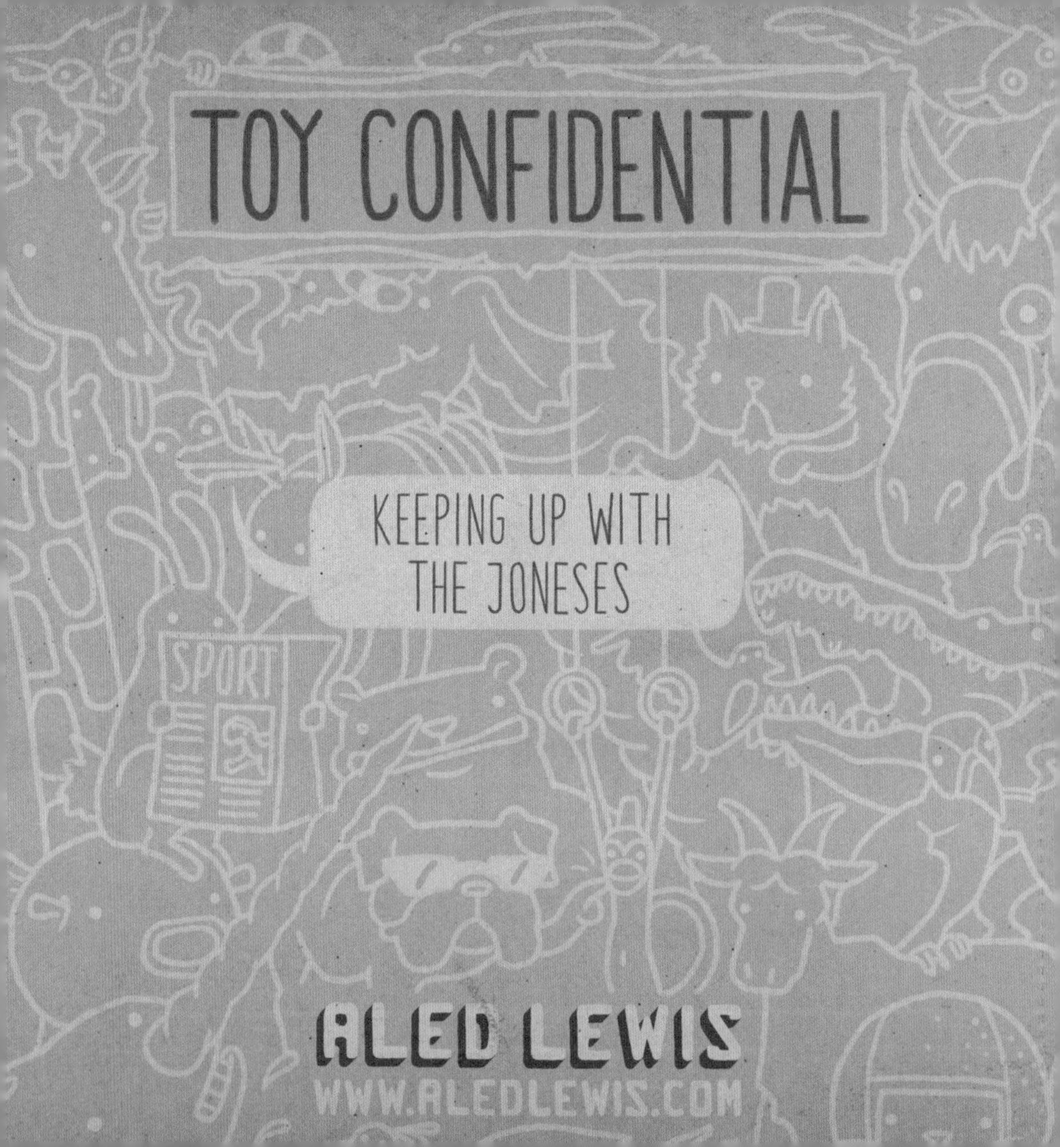
TOY CONFIDENTIAL
KEEPING UP WITH
THE JONESES
SPORT
ALED LEWIS
WWW.ALEDLEWIS.COM

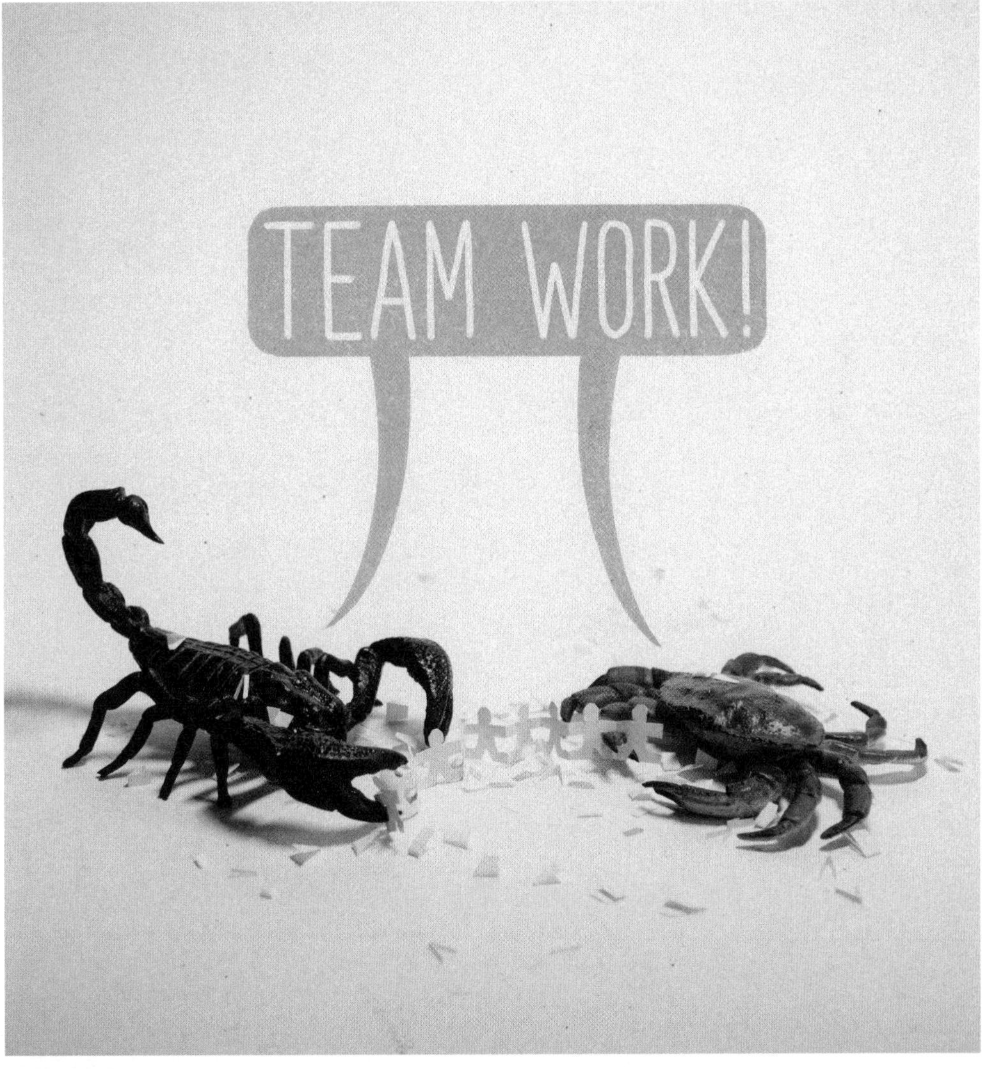
TEAM WORK!

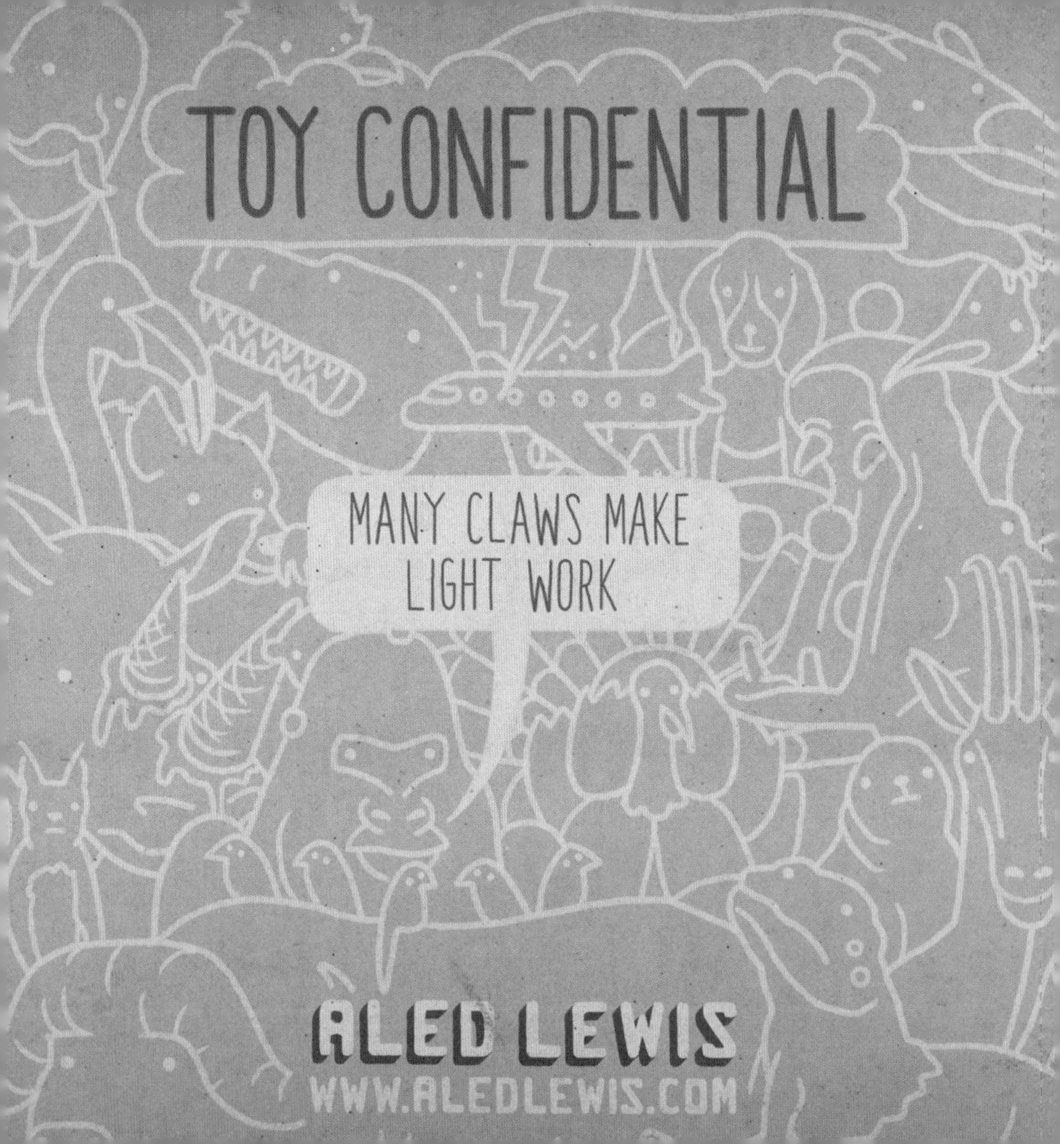
TOY CONFIDENTIAL
MANY CLAWS MAKE LIGHT WORK
ALED LEWIS
WWW.ALEDLEWIS.COM

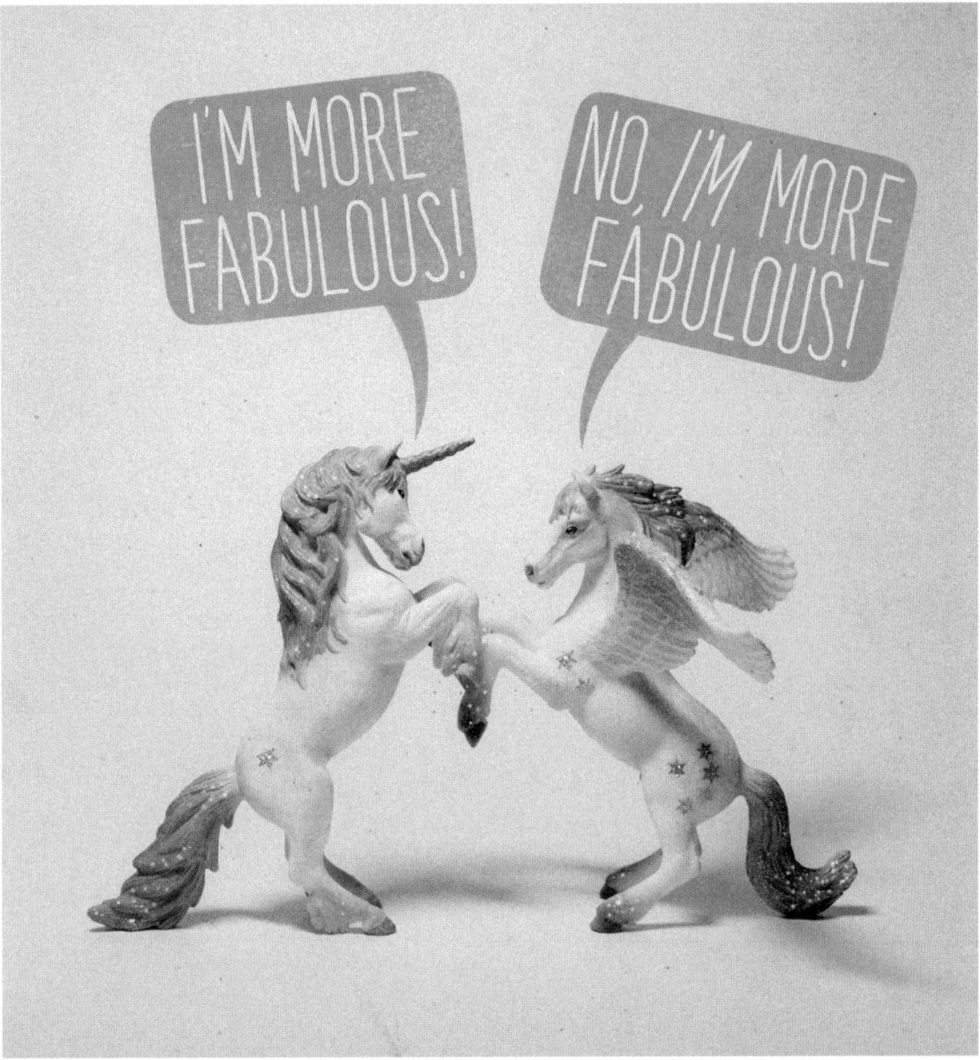
I'M MORE FABULOUS!
NO, I'M MORE FABULOUS!

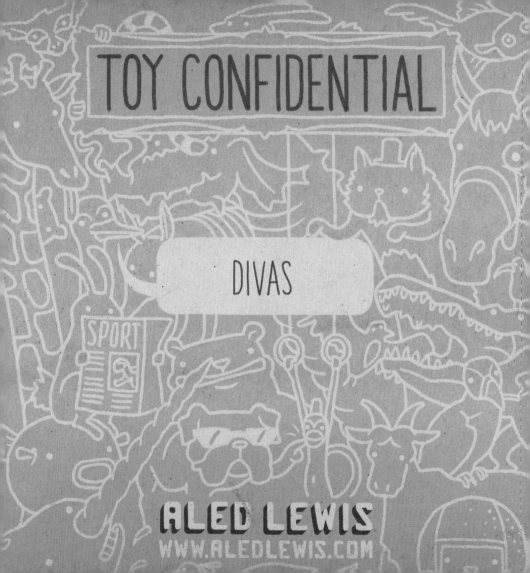

TOY CONFIDENTIAL

DIVAS

SPORT

ALED LEWIS
WWW.ALEDLEWIS.COM

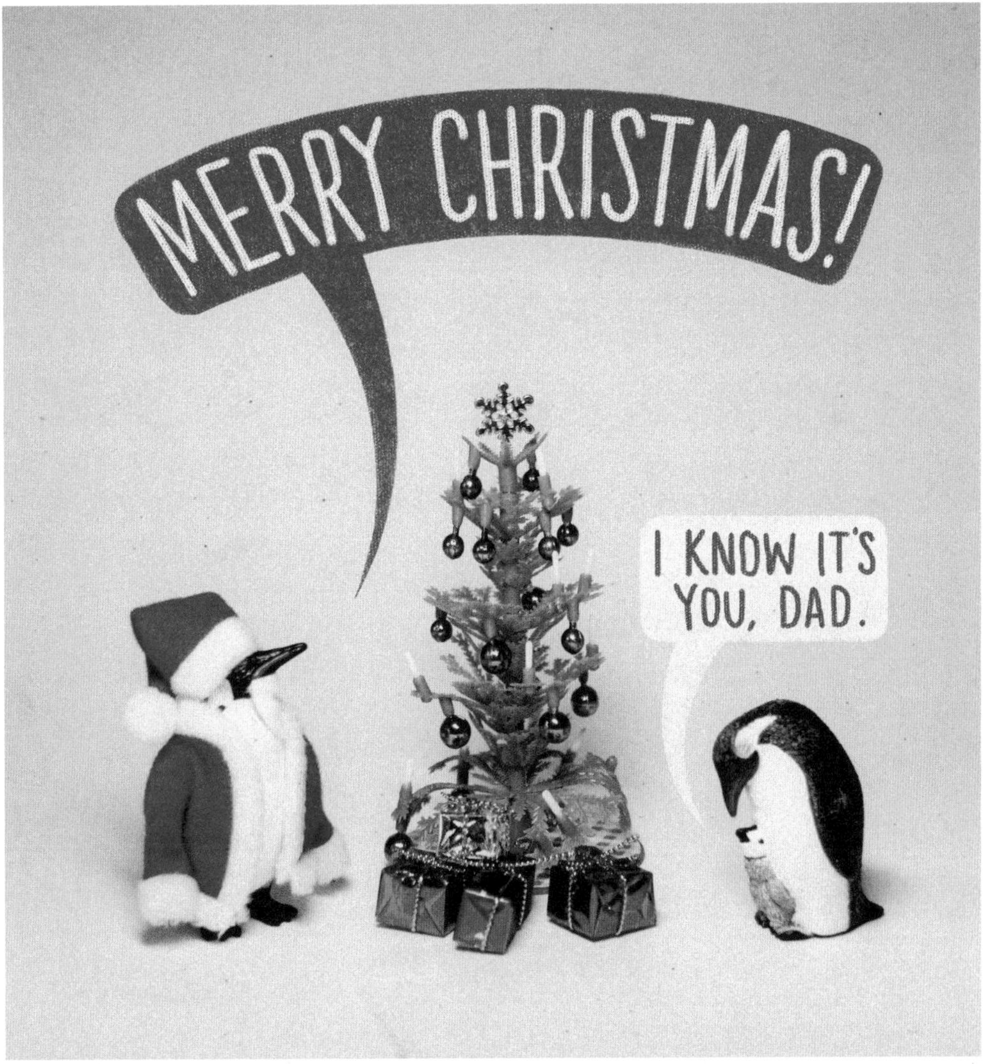
MERRY CHRISTMAS!
I KNOW IT'S YOU, DAD.

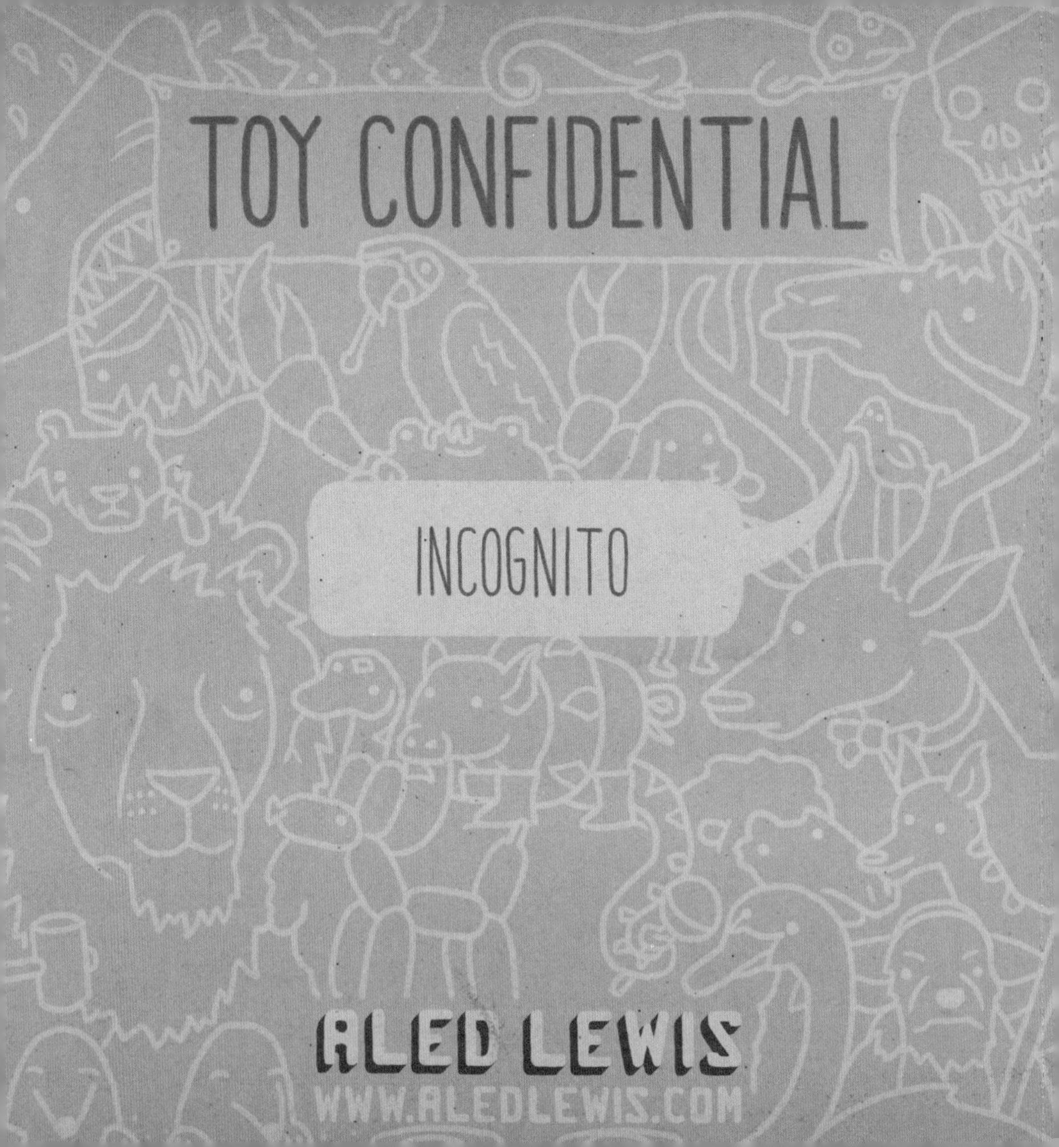
TOY CONFIDENTIAL
INCOGNITO
ALED LEWIS
WWW.ALEDLEWIS.COM

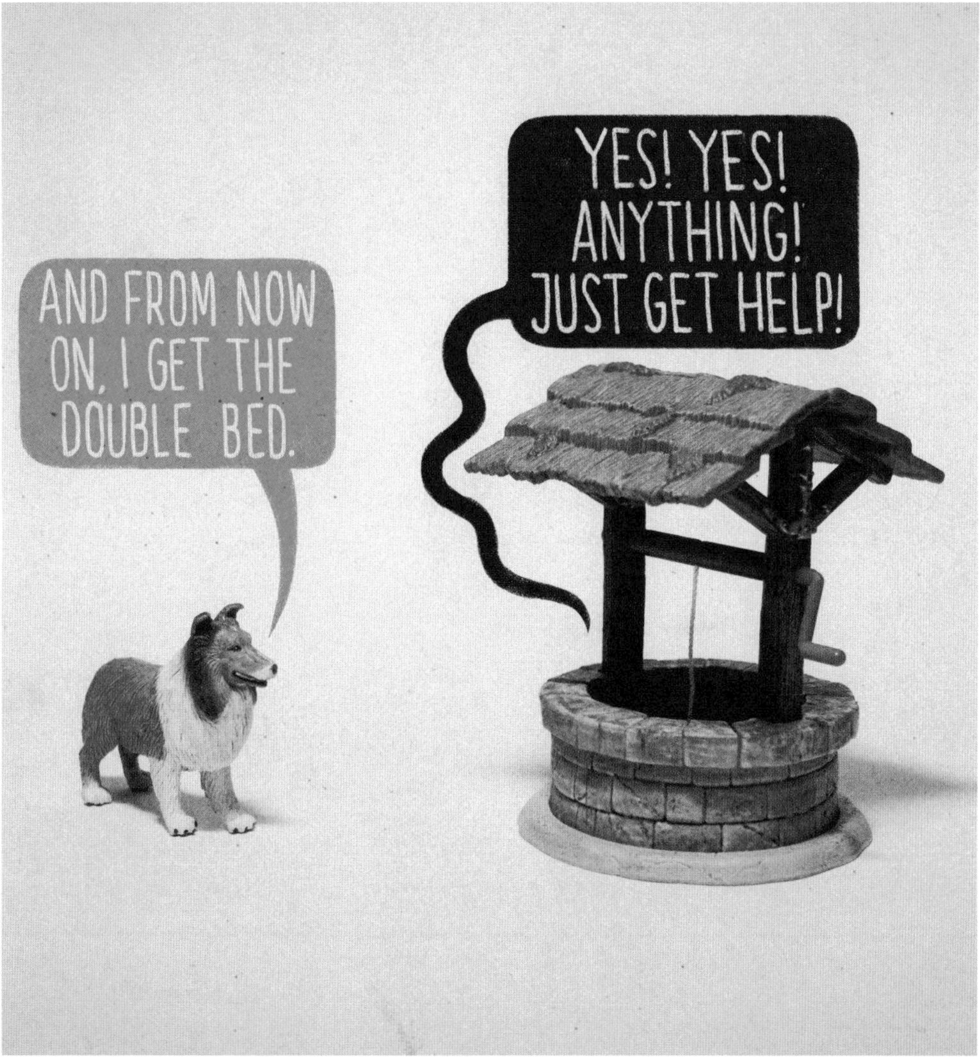
AND FROM NOW ON, I GET THE DOUBLE BED.
YES! YES! ANYTHING! JUST GET HELP!

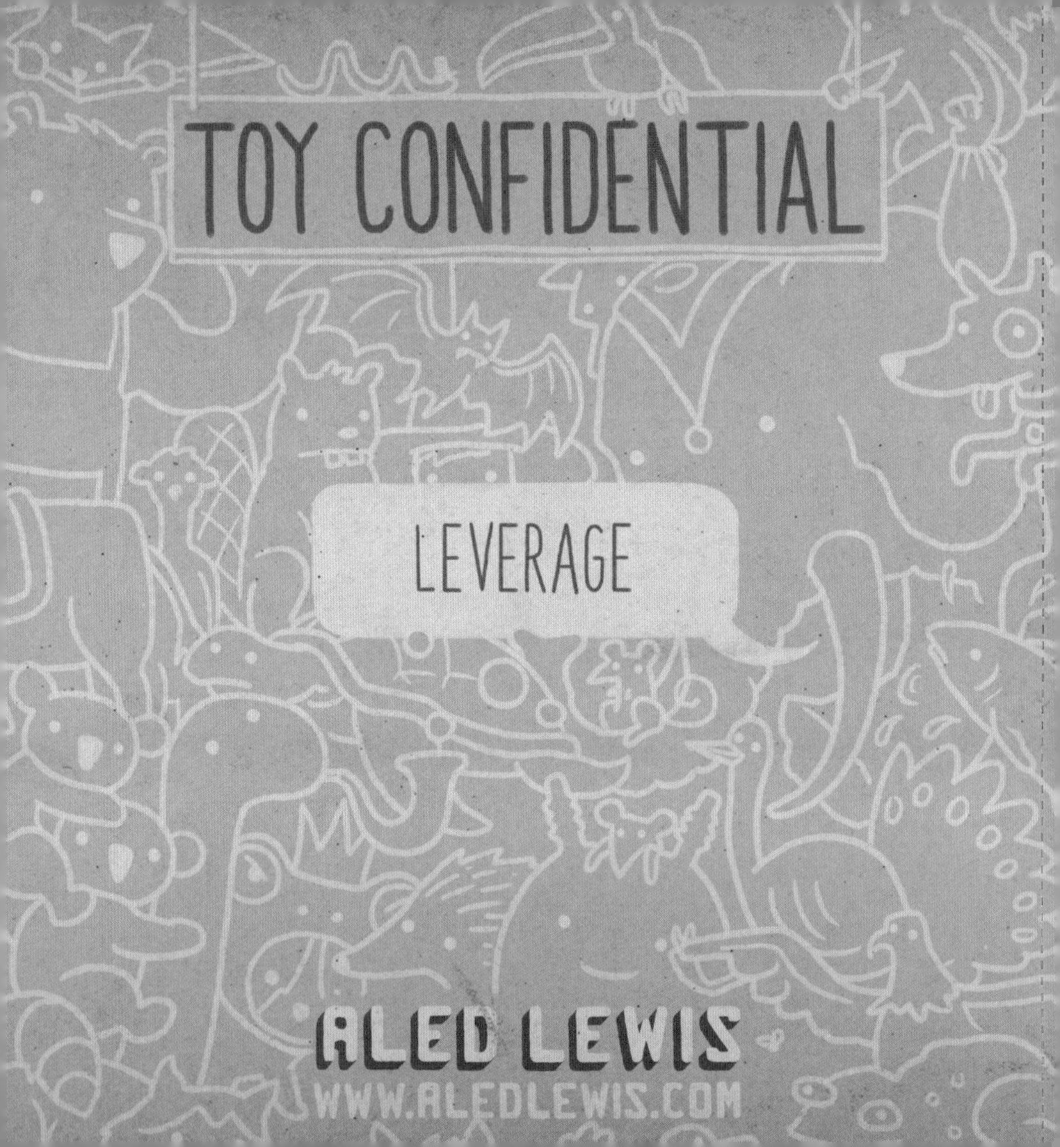
TOY CONFIDENTIAL
LEVERAGE
ALED LEWIS
WWW.ALEDLEWIS.COM

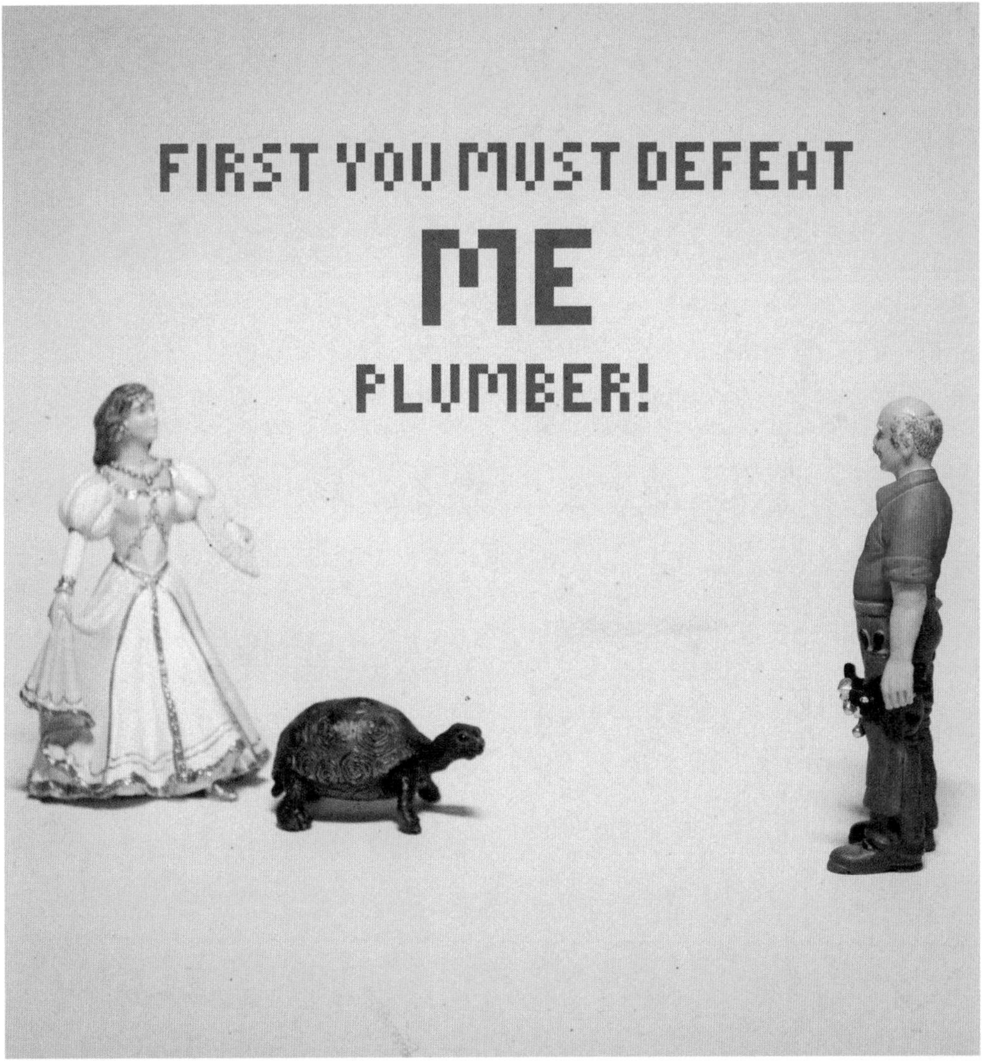
FIRST YOU MUST DEFEAT
ME
PLUMBER!

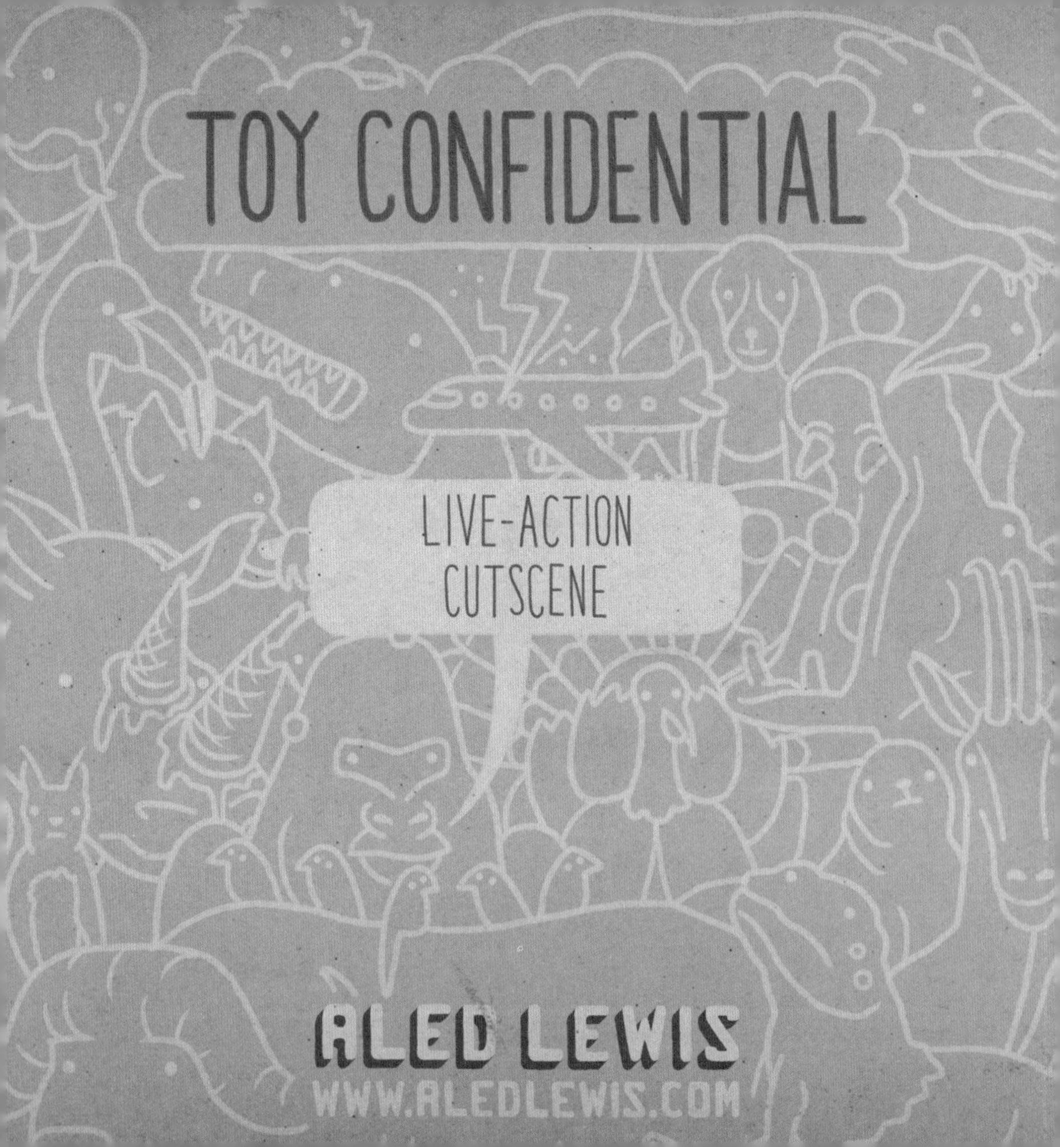
TOY CONFIDENTIAL
LIVE-ACTION CUTSCENE
ALED LEWIS
WWW.ALEDLEWIS.COM

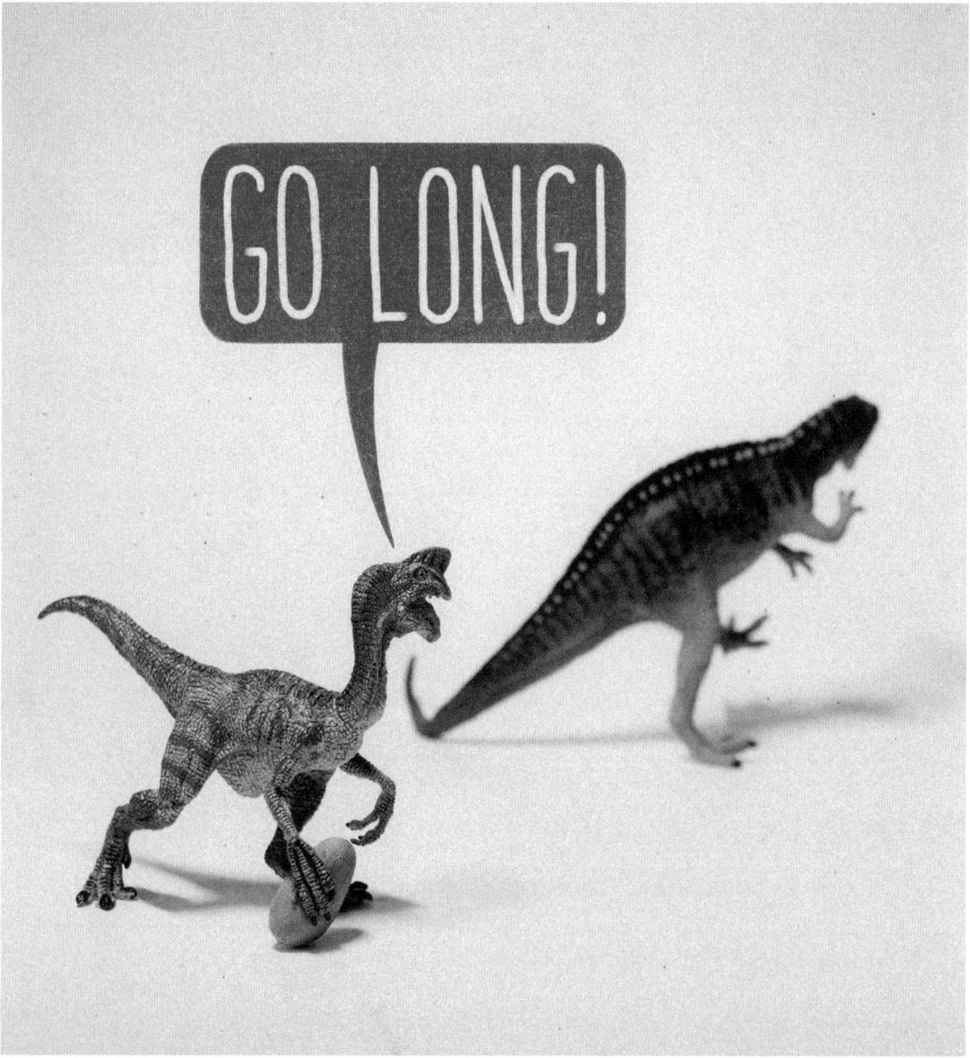
GO LONG!

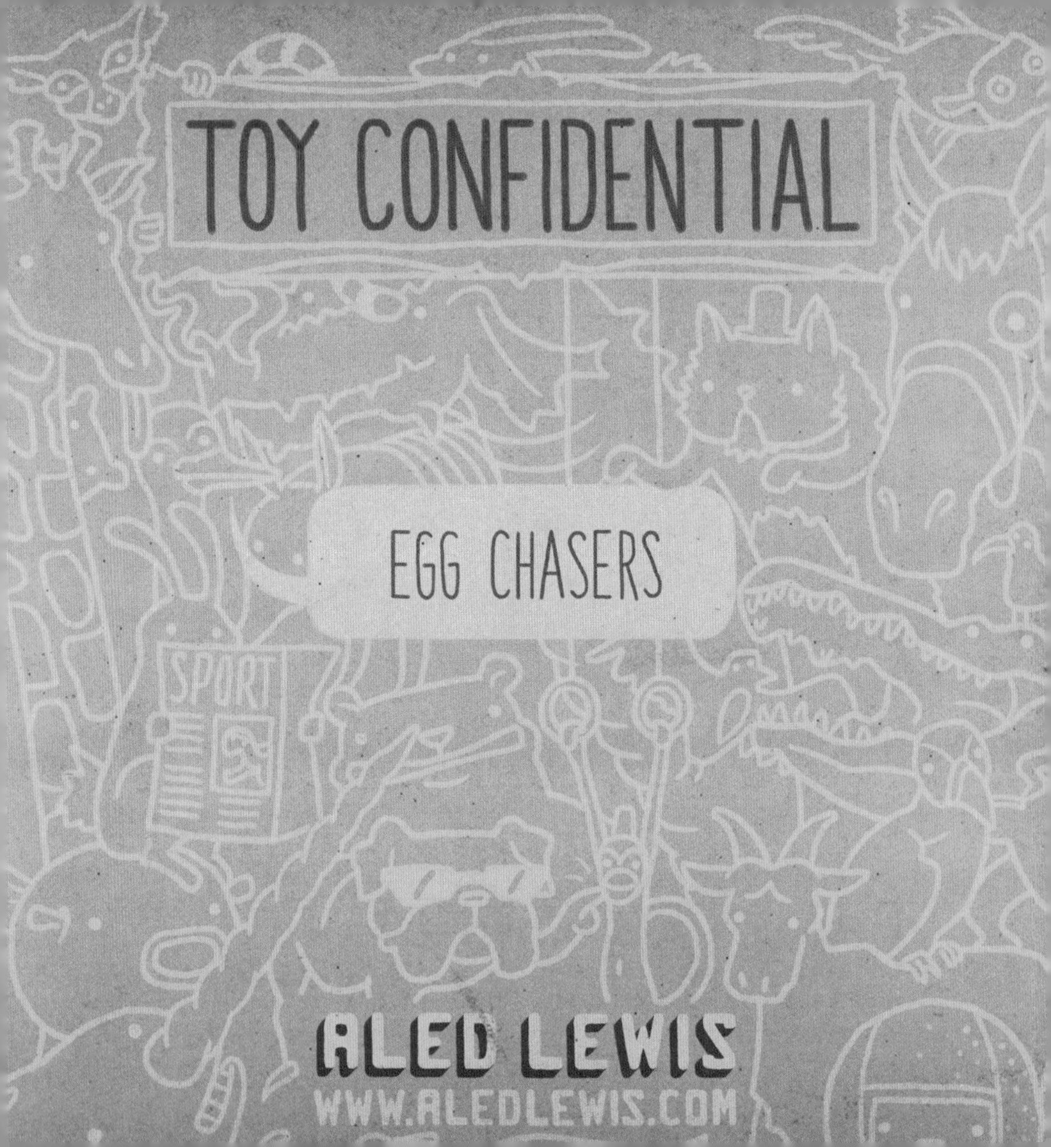
TOY CONFIDENTIAL
EGG CHASERS
SPORT
ALED LEWIS
WWW.ALEDLEWIS.COM

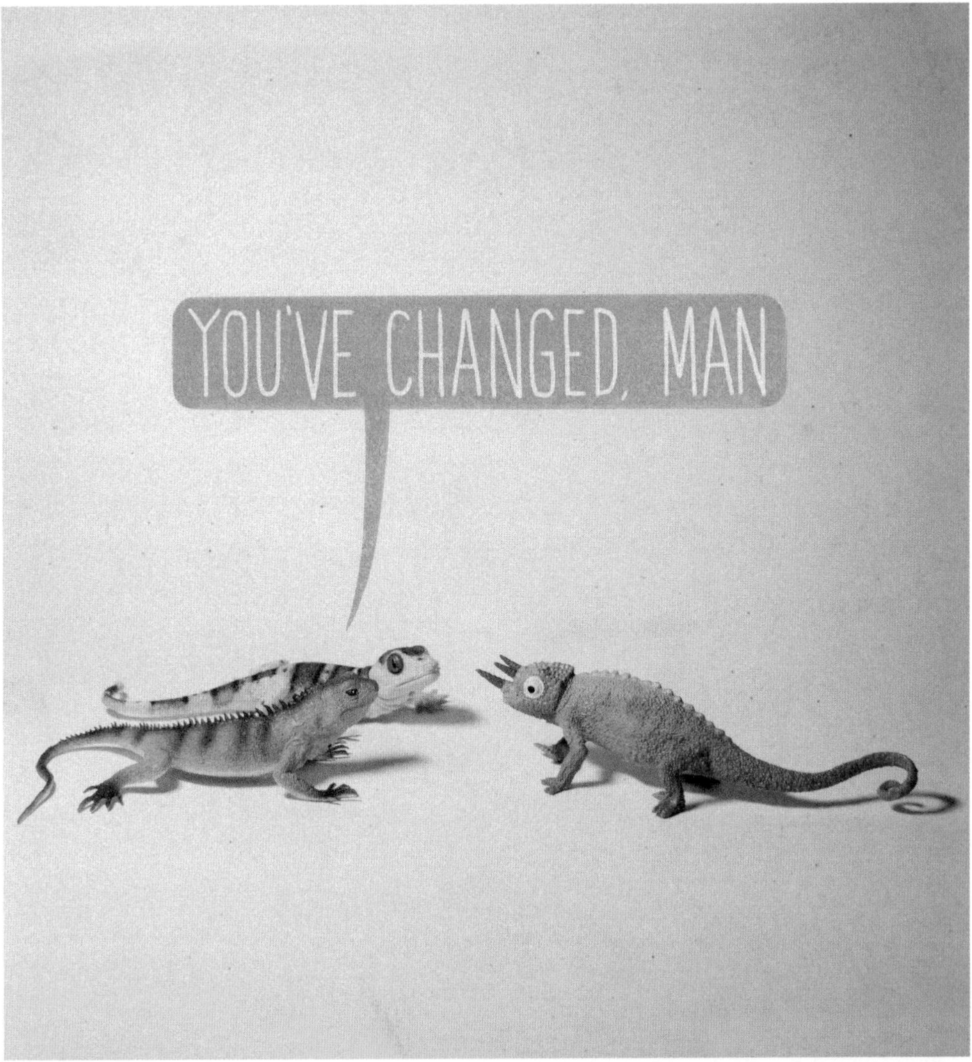
YOU'VE CHANGED, MAN

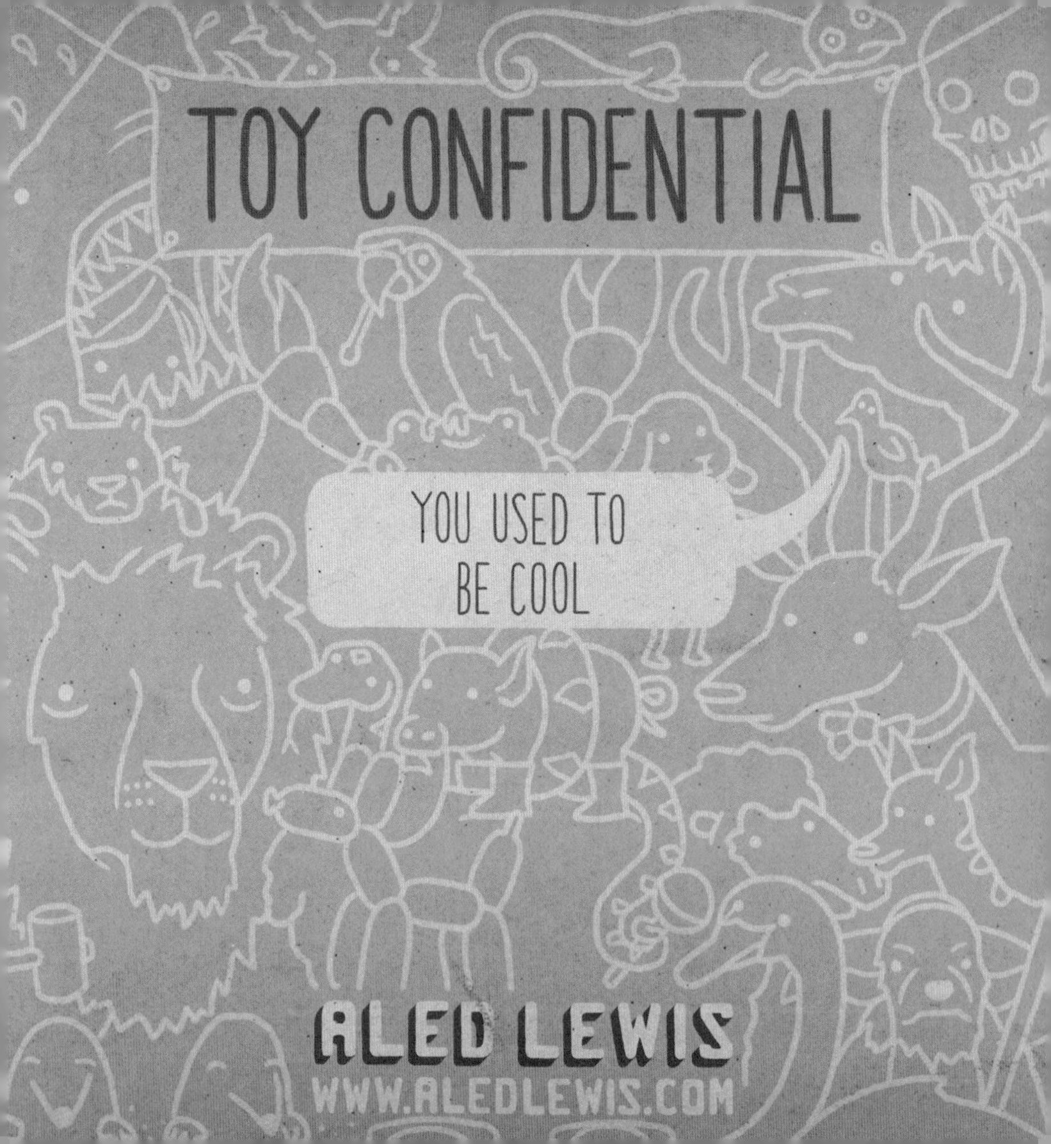
TOY CONFIDENTIAL
YOU USED TO BE COOL
ALED LEWIS
WWW.ALEDLEWIS.COM

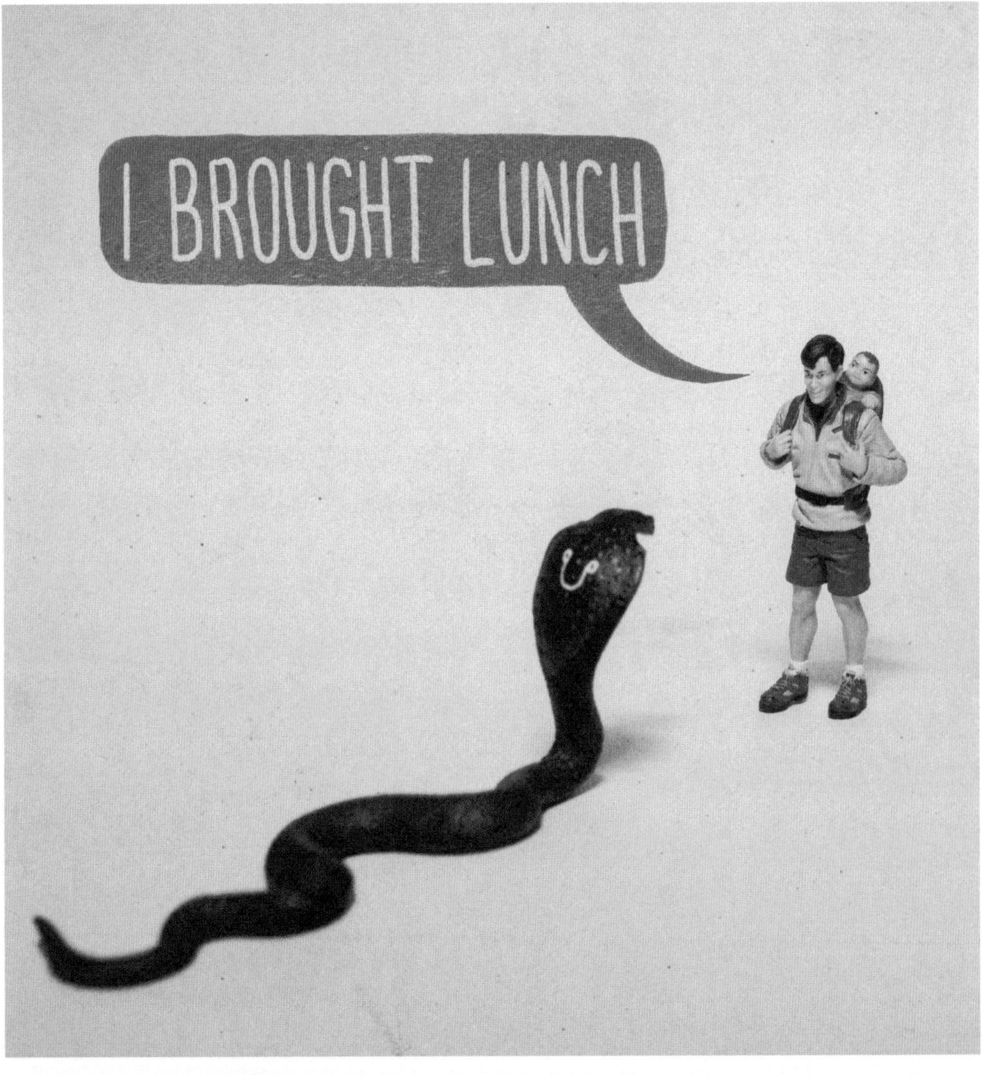
I BROUGHT LUNCH

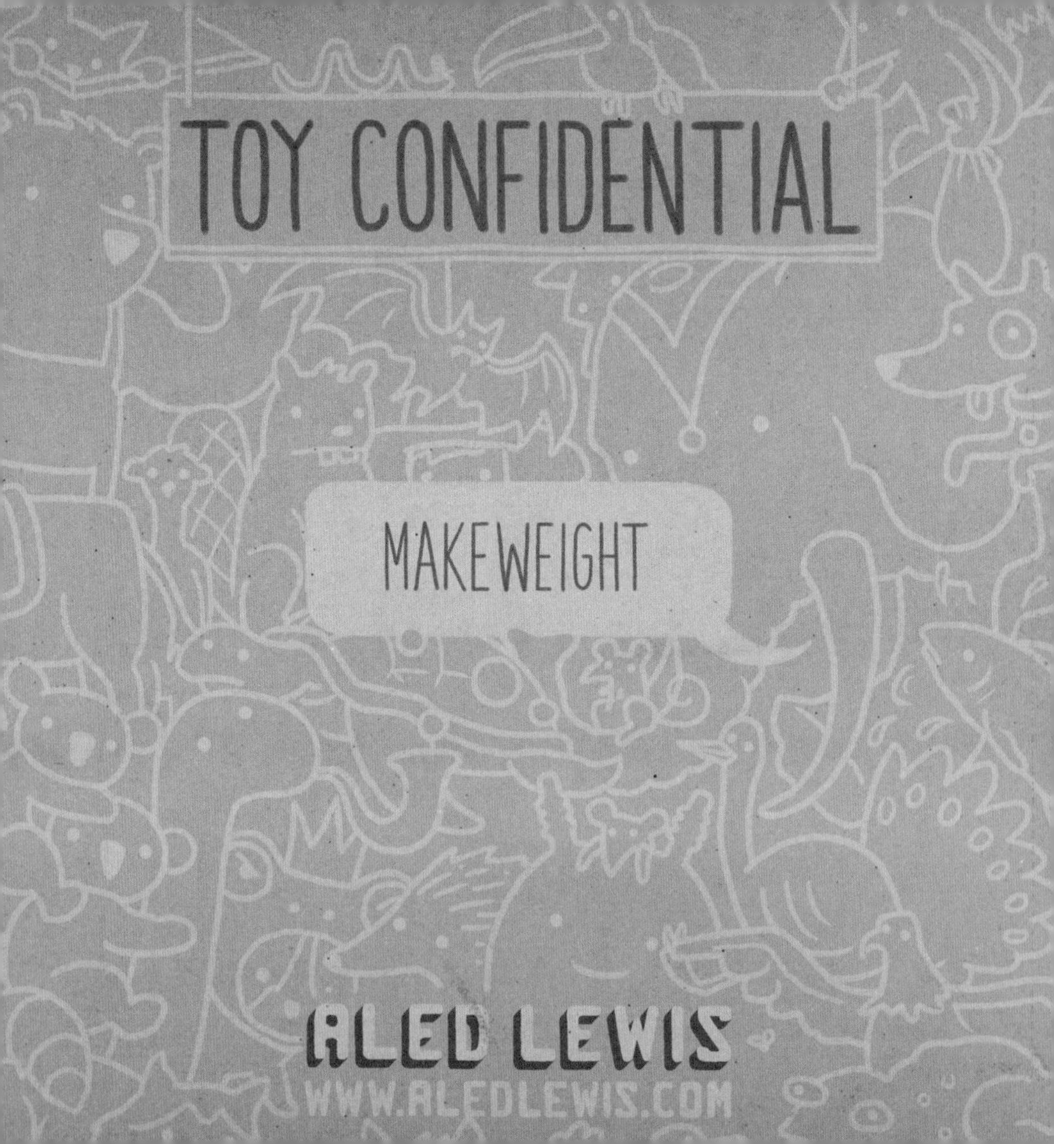
TOY CONFIDENTIAL
MAKEWEIGHT
ALED LEWIS
WWW.ALEDLEWIS.COM

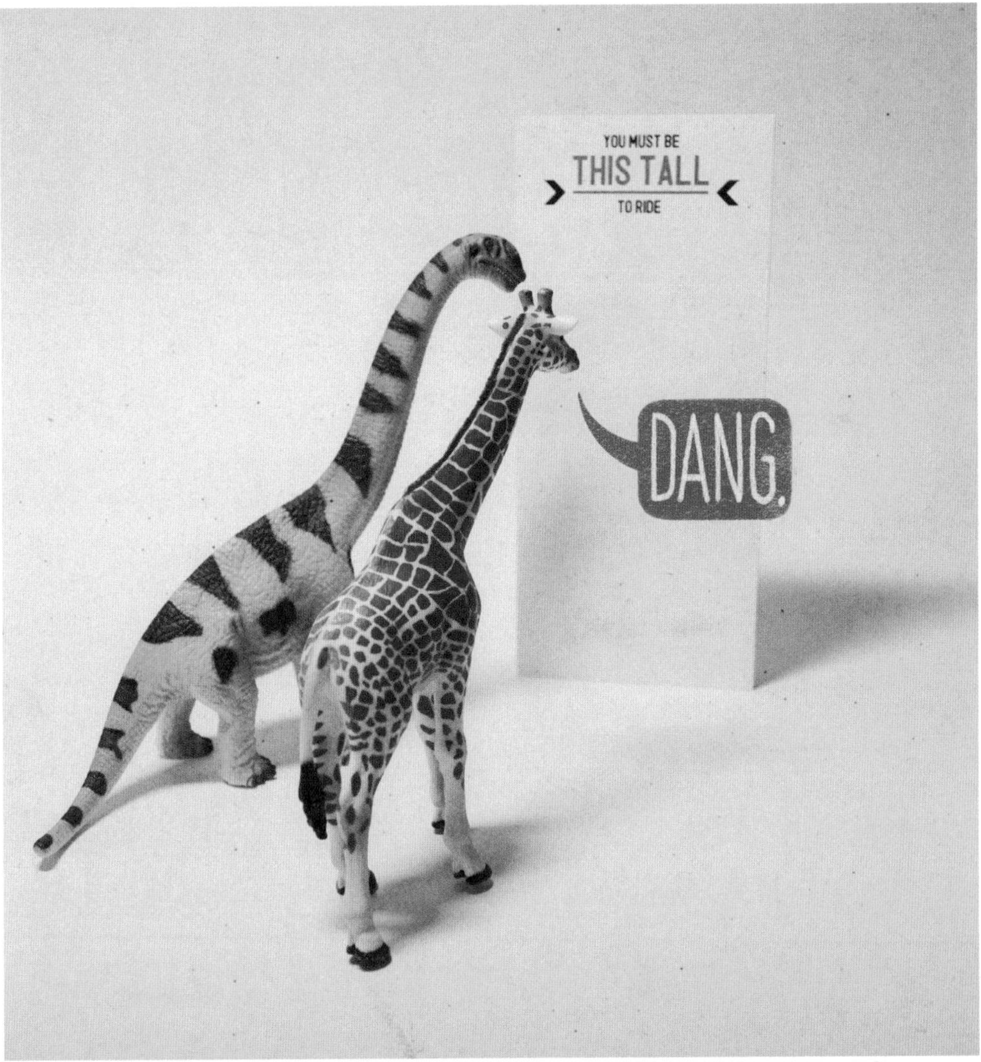
YOU MUST BE
THIS TALL
TO RIDE
DANG.

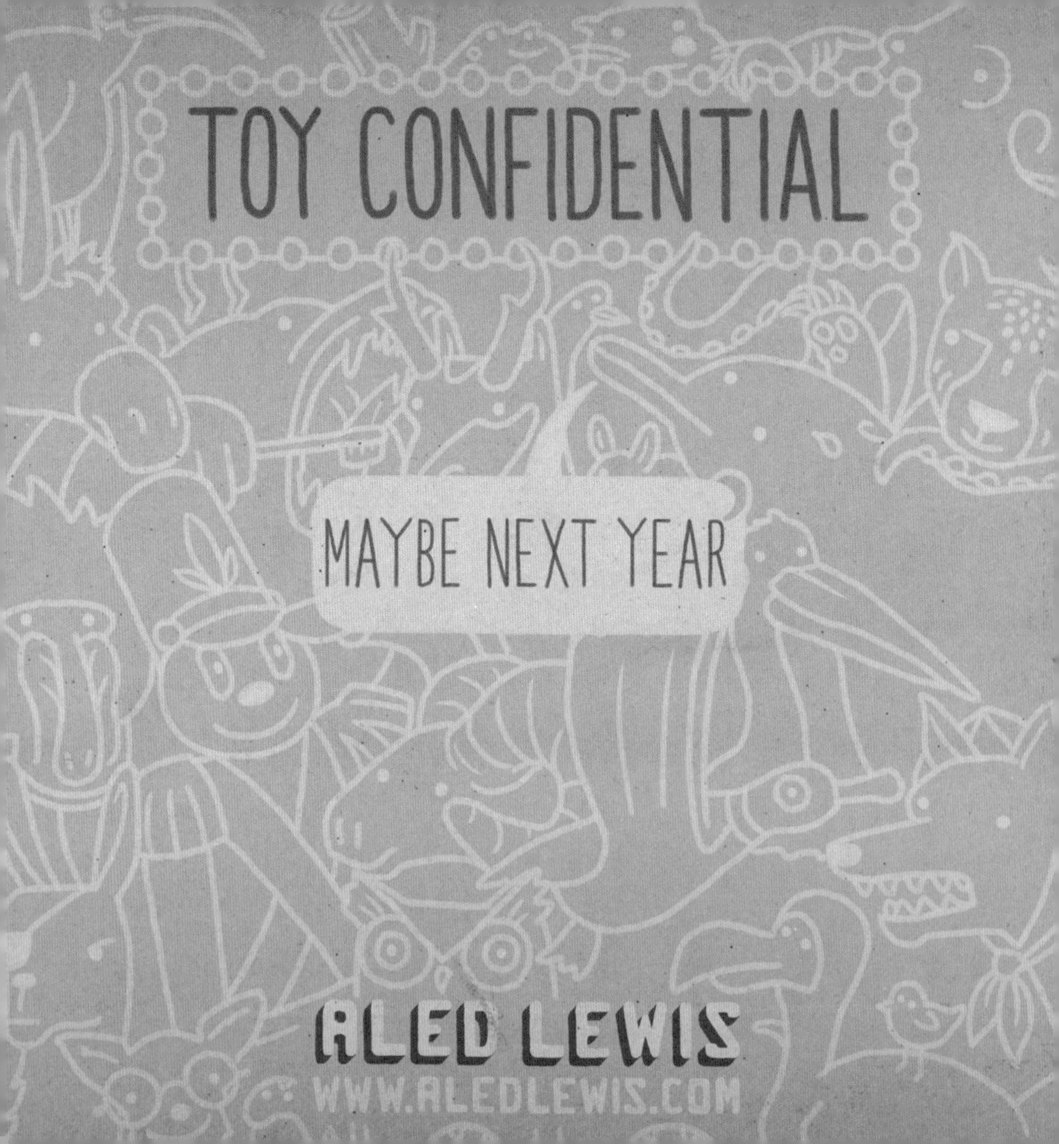
TOY CONFIDENTIAL
MAYBE NEXT YEAR
ALED LEWIS
WWW.ALEDLEWIS.COM

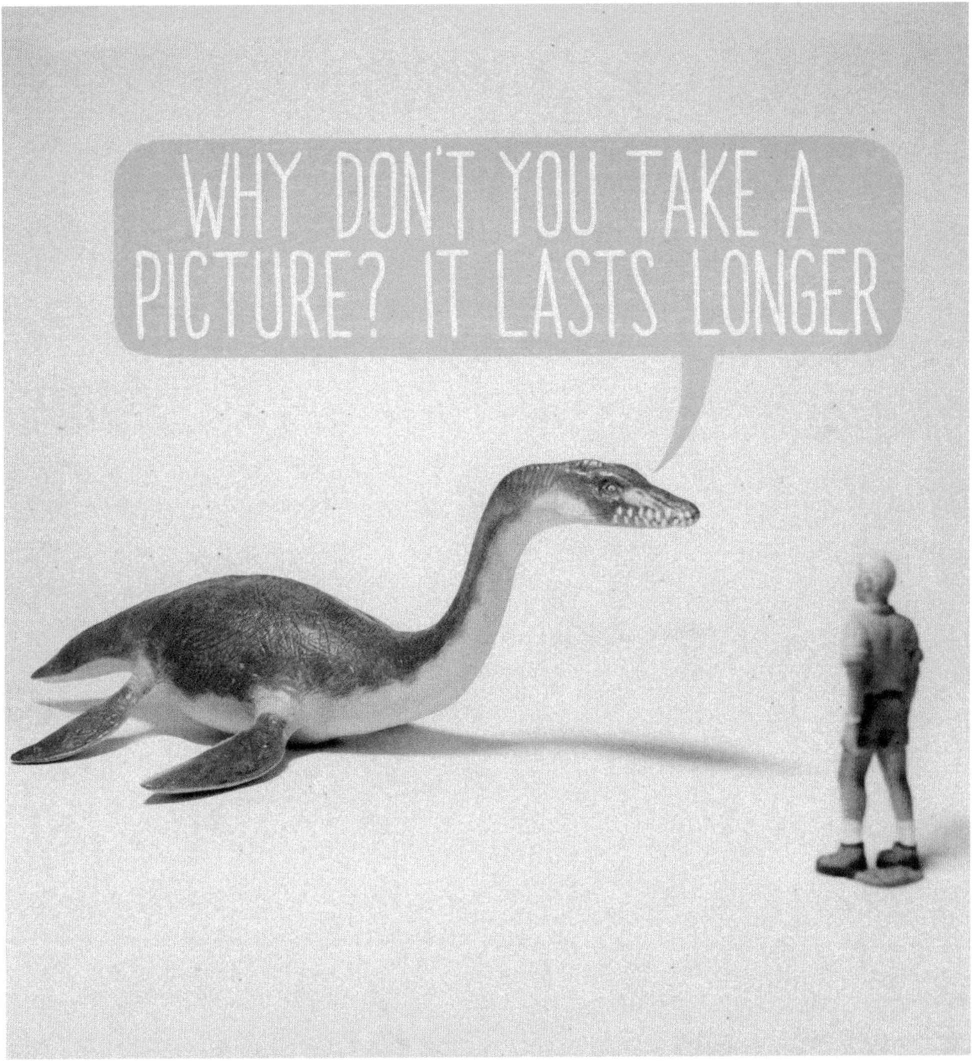
WHY DON'T YOU TAKE A PICTURE? IT LASTS LONGER

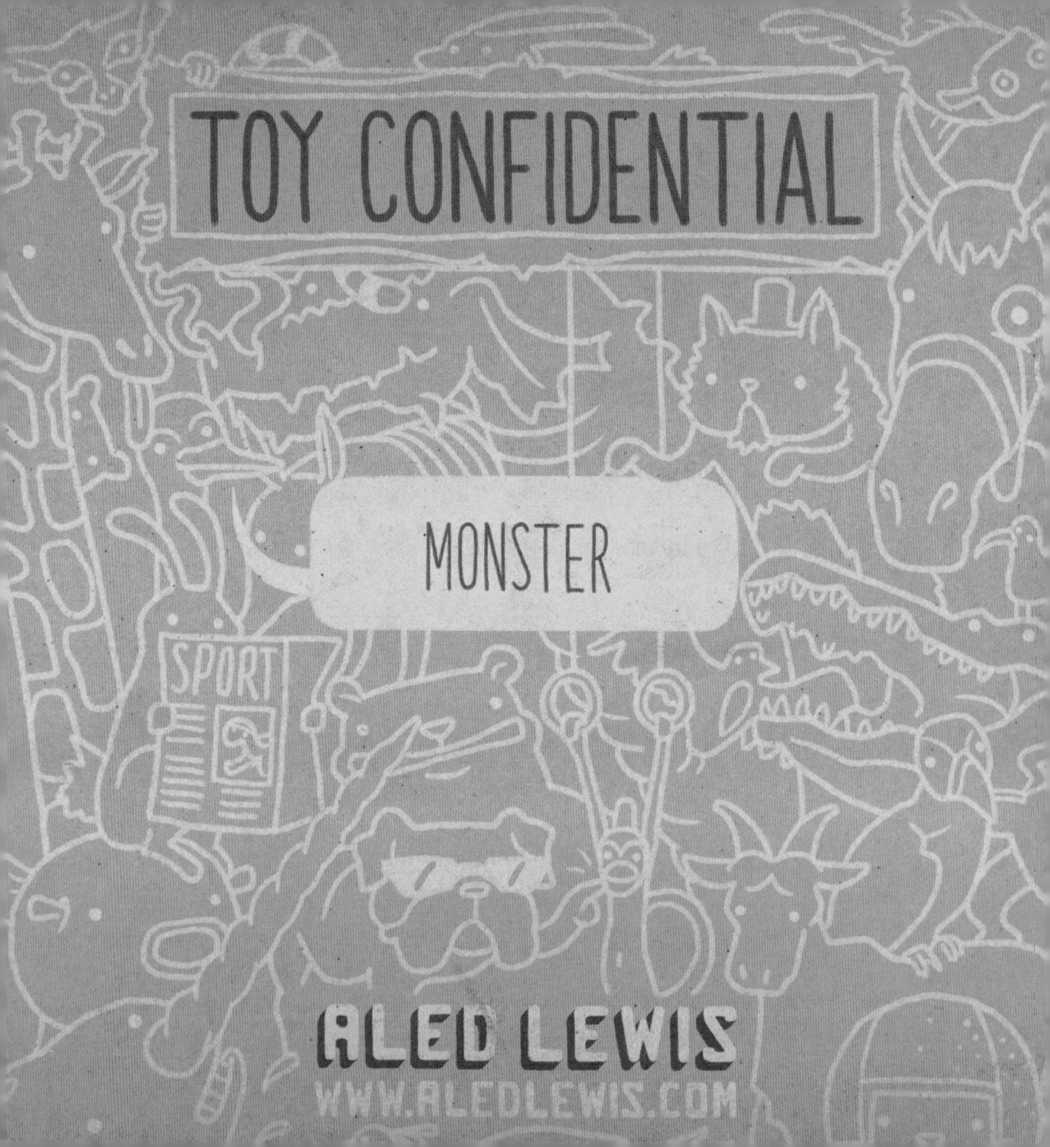
TOY CONFIDENTIAL
MONSTER
SPORT
ALED LEWIS
WWW.ALEDLEWIS.COM

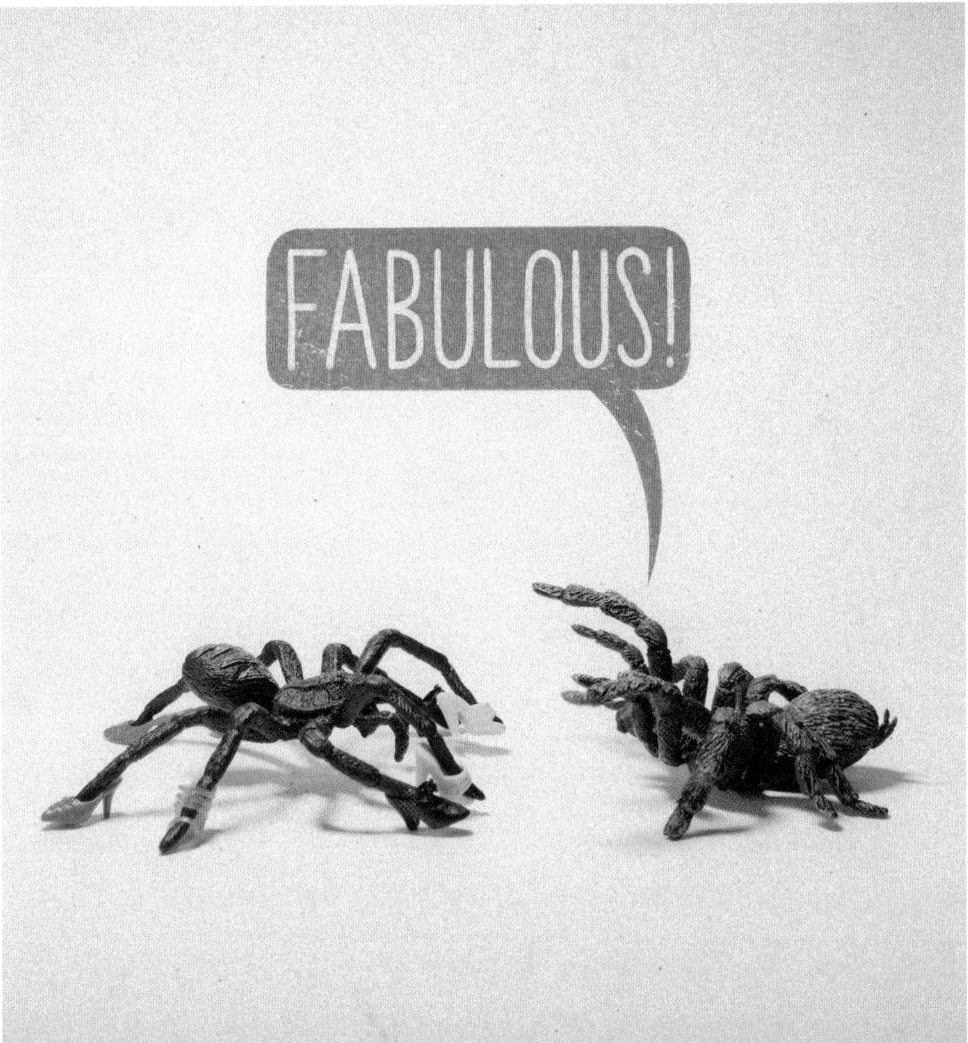
FABULOUS!

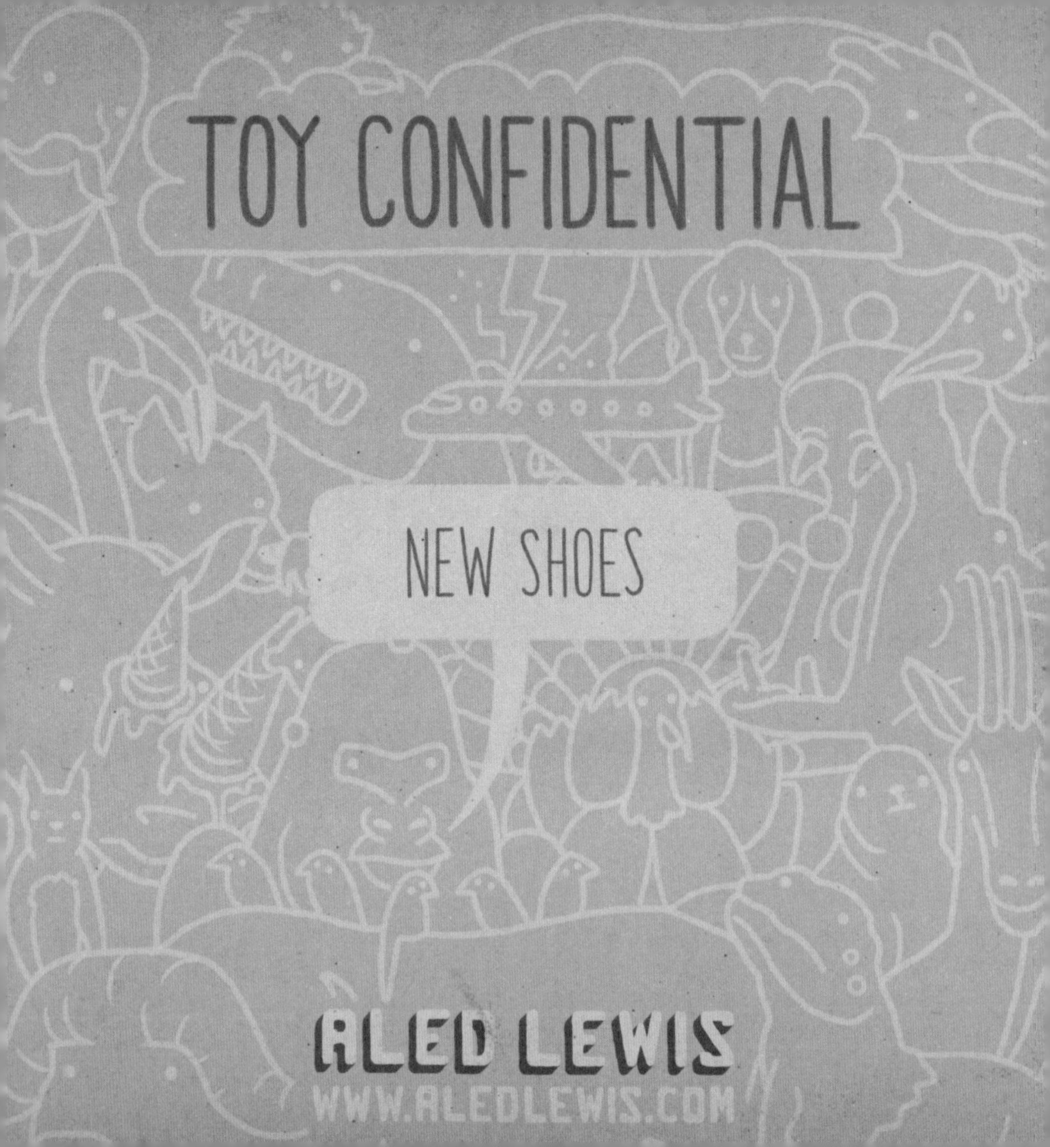
TOY CONFIDENTIAL
NEW SHOES
ALED LEWIS
WWW.ALEDLEWIS.COM

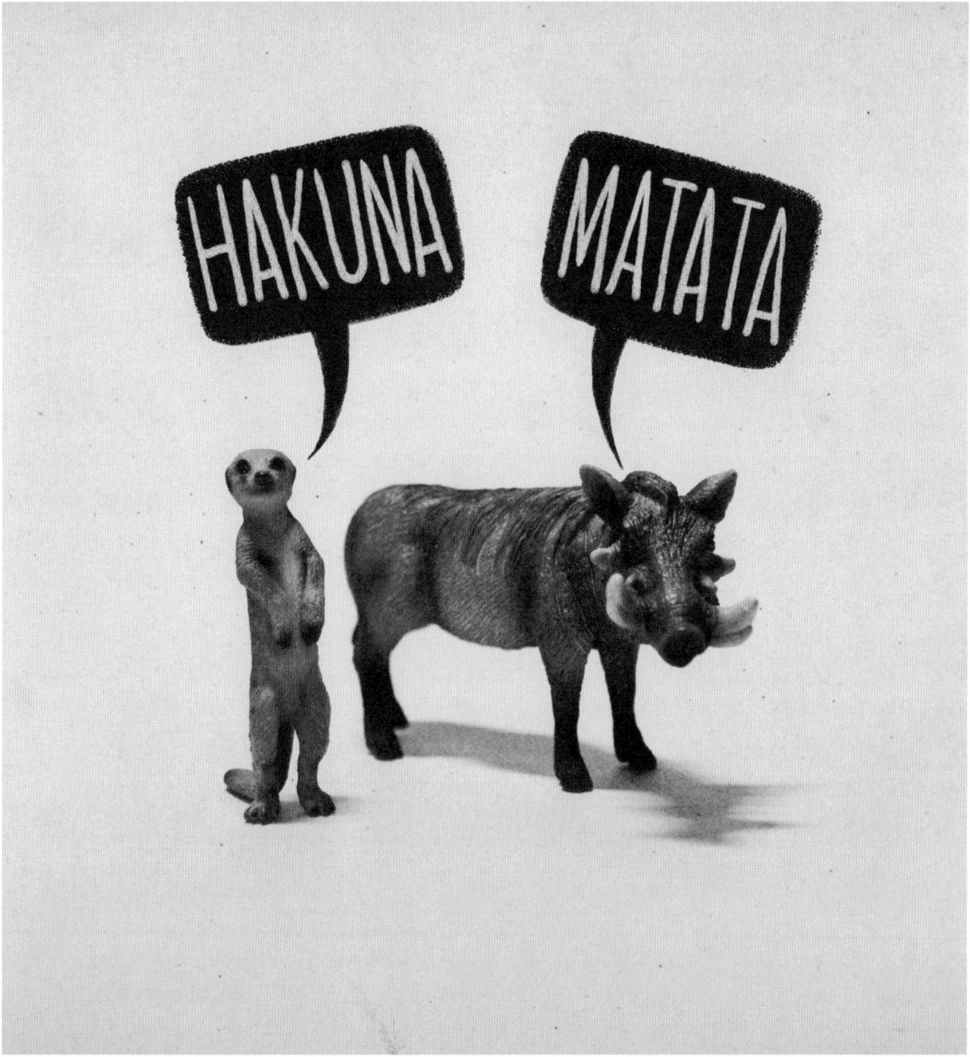
HAKUNA
MATATA

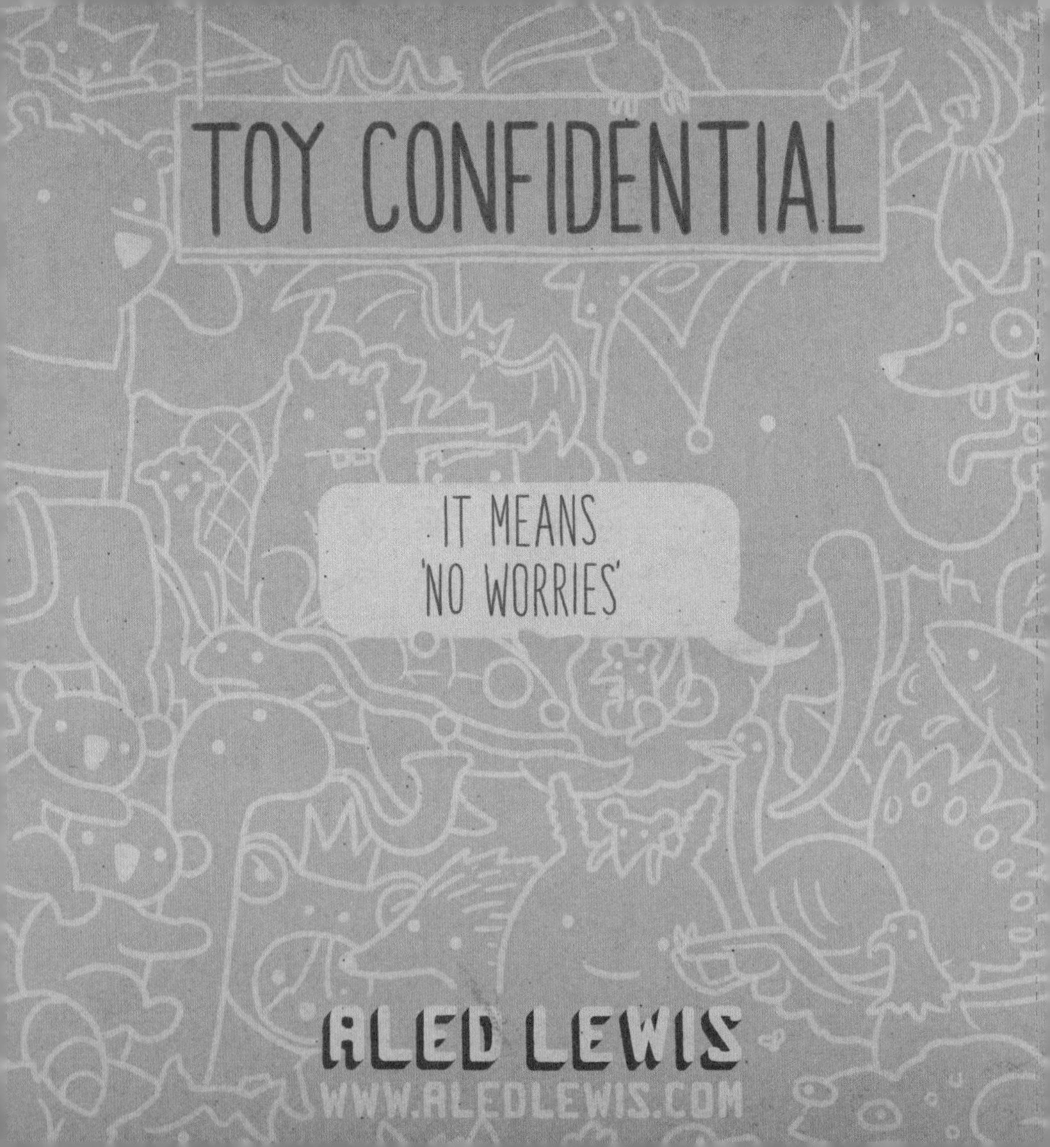
TOY CONFIDENTIAL
IT MEANS 'NO WORRIES'
ALED LEWIS
WWW.ALEDLEWIS.COM

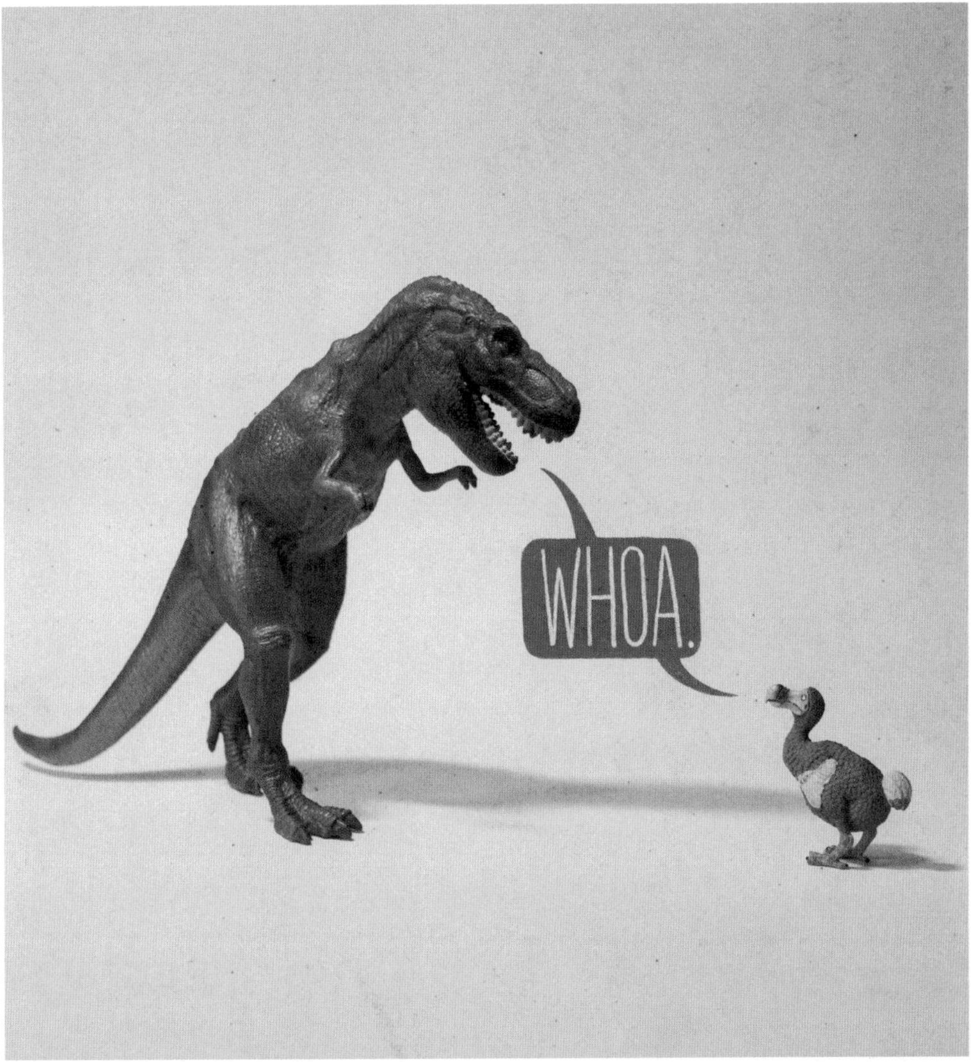
WHOA.

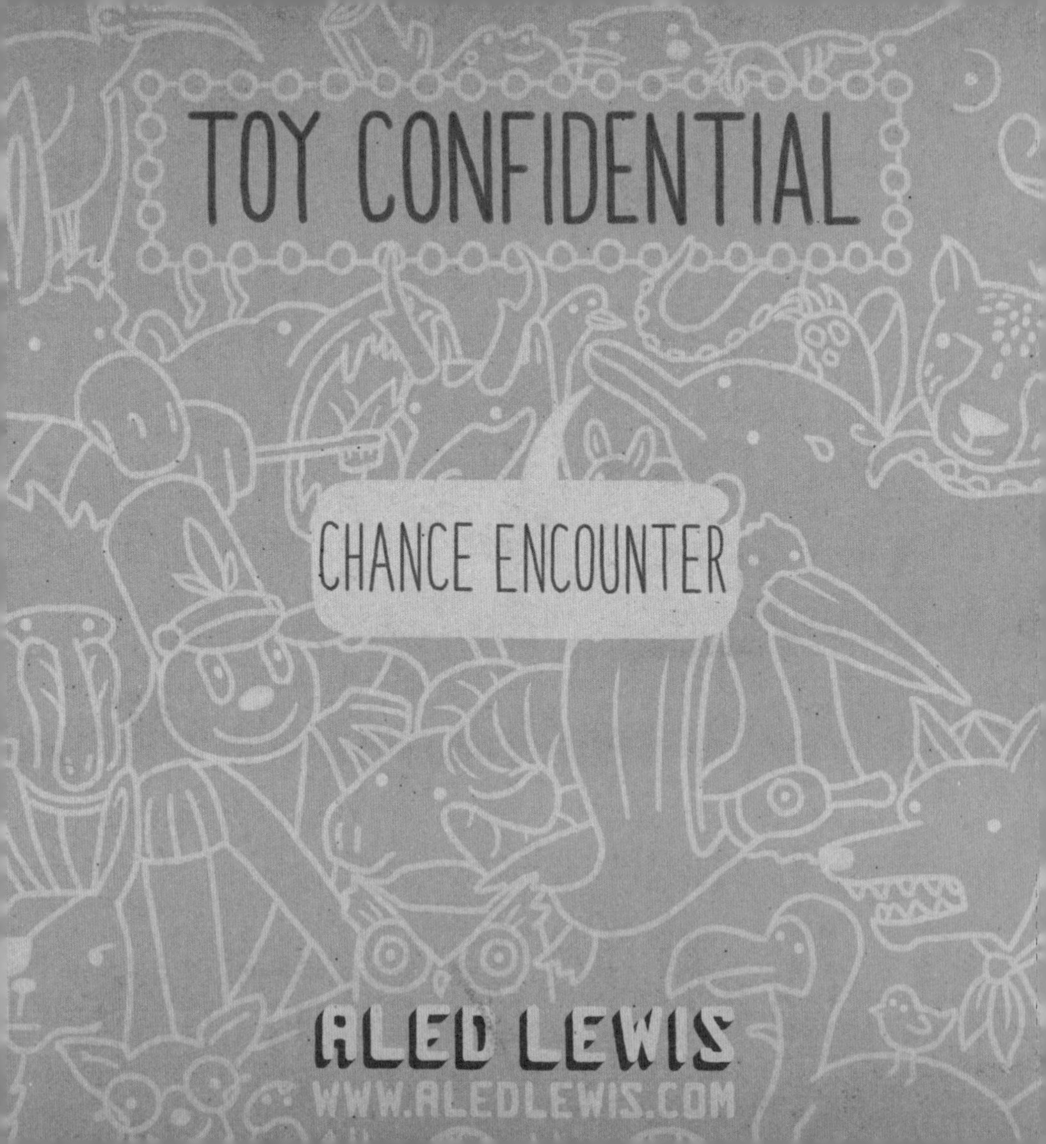
TOY CONFIDENTIAL
CHANCE ENCOUNTER
ALED LEWIS
WWW.ALEDLEWIS.COM

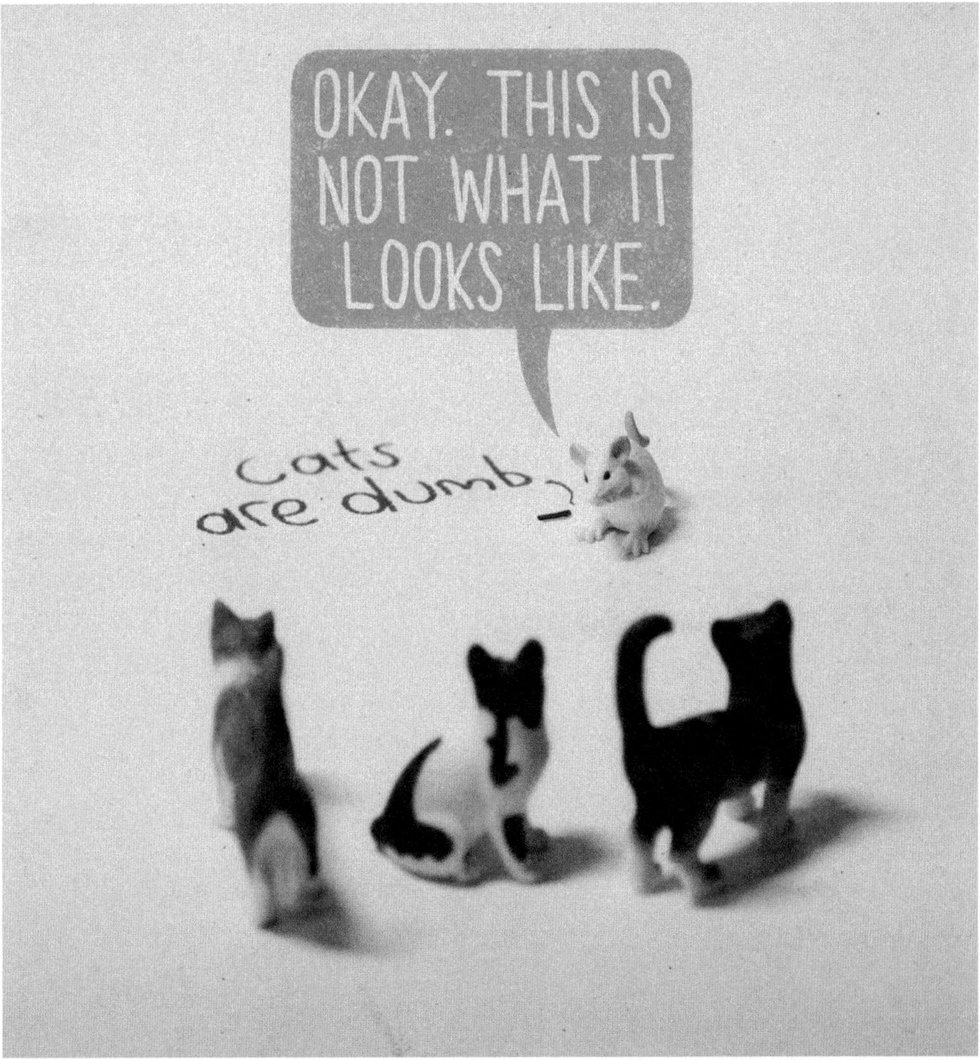
OKAY. THIS IS NOT WHAT IT LOOKS LIKE.
cats are dumb

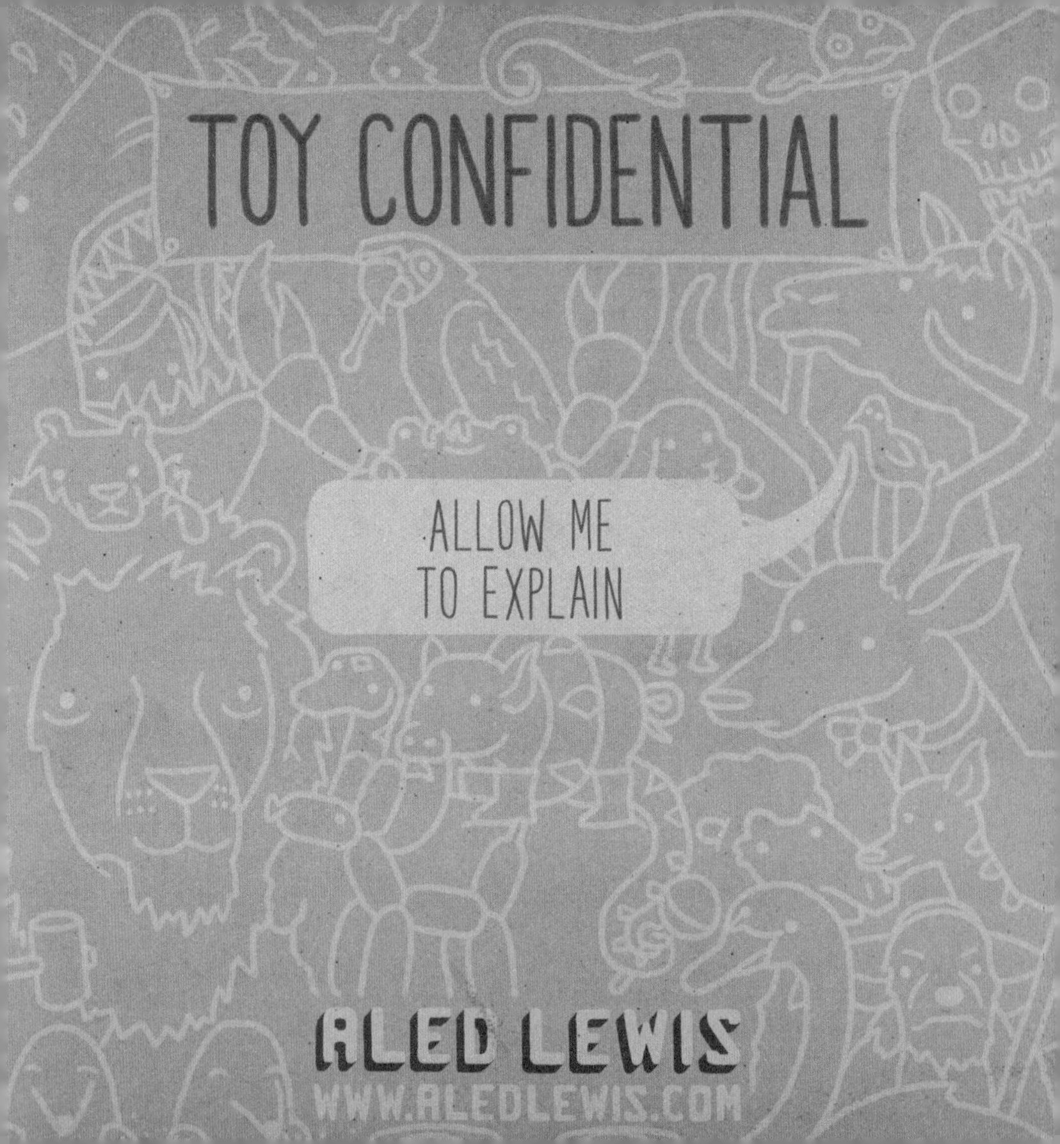
TOY CONFIDENTIAL
ALLOW ME
TO EXPLAIN
ALED LEWIS
WWW.ALEDLEWIS.COM

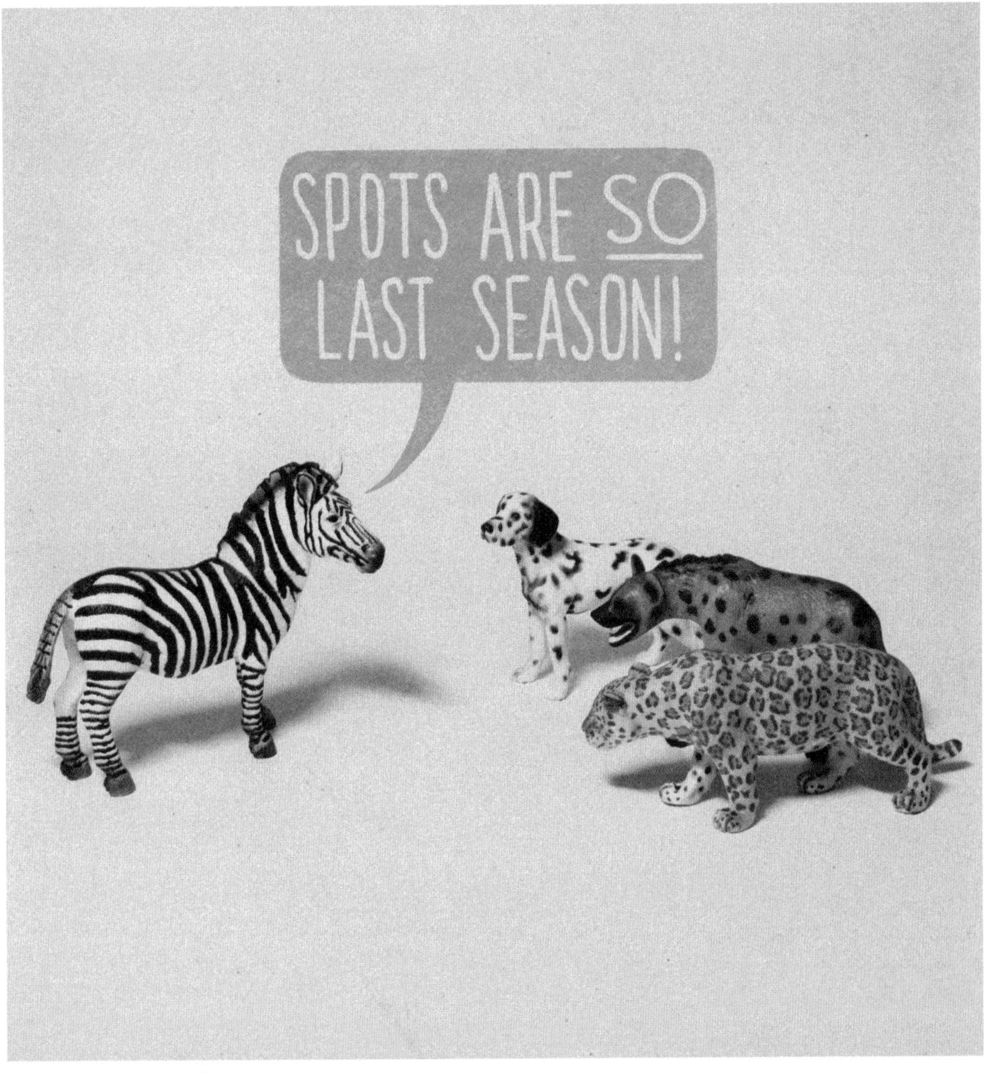
SPOTS ARE SO LAST SEASON!

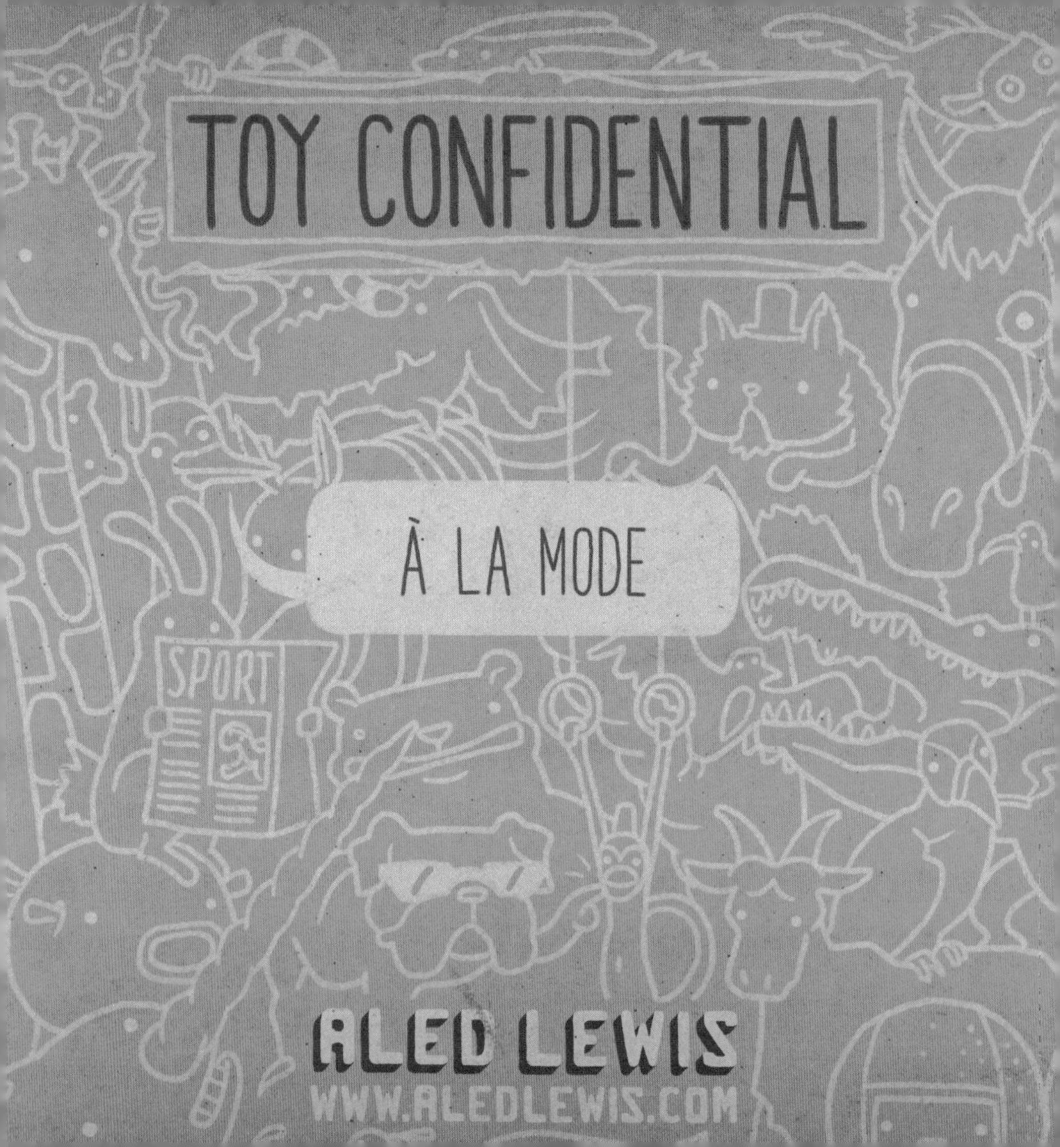
TOY CONFIDENTIAL
À LA MODE
SPORT
ALED LEWIS
WWW.ALEDLEWIS.COM

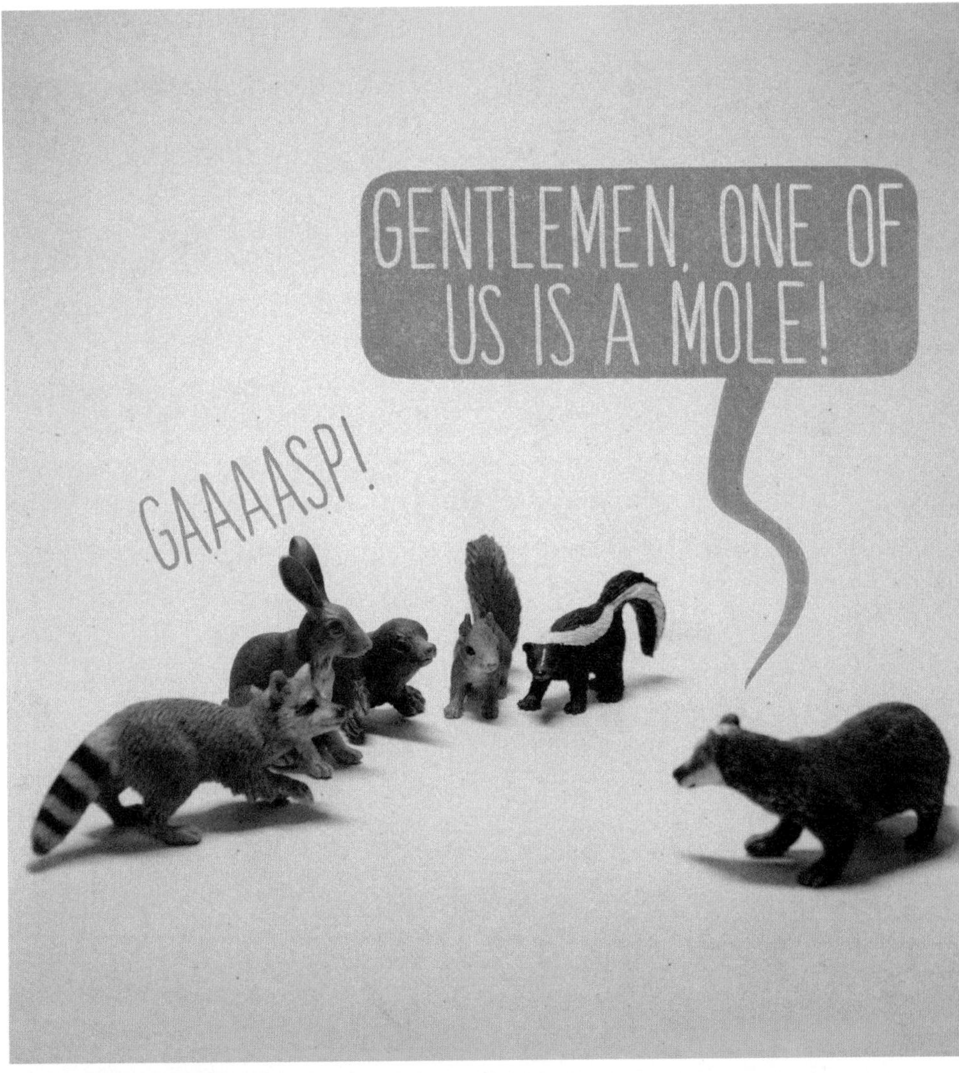
GENTLEMEN, ONE OF US IS A MOLE!
GAAAASP!

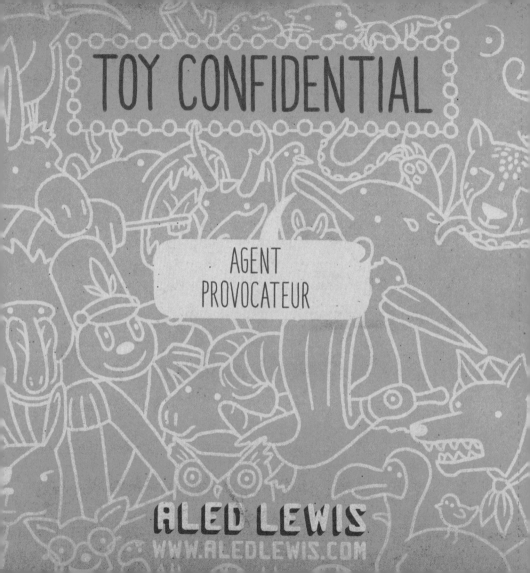

TOY CONFIDENTIAL

AGENT PROVOCATEUR

ALED LEWIS
WWW.ALEDLEWIS.COM

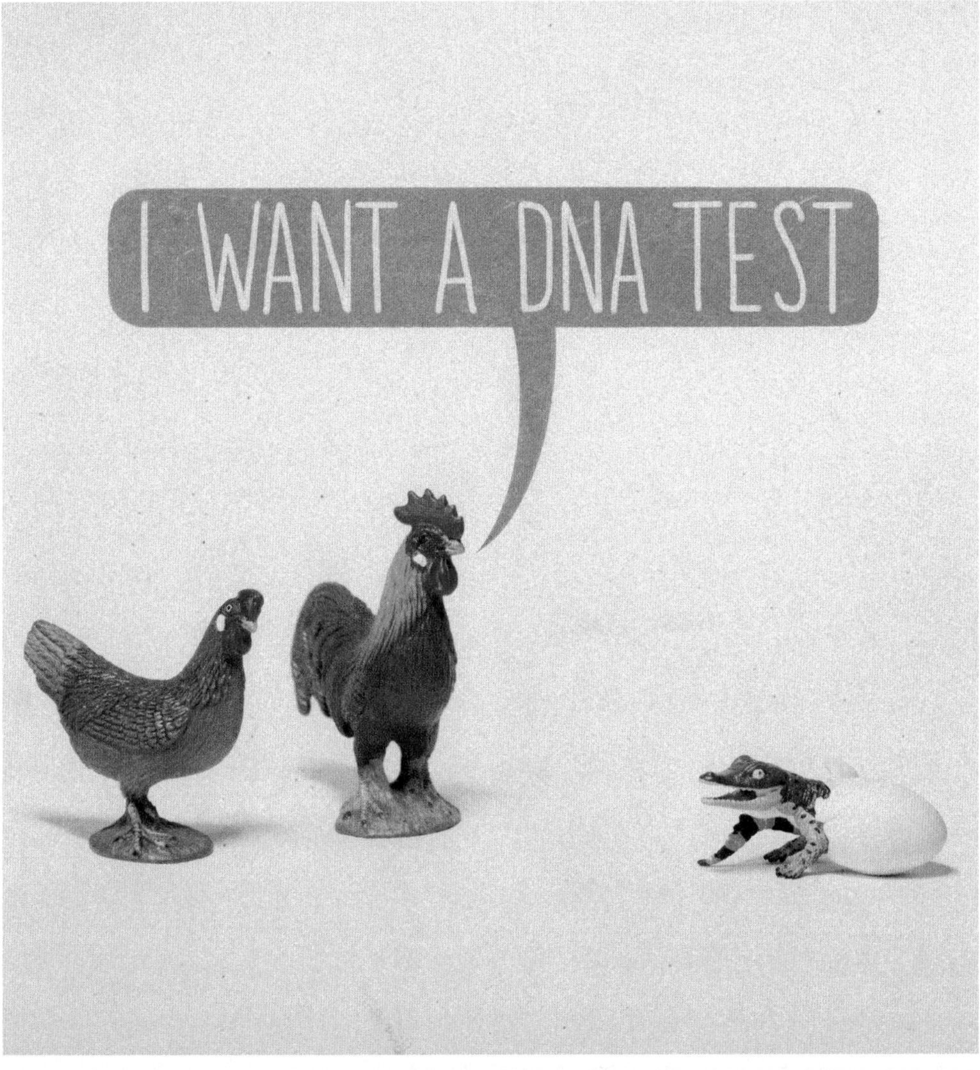
I WANT A DNA TEST

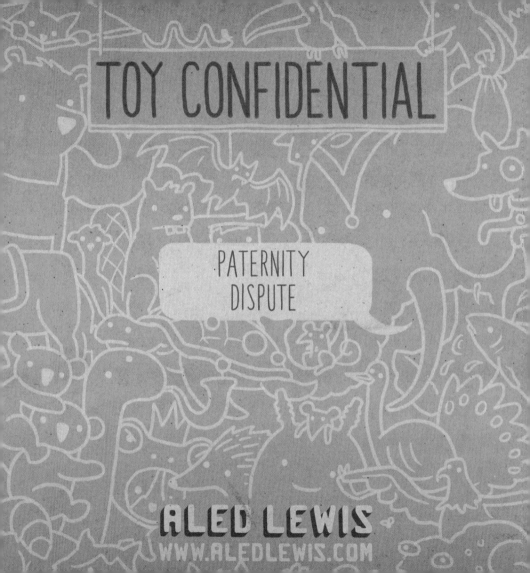

TOY CONFIDENTIAL

PATERNITY
DISPUTE

ALED LEWIS
WWW.ALEDLEWIS.COM

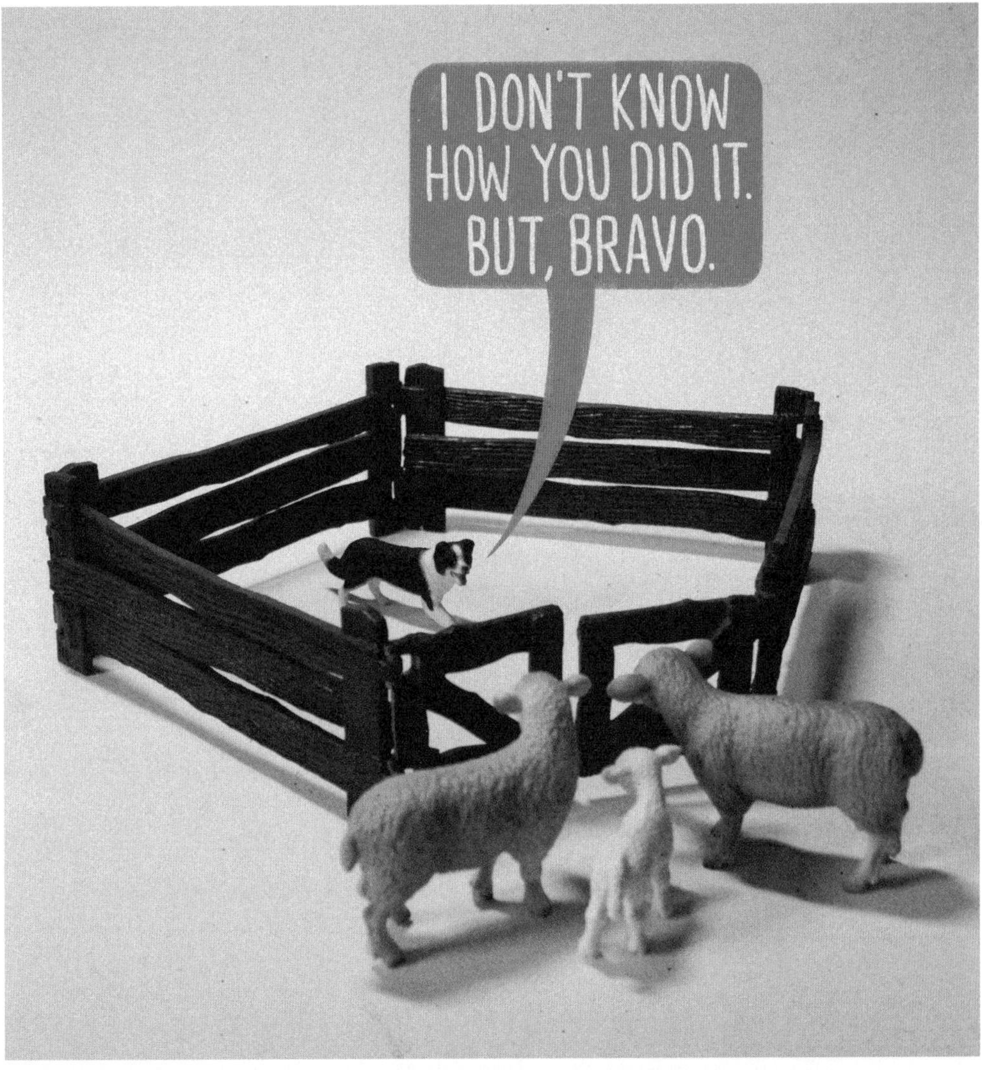
I DON'T KNOW HOW YOU DID IT. BUT, BRAVO.

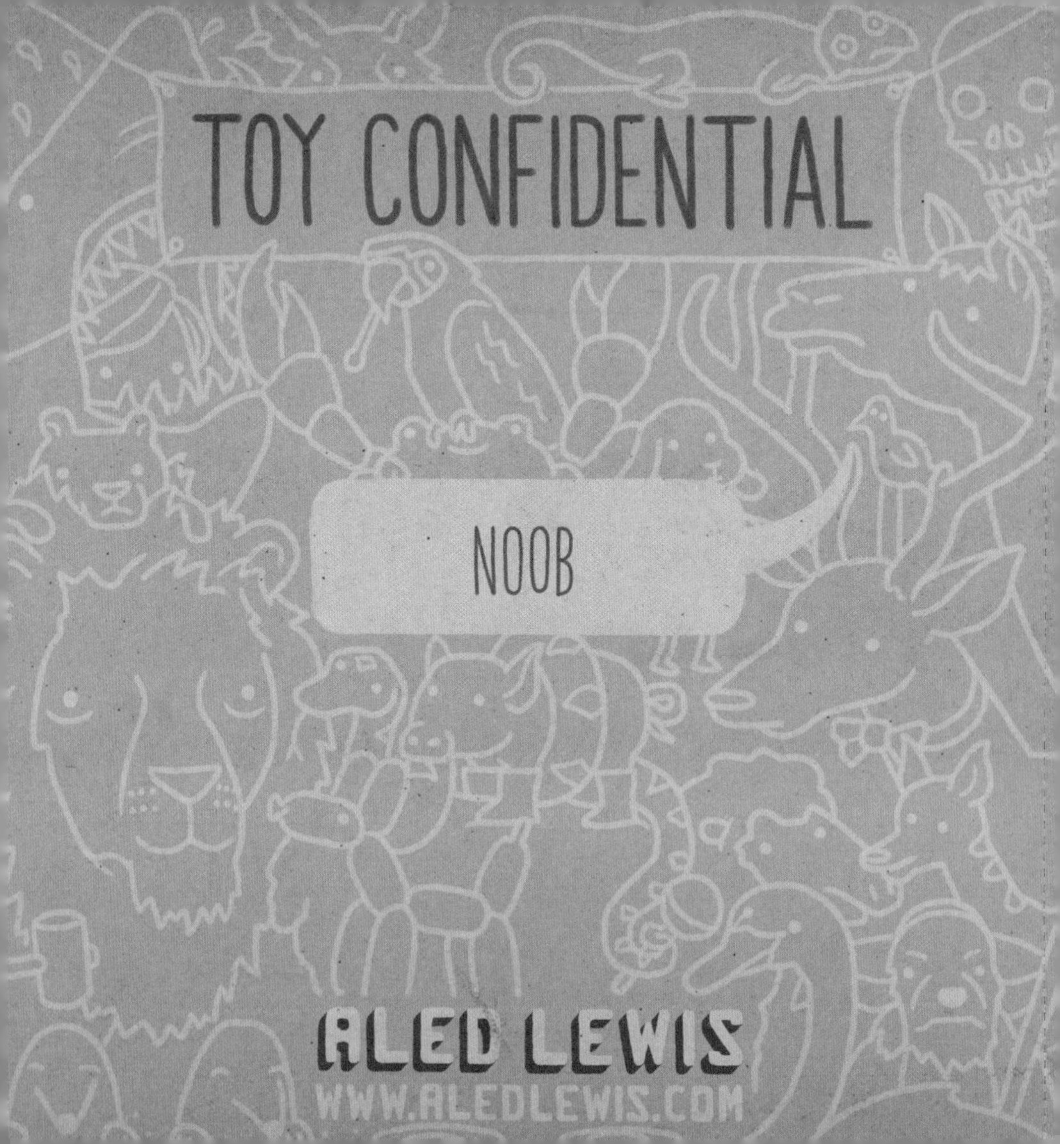
TOY CONFIDENTIAL
NOOB
ALED LEWIS
WWW.ALEDLEWIS.COM

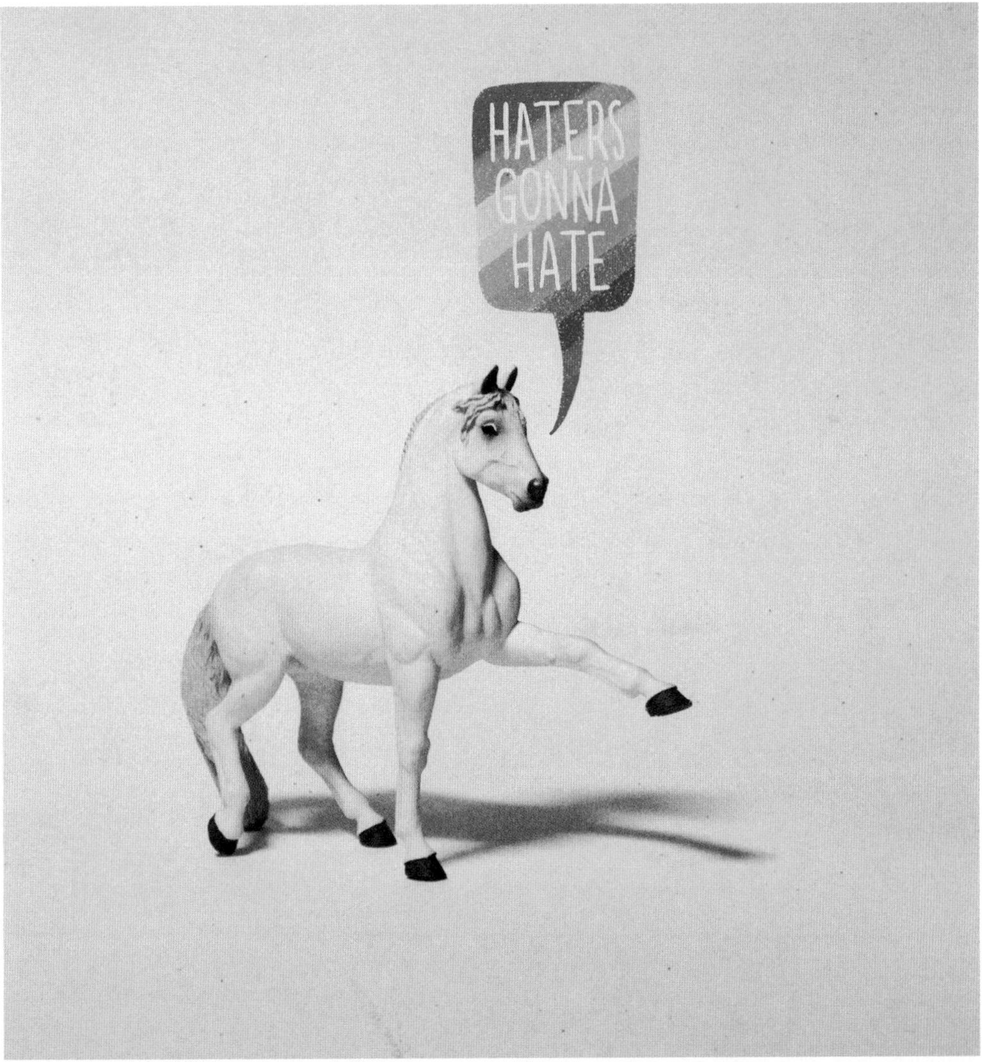
HATERS GONNA HATE

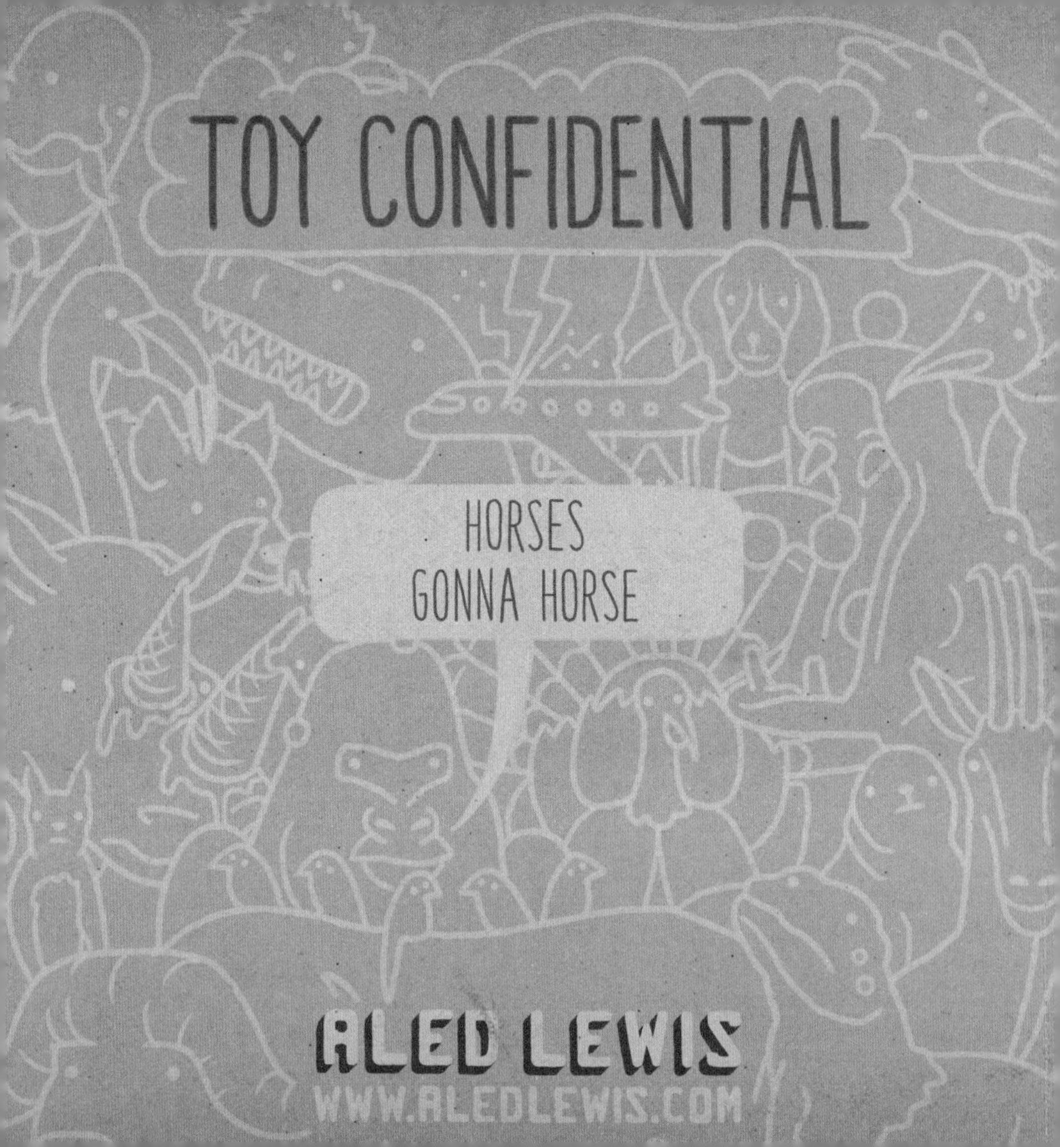
TOY CONFIDENTIAL
HORSES GONNA HORSE
ALED LEWIS
WWW.ALEDLEWIS.COM

ABOUT

Aled is a designer and illustrator living in London, England. He is
a Graphic Design graduate and a life-long gamer influenced and
inspired by comics, film, music and television. He began designing
t-shirts in 2006 before becoming a commissioned illustrator.

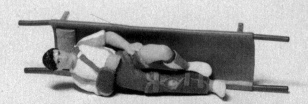

MORE FUN TITLES FROM HOW BOOKS

Kawaii Not
By Meghan Murphy

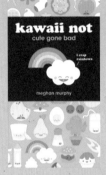

This collection features 100 original comics from the hysterical Kawaii Not comic strip, which depicts cute versions of everyday objects doing and saying some crazy stuff. What exactly is kawaii? Well, kawaii is the Japanese term for cute, as in, "look at the fuzzy kitten, he's so kawaii", and not is an English term meaning "not". It's that simple. AND, the book includes stickers! Nothing is more kawaii than stickers.

Kawaii Not, Too
By Meghan Murphy

After the success of the first Kawaii Not book, fans have been begging for more. And now, cute gets even badder! The more you're looking for? It's here. More twisted pretzels. More talking bacon strips. More anthropomorphic cupcakes. Funny and strange, this book is sure to brighten your day. Or possibly take you to a slightly darker place—albeit a cute one!

Find these books and many others at **MyDesignShop.com** or your local bookstore.

Special Offer From HOW Books!

You can get 15% off your entire order at MyDesignShop.com! All you have to do is go to www.howdesign.com/howbooks-offer and sign up for our free e-newsletter on graphic design. You'll also get a free digital download of HOW magazine.

For more news, tips and articles, follow us at Twitter.com/HOWbrand

For behind-the-scenes information and special offers, become a fan at Facebook.com/HOW-magazine

For visual inspiration, follow us at Pinterest.com/HOWbrand